In the Beginning

THE UNIVERSITY OF NORTH CAROLINA PRESS Chapel Hill

In the Beginning

FUNDAMENTALISM, THE SCOPES TRIAL,
AND THE MAKING OF THE ANTIEVOLUTION
MOVEMENT   MICHAEL LIENESCH

© 2007 The University of North Carolina Press

All rights reserved

Set in Quadraat types by Keystone Typesetting, Inc.

Manufactured in the United States of America

This book was published with the assistance of the
H. Eugene and Lillian Youngs Lehman Fund of the
University of North Carolina Press. A complete list of
books published in the Lehman Series appears at the
end of the book.

The paper in this book meets the guidelines for permanence
and durability of the Committee on Production Guidelines for
Book Longevity of the Council on Library Resources.

Library of Congress Cataloging-in-Publication Data
Lienesch, Michael, 1948–
In the beginning : fundamentalism, the Scopes trial, and the
making of the antievolution movement / Michael Lienesch.
    p. cm.
Includes bibliographical references (p.   ) and index.
ISBN 978-0-8078-3096-3 (cloth: alk. paper)
1. Evolution (Biology)—Religious aspects—Christianity—History.
2. Creationism—History. I. Title.
BT712.L54 2007
231.7′65209—dc22   2006034396

A CARAVAN BOOK.

For more information, visit www.caravanbooks.org.

11 10 09 08 07   5 4 3 2 1

To Nick and Elizabeth

Contents

Illustrations

Acknowledgments

I would like to be able to say that this book was intelligently designed, but the truth is that the process of writing it has been more of an evolutionary one, not only in the enormous amount of time it has taken but also in the countless modifications, the occasional leaps of progress, and the long, slow struggle in bringing it to where it is today. Along the way, many people have been part of the process, contributing their advice, knowledge, and support.

This being a book about origins, I should say right off that I am not at all sure when I began to write it. I do know that whenever I started, now well over a decade ago, I thought I was writing a completely different book. I realized that it was this one during a memorable year at the National Humanities Center that was made possible by a fellowship from the Lilly Endowment. For their gracious hospitality and support during that time, I wish to thank Robert Connor, Kent Mullikin, Alan Tuttle, Jean Houston, Eliza Robertson, and the Center staff. I also want to thank the other fellows in residence with me who were kind enough to ask what I was doing, to listen to what I said, and to help me see what I wanted this book to be.

Over the years I have learned the painful lesson that writing takes time, and I am grateful to the institutions that have provided it for me, as well as to the individuals whose patience and encouragement have made it pass easier and faster. At the University of North Carolina, I have received support from the Department of Political Science, the Institute for the Arts and Humanities, and the University Research Council. Particularly important have been the colleagues who were kind enough to criticize my early drafts, to send me articles and citations, or simply to care enough to keep asking how it was going. For these kindnesses I thank Pete Andrews, Susan Bickford, Jean DeSaix, Leon Fink, Virginia Gray, Jonathan Hartlyn, Joel Kingsolver, Steve Leonard, Bill Lycan, Laurie Maffly-Kipp, Tim Marr, Don Mathews, Warren Nord, Tony Oberschall, Dick Richardson, John Sanders, Christian Smith, Jeff Spinner-Halev, George Tindall, Ruel Tyson, and Charles Waldrup. I also want to thank the many others, both fellow faculty and friends, who over the years have expressed their interest and encouragement. I apologize to those I should have thanked but have forgotten. To those who have helped me in ways I will never know, I send my sincerest thanks.

In researching and writing, I have come to see better than before that books like this one do not stand by themselves, that they are part of a long line of scholarly studies that taken together tell a larger and truer story than any one work alone. In looking back, I realize that I knew very little about this topic when I started to study it, and that I have learned an enormous amount from other scholars—so much from so many that I could never possibly remember them all by name. But I do want to single out one group for special mention, those far-flung colleagues to whom I am doubly beholden, both because I have learned so much from their work and because they have taken the time to comment on earlier versions of mine. I am especially grateful to Joel Carpenter, Clarke Cochran, John Green, Edward J. Larson, George Marsden, Ken Miller, Randy Moore, Ron Numbers, Sidney Tarrow, Grant Wacker, Clyde Wilcox, Charles Reagan Wilson, and Robert Wuthnow.

In the same way, I have become more aware than ever of how present scholarship relies on past sources, and how much is owed to those dedicated and usually unsung archivists and librarians who keep the records that become the basis for so much of what we write. For allowing access and aiding me in using these sources, I want to express gratitude to the directors and staffs of the archives, special collections, and libraries at the Arkansas Historical Collection, Billy Graham Center, Bryan College, Duke Divinity School, Fuller Theological Seminary, Furman University, Library of Congress, Moody Bible Institute, North Carolina Baptist Historical Collection, Northwestern College, Southern Baptist Historical Library and Archives, Tennessee State Library and Archives, University of Kentucky, University of Tennessee, University of North Carolina, Vanderbilt University, Wheaton College, and Wake Forest University.

Although I have written books before, in writing this one I have begun to see publishing as an evolutionary process of its own, a complex and subtle operation involving many people with many different skills who work together to transform early ideas and rough proposals into final polished products. For presiding patiently over the process that led to the publication of this book, I wish to thank Kate Torrey, David Perry, and especially the estimable Chuck Grench, along with the fine staff at the University of North Carolina Press who have brought their skills to bear in making it happen.

Finally, because life continues to evolve even while books are being written, I want to thank those who have lived with me while I was writing this one: Ann, for her love and constant support (not to mention her always excellent editorial advice); and Nick and Elizabeth, who have been doing some evolving of their own in the meantime, growing from children into wonderful young adults, to whom this book is dedicated.

In the Beginning

Introduction

I suppose I should not have been surprised ten or so years ago when my son, then in middle school, reported at the dinner table on what had happened that day in his science class. The lesson had been on scientific classification and how it is used to group members of the animal and plant kingdoms into phyla, classes, orders, families, and so forth. At the end, he put up his hand to ask whether the fact that gorillas and humans were both members of the hominid family meant that they were related to one another. The question was innocent enough, and he was not trying to be controversial. After all, he had already learned a little about evolution in school, to say nothing of all those PBS nature shows, and it must have seemed to him that everyone believed in it, or at least everyone in our liberal (albeit southern) college town. Besides, it was in the textbook and was a standard component of the science curriculum in his award-winning public school. So the response of the teacher—a seasoned veteran with more than two decades of experience in the classroom—confused him, and it surprised me. Without missing a beat, she had looked my son straight in the eye and answered evenly: "*If you believe in evolution, the answer is yes.*"

"*If you believe in evolution, . . .*" I should not have been surprised because at the time I was beginning to write this book, and I was already well aware that evolution was a sensitive topic, particularly in the public schools. As early as 1982, when George Gallup began to ask questions about creation and evolution in his national opinion surveys, polls had consistently shown that almost half of all American adults believed in the creation story as told in the Book of Genesis, in which God made the world in seven days less than ten thousand years ago. In 1988 the Williamsburg Charter Survey had reported that seven of ten Americans thought that public schools should teach both creation and evolution, and the responses were consistent across all regions, education levels, and age groups, including high school students. Studies from the same time showed that significant numbers of biology teachers—in some states approaching one-third— were teaching creationism alongside evolution in their classrooms. Among those teachers who emphasized evolution, many were reporting resistance from students, parents, and church pastors who demanded that students be allowed to leave the classroom during discussion of the topic. By the mid-1990s, when my son was in middle school, efforts were under way in several states to restrict the teaching of evolution and to include creationism alongside it in the curriculum. Under the circumstances, it was understandable that his teacher had chosen her words carefully.[1]

Even so, I was surprised then, and I continue to be surprised now, not only by how deep and wide the distrust of evolution seems to run in this country, but also by the ability of its critics to make themselves heard on the issue. In fact, having studied antievolution activists for the last decade, I have to admit a certain admiration for them, even while confessing at the start that I agree with almost none of their views. Among modern American political movements, antievolutionism —or creationism, as it more commonly came to be called from the 1960s on—has been one of the most enduring, continuing through periods of activism and quiescence from the beginning of the twentieth century down to today. Admittedly an argument can be made that its endurance has followed from its failure, since part of the reason antievolution activists have been so persistent is that they have not succeeded in casting evolution out of the schools and installing creation in its place. Yet the movement has had more than its share of successes, at least at the state and local level, and the effect has been that in many of parts of this country remarkably little evolution has been taught in the public schools over the last century. In our own time, creationists have continued to champion their cause in schools across America, and those who study and track their efforts insist that the movement is as strong now as at any point in its past.

So I began by asking how antievolutionists had done it: how they had built a movement that has endured for almost a century, that has had a significant influence on public policy over that time, and that shows no signs of slowing today. In looking for answers I found no shortage of sources. Over the last fifty years, beginning with Norman Furniss's The Fundamentalist Controversy, scores of studies have detailed the creation, development, and continuing influence of the antievolution movement.[2] Among the best are the works of George Marsden, Ronald Numbers, and Edward J. Larson, who have described the debates over evolution that have continued from the early twentieth century to today, locating them in the religious, scientific, and legal landscape of our time.[3] But these are only the beginning, since few topics have attracted the attention of so many scholars, let alone those from such disparate disciplines. Historians have analyzed the intellectual roots of the antievolution movement; anthropologists and sociologists have studied its development, describing how organizations were created and members mobilized; political scientists have investigated how activists learned how to manipulate the levers of political power and influence public policy.[4] Science educators, who have a special interest in the issue, have followed the influence of creationism into the classroom, charting its effect on curriculum and teaching practices.[5] Journalists have provided details on flash points and personalities.[6] Partisans from both creationist and evolutionist camps have poured out a steady stream of analysis, criticism, and polemics.[7] And this is not even to mention the movies, plays, and television documentaries that have introduced antievolutionism's most famous moment, the 1925 Scopes "monkey" trial, to millions of viewers.[8]

Yet despite all of the studies, there continue to be considerable disagreements in telling the story of the antievolution movement, let alone in trying to explain and interpret it. Antievolutionism is a controversial topic, and on this count alone some argument can be expected. But as Ron Numbers has recently lamented, the controversies that have characterized its study have arisen in large part because of the stubborn persistence of what he calls "myths and misperceptions." As Numbers sees it, scholars from Furniss on have contributed to a stereotypical understanding—really misunderstanding—of the movement. Taking the 1925 Scopes trial to be antievolution's defining moment, they have tended to shape their studies around it and, as a result, have spent too little time treating either its early development or later transformation. While William Jennings Bryan, the movement's most prominent personality, receives too much attention, other leading antievolutionists such as William Bell Riley, John Roach Straton, and J. Frank Norris receive too little. Tennessee, where antievolutionists won, becomes the focus, while events in other states, where they occasionally won but more often lost, are all but forgotten. In addition, Numbers argues that too many scholars continue to accept the conventional account of the Scopes trial as a battle between rural South and cosmopolitan North. Consequently, they have shown an almost instinctive tendency to depict the antievolution movement as existing for all practical purposes entirely in the South, rather than in the big cities of the North, where it began and where it carried out some of its most important campaigns. Above all, Numbers makes the point that by embracing the stereotype, these scholars have implicitly ignored other explanations for the movement, foregoing intellectual, political, and religious reasons in favor of social and economic ones. Predictably, when others have challenged the Scopes stereotype, or tried to move the study of antievolutionism beyond it, there has been conflict— what Numbers calls "continuing historiographical disagreement about even the most basic issues."[9]

Thus it became clear to me that in order to discover how antievolutionists had done it, I would have to find a way to get beyond the continuing debates. The first task was to describe the movement, telling its story in such a way as to avoid as many of the old preconceptions and stereotypes as possible. The second and bigger one was to explain and interpret it, bringing to bear whatever theories or explanatory tools that would help me make sense of its success. My own background was in political theory, or, more precisely, in the history of American political thought. For the better part of two decades I had studied the connections between politics and religion in the United States, concentrating on conservative politics and conservative religion. I had written a book on the New Christian Right of the 1980s. But that book was primarily a study of ideas, based mostly on an analysis of the thinking of Christian conservative writers. This time I wanted to say more about how ideas were put into practice, how the thinking of the writers came to be applied in the agendas of the activists, in the character of the groups and organizations they created, and in the choices of the strategies they used to pursue their cause. That is to say, I wanted to study antievolutionism not only as a political ideology but also as a political movement. With this purpose in mind, I turned to social movement theory.

For at least a century scholars have been examining social movements, searching for explanations for how and why people come together to change their societies. In many of the earliest studies, movements were described in highly critical terms, as irrational products of the kind of mass behavior that inspired nineteenth-century mobs and twentieth-century totalitarian political parties. By the 1960s, responding to the labor and civil rights protests of the time, scholars had begun to treat movements more sympathetically, depicting them as the rightful efforts of rational people seeking their own economic interests and political rights. But it was in the 1970s and 1980s, inspired by the explosion of groups advocating causes such as environmentalism, feminism, gay and lesbian liberation, and nuclear nonproliferation, that social movement theory really came into its own. Turning their attention to these so-called new social movements, European social theorists began to argue that they were distinctly different from older ones in that they existed not to achieve class-based economic ends but rather to pursue broader cultural and psychological goals such as building a sense of shared identity or improving the quality of life.[10] At about the same time, American academics, many of them studying similar movements in this country, began the shift from older Durkheimian theories to what they called a "political process" perspective, analyzing how these new-style groups and organizations operated within existing political systems to transform protest into policy.[11] Scholars from both schools concentrated their studies on late-twentieth-century movements, but some applied their assumptions to earlier ones as well, finding similarities between "new" social movements and "old" ones such as the moral reform movements that were common in the nineteenth and early twentieth centuries in the United States.[12] Although almost all of the studies were of liberal and left-leaning groups, a few treated conservative and right-wing ones as well.[13] On rare occasions, conservative movements that were not only political but also religious even came in for review.[14]

As social movement theory flourished, however, it struggled to come together. Throughout the 1980s the field was in disarray, as "new social movement" and "political process" schools seemed to move into competing camps, with little communication between them. Those associated with new social movement theory maintained that movements could be understood best by considering how they gave meaning to the personal lives of their members. Concentrating on the concept of collective identity, these thinkers investigated how activists managed to create and sustain a shared sense of themselves (as people of color, as gays and lesbians, as women, etc.) by developing common cultural codes and distinctive discourses. For them, the internal dynamics of movements, including the emotional dynamics, were more important than any external ones.[15] By contrast, those associated with the political process model argued that movements should be seen in more political terms, as groups and organizations existing within elaborate social and political systems. These scholars focused on how movements mobilized resources, on how they took advantage of opportunities, and on how they operated within the constraints and possibilities of the political environment around them. Their perspective was more external than internal, focusing on how larger political forces—parties, states, even other movements—affected the success of political movements.[16] To some extent, the different perspectives reflected different academic traditions, with European scholars being attracted to a more cultural and philosophical perspective, while their American counterparts took a more institutional and instrumental one. Disciplinary differences—among historians, sociologists, political scientists, and so forth—exacerbated the divisions, as did methodological ones. Even within schools scholars analyzed different movements at different levels, with some concentrating on activists, others on organizations, and still others on state or even international systems. For that matter, studies of the same or similar movements sometimes came to contrasting conclusions depending on where in their histories they were studied, since movements can be very different in the early stages of mobilization than when they have arrived at maturity or are coming to a close.[17]

More recently, a rising chorus has begun to call for the creation of a more synthetic perspective. Denouncing false dichotomies between culture and structure, a new generation of social movement scholars, many of them associated only loosely (if at all) with the older schools, has come to draw simultaneously from both.[18] Theoretical differences remain, as do disciplinary and methodological ones, but boundaries seem increasingly to be blurred. Encouraged by collaboration between scholars in Europe and the United States, identity theorists have begun to pay more attention to the role of institutions and political processes, exploring how the creation of identities in social movements is frequently shaped by the state, with its power to recognize some identities and repress others.[19] Political process thinkers have started to take more seriously what goes on inside movements, looking more closely at how institutions can influence the attitudes, concerns, and even emotions of movement members.[20] Disciplinary divisions are being overcome. As movements are analyzed at different levels and at different points in their development, scholars on all sides have come to see them as more complex and multilayered, as well as more dynamic, constantly adapting and transforming themselves in response to pressures both within and without.[21] Much still remains to be done, but as sociologist David S. Meyer has suggested in a recent essay, the state of social movement theory is that scholars have begun to create "synthetic paradigms," building bridges between what were once competing perspectives to create more comprehensive theories.[22]

It is in this spirit that I have written this book. In addition to telling the story of the antievolution movement, my aim has been to analyze it, considering it as a whole, from beginning to end, top to bottom, inside and out. To provide some structure to that substantial task, I have adopted some of the most significant concepts of social movement theory, drawing more or less equally from identity theorists and political process thinkers in an attempt to arrive at a more comprehensive account. Applying ideas of identity, mobilization, and framing, I have analyzed how antievolutionists of the early twentieth century created an identity for themselves, how they mobilized and organized their ranks, and how they framed evolution into an issue central to their cause. Using concepts of frame alignment, political opportunity structures, and strategic staging, I discuss how activists and their allies developed their movement during the first part of the 1920s, adapting to changing constituencies, taking advantage of political openings, and presenting their message to the media on the dramatic stage of the Scopes trial. Introducing a cyclical theory of protest, I track the course of events that followed the trial, describing how antievolution protest rose and fell as it came to a climax at the end of the decade. Finally, using insights into how movements survive over extended periods, I show how antievolutionists have managed to continuously renew their movement since the 1920s, maintaining it through several periods of retreat and revival over the course of the twentieth century and into the twenty-first. In the conclusion I even attempt a few predictions about its future. The book considers the antievolution movement as it existed at the national, state, and local levels. It examines both its leaders and its rank-and-file followers. It treats its successes and its failures, its highs and its lows. It is a study of one movement, and the findings cannot be applied universally. But for this one movement, it tries to tell the whole story.

In telling that story, I have relied as much as possible on the words of its members. Political movements are complex creations, but they are held together with words. As William Gamson has described, movements are the product of discourse, which he broadly conceives to include not only the written and spoken word but also symbolic acts and ritualized practices.[23] Robert Wuthnow calls them "communities of discourse," groups of like-minded talkers who develop their own ways of articulating common beliefs, goals, and visions of the future.[24] Moreover, as Ann Swidler and others have shown, movements use their distinctive discourses to act as well as talk, since discourse serves not only to construct collective identity but also to inspire and channel collective action.[25] In the anti-evolution movement, whose roots run deep into Scripture and sermon, words have seemed particularly important, and I have tried to take them seriously. With this in mind I have made use of a wide variety of printed sources, including not only books, pamphlets, and speeches, but also correspondence, court records, debate transcripts, news reports, opinion pieces, letters to the editor, and (for more recent creationists) Web sites. In all of these, I have sought out a variety of voices, recognizing that movements consist of multiple views. On occasion, when the voices seemed too self-serving, I have added the perspective of critics and outside observers. Whenever possible, however, I have allowed anti-evolutionists to speak for themselves.

Finally, I would like to say one last word to readers. In each of the books I have written, I have attempted to address both specialists and generalists, those inside the academy and those outside it. In this one, I have found the challenge of reaching such a diverse audience to be especially daunting. On the one hand, this is a book of theory, an attempt to apply some of the best theoretical tools that scholars have devised in order to understand political movements. I am acutely aware that much of this theory is abstract and sometimes awkward in its terminology. Some may find it a distraction. On the other hand, it is also a book about the practice of politics, complete with colorful characters and detailed descriptions of events. No doubt there will also be those for whom such descriptions seem tedious. I ask that you all bear with me. What I am attempting to do here is to connect theory to practice in such a way that each can inform our understanding of the other. Making this connection has been the biggest challenge in writing this book. But it is also the best way to understand this movement. And we need to understand it, because however we feel about it, antievolutionism is not going away any time soon.

1 : Identity

FUNDAMENTALIST FOUNDATIONS

It began with a sermon. A. C. Dixon was a powerful speaker, whose soul-stirring preaching often drew audiences of up to ten thousand at Chicago's Moody Church. But his message must have been particularly moving on the warm Sunday afternoon in August 1909, when he brought his Southern California revival campaign to Los Angeles. In the audience that day at the art nouveau Temple Auditorium were many of the city's most prominent conservative evangelicals, among them millionaire oilman Lyman Stewart, who had come with the growing conviction that something had to be done to bring the Bible's true message to its most faithful believers. As he listened to Dixon, Stewart realized that he was being called to carry out that mission. Within days, aided by his brother and business partner Milton, he had laid out plans to publish a series of inexpensive paperback books containing the best teachings of the best (meaning the most conservative) Bible teachers in the world. Dixon would serve as editor of the series. The volumes would be distributed free of charge to church people across the country. They would be called *The Fundamentals*.[1]

To the extent that it is possible to locate a single moment when the anti-evolution movement could be said to have been born, it was then, because anti-evolutionism arose out of fundamentalism, and because fundamentalism became possible only because of *The Fundamentals*. As a set of ideas and even as an ill-formed ideology, antievolutionism had existed ever since the time of Charles Darwin (1809–82), and critics of evolutionary theory had flourished on and off throughout the late nineteenth century in the United States, especially in its most conservative churches. But as a movement, antievolutionism appeared much later, in the 1920s, as a product of the religious and political protest that would come to be called fundamentalism. For decades, conservative evangelicals had been growing restive, alarmed at the liberalizing tendencies in their churches and in the larger culture around them. Their concerns went mostly unnoticed, however, primarily because their protests tended to be localized and sporadic. Divided by denomination, fragmented into countless church congregations, these disillusioned conservatives lacked any real sense that they shared similar views, let alone that they constituted a common cause. What brought them together for the first time was not a leader or an organization, but Stewart's set of twelve paperback books. Appearing between 1910 and 1915, The Fundamentals did more than give fundamentalists their name. Announcing articles of belief, communicating a distinct style of discourse, defining differences between themselves and others, the project gave them a common identity, a shared conception of themselves that told them who they were and what they were about. That identity formed the fundamentalist foundations on which creationism would be built.

Although the idea of identity is a relatively recent addition to social movement theory, it has become a central concept in the study of contemporary political movements. Inspired by the appearance in the late twentieth century of groups committed to cultural change and personal transformation, some social movement scholars have suggested that many movements exist almost exclusively to provide their members with a sense of belonging, along with an image of themselves as part of a larger community of common purpose. Among these scholars, Alberto Melucci was one of the first to argue that the chief characteristic of many contemporary movements is that instead of providing economic benefits for their members, they offer them the cultural tools to give meaning to their everyday lives—what he called "the right to realize their own identity."[2] According to Alain Touraine, Jean Cohen, and others, this identity is consciously constructed and communicated as movement members come together to arrive at an understanding of who they are, what they have in common, and how they differ from others in the dominant or mainstream culture.[3] Sociologists Verta Taylor and Nancy Whittier have analyzed the process by which such collective identities are constructed, arguing that it consists of three separate but related steps: (1) the active creation of collective *consciousness*, or a shared sense of self; (2) the development of social and psychological *boundaries* between movement members and others; and (3) the insistence on *negotiation* (or what Karen Cerulo has called *politicization*), in which members move from the personal to the political in order to define differences between themselves and those they depict as their political enemies or opponents.[4]

For as long as scholars have been studying fundamentalism, they have been describing it as being based on ideology rather than identity. The first histories of the movement, written by Norman Furniss and Stewart G. Cole, portrayed it as the product of a set of basic beliefs, the famous "five points," consisting (with some variation) of belief in (1) the Bible's infallibility, (2) Christ's divinity (or virgin birth), (3) his atonement, (4) resurrection, and (5) second coming. Adapted from a 1910 declaration of the Presbyterian General Assembly, these five points would assume something like creedal status over time, eventually coming to be seen as the essential articles of fundamentalist faith.[5] But in the years leading up to World War I, before fundamentalism had emerged as a full-fledged political movement or even found a name for itself (the term would not become popular until the early 1920s), its advocates were less concerned with creating creeds than with constructing community, and less interested in developing a doctrine or ideology than in establishing a sense of identity for themselves. With the publication of The Fundamentals, they began to create that identity.

Consciousness

Movements begin by creating collective consciousness. Informing individuals of their common interests, attributing discontent to structural rather than personal reasons, collective consciousness allows people to see that they are not alone and that their problems are not entirely the result of their own failings. Although commonly conceived in class terms, consciousness can be created whenever individuals and groups feel marginalized as a result of domination by an established order. Its character is dynamic, changing over time as groups reevaluate their roles and expectations. But in its inception, as Taylor and Whittier argue, collective consciousness tends to be imparted canonically through a formal body of documents, speeches, or writings.[6]

For early fundamentalists, The Fundamentals was this canon, a body of writings designed to create a collective consciousness, a shared sense of themselves, among the most orthodox and traditional of America's evangelicals. Throughout the early twentieth century, conservative discontent had been building in Protestant churches, primarily as a reaction to the liberal theology that was making its way into many major church denominations. Yet while widespread, the discontent was diffuse, in large part because conservatives were deeply divided among themselves along theological and denominational lines. It was Lyman Stewart, a businessman rather than a church leader, who proposed to transcend the doctrinal and denominational divisions by making use of modern communication and marketing methods. Inspired by Dixon's sermon, he developed plans to not only publish but also directly distribute the twelve volumes that would eventually comprise The Fundamentals. To underwrite the project, which would require the printing and mailing of almost three million copies over the next five years, he established a fund of about $300,000, a substantial sum at the time, even for the president of the Union Oil Company. Nevertheless, Stewart was certain of his calling. "It is for us to send out the 'testimony,' " he wrote to his brother Milton, who agreed to share half of the expense, "and leave the results to God."[7]

In planning The Fundamentals, Stewart was determined to avoid the differences that had divided conservatives in the past. As editor he had chosen the widely respected Dixon, who proceeded to recruit an editorial committee of clergy and lay leaders that included prominent Baptists, Presbyterians, and independent evangelicals. The committee, in turn, selected a diverse group of sixty-four authors to write the ninety essays that would comprise the twelve volumes. Among the American, British, and Canadian authors were some of the leading orthodox theologians and scholars of the time, along with well-known evangelists, ministers, and lay leaders. Although affiliated with numerous denominations (and in a few cases with none), their chief ties tended to be nondenominational in that most were closely associated with independent Bible conferences, revival ministries, and missionary organizations. Theologically they represented a broad spectrum of evangelical thought, ranging from conventional Calvinists to esoteric dispensational premillennialists. At Dixon's urging, the authors were asked to avoid doctrinal arguments, emphasizing instead commonly held articles of faith and shared religious values. The books were distributed in the same inclusive spirit, with the intention of reaching as many readers as possible. Copies were to be sent out by the tens of thousands, free of charge, "to every pastor, evangelist, missionary, theological professor, theological student, Sunday school superintendent, Y.M.C.A. and Y.W.C.A. secretary in the English speaking world, as far as the addresses of all these can be obtained."[8]

Appropriately enough, The Fundamentals began with the Word, as scriptural text provided the primary source and principal topic of most of the early essays. Throughout the first volumes, many articles consisted of biblical exegesis, including commentaries on various books of the Bible. Almost all quoted Scripture frequently and on occasion extensively, and a few were little more than strings of Bible verses. Although the Gospels and Paul appeared frequently, citations came from almost every Book including on occasion the Apocrypha. In citing the Bible, all of the authors took it to be true, accepting it as both inspired and inerrant. (In keeping with this assumption, The Fundamentals was subtitled "A Testimony to the Truth.") Believers in inerrancy, an idea they had adopted from nineteenth-century Princeton theology, and in particular from the commonsense realism of Princeton theologian Charles Hodge, they assumed that Scripture consisted entirely of words whose meanings were clear and unchanging. Thus they supposed that by reading the same text all sincere believers would arrive at the same conclusions, those being the accepted and customary ones. It followed that the primary role of biblical scholarship was to authenticate the Scripture, ensuring that passages were contained in the original texts and that they had not been tainted by later human interpreters.[9]

In the opening essay of the first volume, Scottish theologian James Orr of Glasgow College demonstrated this approach to the text, using it to defend Christ's divinity, which he took to be the central tenet of the Christian faith. Turning to "*the Scripture itself*," Orr worked his way from the Old to the New Testament, making sure that the narratives were truthful by testing to see that they were original parts and not "late and untrustworthy additions" to the Bible. He described the process:

> The narratives of the nativity in Matthew and Luke are undoubtedly *genuine parts* of their respective Gospels. They have been there since ever the Gospels themselves had an existence. The proof of this is convincing. The chapters in question are found in every manuscript and version of the Gospels known to exist. There are hundreds of manuscripts, some of them very old, belonging to different parts of the world, and many versions in different languages (Latin, Syriac, Egyptian, etc.), but these narratives of the virgin birth are found in all.

Comparing the sources for content and style, and finding them to be consistent, Orr confidently declared them to be definitive texts, bearing "the stamp of truth, honesty, and purity," and therefore providing proof of Christ's divinity.[10] In another essay in the first volume, the highly respected Princeton theologian Benjamin B. Warfield acknowledged that Scripture was not the only source for proving that Christ was divine, and that "proof texts and passages" should be supplemented with other kinds of evidence, including "the impression Jesus has left upon the world."[11] Nevertheless, all of the authors of The Fundamentals would have agreed with Canadian pastor and professor of theology Dyson Hague when he announced in the opening volume that the Bible "does not merely *contain* the Word of God; it *is* the Word of God." Assuming inerrancy, they took it as axiomatic that the Scriptures contained, as Hague put it, "the truth, the whole truth, and nothing but the truth." Moreover, because the Bible was authentic and true, they saw it as providing absolute authority, along with an assurance of certainty about the correctness of traditional Christian teachings. All that believers had to do was accept it, "receiving the Scriptures," explained Hague, as "the Word of God, without objection and without a doubt."[12]

While many of the early essays were built around biblical exegesis, others consisted of personal testimonies, written in the style of contemporary sermons. Among the authors chosen to contribute to The Fundamentals were some of the best-known revivalists of the day, including Reuben A. Torrey, Arthur Pierson, and James M. Gray, all of whom were protégés of Dwight L. Moody, the revered founding father of the evangelical urban revival movement of the late nineteenth century.[13] Writing in the high Victorian style of the big-city revival sermon, and seasoning their essays with healthy doses of sentimentality, these authors told stories of lost and troubled souls rescued by the loving hand of the Holy Spirit. Torrey, for one, dusted off the tried-and-true revivalist trope of the wandering boy lost in the sinful city, introducing it into his essay "The Personality and Deity of the Holy Spirit":

> How many a young man, who has gone from a holy, Christian home to the great city with its many temptations, has been kept back from doing things that he would otherwise do by the thought that if he did them his mother might hear of it and that it would grieve her beyond description. But there is One who dwells in our hearts, if we are believers in Christ, who goes with us wherever we go, sees everything that we do, hears everything that we say, observes every thought, even the most fleeting fancy, and this One is purer than the holiest mother that ever lived.

As conversion narratives go, Torrey's testimony was fairly conventional, save for the fact that sin did not seem particularly prominent in it. Instead of sin, secularity and the allure of success and worldly wealth loomed large as motivating factors in his salvation. Torrey's story was already well known to American evangelicals: how as a student at Yale he had lived a life of dancing, gambling, and religious skepticism, only to find himself depressed at the emptiness of his existence and on the verge of suicide. As his mother, miles away, prayed fervently for her son at her bedside, Torrey fumbled with his razor only to collapse in prayer, begging to be saved and promising to dedicate his life to preaching. For the authors of The Fundamentals, his conversion was a model, a modern narrative in which salvation was less an absolution of sin than a release from the alienation of mass society, a "cure for loneliness," as Torrey described it in his essay, that would "save us from all anxiety and worry."[14]

Throughout the early volumes of The Fundamentals, other testimonies followed the same pattern in depicting conversion as a cure for the discontent that was endemic in modern secular society. Among the most striking of these stories was that of Philip Mauro, a wealthy New York City patent attorney, who described how social and professional success had led him to doubt and depression, "becoming more and more an easy prey to being plagued by gloomy thoughts and vague, undefinable apprehensions." Attempting to allay his discontent by attending a Broadway play, Mauro found himself being led "by an unseen hand" from the lobby of the theater, crowded with well-dressed playgoers, toward a drab urban mission where a prayer meeting was taking place among "exceedingly plain, humble people, of little education" who were "not in the social grade to which I had been accustomed." Put off by the poverty of the place and its people, and unwilling to give up anything in the way of wealth or worldly sophistication, Mauro left the meeting unmoved, only to be drawn back time after time until he finally came forward to kneel at the front of the room, where he confessed his need for the grace of God. At that moment, a complete and unexpected change took place, as "all my doubts, questionings, skepticism and criticism" were "swept away completely." For Mauro, conversion brought absolute assurance. It also provided a cure for the stresses and strains of modern life, "what is called 'nervous prostration,'" as he put it, "from which so many are suffering in these times of high pressure."[15]

In addition to being biblical and evangelical, the language of The Fundamentals was also prophetic, in that it was shaped by the expectation that the world would soon come to an end. As shown by Ernest Sandeen, dispensationalism was an important influence on the forebears of fundamentalism, many of whom had been introduced to the idea at one of the many prophecy conferences that were taking place at the time. In the teachings of John Nelson Darby, a mid-nineteenth-century English preacher and writer, the conventional idea that the history of the church could be understood as a series of distinctive ages or "dispensations" was given a strongly prophetic reading, complete with the prediction that the apostasy of the present age would soon give way to Christ's Second Coming. Unlike earlier expositors, who believed that Christ would return at the end of the millennium, or the thousand years of peace promised in apocalyptic Scripture, Darby maintained that the Second Coming would take place at its beginning and would be preceded by a period of tribulation in which true believers would be carried to heaven in a redemptive moment called the rapture. Adopted in America by Moody, and inserted by Cyrus Scofield into his 1909 Scofield Reference Bible (which would become the standard fundamentalist version of the Scriptures), this "premillennialist" reading encouraged an attitude of expectancy among conservative evangelicals, assuring them that the end of the world was near and that Christ's Second Coming was imminent.[16]

While premillennialism was by no means pervasive in The Fundamentals, it was a presence even in the first volume, where English pastor G. Campbell Morgan introduced the idea in his essay "The Purposes of the Incarnation." Although Morgan treaded lightly, aware that not all of those involved in the project were premillennialists, he assumed that there was almost universal agreement among Christians that Christ would return in the Second Coming. "There may be diversities of interpretations as to how He will come, and when He will come; whether He will come to usher in a millennium or to crown it; but the fact of His actual coming is beyond question." More important, he asserted that Christians had believed from the beginning that Christ would return soon: the idea "gave the

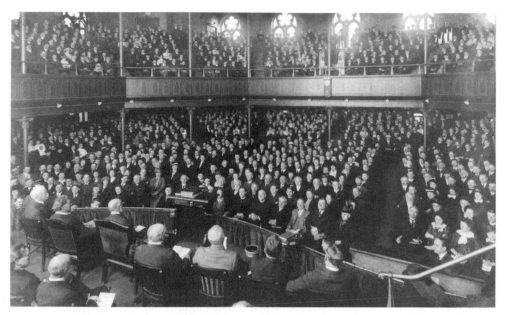

An early prophecy conference, 1914 (Moody Bible Institute Archives)

bloom to primitive Christianity, and constituted the power of the early Christians to laugh in the face of death, and to overcome all forces that were against them." As for those in modern times, Morgan insisted that anticipation of an actual second advent was absolutely essential and that "there is nothing more necessary in our day than a new declaration of this vital fact of Christian faith." He elaborated on the theme: "Think what it would mean if the whole church still lifted her face toward the east and waited for the morning; waited as the Lord would have her wait—not star-gazing, and almanac examining, but with loins girt for service and lamps burning. . . . If the whole Christian church were so waiting, she would cast off her worldliness and infidelity, and all other things which hinder her march to conquest." Though Morgan was one of the most outspoken, other authors echoed his millennial message, giving The Fundamentals a tone of anticipation and anxiousness about the coming tribulation, combined with the certain conviction of ultimate redemption. Morgan captured the feeling, a complex mixture of impatience and confidence: "Heaven is waiting for it. Earth is waiting for it. Hell is waiting for it. The universe is waiting for it," he concluded. "Christ shall appear."[17]

Already in the first volume of The Fundamentals, the authors had begun to create the community of discourse that would become the basis of early fundamentalism. The process was not only rhetorical but also philosophical and psychological, providing readers with new ways of talking and thinking, especially with new ways of thinking about themselves. Blending approaches that were biblical, evangelical, and prophetic, and combining assumptions from Princeton theology, urban revivalism, and dispensational premillennialism, the discourse was distinctive in content, being characterized by absolute belief in biblical authority, certitude about the power of the Holy Spirit to redeem secular society, and faith in Christ's imminent return. It was also distinctive in style and tone, sounding at once authoritative, confident, and eagerly expectant. Talking and thinking in this way, the authors communicated with one another and with their readers, but they also connected with them, creating a consciousness of themselves as part of a larger body of like-minded Christian conservatives. Thus as early as 1910, before there was a movement or even a name, fundamentalists had begun to coalesce into a self-conscious community, a very self-assured and purposeful one, what Dyson Hague was already calling "the noble army of truth-lovers."[18]

Boundaries

In addition to creating consciousness, movements must build boundaries, demarcating the differences between themselves and those who oppose or oppress them. Asserting a sense of "who we are" and "who we are not," boundaries clarify commonalities among movement members while deepening perceived dissimilarities between insiders and outsiders. They also affirm the beliefs and values of the movement, while devaluing those of the dominant order. Above all, boundaries are not self-evident or set in stone. Pliable and porous, they must be consciously constructed, and they can change.[19]

In *The Fundamentals*, boundary building was evident everywhere, as the authors repeatedly distinguished themselves from other more mainstream religious thinkers. At its inception the lines were not completely clear, not only because no one had ever sought to draw them before but also because there was considerable overlap between conservative and mainstream—even liberal—evangelical views. The challenge was to create boundaries that were both broadly inclusive and selectively exclusive, admitting as many moderate-to-conservative evangelicals as possible into the conservative camp while at the same time identifying and isolating the liberals and modernists among them. Thus, as Milton Rudnick has argued, the authors were on the whole surprisingly civil, at least in the early volumes, more concerned with attracting moderates and fellow conservatives than with excoriating liberals. In general their essays tended to be scholarly, sometimes pedantic; extreme statements were relatively few and far between; name-calling was almost nonexistent. On occasion, as Rudnick points out, the authors could even be self-critical, condemning fellow conservatives for going overboard with their orthodoxy.[20]

From the start, *The Fundamentals* were intended to reach out to as many readers as possible. By the time the third volume appeared, they were already a success. With each installment the audience grew, as lay readers began to inquire how books could be sent not only to church leaders but also directly to the people in the pews. To meet the demand, the publishers offered to provide future publications at low cost (fifteen cents per copy, eight copies for one dollar, or one hundred for ten dollars—"Do not send currency or personal checks"). Apparently taken aback by the popularity of the volumes, and beginning to realize the potential to reach an even larger mass audience, they also began to encourage lay leaders to purchase and circulate copies within their churches and communities, as well as to form prayer groups in support of their publication. For the first time, the editorial committee began to refer to the project, albeit awkwardly, as a "movement."[21] Writing at the beginning of the third volume, the editors expressed delight at their success, explaining that they had been "greatly encouraged by the more than 10,000 letters of appreciation, which have come from all parts of the world." They even seemed happy to have received a few critical letters: "The adverse criticisms have been almost equally encouraging," the editors went on, "because they indicate that the books have been read by some who need the truth they contain, and their criticism will attract the attention of others."[22]

The boundary building began with theology, or more precisely with biblical exegesis, as the authors asserted their belief in inerrancy against the trend toward interpretivism that had become commonplace in contemporary biblical studies. They began by drawing clear contrasts between themselves and the so-called higher critics, the school of biblical scholarship—introduced in Germany by Friedrich Schleiermacher, David Friedrich Strauss, and Ludwig Feuerbach, transported to England and America over several decades by German-trained scholars and university students—which contended that the Bible could be understood best in historical context, by taking into account the authorship, dating, and original purpose of each of its various books. To make their case they turned to their most prominent biblical scholars, those like Dyson Hague, a student of apologetics and exegesis trained at the University of Toronto, who had studied the higher criticism and took it seriously, going so far as to admit that it was at least in theory "a very valuable branch of Biblical science." Hague argued that the earliest higher critics had been reverent and responsible scholars, but that the later ones, mostly German rationalists and unbelievers, had turned away from the original purpose of authenticating the Scriptures and were now criticizing and discrediting them instead. In the hands of these critics (Hague's list was long, including "French-Dutch," German, and American scholars), the Bible became little more than a collection of ancient fables and myths, passed along by any number of anonymous authors whose writings were marred by misinterpretation, omission, and outright forgery. Far from inspired, it was an all-too-human text. Hague described their view: "It is not the Word of God in the sense that all of it is given by the inspiration of God. It simply *contains* the Word of God. In many of its parts it is just as uncertain as any other human book. It is not even reliable history." The implications were crystal clear, and they were disturbing. Instead of accepting biblical text as truth—an axiomatic assumption for most Christian churches of the time—believers would now have to test its truth by applying the standards of modern scholarship. Therefore, "every text and chapter and book will have to be inspected and analyzed in the light of its date, and origin, and circumstances, and authorship, and so on, and only after it has passed the examining board of the modern Franco-Dutch-German criticism will it be allowed to stand as a proof-text for the establishment of any Christian doctrine."[23]

Yet for all his criticism of the higher critics, Hague stopped short of a more sweeping attack on contemporary biblical scholarship. It would be easy enough, he confessed, for believers to close their minds, contenting themselves with the simple meaning of the text, while accepting the authority of the Bible as true and altogether unquestionable. Such an attitude, however, would consist of nothing more than "obscurantism," and "no really healthy Christian mind can advocate obscurantism." Instead, it was the duty of all Christians to test the truth of Scripture for themselves. Admitting that the higher critics came with the best academic credentials, Hague warned against being overly impressed, since all believers, even those who were "technically speaking, unlearned," had the right to seek the truth for themselves rather than accepting another view "simply because it is that of a so-called scholar." Still, his warning was not an invitation to anti-intellectualism, since he went on to argue that the best way to confront the errors of the critical scholars was with sounder and more traditional scholarship. It would be a serious mistake, wrote Hague, to assume that "the old-fashioned conservative views" are held only by "the ignorant, the prejudiced, and the illiterate." Far from it: pointing to the common practice of the biblical critics in citing imposing lists of scholars who were on their side, Hague offered a list of his own, consisting of no less than a dozen German, English, and American academics— each an example of "enormous learning"—who had championed a traditional approach to the Bible. In short, he made the case that conservatism was not inherently anti-intellectual, let alone unscholarly, and that "the old-fashioned views are as scholarly as they are Scriptural."[24]

Other authors picked up the theme, blasting the biblical critics while celebrating their own brand of conservative scholarship. Throughout the early volumes of The Fundamentals one author after another took aim at the higher criticism, denouncing its assumptions as "biased," its methods as "partial," and its results as "one-sided and untrustworthy."[25] Applying traditional textual methods and citing passage after passage from every part of the Bible, they analyzed the claims of the higher critics, categorizing their conclusions as "mere hypotheses, imaginings and assertions, brought forward often without even the shadow of proof."[26] They went on to challenge the scholarly standing of the critics themselves, chastising them for their academic "snobbery," the "sublime contempt" and "splendid scorn" they showed for all opinions other than their own, while also asserting that "many leading scholars are with them, but a majority of the most reverent judicious scholars are not."[27] Throughout, they attempted to consign the critics to the margins of biblical scholarship, while at the same time placing themselves squarely in the mainstream. (Far from "an unintelligent literalism," as one of the writers put it, their own brand of conservative biblical criticism was in fact "a true and reverent criticism.")[28] Some went so far as to suggest that the higher criticism was already doomed, an academic fad that was destined for the dustbin of theology. Observed J. J. Reeve, a professor at Southwestern Theological Seminary in Fort Worth, Texas, "Conservative scholarship is rapidly awakening, and, while it will retain the legitimate use of the invaluable historical method, will sweep from the field most of the speculations of the critics."[29]

The boundary making continued with philosophy, as the authors contrasted their own religious principles with the secular thinking of modern writers. Admittedly, only a few seemed prepared to take up the topic, and none of the writers offered a sustained treatment of any school of philosophical thought. But these few were eager to draw distinctions between themselves and secular scholars, aiming in particular at those who taught in America's leading universities. In the forefront of the effort was the New York attorney Philip Mauro, whose essay "Modern Philosophy" showed a deep suspicion of secular scholarship, along with an only too obvious resentment of college professors and their universities. Citing St. Paul and drawing a sharp distinction between faith and reason, Mauro began his essay with the premise that philosophy and religion were inherently at odds and "utterly irreconcilable." After a breathtakingly brief review of the status of present-day philosophy, in which he selectively quoted (while thoroughly misreading) William James's essay "The Present Situation in Philosophy," he surmised that something was wrong in American and English universities, where serious study of the Scriptures had been replaced by a fleeting infatuation with contemporary philosophers who preached nothing less than "the brutalizing and degrading doctrines of pantheism." Introducing arguments that would become commonplace in the antievolution movement over the next decade, he went on to caution Christian parents of the dangers to which their children were being exposed, and to threaten teachers with reprisal, reminding them (in words that William Jennings Bryan would echo in years to come) that "by the very constitution of a democratic social order the teachers *must* teach what the people like to hear, or else give place to those who will." When it came to placing blame, Mauro was explicit, warning balefully that the greatest enemy of the Christian faith at that time was "the smooth-tongued, learned and polished professor."[30]

Yet among the authors in the early volumes, Mauro was atypical. Whatever their views on secular philosophy, these writers were respectful of academic authority, as seen by the conspicuous display of their own degrees, titles, and institutional affiliations. Moreover, they were impressed by intellect, showing a distinct deference to what they called "brainy men," including even those "not known as active Christians."[31] On the whole they seemed less similar to Mauro than to E. Y. Mullins, the widely known and well-respected president of Southern Baptist Seminary, whose essay "The Testimony of Christian Experience," appearing in the third volume of The Fundamentals, seemed to be a response to Mauro's bombastic screed. In his carefully crafted essay, Mullins examined the relationship between Christianity and philosophy, arguing that each was the product of human experience and that the two could be complementary rather than remaining always at odds. When it came to secular philosophers he had no illusions, concluding that many of them (he listed Spinoza, Hegel, and Schopenhauer as examples) set their sights too high, creating abstractions and engaging in "excessive star-gazing, metaphysical cliff-climbing and transcendental soap-bubbleblowing." By contrast, Christianity was grounded in everyday experience and therefore provided answers to practical problems. Rather than dismiss philosophy, however, Mullins tried to make connections to it, suggesting a "point of contact" between Christianity and the new philosophy of pragmatism, which took as its ultimate task "not to solve the insoluble riddle of the universe but to save men from pessimism." (Mullins appears to have actually understood William James.) Far from renouncing reason, as Mauro did, Mullins saw it as complementary to revelation. Unlike Mauro, who insisted that faith was at odds with philosophy, Mullins argued that it completed it. As for the contemporary philosophers whom Mauro defined as enemies, Mullins saw them as collaborators and potential converts. Over the course of the next decade, it would be Mauro's views that would win out, and Mullins would eventually be drummed out of the fundamentalist fold. But during these early days, the authors of The Fundamentals were not willing to write off all secular thinking. Indeed, being less combative and less pessimistic than later fundamentalists, many of them held out hope for contemporary philosophy, agreeing with Mullins when he predicted that "ere long the philosophers will see the gleam on the gates of pearl and the sparkle of the jasper walls of the city of God."[32]

Somewhat surprisingly, in attempting to draw boundaries between faith and science, the authors sometimes seemed unable to make clear distinctions between them. Throughout the volumes a diffuse skepticism about science could be detected, and from time to time an essay would contain some sharp criticism of scientific assumptions or practices. More often, however, the authors went out of their way to associate themselves with scientific thinking (admittedly broadly defined), and to reject the popular perception that Christianity and science were somehow at odds. The most articulate on this count was Glasgow's James Orr, who in his "Science and Christian Faith" argued that religion and science were neither contradictory nor in conflict, and that the two had in fact begun to come even closer together in recent times. Tracing the relationship, he pointed out that most of the founders of modern science—Galileo, Kepler, Bacon, Newton, Faraday, Brewster, Kelvin, and "a host of others"—had been "devout Christian men." Orr admitted that in the past the church (presumably he meant the Roman Catholic Church) had sought to stifle the scientific process, sometimes out of ignorance and occasionally because the theories themselves were "hasty and unwarrantable." Yet through it all truth had prevailed. Although Galileo was imprisoned and persecuted, his conception of the solar system came to be accepted as correct, and today every Christian "rejoices that he understands nature better, and reads his Bible without the slightest sense of contradiction."[33]

Many of The Fundamentals' early essays conveyed the same spirit, and several showed specifically how biblical truths had been proven through advances in science, especially archaeological science. The most convincing of them was the report by Oberlin College's eminent geologist George Frederick Wright, who cited some of the most spectacular recent evidence—the 1868 discovery of the Moabite Stone at Dibon in Transjordan, the 1887 finding of the Tell-el-Amarna Tablets south of Cairo, and the 1906 uncovering of the royal record office of the Hittites east of modern Ankara, Turkey—as providing irrefutable proof that the Bible was scientifically sound. As Wright saw it, these disparate discoveries—coming at separate places and times—were nothing short of providential, conclusively demonstrating that modern science could not just confirm Christian faith, but actually revitalize it. "When the faith of many was waning and many heralds of truth were tempted to speak with uncertain sound," he wrote poetically, "the very stones have cried out with a voice that only the deaf could fail to hear."[34]

For the authors who attempted to clarify the differences between faith and science, the theory of evolution proved unusually troublesome. Although Darwinism had begun to be criticized more openly by American scientists in the decade after 1900, primarily because of the growing popularity of alternative scientific theories, The Fundamentals contain surprisingly little of this criticism. Most essays in the early volumes do not even mention the topic, and those that do discuss evolution treat it gingerly. It is true that some of the writers viewed the theory skeptically from the start. The Texas Baptist Reeve, for example, described contemporary biblical criticism as not only materialistic and naturalistic but also evolutionary and therefore "fundamentally contradictory to the Biblical and Christian point of view."[35] At the same time, however, there were also advocates for evolutionary theory among the authors, including Oberlin's Wright, who—following in the footsteps of his mentor Asa Gray, the great Christian Darwinist—was a committed theistic evolutionist who saw evolution as a divine process guided by the hand of God. More often, the authors seemed to be confused about evolution, accepting many of its assumptions, at least tentatively, while trying to draw clearer distinctions between Christian and Darwinian versions of the theory.

Among these was Orr, a theistic evolutionist who contended that evolution was entirely compatible with biblical accounts of creation. Orr admitted that the findings of modern geology that the earth was immensely older than the traditional six thousand years did appear to pose problems for Bible believers. Applying his own variation on the popular "day-age" theory, however, he argued that the "days" of Genesis could easily be considered to be " 'aeonic' days"—vast cosmic periods—during which the earth evolved as predicted by evolutionary theory. As to the origins of life, he was equally certain that plants and animals had been both created and evolved, since, although evolution was "not yet *proved*," there was growing evidence "of some genetic connection of higher with lower forms." Orr was not prepared to take his assumptions to their logical conclusion, as he went on to specify that as far as evolution was concerned there was a clear distinction between animals and people, with the human body and soul being the product of a special creation. In particular, he was dubious about the Darwinian assumption that humans descended from nonhuman species, because it was not only unscriptural but also scientifically unproven, given "the absence of all reliable evidence of those ape-like intermediate forms which . . . must have intervened between the animal progenitors and the finished human being." Even so, Orr was confident that Darwin's ideas were being superseded by a new and improved evolutionary theory, in which random mutation was coming to be seen as more purposeful, natural selection as less pervasive, and the rate of evolutionary change as more variable, allowing for rapid and sudden change as well as slow but steady development. Certain that science and faith were complementary, and confident that the best scientists were approaching their work in ways that were more open to the divine and transcendent, Orr proceeded to draw distinctions and simultaneously to blur them, distinguishing Darwinism from improved ideas of evolution while conflating biblical and scientific theories. " 'Evolution,' " he concluded, "in short, is coming to be recognized as but a new name for 'creation,' only that the creative power now works from *within*, instead of, as in the old conception, in an *external*, plastic fashion. It is, however, creation none the less."[36]

Ultimately, the boundary-making process worked two ways, involving both writers and readers. Throughout the early volumes of The Fundamentals, the essayists attempted to define differences between themselves and their opponents while admitting as many as possible into their own conservative camp. Their task was complex: attacking theologians, scholars, and scientists while claiming to represent the best theology, scholarship, and science themselves. For their readers, the process was simpler, because it allowed them to come away from the essays with their own less complicated interpretations. At the end of the fifth volume, the publishers enclosed a letter from an anonymous reader, one "more or less similar" to the "many thousands" they had received "from all parts of the world." The letter—from a missionary in British Columbia—expressed appreciation for "this Testimony movement which you have started." Using terms that were implicitly democratic and explicitly anti-intellectual, the writer went on to thank the Christian laymen who had provided funds for the project, describing their efforts as a "well directed blow at the enemy":

> Hitherto the critics have had everything their own way. Fenced around with great learning and scholarship, ordinary men have shrunk from attempting any attack upon their position. We have been looking long to Christian scholarship to give us a lead, but its utterance was not only uncertain but tinged with compromise. . . . It seems to me we have shown too much deference to human scholarship and mere worldly wisdom or learning. In all the churches it has been set above that wisdom which cometh from above. Worldly scholarship has been put in place of the Holy Spirit, and now our chief seats of learning have become hotbeds of infidelity and materialism!

As the lone letter printed in any of the twelve volumes, it was apparently considered by the editors to be the best short statement of the reaction of their readers. Thus it was portentous that the missive ended by asking the publishers to establish "some sort of union or league for the enrollment of all those who are on the Lord's side." Having drawn the boundaries between themselves and others, fundamentalists seemed to be preparing to police them. "Let all of us who are on the Lord's side come out and show ourselves," concluded the letter writer.[37]

Politicization

At some point, movements must turn from "being" to "doing." Having built boundaries to distinguish themselves from others, movement members must contest and defend them. The process requires politicization, as members come to see private concerns as public ones. It also assumes agency, that movements have the ability to act, creating and coordinating strategies to bring about political reform. As Taylor and Whittier point out, politicization does not happen all at once; it is a process that requires movement members to negotiate new ways of thinking as well as acting. Still, if movements are to have any enduring effect on their world, they must be able to act politically.[38]

In The Fundamentals, the politicization process seemed to develop slowly, and it was only in the seventh volume, published in 1912, that the essays began to take on a more pointedly political character. Biblical scholars and theologians began to be replaced by lay writers and local ministers. Essays concentrated less on theory and more on practice, addressing everyday themes like prayer, sin, or how to use one's money. Conversion gave way to criticism, as the original plan of concluding each book with the testimony of a prominent Christian convert was abandoned in favor of a format in which each of the succeeding volumes ended with critical commentaries—sometimes all-out attacks—on other religious and political groups. Above all, the essays in the later volumes seemed more concerned with confronting and combating enemies. While the new perspective was in part the product of editorial policies (A. C. Dixon had been succeeded as series editor by Louis Meyer in 1911 and R. A. Torrey in 1913), it reflected broader changes as well, as fundamentalists began to assume a more active and combative attitude at this time.[39] Premonitions had appeared at the beginning of volume six, the last to be edited by Dixon, in which the foreword suggested the new stance: "May it [the sixth volume] be as abundantly blessed as its predecessors have been by the grace of God, unto the strengthening of saints, unto the defense of the truth against the insidious attacks of the present day, and unto the conversion of sinners."[40]

In one way or another, almost all of the later authors took up the challenge to Christianity posed by a host of enemies. They began with the religious ones, and, predictably, the biblical higher critics stood at the top of the list. Starting with the seventh volume a small phalanx of scholars went on a renewed offensive against them, defending the Bible as absolute in its authority and rejecting the claims of the critics as contrary to Christian teachings.[41] In these later volumes, the idea of inerrancy came to the fore, as essayists like George Bishop, a Princeton-educated Presbyterian minister, developed the so-called dictation theory, arguing that God had authored the Scriptures down to the last line, and that the Bible was nothing less than "a Book dropped from heaven."[42] (So strong was the idea of inerrancy that even a moderate like Old Testament scholar Griffith Thomas would chime in with his support, admitting the need for "sober, necessary, and valuable criticism," but exempting from it all statements of Christ, since "where Christ has spoken, surely 'the matter is closed.' ")[43] As for the higher critics themselves, they were no longer described as mistaken, but as deliberately deceitful and "evil," according to the late Howard Crosby, who in a sermon reprinted in the eighth volume called on Christians to drive them out "before the whole Church is poisoned by this insidious influence."[44]

The authors described Christianity as being beset by numerous other religious enemies as well. These consisted of a diverse contingent of anti-Christian "cults" that included Mormonism ("strongly anti-American" and "thoroughly anti-Christian"), Christian Science (a "farrago of irreligion and nonsense"), Adventism ("essentially polytheistic"), and Spiritualism ("in reality demonism").[45] Another adversary was the Catholic Church, the oldest Christian denomination, which was described by one writer as "so different from, and so hostile to, real Christianity, that it is not, in fact, Christianity at all."[46] Nor did the enemies list end there, for the authors of The Fundamentals found potential opponents lurking even in the pews of their own Protestant churches. A sermon by Anglican bishop J. C. Ryle, also recently deceased, was dusted off to warn in the most dire terms of these enemies within: "All were not Israel who were called Israel, and all are not members of Christ's body who profess themselves Christians. Take notice, you may be a staunch Episcopalian, or Presbyterian, or Independent, or Baptist, or Wesleyan, or Plymouth Brethren—and yet not belong to the true Church. And if you do not, it will be better at last if you had never been born."[47]

Turning from religion to society, the essayists found even more enemies, portraying Christianity as threatened by secular philosophy and at odds with contemporary culture. Unlike the earlier essays, which had shown at least some respect for secular scholarship, the later ones were consistently critical and frequently dismissive of it. A few authors were conspicuously anti-intellectual, proudly boasting that they spoke for "less learned folk."[48] Not content to criticize specific thinkers, the writers in these volumes derided thinkers in general; Salem, Virginia, preacher A. W. Pitzer dismissed them as "the wise men of this world, filled with philosophy so-called." In an essay entitled "The Wisdom of the World," Pitzer traced the roots of contemporary philosophy through several ancient societies, giving special attention to Athens, a civilization where "godlessness and vice, irreligion and immorality, went hand and hand," and which as a result "perished of its own inherent rottenness."[49] Presbyterian pastor George F. Pentecost extended the critique of classical culture into modern times. "Read Homer and Milton, Shakespeare and Dante, read Bacon, Macaulay, Addison and Carlyle, go through all the best literature of all ages," he expounded grandiloquently, "and it will fall infinitely short of the purity, beauty and grandeur of thought and expression found in God's Word."[50] The prominent Presbyterian lay leader Robert E. Speer brought the argument up-to-date by depicting contemporary culture as godless and morally debased—"a vain and empty thing."[51] Some warned of anarchy, describing secular society as lawless and licentious, and cautioning readers not to be "mastered by the mob."[52] Others took a more ideological stand, suggesting that the greater threat was from state-sponsored socialism. Although usually a moderate voice, Princeton theologian Charles R. Erdman was unequivocal on this point, insisting in the closing essay of the final volume of The Fundamentals that Christianity and socialism were antithetical and could never under any circumstances be reconciled, since " 'Christian socialism' is neither Christian nor Socialism."[53] All of the authors could agree that Christianity was threatened by the spread of secularity and that if nothing were done to stop it, the consequences would be dire. Thus the Reverend Daniel Hoffman Martin, a minister from Glen Falls, New York, made the case for Sunday closing laws, arguing that the Sabbath should be protected from "the contaminations of a wicked world": "We are not pleading for a Puritan Sunday of bigotry or intolerance. We are not pleading for blue laws. But as between bigotry and a mush of concession give us bigotry every time. And even the bluest of blue laws would be preferable to red anarchy."[54]

In these later volumes, the relationship between faith and science appeared more troubled than before. Acutely aware of the advances of modern science and confident that Christian teachings had been confirmed by the best scientific research, the authors persisted in claiming that there was no inherent conflict between faith and science. At the same time, they were disturbed by the increasing secularity of science and specifically by what they perceived to be a growing godlessness among scientific professionals. Thus they began to amend the contention that there was no conflict between faith and science, arguing more along the lines of Pitzer when he claimed that there was no conflict "provided each one acts in his proper role." In consigning faith and science to separate spheres, the authors drew clearer boundaries than before, requiring that science concern itself exclusively with the observable world, and insisting that it "has passed out of its proper sphere when it invades the domain of the Invisible and the Infinite." More to the point, they demanded sharper distinctions between reason and revelation (what Pitzer called "the boundary of the known"), refusing to accept that science had any authority at all "when it assumes to deny that the infinite God has revealed or can reveal Himself in His Word, His Son, His Spirit."[55] In essence, the authors seemed willing to accept the findings of science, but only as long as the findings confirmed and did not criticize or question any assumptions of their religious faith.

Furthermore, several writers wanted to have nothing to do with science whatsoever. This view was stated best by Howard Crosby in his "Preach the Word," where he counseled ministers in no uncertain terms to "leave science alone." As a biblical scholar and professor of Greek who served for more than a decade as chancellor of the University of the City of New York (later New York University), Crosby was far from a simpleminded critic of all things scientific. Even so, he saw religion and science as separate spheres. "All the knowledge of the material world, which science deals in," he wrote, "has nothing to do with the soul's salvation." He allowed that it was entirely proper for the preacher to have some knowledge of the natural world, including the main principles of natural science, if only to be considered "an educated man." But, he cautioned, for the minister, the study of science could be a distraction to the teaching of heavenly truths, and there was no reason whatsoever "to waste his time on protoplasm, bathybius, and natural selection, into which and the like subjects Satan would gladly draw him." Indeed, faith and science were not only separate spheres; they were also unequal ones:

> Science and religion are too often spoken of as if they occupied the same plane. Both those who say they are antagonistic, and those who say they are at one, equally talk of the two as on a level. You might as well talk of bread-baking and religion as if they were co-ordinates. Of course there is a connection between science and religion. So there is between bread-baking and religion. The scientific man ought to be religious. So ought the bread-baker. Science can furnish examples of God's wonders in nature. So can bread-baking. But such connections cannot put the subjects on the same level.

For Crosby, who was at heart a Presbyterian preacher, the supernatural realm was clearly superior to the scientific, since science could never comprehend let alone offer comfort to the soul. "Science," he wrote, "at its utmost reach can never touch the sphere of the soul's pressing wants." Why then, he asked rhetorically, "meddle with it in the pulpit?" As for those preachers who did, he was unsympathetic, accusing them of blasphemy and predicting that their preaching would become barren and lifeless. "The Word is supernatural," he concluded, "and woe to the preacher who leaves the supernatural for the natural."[56]

When it came to evolution, the authors in these later volumes took an even harder line, anticipating arguments that would become commonplace among antievolution activists over the next decade. In contrast to the essayists from the earlier volumes, who had criticized Darwinism while accepting other theistic forms of evolution, these later writers tended to collapse almost all evolutionary theory, rejecting both materialistic and theistic versions more or less equally. In addition, they were clearer than ever about the threat to Christianity and Christian civilization posed by evolutionists, whom they increasingly defined as enemies of religion and society. Ironically, it was the theistic evolutionist Wright who made the argument first, claiming in "The Passing of Evolution," the lead essay of the seventh volume, that Darwin himself had never meant to exclude design, but that later Darwinists—he did not name any names—had transformed his science into theology by assuming that his naturalistic methods required a materialistic (and atheistic) theory of the universe. Thus Wright found himself in the awkward position of defending Darwin against the Darwinists, describing how they had carried the concept of natural selection to "illogical conclusions" in which chance and time had been allowed to take the place of a designing deity. To defend Darwin, however, he had to describe him more as a creationist than an evolutionist, going so far as to suggest that the author of *The Descent of Man* believed that humans came into existence "as the Bible represents, by the special creation of a single pair." As Ron Numbers has shown, Wright considered himself to be consistent in seeing creation and evolution as almost synonymous, part of an ongoing evolutionary process into which God stepped to create humans from apelike creatures. Even so, Wright's thinking at this time was clearly moving away from Christian evolutionism toward fundamentalist conceptions of creation. After all, he concluded his essay, "the evidence for evolution, even in its milder form, does not begin to be as strong as that for the revelation of God in the Bible."[57]

Others, including a trio of authors writing in the eighth volume, were even more critical of Darwinism and, by extension, of evolutionary theory of any and all kinds. Adopting arguments that had been advanced by the scientific critics of Darwin, and drawing heavily on several popular pamphlets—Alexander Patterson's *The Other Side of Evolution* (1903), Eberhard Dennert's *At the Deathbed of Darwinism* (1904), and Luther T. Townsend's *Collapse of Evolution* (1905)—that had been circulating widely among conservative clerics of the time, these writers described Darwinism as a discredited theory that had lost all hope of scientific validation. More important, having no real reason to defend theistic evolution, they categorically denied any relationship between creation and evolution. The Anglican curate Dyson Hague summarized their views: "Man was created, not evolved," he stated flatly. "That is, he did not come from protoplasmic mud-mass, or sea ooze bathybian, or by descent from fish or frog, or horse, or ape; but at once, direct, full made, did man come forth from God." Painting with a broad brush and cribbing freely from Townsend's *Collapse of Evolution*, Hague listed the principal points against evolution, arguing that both Scripture and science had proven that (1) there was no such thing as a universal law of development; (2) no new type had ever been discovered, and generation took place "after their kind" or species by species ("the trilobite never produced anything but a trilobite"); (3) there could never be a transmutation of species, since "a man cell develops into a man and the monkey cell develops into a monkey"; and (4) "the missing link"—the transitional connection between ape and human that scientists had been seeking ever since Darwin suggested its existence—had never been found. Elaborating on the last point, he reminded readers that men were not monkeys, passing on the popular misrepresentation of Darwin's ideas that his enemies had been using, much to the delight of appreciative audiences, ever since Wilberforce had debated Huxley. "A man does a thousand things every day," wrote Hague, "that a monkey could not do if he tried ten thousand years. Man has the designing, controlling, ordering, constructive, and governing faculties. Man has personality, understanding, will, conscience. Man is fitted for apprehending God, and for worshipping God." The last point was crucial, because humans were not simply superior beings but spiritually superior ones, "made in the image of God." The problem with evolution—even in its theistic versions—was that it denied this spirituality, effectively removing any reason for revealed religion. "The Genesis account of man," Hague concluded, was "the only possible basis of revelation." Moreover, it was the only hope for salvation, "the only rational basis for the doctrine of regeneration."[58]

Even more adamant was the pseudonymous article "Evolutionism in the Pulpit," written by "An Occupant of the Pew" and reprinted in the eighth volume of The Fundamentals from a 1911 piece appearing in a Presbyterian Church publication. The essay was nothing less than a full-scale assault on Darwinism, which the author described as not just dying but "already dead." It was also a classic example of antievolution writing, introducing themes that would continue to appear in creationist speeches and pamphlets for decades to come. The essay began with a basic statement of Baconian science, describing the evolutionary theory of Darwin, Huxley, and Spencer as "a system based upon hypothesis only" that even after forty years was "without a single known fact to support it." In a quotation that William Jennings Bryan would repeat regularly in his speeches and writings, the author claimed that in Darwin's two principal works alone, the expression "we may well suppose" occurred over eight hundred times. (While completely false, the claim continues to be recited by critics of Darwinism even today.) Comparing Darwin to Jules Verne, the author dismissed Darwin's science as science fiction, which even "the average man" finds "little less than farcical." Apparently drawing on Townsend, "Occupant" went on to make use of a literary device that would become almost universal among antievolution writers, providing a list of anti-Darwinist scientists, "distinguished in their respective departments," each of whom offered "unequivocal testimony" that the Darwinian theory of descent had "not a single fact to confirm it." It did not seem to matter to the writer that several of the scientists listed were either discredited or unknown, or that others in fact accepted some version of the theory of descent. The point was to discredit Darwinism and even more to show that its assumptions were thoroughly at odds with the fundamentals of Christian faith, since "such a system can have no possible points of contact with Christianity."[59]

In addition to discrediting Darwinism, however, "Occupant's" primary purpose was to banish it from the church by removing those ministers who continued to preach it. Writing from his place in the pew, the author expressed astonishment that so many clergy still clung to the theory, apparently because they were afraid of being ridiculed as unscholarly, even though "scholarship can no longer be pleaded as an excuse for clinging to Darwinism." Contrasting the laity with their church leaders, he maintained that "the ordinary individual" experienced "a feeling akin to disgust" at those clergy who used "intellectual subtleties and plausible sophistries" to rationalize their views, "all of which, to this untrained and practical mind, sounds like unmitigated and pharisaical cant." Under the circumstances, it seemed only right to demand that these errant clergy have the "common honesty" and "sense of honor" to step down from the pulpit, "taking with them those of their flocks who think like them and wish to follow."[60]

Finally, in a rambling essay called "The Decadence of Darwinism," Colorado minister Henry Beach took one final step in politicizing the issue. Beach had little to offer on evolutionary theory, confessing that "as a purely academic question" it meant nothing to him. ("Who cares," he asked, "whether a protoplastic cell, or an amoeba, or an ascidian larva, was his primordial progenitor?") But he had a lot to say about evolutionary practice, the application of Darwinian assumptions to religion and society, since he believed that the theory had implications that were anti-Christian and antimoral. "Darwinism," as he put it simply, "degrades both God and man." Trying his hand at science, and taking his definitions from the encyclopedia, the Colorado minister used commonsensical observations to deduce that the theory of natural selection was self-contradictory and impossible, since "it is false that man is derived from a brute and a brute from a vegetable." His science (such as it was) notwithstanding, Beach made a better case when it came to ethics, where he criticized Darwinism for its "poor morals." Articulating concerns that were appearing in response to growing German militarism on the eve of World War I, he seemed to mistake Darwinism for Social Darwinism, describing it as a theory that sanctioned the domination of might over right. "A theory of nature must be ideal to be true," he explained. "Natural selection is a scheme for the survival of the passionate and the violent, the destruction of the weak and defenseless. To be true, black must be white, and wrong must be right, and God an Ivan the terrible." As for what should be done to counter the danger that Darwinism posed to society, Beach was uncertain. A minister himself, he did not appear particularly troubled by the preaching of evolution from the pulpit. But he was concerned with the schools, where "the teaching of Darwinism, as an approved science" had become "the most deplorable feature of the whole wretched propaganda." Raising for the first time a specter that would dominate the thinking of antievolutionists throughout the coming decade, Beach warned that Darwinian doctrine was already present in the schools, and that even now it was working its way into the minds of the children and youth, "like the revenge of the Pied Piper of Hamlin Town."[61]

Taken together, the essays sounded like an alarm bell awakening fundamentalists to the threat posed by their Darwinist enemies. Yet having raised the warning, the authors of The Fundamentals appeared to lose interest in the issue. In the last four volumes, not a single essay on evolution was to be found, with writers instead emphasizing the need for evangelism and focusing on more conventional enemies like Catholics and socialists. David Livingstone has suggested that this apparent retreat may have been due to decisions made by Torrey, editor of the final volumes, who was a firm believer in the harmony of Scripture and science, and who personally accepted theistic versions of evolution. George Marsden thinks that the battle lines were not yet firmly fixed, since there was still no clear consensus among fundamentalists on the dangers of biological evolutionism. Ron Numbers has found more agreement on the perceived threat, but he notes that even those who had made up their minds that Darwinism was a danger to society were not ready to move against it. "Fundamentalists may not have liked evolution," he explains, "but at this time few, if any, saw the necessity or desirability of launching a crusade to eradicate it from the schools and churches of America."[62]

Yet even while avoiding the issue of evolution, the essays in the final volumes of The Fundamentals contributed to what would become a more combative brand of conservatism among American fundamentalists. Published in 1915, the last three volumes in particular were marked by a growing sense of eschatological expectancy, a feeling of foreboding expressed in the premillennial predictions of Arno C. Gaebelein, who wrote in the eleventh volume that the last days of the world were at hand and "the time of the end is here."[63] With World War I already under way, martial metaphors had become more common, with frequent references to the Bible as an "armory" and a "weapon," to Christians as an "army" of "warriors," and to the church's mission as "conquest" and "victory."[64] The discourse also was more pessimistic, as events unfolding in Europe seemed to encourage skepticism about the likelihood of political progress in the future, leading several of the authors to advocate a turn away from political reform in favor of a more personal approach to solving the problems of the world.[65] Among these was Charles G. Trumbull, editor of the influential Sunday School Times, who argued that churches should avoid social programs and act instead to save souls one by one, cautioning that "the salvation of society regardless of the salvation of the individual is a hopeless task."[66] Even the most moderate of the writers, like Speer, a leading advocate of foreign missions, took on a more confrontational tone, calling for a missionary faith that was based "not on compromise, but on conflict and conquest."[67] The most militant authors, like George Pentecost, who as a young man had been a chaplain during the Civil War, pulled out all the stops:

"The Christian's calling in the world is that of the soldier," he told readers. "He must fight the good fight of faith."[68]

In any case, the project had done its work. By 1915, with the publication of the final volume of *The Fundamentals*, a fundamentalist identity had been constructed, a way of talking and thinking that brought Christian conservatives together into a community of discourse and allowed them to begin thinking about themselves as a political movement. In *The Fundamentals* they had found a common consciousness, a definition of the boundaries that would distinguish themselves from others, and an emerging sense of political purpose, a predisposition to do battle against an ever-growing list of enemies. Among those enemies, evolution was waiting in the wings, a concern that had not yet become a cause. But before fundamentalism could generate an antievolution crusade—indeed, even before it could give birth to what eventually became a full-fledged fundamentalist movement—activists had to turn from creating identities to building institutions, mobilizing and organizing for what would become the biggest political struggle of the 1920s.

2 : Mobilization

ACTIVISTS AND ORGANIZATIONS

William Bell Riley had expected a crowd, but nothing like this one. For more than a year he had been recruiting conservative church leaders to join him in Philadelphia in May 1919 for what he had been calling a "World Conference on the Fundamentals of the Faith." But as the meeting approached, Riley and his local conference organizers began to realize that they had seriously underestimated the more than six thousand participants who poured into the city from forty-two states and most of the Canadian provinces, as well as seven other countries. Over the course of the week, the crowds grew larger each day, filling the grand opera house of the Academy of Music and flowing over into Philadelphia's largest theater and several of its biggest churches. As he rose to welcome the throngs, Riley seemed overwhelmed at the turnout. "The importance of this occasion," he began his opening remarks, "exceeds the understanding of its organizers."[1]

In The Fundamentals, evangelical conservatives had discovered an identity, along with a mounting sense of political purpose. But before they could begin to act on their common concerns, they had to assemble the activists and build the organizations that would become the backbone of their movement. With the war no longer delaying the expression of their discontent, Riley and his colleagues had set to work. At Philadelphia, they not only mobilized religious conservatives in unprecedented numbers, but they also began to organize them by establishing what soon became the World's Christian Fundamentals Association (WCFA), the first and most formidable of the early fundamentalist groups. By 1920, led by the WCFA and its teams of organizers, fundamentalists had transformed themselves from a community of like-minded conservatives into an organized opposition, a change that was captured when Baptist editor Curtis Lee Laws coined the term "fundamentalism."[2] Within a year they had become a full-fledged political movement, commonly referred to by themselves and others as the "fundamentals movement."[3] By 1922, they had carried their movement across the continent, holding annual meetings in Philadelphia, Chicago, Denver, and Los Angeles. The following year they met in Fort Worth, Texas, a site symbolic of a new campaign to bring their message to the American South.[4] At every step the movement grew, attracting activists and spawning new organizations, mobilizing support not only for fundamentalism but also for the antievolution movement that would emerge from it.

Among social movement scholars, mobilization has been a hotly contested concept. All agree that, to succeed, movements must attract activists and construct groups and organizations to support and sustain them. As to how to go about mobilizing, however, there has been considerable disagreement. Advocates of resource mobilization theory maintain that the process consists principally of the accumulation and application of resources, including not only time, facilities, money, and people, but also intangible assets such as access, experience, and legitimacy.[5] Critics have pointed out problems with the theory, with new social movement theorists concerned that it ignores the personal and psychological aspects of movement participation, and political process thinkers finding fault with its failure to consider the role of the larger political system.[6] Others, including those who study network structures, have taken a different tack, stressing the importance of the social relationships that come into play when members are mobilized, and examining the complex webs that tie together the people, groups, and organizations that make up movements.[7] Amid the disagreements, a few scholars have sought to shift the focus by turning their attention to the mobilization process itself. Among them is sociologist Bert Klandermans, who in a series of studies has argued that the best way to analyze mobilization is by recognizing it as a multistep process that requires (1) the activation of mobilization potential, (2) the development of recruitment networks, (3) the generation of motivation to participate, and (4) the removal of barriers to participation. The steps are distinct, dealing with different aspects of mobilization, but they have a cumulative character, and they interact with one another. Although different movements will approach each step differently, all must negotiate some version of the larger process. In several studies of European protest groups, Klandermans has found that the steps can be steep, with many chances to stumble along the way. As a result, the movements that mobilize successfully tend to be few and far between, whereas those that fail to get off the ground are all too common.[8]

Fundamentalists were among the successful ones: the question is, How did they do it? Beginning with Norman Furniss, the first students of the fundamentalist movement said little about mobilization, attributing its appearance to broader societal considerations: conflicts between traditional theology and new trends in science, concerns about the influence of modernism and evolution on society, doubts about the inevitability of progress created by the war.[9] Many followed Richard Niebuhr in emphasizing the importance of social and economic factors, depicting the movement as an agrarian protest against urban society.[10] Other scholars, like Richard Hofstadter, adopted a more sociological and psychological approach, describing the movement as a manifestation of anxiety about the loss of social status, along with the paranoia that resulted when conservatives began to feel threatened by the modernizing trends taking place in their churches.[11] Almost all of these observers viewed fundamentalism as an explosion of popular protest that occurred more or less spontaneously, the product of an intense and often irrational response to the modern world. But the fundamentalist movement was not a popular protest, at least in the beginning, and it was certainly neither spontaneous nor irrational in its origins. Rather, it began as an elite enterprise, brought into being by a careful and self-conscious process of political mobilization.

Activating Potential

When movements mobilize they start with what is already there, building from a preexisting base of potential support. Even before any activity begins, there are resources to draw upon: attitudes and identities among a sympathetic part of the population, indigenous social networks, sometimes already established institutions. This reservoir of resources, what Klandermans calls the "mobilization potential" of the movement, is the seedbed from which it will flower.[12]

For fundamentalists, the reservoir was rich, consisting not only of a collective identity already inspired by The Fundamentals, but also an impressive array of conservative evangelical institutions and interrelationships. From the 1880s on, conservative evangelicals had been building Bible colleges—Chicago's Moody Bible Institute, Minneapolis's Northwestern Bible School, the Bible Institute of Los Angeles (Biola) were among the biggest and best known—which by the early twentieth century were educating thousands of conservative ministers and church workers.[13] At about the same time, Bible conferences had started to meet regularly in summer retreat settings, bringing together conservatives from different denominations and distant parts of the country. Inspired by the Bible conferences, dispensationalists had begun to sponsor their own prophecy conferences, where millennialist ministers addressed audiences eager to study the prophetic books of the Bible, especially Daniel and Revelation, and where large crowds gave them a sense of their growing strength.[14] Conservative evangelical publications were expanding rapidly as well, with magazines like Moody Monthly, Our Hope, and the Sunday School Times reaching readers in the tens of thousands.[15] Increasingly, all of these institutions were becoming interrelated, with the Bible colleges sponsoring Bible and prophecy conferences, with ministers from one meeting appearing at the next, and with the religious periodicals providing publicity. By 1918, at the close of the war, a broad conservative evangelical network—what Riley called "a new fellowship"—was already being built. "Individuals and organizations," he observed, "are, by the law of attraction, flowing into it."[16]

At the heart of this network were the ministers. Ministers were a constant presence in the early days of the fundamentalist movement, establishing Bible colleges, organizing Bible and prophecy conferences, and editing conservative evangelical publications. In addition to planning the earliest conferences and meetings, they appeared on the platform to deliver soul-stirring sermons and counsel those who responded to the altar calls. They also took their places in the audience and congregated in the halls outside the sessions, comparing notes with old colleagues and meeting new ones. In their ranks were some of the most famous preachers of the day, including Moody protégés A. C. Dixon, James M. Gray, and R. A. Torrey. Baptists (W. B. Riley, John Roach Straton, Jasper C. Massee, T. T. Shields), Methodists (Leander W. Munhall, Arno A. Gaebelein), and Presbyterians (C. I. Scofield, Clarence E. Macartney) were most frequently represented, but clergy came from almost every Protestant denomination (Adventists, Anglicans, Congregationalists, Dutch Reformed, and Lutherans all attended early meetings); some participants were associated with no denomination at all.[17] Denomination aside, many of the ministers presided more or less independently over their own churches, which served some of the country's largest congregations, early-era megachurches like Boston's Tremont Temple, New York City's Calvary Baptist Church, or Philadelphia's Arch Street Presbyterian Church. Although a few (such as Fort Worth's J. Frank Norris) were lifelong southerners and others (like Riley and Straton) had been born in the South and retained strong southern ties, most were from the North (counting also Canadians like Shields, who hailed from Toronto).[18] By the standards of their time, they were well educated and well traveled, and they represented a surprisingly broad band of opinion. Together, they comprised a formidable nucleus to the emerging fundamentalist network. "Hundreds of the most eminent preachers of the world," wrote Riley in 1918, "eminent because of their confidence in Christ, and their unshaken belief in the Bible, recognize themselves as already members of the new brotherhood."[19]

Surrounding and supporting the ministers were the members of their congregations. In his classic study The Fundamentalist Controversy, Furniss asserted that fundamentalism was a product of the rural South, its adherents consisting mainly of the poor and illiterate. In fact, at least in its early years, it was quite the opposite, a movement of metropolitan northerners who were in most cases of the middle class and moderately educated. These congregants of big city churches were prosperous and respectable people: photographs from early meetings invariably show men in business suits and women in discrete but fashionable Victorian traveling dresses. George Marsden has suggested that because fundamentalist churches grew by conversion, their congregations were probably somewhat younger than those in older, more established churches, with more members who were recent arrivals to the city and still making their way into the middle class. That said, Marsden also emphasizes that even among the church members who would be considered of the working class, fundamentalism appealed to those who in their aspirations and values were essentially bourgeois and Victorian. He points out that many of the first fundamentalists were Anglo-Americans of English and Scottish ancestry, who may have seen the movement as a way to separate themselves from more recent immigrants as well as to shore up conventional norms against the challenges of an increasingly secular society. In any case, it is clear that early fundamentalists were far from the fringes of society. Over time, as the movement turned its attention from North to South, it would attract more support among southerners, including poorer rural ones. Yet even in the South, fundamentalists in the 1920s tended to find their greatest advocates in cities and larger towns, and among the same kind of middle-class people who comprised the movement in the North.[20]

Although men played the most prominent part in the movement, women were among its strongest supporters. As Margaret Bendroth has shown, fundamentalist attitudes toward women tended to be complex and contradictory, a mixture of appreciation of women's unique spiritual gifts and suspicion of their innate sinfulness. Bendroth and Betty DeBerg have demonstrated how leaders of the movement encouraged women to be active in certain roles, particularly as Sunday school teachers and leaders of missionary societies, though allowing them almost no official authority or status in fundamentalist organizations. Though they attended the early Bible and prophecy conferences, usually accompanying their husbands, women seldom appeared on programs or as members of conference committees. Almost without exception, officials of the WCFA were men; even the association's committee on Sunday school literature consisted entirely of males. The woman's auxiliary, created in 1930, seemed to have had no real presence—let alone any power—in the WCFA. Indeed, both Bendroth and DeBerg have argued that during the 1920s fundamentalism became more suspicious of women, who were increasingly described as too sympathetic to liberalizing trends (including what was seen as an emerging feminism) in the church and society. Nevertheless, women would continue to be active in the movement, appearing alongside their husbands at meetings and services, lobbying church and political leaders, and writing letters to their local newspapers in support of fundamentalist causes. At the time of the Scopes trial in 1925, one reporter estimated that 70 percent of all fundamentalists were women.[21]

Similarly, although fundamentalism was initially a lily-white movement and remained overwhelmingly white and in most places segregated, some African Americans did support it. By and large, black churches of the period tended to be theologically orthodox, and many of their ministers were biblical literalists who held strong dispensationalist sympathies. As Jeffrey Moran has shown, concerns about evolution, which they saw as a threat to revealed religion, led many African American church leaders to find allies within the fundamentalist ranks. Although Moran found no public expressions of the sentiment, he speculates that these church leaders may also have considered evolution to be a threat to their race, since it had for some time been associated with certain strains of scientific racism, and since some of America's leading evolutionists were among the strongest promoters of the international eugenics movement that was thriving during that period.[22] Throughout the 1920s black preachers frequently expressed their opposition to evolution in their sermons, insisting, like Baltimore's Reverend A. B. Callis, that there "couldn't be any relation between man and monkey. A monkey has no soul, therefore has no salvation. But man has both a soul and a salvation."[23] In 1925 large numbers of black believers rallied behind William Jennings Bryan at the Scopes trial. "The negro commends . . . Bryan for his solid stand for the fundamentals of our faith," stated the Reverend George Washington Sandefur, one of a delegation of black Baptists ministers who attended the trial. Sandefur went on to say that he "did not know a single minister among my race in Tennessee who is an evolutionist."[24] After that time, black church leaders would voice a growing suspicion of fundamentalism, especially in the latter 1920s, when it came to be increasingly identified with southern white racism. Nevertheless, while African Americans remained on the outside of fundamentalism's strictly segregated organizations, many (Moran suggests a majority) may have considered themselves to be fundamentalists.[25]

Although the diversity of the movement can be overstated (the fact remains that it was and would continue to be dominated by white middle-class males), fundamentalism had more potential supporters than anyone at the time seemed to realize. In their early meetings, leaders could always count on the ministers who made up the core of the movement, along with the members of their congregations who accompanied them. More surprising to them were those in the audience who had arrived on their own—without any preexisting connections to conservative churches or conferences. By and large, these people were "closet" conservatives, members of mainline churches who had become disaffected by liberalizing trends in their own denominations. For such alienated conservatives, the early meetings would provide a means by which they could move from their moderate or liberal congregations to more orthodox ones. From all accounts, they appeared in astonishing numbers. Riley reported that when organizers of the 1918 New York Prophetic Bible Conference rented Carnegie Hall as the main site for their meeting, "many hundreds" of ministers opposed the action, declaring it "almost a presumptuous sin since there would be so few present." When the meeting convened, however, the hall was packed three times a day for four straight days, and every evening overflow auditoriums had to be opened in nearby churches, with speakers and singers dispatched to lead the satellite sessions. By the close of the conference, Riley would later boast, the same ministers who had scoffed at the idea of renting Carnegie Hall were expressing "open astonishment that the Hall was not sufficient to hold the crowds."[26]

For fundamentalism to become a movement, it would need to activate this potential support. Movements require mobilization, and mobilization requires mobilizers. Among these, William Bell Riley was unsurpassed. As a biblical inerrantist, a born-again evangelical, and a staunch dispensational premillennialist, Riley's fundamentalist credentials were impeccable. A gifted preacher, a skilled administrator, and a successful fund-raiser, by World War I he had built a small evangelical empire in Minneapolis around his First Baptist Church and Northwestern Bible and Missionary Training School.[27] Riley was also an experienced revivalist who was in constant contact with an ever-expanding national network of conservative preachers and congregations. Above all, he was a man who made things happen. Most histories of the movement date the founding of fundamentalism to a 1917 meeting at Montrose, Pennsylvania, that was attended by Dixon, Torrey, Riley, and others. But as Ferenc Szasz has pointed out, eighteen months of inaction followed that gathering, and fundamentalism only really began to become a reality when Riley took matters into his own hands.[28] Using the 1918 Carnegie Hall conference as a base of operations, he worked the halls tirelessly, taking notes on organization, buttonholing financial supporters, and convincing anyone who would listen of the need for a more ambitious meeting, a national and even international gathering of the growing forces that would make up fundamentalism. For the next six months, he was in constant motion as he laid plans for the proposed meeting, contacting pastors from across the county and abroad, drawing up an extensive program, establishing a committee on arrangements, and sending announcements to church publications across the country. Proclaiming that a "World Conference" would take place in Philadelphia in the late spring, the expansive Riley described it as the biggest and most important event of its kind ever held. "The whole Christian world will be interested in this Conference," he wrote in a preconvention advertising broadside. "In proportions it will exceed anything that has yet taken place on American soil."[29]

In calling the conference, Riley was not only arranging a meeting but also beginning to construct an organized movement. Working closely with Philadelphia pastor J. Davis Adams, who was in charge of local arrangements, he established a conference executive committee whose members represented a broad conservative constituency. Program speakers were chosen carefully, with an eye to both doctrinal and denominational considerations. "Premillennial Methodists are scarce," Riley wrote to Adams in April, "and [the Moody Bible Institute's Dr. Henry] Ostrom might be worthy [of] consideration by the Committee." Egos frequently had to be assuaged: "I have a letter from Brother [Arno C.] Gaebelein and he feels deeply grieved that he has not been asked to take a place in the program."[30] The arrangements called upon all of his formidable diplomatic skills ("It is exasperating, to say the least," he confided to Adams, "to deal with men who cannot do anything to suit anybody else"),[31] but by April he had managed to persuade most of America's leading conservative preachers to attend the meeting. Equally essential were the plans to establish the conference as a continuing organization, complete with officers, committees, and permanent membership. Here Riley was again intimately involved, setting out plans for standing committees and personally choosing the people who would chair them. (In December 1918 he had presided over the creation of the Northwestern Prophetic Association, a Minnesota premillennialist group that had adopted its own constitution and declaration of faith, along with an organizational structure of officers, committees, and membership dues.)[32] Yet he spent the bulk of his time planning for what would come after the conference itself, developing an ambitious scheme to send out speakers to no fewer than seventy-five locations across the country, thereby transforming the conference into a continuing national organization. "You think that you have a big job on your hands with this one conference," Riley wrote to Adams, "and you have; but, man alive! think of me trying to get twenty five of these, yea seventy five, arranged and going. It is simply maddening."[33]

The planning paid off. Arriving in Philadelphia for the May conference was an all-star cast of conservative clergy, among them some of the English-speaking world's most famous preachers. During the week more than twenty of these dignitaries addressed the convention. Beyond the speeches and sermons, however, the real work of the conference took place in several days of business sessions. In these meetings, organizers adopted a nine-point doctrinal statement (written by Riley) that was broad enough to reach across denominational divisions, while avoiding the common points of conflict between the various versions of dispensationalism. Five standing committees were created, and the chairs of these bodies constituted an executive committee, with Riley presiding. Membership was offered at both associate and active levels, and active members paid five dollars yearly to be able to vote and hold office. Institutional memberships were available as well, not only to churches but also to Bible schools and conferences, suggesting a strategy by which the conference would attempt to encompass the emerging network of fundamentalist groups. Perhaps most important, in establishing an ongoing organization—what would come to be called the World's Christian Fundamentals Association—the Philadelphia conference had brought together what were previously unorganized protests into a unified movement, giving "positive expression," as Riley put it, "to one of the greatest movements of modern times, a movement that is indisputably from God."[34]

Building Networks

No matter how well movements activate potential, they cannot recruit new members unless they have access to the networks where recruitment takes place. Social networks come in many forms, ranging from friendship ties to organizational memberships, and they include the invisible connections that can be built through media or direct mail. Personal and organizational networks have been shown to be most important, since people are more likely to join groups if they have been recruited by those whom they know and trust. Thus movements must create new networks and connect to existing ones, primarily by recruiting activists at the local level and forming coalitions among face-to-face groups.[35]

For the newly formed WCFA, the process of building networks began even before the Philadelphia convention had ended. Each of the five standing committees created there was designated a "Committee on Correlation" to ensure closer cooperation between (1) Bible schools, (2) colleges, seminaries, and academies, (3) religious periodicals and magazines, (4) Bible conferences, and (5) interdenominational foreign missionary societies. Although a few of the committee reports suggested the need for greater centralization (James M. Gray's Committee on Bible Schools, which set out to standardize their curricula and creeds was the most ambitious), most concentrated on building better communication and cooperation between existing bodies and groups. The intention, as the Resolutions Committee put it, was not so much "federation" as "fellowship."[36]

The real work of network building fell to the Committee on Bible Conferences, whose role was to carry out Riley's plan to establish local conferences across the country by using a system of traveling speakers. For years, local communities had been sponsoring Bible conferences, and Bible institutes like Moody, Northwestern, and Biola each ran successful regional programs. Occasionally, two or more of these programs competed for participants. In fact, the organizers of the Philadelphia meeting had feared that attendance would be limited there because several other conferences were scheduled in East Coast cities at roughly the same time.[37] Now, however, the Committee on Bible Conferences, whose leadership Riley himself assumed, was determined to bring order to these previously disconnected programs. Roughly copying the Chautauqua circuit, which had brought popular adult education and entertainment to Americans for decades, the committee proposed the creation of four or five routes along which speakers would travel in small groups, coordinating conferences on each route. The speakers would move to the next stop as soon as they had finished their part at the previous one, thereby saving time and money. At least in theory, the design appeared to be extraordinarily efficient. "We are persuaded," the committee explained, "that these assemblies can be so arranged in complete and adaptable circuits as that a company of speakers given such a circuit could cover within a month from ten to twenty centers without the loss of time on the part of any speaker and with the least possible expenditure in travel and entertainment."[38]

Although its execution was far from perfect, the conference circuit was essential to the formation and coordination of an extensive new network of future fundamentalists. Almost as soon as the Philadelphia meeting adjourned, Riley had put the plan into operation, venturing forth with some fourteen speakers on a cross-country tour that would eventually cover about seven thousand miles and reach eighteen cities. Moving westward in a three-pronged sweep, the group—which included such well-known preachers as A. C. Dixon, J. C. Massee, and Charles A. Blanchard—spoke in teams of four or five, holding three- to six-day conferences for six weeks as they made their way from coast to coast. The financial and logistical problems posed by the continentwide campaign were daunting, and at points Riley's year-long planning broke down in execution. But the conference campaign was a brilliant way to build recruitment networks.[39] Everywhere the speakers stopped, pastors were recruited, local fundamentalist groups were established, and plans for regional conferences were implemented. Letters poured in from across the country testifying to the campaign's success. "The sessions of the conference were largely attended," wrote Biola's superintendent about the meetings in Southern California; "the newspapers gave extensive publicity, and scores of pastors were present from different sections of the State."[40] Nor did the campaign stop there. By the end of August 1919, Riley had recruited a fresh team to carry out a six-month circle of the continent, this time going south as well as west and including a hundred more stops, fifty of which were smaller towns (Berne, Indiana; Owensboro, Kentucky; Alcolu, South Carolina; Waxahachie, Texas; etc.). Everywhere along the way, amid reports of great crowds and enthusiastic audiences, there was a growing impression that conservative congregants were for the first time experiencing a sense of themselves as part of a larger movement, and that they were committing themselves to it. Moreover, the movement was clearly building on its own success. "In addition to the decision of every point visited to be reached again within a year, scores of adjoining cities have placed requests with the committee to be remembered when consideration is being given to future circuits," wrote Riley.[41]

By building these networks, the WCFA established itself as the most formidable of the early fundamentalist organizations. Over the course of its first four years, the association held annual meetings in Philadelphia, Chicago, Denver, and Los Angeles, with new members recruited at each location. The committees reported regularly, announcing initiatives that included alliances between conservative denominational publications, construction of a Bible-based Sunday school curriculum, and investigations of modernist influences on church mission boards, in divinity schools, and at several denominational colleges. The Committee on Bible Conferences was by far the most active, continuing to sponsor continentwide campaigns and adding its own business manager to operate the increasingly intricate system of speakers.[42] Membership rules were clarified and dues introduced and collected.[43] Publicity poured out from the organization's offices, with reports on the WCFA appearing in a growing number of religious publications.[44] For his part, Riley was active in almost every aspect of the organization and stretched so thin that the 1921 Denver meeting voted him a salaried secretary to lighten the load.[45] In keeping with the original concept of the WCFA as a federation of groups, state chapters began to be organized, with the Iowa association developing a model constitution.[46] By the fall of 1922 Riley predicted that "another year would give us a State organization in every state of the Union."[47] At its Los Angeles meeting the same year, the WCFA could rightly celebrate its role in organizing what was now popularly called the "fundamentalist movement." "The time is at hand," announced a delighted Riley in his keynote address, "when we no longer need to advertise ourselves or our 'Association'; it is the best known movement of the twentieth century."[48]

Yet within fundamentalism, the WCFA was only one of many overlapping organizations. While a few early fundamentalists were determinedly nondenominational, most were active in their own denominations. In spite of their separatist tradition, Baptists were among the most loyal to their church conventions. In 1920 conservatives concerned about the direction of the Northern Baptist Convention organized the Fundamentalist Fellowship, composed exclusively of Northern Baptists. Although working independently of the WCFA, the group shared many members with it, including leaders like Dixon, Massee, and the omnipresent Riley. Determined to wrest power from liberals in the denomination, the fellowship adopted a conservative creed, called the "New Hampshire Confession," and began to lobby for its acceptance at the convention's 1922 annual meeting. Turned back at the meeting by a coalition of moderates and liberals who took advantage of long-standing Baptist suspicion of creedal statements, fundamentalists seemed stunned.[49] Increasingly convinced that some of his conservative colleagues had been too willing to compromise their principles for the sake of denominational harmony, a frustrated Riley abruptly resigned from the Fundamentalist Fellowship in order to organize a more militant group. Founded by Riley and fellow firebrands J. Frank Norris and T. T. Shields, the Baptist Bible Union (BBU) was designed to unite all Baptist fundamentalists in North America, with Riley symbolically representing the North; Norris, the South; and Shields, Canada. Committed to denominational reform, the BBU was also willing to consider establishing its own Baptist agencies, acting like (but not calling itself) a new Baptist denomination. The BBU was present at the state (in Canada, the provincial) level as well, organizing active chapters in many states and provinces, and holding regular meetings simultaneously with Baptist state and provincial conventions.[50] In addition, Baptist fundamentalist groups flourished at the local level, many of them independently of national and state Baptist organizations. For example, while John Roach Straton was a charter member of the WCFA, the Fundamentalist Fellowship, and the BBU, he was most active in his own Baptist fundamentalist organization, the Fundamentalist League of Greater New York.[51] From time to time the existence of overlapping organizations led to tensions between groups, with fundamentalists dividing their energies and working at cross purposes. On the whole, however, the explosion of organizations created multiple means for bringing members into the movement. As the 1923 WCFA platform put it, fundamentalism was an alliance of armies, uniting "souls from hard-fought battlefields, who are fighting for the same cause, for the same blessed truth under the same Captain."[52]

Of all the groups, the most ambitious builders of networks were the antievolution organizations. Fundamentalists would take up the issue of evolution for a variety of reasons, including institutional and organizational ones. Throughout the early 1920s the major Protestant denominations had proven themselves remarkably resilient in fending off fundamentalist initiatives. As early as 1922, following the crushing defeat by Northern Baptists of the conservative New Hampshire Confession, W. B. Riley had become all too aware of the difficulties in carrying out denominational reform. Though appreciating the long-standing loyalty that fundamentalists often felt to their church denominations, Riley was frustrated by their willingness to compromise on individual issues for the sake of denominational peace.[53] Thus he began to investigate the possibilities of inter-denominational reform. With critics of evolution beginning to attract attention in many churches, he saw antievolutionism as an issue that could bring together fundamentalists from across denominational lines. In 1923, working in his home state of Minnesota, he invited ministers from no fewer than eight denominations to help found the Anti-Evolution League for the purpose of opposing the teaching of evolution in the state's public schools.[54] The group drew up a constitution, elected officers (Riley, of course, was president) and a board of directors, and set membership dues at one dollar per year.[55] A mass meeting was held in March at the Swedish Tabernacle, the largest church in the Twin Cities, where the new league passed resolutions calling for the removal of textbooks from the public schools of Minnesota. The next day similar resolutions were passed by the Presbyterian Minister's Association of Minneapolis and within weeks by several other ministerial groups.[56] The Anti-Evolution League provided a prototype, as similar groups appeared in other states. By 1924 a national association, the Anti-Evolution League of America, led by John W. Porter of Kentucky and T. T. Martin of Mississippi, was formed to coordinate the state organizations.[57] In its ability to establish extensive networks of supporters, the national league seemed to have almost unlimited potential, reaching beyond conservative evangelicals to "American citizens," "tax payers," and "parents." Admittedly, antievolutionism was a late addition to the fundamentalist family and was still only emerging in 1923. But even at its inception, the league was already viewed by the membership as more than an offshoot of fundamentalism. Its creation, wrote one of its organizers, was "an initial step in what is destined to be a nation-wide movement of tremendous moment."[58]

Motivating Participants

To mobilize, movements must motivate their members by convincing them that there are more benefits than costs to participating. According to standard social choice theory, movements seldom succeed because the benefits that come to any individual, when averaged out among all of the participants, almost never exceed their costs. It follows that participation is not a rational choice for most movement members, since it makes more sense to be "free riders," allowing others to act for them. But social movement theory suggests that people often become active in movements for reasons that are collective and social rather than selective and self-interested. Moreover, studies of actual movements confirm that members participate more often when they see themselves as pursuing a common cause with other like-minded persons. Thus it is essential that movements communicate to their members the sense that others are active alongside them.[59]

For early fundamentalists, this communication took place constantly, as leaders sought to motivate members with glowing accounts of the movement's growing strength. Throughout its first two years, the WCFA kept up a steady stream of publicity on the success of its conference circuits, with every item depicting auditoriums and churches teeming with enthusiastic supporters. A typical report described meetings held in late 1920 throughout the Midwest and South, where "great crowds assembled" all along the line. In Cleveland, the Euclid Avenue Baptist Church was "packed night after night, and well filled in the day services." Even where the turnout began small, as in Elgin, Illinois, it built steadily, "finally filling the house." Only in Columbia, South Carolina, could the attendance be considered no more than "fair." Audiences were diverse, representing a broad cross section of evangelicals from different denominations. In Jefferson City, Missouri, for example, "the meetings were in the Baptist, Methodist and Christian churches, moving from building to building to accommodate the crowds."[60] The crowds were enthusiastic. By 1921 the WCFA was claiming that "hundreds, and even thousands of people, who were either indifferent to the articles of our Faith or in opposition to them, have been converted into ardent advocates of that declaration."[61] Financial support seemed to be growing as well, as reports from the same year showed that the movement had managed to create a national organization, sponsor hundreds of conferences, and produce a growing stream of publications, all by "free will offerings."[62] Perhaps most significant to leaders like Riley, the movement had come to be noticed not only in church publications but also in the popular press. "The Christian Fundamentals movement is stirring the nation from sea to sea," wrote Riley in the summer of 1922. "Within the last sixty days more articles have been written upon this subject than upon any other single subject of religious concern."[63]

While fundamentalism found support from the conservative evangelical press, the movement relied on its own periodicals to motivate its members. These home-grown publications were primarily church-based papers, some with a large regional readership. The most prominent were Riley's *Christian Fundamentals in School and Church* (later called *The Christian Fundamentalist*), Curtis Lee Laws's *Watchman-Examiner*, and J. Frank Norris's *The Searchlight*.[64] As the official organ of the WCFA, *Christian Fundamentals in School and Church* was the movement's organizational voice, not only carrying on its first page the WCFA's seal (designed by Riley himself) and its distinctively Midwestern motto ("Prairie fires are stopped by starting opposing fires to meet the on-rushing flames"), but also featuring regular reports from WCFA committees and officials.[65] The *Watchman-Examiner*, edited by Brooklyn, New York, pastor Laws, embodied the mind of the movement, consisting principally of carefully crafted editorials and opinion pieces.[66]

Seal of the World's Christian Fundamentals Association
(from Christian Fundamentals in School and Church, 1920)

But it was Norris's *The Searchlight* that captured the movement's emotion and energy, while also introducing a more innovative style of journalism to fundamentalist publishing. Originating (like most of the early fundamentalist papers) as a church newsletter, complete with regular reports on Sunday school attendance, building campaigns, and upcoming church picnics, *The Searchlight* underwent a transformation after 1920, when Norris surfaced as a movement leader. Following Riley's example, Norris expanded his paper by reprinting articles from other fundamentalist publications, while at the same time sending pieces from his paper to be reprinted by them, contributing to what was rapidly becoming a fundamentalist newspaper network. A tireless self-promoter, Norris included regular updates on when and where *The Searchlight* had been reprinted, along with correspondence from other movement leaders complimenting him on his publication. ("I have enjoyed reading in the Searchlight your 'red-hot' discussion," wrote A. C. Dixon. "It cannot fail to do good.")[67] Not content with the staid style of the church newsletter, Norris adopted techniques from mass circulation newspapers: splashy headlines, editorial cartoons, and eye-catching advertisements (including those featuring tourist packages for WCFA conventions).[68] Yet Norris's true gift was in marketing. Selling subscriptions at one dollar per year, *The Searchlight* consistently published letters from satisfied customers, many of them asking for sample copies and subscription blanks to give to their friends. The letter writers made it clear that by buying copies, they were helping to build the fundamentalist movement. Norris echoed the sentiment: "The circulation is increasing by leaps and bounds. Every mail brings in new names. Only a dollar a year. Let everyone who believes in the whole truth and who wants to see all heresy and isms [sic] exposed, help to circulate the paper."[69]

The process of motivating members was more systematic than it seemed. Although editors were eager to attract any and all readers, their efforts tended to focus on specific constituencies, taking advantage of existing networks and organizations. Because the main newspapers of the movement were Baptist, they turned first to their Baptist readers, addressing their denominational concerns and leadership. In his *Watchman-Examiner*, for example, Laws concentrated almost entirely on issues involving the Northern Baptist Convention, while also actively recruiting for the Fundamentalist Fellowship that he had helped to organize within it.[70] By contrast, Riley's *Christian Fundamentals* reflected the editor's more complex denominational views. A devoted (if deeply disgruntled) Northern Baptist who was a power in his own state convention, Riley was also committed to building an alliance between fundamentalists within the Northern and Southern Baptist Conventions. Thus in the early 1920s he frequently printed stories examining conflicts among Southern Baptists, while at the same time reminding his

ARE YOU COMING ?

to the

Sixth Annual Convention

of the

Christian Fundamentals Association

JUNE 8-15

in

MINNEAPOLIS, MINN.

SPEAKERS:

William Jennings Bryan, J. Frank Norris, Hugh White, Leander S. Keyser, Sidney T. Smith, John G. Inkster, W. B. Riley, C. G. Trumbull, A. C. Gaebelein, P. W. Philpott, T. T. Shields, O. F. Bartholow, L. W. Munhall and others.

Summer Tourist Rates on all Railroads

Write:

L. M. Aldridge,
Publicity Director,
Fort Worth, Texas.

Ethel H. Blake
Coresponding Secretary,
Minneapolis, Minn.

Advertisement for an early WCFA conference (The Searchlight, 1924)

readers that "the great body of Baptists, North and South, is loyal to the fundamentals of the faith."[71] For his part, Norris took a more confrontational route
with The Searchlight, conducting unrelenting campaigns against both the Southern
Baptist Convention and the Baptist General Convention of Texas. Censured by his
own state organization in 1922, Norris began to seek out ties to northern fundamentalists, primarily in the BBU. He also began a close correspondence with
Riley. As the most active and visible fundamentalists within the Northern and
Southern Baptist Conventions, the two leaders represented the potential for a
conservative alliance that could transcend the historical divisions that had divided
Baptists since before the Civil War. Using their newspapers, they began to introduce one another to their respective readers by advertising pulpit exchanges,
printing biographies and pictures, and highlighting their activities and awards.
Each strongly supported the other. (Although they would later experience a falling out, during most of the 1920s they considered themselves to be "dear and
appreciated friends.")[72] Above all, both men regarded Baptists as the core of the
fundamentalist movement. "We be Baptists," wrote Riley in The Searchlight, "and
there are some of us in the North who earnestly crave the fellowship of the great
Southern hosts who hold the Bible to be the inspired Word of God."[73]

But mobilizing Baptists was just the beginning. With their strong tradition
of independent publications, Baptists tended to dominate the fundamentalist
press. Because so many of them were unrestricted by denominational ties, the
Baptist publications seemed more disposed to reach out to readers from other
denominations, going out of their way to address issues of interest to Methodists, Presbyterians, and others. In 1921, when Norris campaigned to remove
biblical critics from the faculty of Southern Methodist University (SMU), he consciously courted what he called "old-fashioned, John Wesley, orthodox, God-
fearing Methodists."[74] Riley followed fast on his heels, providing extensive coverage in his Christian Fundamentals of Norris's charges against SMU; he also published claims that Methodist bishops had "gone over, in a body, to modernism."[75] Conservative Methodists then began to speak for themselves, led by those
like Leander Munhall, editor of the Eastern Methodist, who denounced the Northern Methodist Church for "the unMethodistic teaching in her schools."[76] Within
a year, Baptist and Methodist fundamentalists were working together closely in
the newfound Council of Church Schools of the South, where they "fraternize,"
according to Norris, "in perfect fellowship."[77]

Meanwhile, Northern Baptists and Northern Presbyterians were finding com-
mon ground in their attempts to discredit the outspoken liberal Harry Emerson
Fosdick, an ordained Baptist minister who served as pastor of New York City's
Park Avenue Presbyterian Church.[78] As connections between Baptist, Methodist,

and Presbyterian fundamentalists grew closer, those from other denominations came on board, including Congregationalist conservatives in the Churches of Christ.[79] The mobilization process had its limits: few of the early fundamentalist publications made any mention of Adventists, Pentecostals, or holiness groups, many of which would later be associated with the movement.[80] Catholics, of course, were beyond the pale and not even considered as potential collaborators. Nevertheless, within broadly Protestant boundaries, early fundamentalism showed a surprising openness. "This movement," wrote an agitated Riley, responding to depictions of fundamentalists as narrow sectarians, "represents no single doctrine, nor has it at any time laid any unusual emphasis upon any particular phase of truth."[81]

By 1923 the movement was reaching beyond church-based mobilization. Over the course of its first four years, fundamentalism had built a strong base of support within the largest Protestant denominations. At the same time, its attempts to assume control of the denominations had consistently ended in failure. Consequently many in the movement had come to advocate broader coalitions with activists from other churches, as well as those not associated with any church. At its 1922 convention, for example, the WCFA had resolved to create a Layman's Movement, with William Jennings Bryan at its head, to operate alongside its clergy-dominated committee structure. Although Bryan adamantly refused to serve, his selection was symbolic. The son of a Baptist father and a Methodist mother who himself converted to Presbyterianism, he seemed at home in any Protestant church. Moreover, he was adept at bringing his broadly evangelical message to almost any audience, including relatively nonreligious ones. Above all, Bryan was a national figure who could reach out to supporters in every part of the country. "The Christian Fundamentals Association," insisted Riley, "regards neither the Mason and Dixon line, nor any denominational line, in its contention for the faith one for all delivered."[82]

But the broadening of the movement was symbolized even more by the decision of the WCFA to hold its 1923 convention in Fort Worth. A movement born in the big cities of the North, fundamentalism came to the South cautiously and only after building bases of support in the Midwest and West. Many of its members seemed to view the South in stereotypical terms, as a backward and provincial place. Few had any close ties to the largest southern denominations, which were deeply conservative but not particularly sympathetic to fundamentalism, in large part because there was so little liberalism to threaten the southern churches. Even so, encouraged by Norris, WCFA leaders became convinced that they could bypass the southern denominations by taking their message directly to what one called "the plain, common people of the South."[83] At Fort Worth, their expectations were met and far surpassed. Meeting in the auditorium of Norris's First Baptist Church, which held between five and six thousand persons, the sessions were regularly filled. More important, however, was what went on outside the convention halls. "On the street cars, in the banks, in hotel lobbies, in the factories, on business corners, in the houses, in clubs, everywhere people are discussing the fundamentals convention," reported an excited Riley.[84] Mobilizing members wherever they found them, fundamentalists at Fort Worth began to think of themselves for the first time as a truly national movement. "Our appeal," the convention concluded in its final resolutions, "is not only to the members of evangelical churches, but to the great body of men and women whose homes and whose hearts and lives are involved."[85]

Removing Barriers

In addition to motivating their members, movements must remove the barriers that prevent them from participating. Barriers can often consist of concrete concerns—time, money, other obligations—that discourage even the most motivated from becoming actively involved. But barriers can be psychological and emotional as well, and as a result they are closely and reciprocally related to motivations. Thus removing them is not always simple, and many movements fail to mobilize some of their most likely members.[86]

For early fundamentalists, the psychological and emotional barriers were especially steep. To begin with, most of them were ambivalent about becoming associated with any kind of movement. In his early essays, Riley avoided the term, preferring to call the new alliance of conservative evangelicals a "brotherhood," "fellowship," or "possibly a loose organization."[87] In contrast to conservatives, liberals had created movements, in particular the Interchurch World Movement, an idealistic and ill-fated attempt of postwar reformers to unite the major Protestant denominations behind a common goal of achieving peace and building a better world. More troubling to fundamentalists, they had constructed interdenominational institutions such as the Federal Council of Churches and the Young Men's Christian Association (YMCA), both of which threatened the denominational structure of Protestantism. (Among other dangers, Riley believed that such ecumenical groups would lead inevitably to cooperation between Protestants and Catholics, and on at least one occasion he claimed that the Interchurch World Movement had actually been "courting Rome.")[88] Failing to see the irony in their own interdenominationalism, fundamentalists were confused about denominational loyalties. "We have come to believe that the brotherhood of faith and of teaching is bigger than denominational labels," an uncharacteristically tongue-tied Riley tried to explain, "and while not despising the latter, we are ready to protest against the destruction of honorable denominational titles by a coalition that renders them meaningless to us."[89] When it came to their own denominations, most fundamentalists were highly conflicted in their feelings. On the one hand, they portrayed themselves as champions of their churches, defending orthodoxy and traditional values. "The great heart of the Baptist denomination is yet loyal to the Book and the Blood," wrote Riley to his fellow Northern Baptists. "It is not necessarily too late to recover our reputation."[90] On the other hand, they thought of themselves as holy warriors leading all-out assaults on their church establishments, "allies of faith," as Riley called them, "as confident in their God as were the great Generals of the Entente."[91] The two conceptions of themselves—as insiders and as outsiders—were often at odds, and the juxtapositions were jarring, as when Riley called upon all "orthodox people" to foment "revolutions" in their churches.[92] Above all, fundamentalists were ambivalent about activism. Conventional and conservative in their values, they had a hard time conceiving of themselves as reformers, let alone as radicals. "The orthodox men of the country are not trouble-breeders," observed Riley. Even so, there were times when they had no choice but to act. "Silence sometimes becomes a sin," he had concluded, "and the men who are ready now to speak realize that fact."[93]

Nor were fundamentalists particularly open to organizing. As Protestants, most of whom were associated with congregational or separatist churches, they were historically distrustful of ecclesiastical hierarchy. Even within their own denominations, they preferred leadership to be personalized and membership participatory. Contrasting themselves to their liberal counterparts, they constantly complained that liberal church leaders had adopted strategies of centralization and consolidation from the business world in an attempt to make America's churches as efficient as its corporations. In the Interchurch World Movement, they saw an extreme version of the trend, an attempt to control the churches in the same way that corporate monopolies had gained control over the economy. Riley explained: "They naturally reason that if the great millionaire magnates of the world have been able by consolidation and corporation to either control or crush out all opponents, the principle can be worked in church; and a steam roller can be created before which no man, even the fanatic, would dare attempt to stand."[94]

By contrast, fundamentalists conceived of themselves as a decidedly decentralized group, an amalgamation of mostly independent ministers and their church congregations. Admitting that they lacked administrative support, leaders looked for resources at the local level. As one example, Riley made the case for using church bulletins to counter the propaganda that poured out from the powerful and well-funded denominational publications. Applying military analogies, he described the strategy: "In the process of time the repeating rifle is more effective than the cannon, and while Moderns are constructing their Big Berthas, let Conservatives get busy with their Mausers. Of course these are supposed to be out of date now, as our theology is, but when dexterously employed, they have proven as effective as sound theology."[95]

Indeed, fundamentalists sometimes disclaimed responsibility for organizing their own organizations. In his keynote address to the WCFA convention in 1922, Riley characterized the first four years of the fundamentalist movement as a conscious creation, not an outburst of protest or a "mere tidal wave of excitement consequent upon the late war." Yet as he depicted the movement, it seemed surprisingly spontaneous, the product less of planning than of what he called "certain irresistible forces." He elaborated: "If ever a movement came in answer to prayer, it was this movement. And if ever a large company of men, living at remote distances from one another and laboring under varied circumstances, found themselves animated by a common conviction and pushed forward by a common impulse, it was that company who brought this Association to the birth, and who, without exception, abide as its leaders to this blessed hour." Above all, fundamentalists insisted on seeing their efforts in spiritual terms. As Riley stated in his 1922 address, the movement had come about because "believers by the millions" had "long waited" and "ardently prayed" for "the realization of just such a fellowship."[96]

In the same way, fundamentalists seemed conflicted about seeking financial support for their movement. Although Lyman Stewart's generous funding of *The Fundamentals* had made the movement possible, its leaders consistently claimed that almost all of the financing came from the contributions of small donors. At times, they went so far as to suggest that money did not matter to the movement, and that it was "not financed at all, save as God has put his continued blessing upon it."[97] Here again, they contrasted themselves to their liberal counterparts, blasting interdenominational organizations like the Federal Council of Churches for relying on the main denominations for support, feigning friendship with them, as Riley put it, "in order to be able to filch from the spoils, goodly garments, shekels of silver, wedges of gold."[98] Worse, these same liberal organizations had become beholden to the powerful patrons and well-financed foundations that funded them, with John D. Rockefeller and the Rockefeller Foundation Fund being the most obvious offenders. Throughout the early 1920s Riley carried on a sustained campaign of criticism against Rockefeller, a fellow Northern Baptist, maintaining that the denomination and its University of Chicago Divinity School had become captive of the "Rockefeller millions."[99] Indeed, for fundamentalists Rockefeller served as a foil, a symbol of corporate control against which they posed their own independence and widespread popular support. Thus throughout the early years, Riley repeatedly boasted that "no man of means" (he conveniently omitted Lyman Stewart) had been asked to support the fundamentalist movement and "no gift of any considerable amount" had ever been made "by any one man."[100] Even four years into the movement, he asserted that, with only one exception (presumably the $300,000 that the Stewarts had contributed to fund The Fundamentals), the largest gift it had ever received was $150, and that support continued to come entirely through "the multiplied gifts of the people."[101] Yet in almost the same breath Riley admitted that ever-expanding programs had created financial difficulties, and he called for twenty-five donors to contribute a thousand dollars a year each to maintain the solvency of the movement. The request would become a repeated refrain, in later years supplemented by calls for individual donors to give anywhere from $25,000 to $5 million each. That said, it is also true that even in their most dire straits, fundamentalists continued to turn to small donors, passing the collection plate and relying on membership fees to keep the movement financially afloat. Ultimately, they tended to regard financial support as a secondary concern, assuming that God would somehow provide. Said Riley: "If it be His will that the work shall be carried on after this manner, the same Spirit who has sustained us until this good hour, will raise up for us these friends and provide these funds."[102]

There was another problem as well: even when they organized, fundamentalists found it difficult to stay organized. An alliance of independent and strong-minded ministers, the movement was beset by conflicts and disagreements from the start. Over time, as it grew and institutionalized, internal tensions only intensified. Fundamentalist leaders presided over their personal fiefdoms like biblical patriarchs, tending to view one another with jealously and suspicion. Riley felt little affection for Straton, distrusted Shields, and eventually broke with Norris. Straton fought with the more moderate Jasper Massee, calling him an apostate to the fundamentalist cause. At one time or another, Norris managed to alienate virtually every major fundamentalist leader. All of them kept their distance from William Jennings Bryan: only T. T. Martin would go to Dayton, Tennessee, to support him during the Scopes trial.[103] In the same way, denominational differences were never far from the surface, and Baptists came in for frequent criticism from Methodists and Presbyterians for attempting to control the movement. Even among members of the same denomination there were tensions, particularly between those (like supporters of the Baptist Fundamentalist Fellowship) who were committed to working within church structures and those (such as advocates of the BBU) who operated outside of them.[104] Doctrinal disagreements were also common, especially in the early days of the movement. As late as 1922, Riley declared that the contention that the movement was "distinctly premillennial" was "as false as the motivations of the men who make it."[105] Institutional interests also had to be considered, both within the WCFA, where state and local chapters were constantly being created, and outside of it, with the proliferation of offshoot organizations, including the Anti-Evolution Leagues. Finally, by 1923 there were growing divisions concerning the direction of the movement, with many believing that the time had come to turn their attention from working within the churches to changing the broader culture around them. At stake, these partisans argued, was nothing less than "civilization itself."[106] With the movement appearing to go in different directions, leaders expressed frustration. "Some Fundamentalists are laws unto themselves," Riley lamented, "and even those who have no such disposition are not as yet in the close co-ordinated fellowship that would accomplish the best and most to be desired results."[107]

All told, organizing fundamentalists was an overwhelming task. On its face, fundamentalism was a controlled and structured movement, with the WCFA in charge of an intricately interconnected network of activists and groups. When considered more closely, however, it was a decentralized and disorderly conglomeration of often competing constituencies, many of them suspicious or resentful of each other. As early as 1922, WCFA leaders were convinced that they had lost control of the movement. Attempting to bring the growing number of fundamentalist groups under a central direction, they introduced a resolution at that year's convention to divide the continent into nine regions, each administered by a member of the organization's central Advisory Committee. "Believing as we do that our work is so essentially one," the resolution explained, "there can be no overlapping of interests."[108] Apparently no one paid any attention. For his part, Riley struggled valiantly to hold things together. In the first five years of the movement, he had spoken at over 250 conferences, raised almost $200,000, and founded no fewer than four fundamentalist organizations. During that time he had continued to serve as minister of his large Minneapolis church and president of its Bible college. At every step he had made ambitious new plans, including his intention, announced in 1923, to bring 100,000 new members into the movement the next year. Although his energy seemed inexhaustible, his pronouncements grew more strained and shrill, and his appeals for money more frequent.[109] In 1924, following an automobile accident, he collapsed in his pulpit, suffering from what he later described as a "nerve collapse" or "nervous break."[110] Although he would fully recover and live until 1947, he would never regain his position as fundamentalism's preeminent figure, let alone control the movement. Returning from his recuperation, Riley appeared resigned to the difficulties in organizing the fundamentalist forces. "One of the greatest dangers to Fundamentalism is the absolute independence of the average Fundamentalist and his unreadiness to find harmonious ways with the brethren of his own convictions," he wrote. "If Fundamentalists did as good team-work as do Modernists, their success would be far greater."[111]

Nevertheless, fundamentalists had managed to mobilize. Building on existing evangelical institutions, tapping into long-standing networks of ministers and lay leaders, supported by the gifts of a small number of large donors and large numbers of small ones, they had created in a matter of months an extraordinary institutional infrastructure. Now they had to put it to use. Ambivalent about activism, divided among themselves, seemingly incapable of sustaining organizations, they craved an issue that would bring them together in a common cause. In evolution they would find their issue.

3 : Framing

THE CAMPAIGN AGAINST THE COLLEGES

William Jennings Bryan had always felt a little more hopeful about the future when he was speaking to students. For decades he had been a familiar face on America's college campuses, where he drew admiring audiences, often in the thousands, who came to experience his eloquence and stand in line to shake his hand. But in the early 1920s he sensed that something was seriously wrong: the crowds at the colleges seemed smaller, the students more distracted and less enthusiastic. At the same time, he began to receive disturbing letters from parents relating how their children had returned home from college as doubters, having lost their faith. As the letters continued to arrive, Bryan became more and more convinced that American schools were systematically undermining the religious views of their students, and as Mary Baird Bryan described her husband, "his soul arose in righteous indignation."[1]

With peace and prosperity, secularity was spreading, particularly among the young. America's colleges seemed especially vulnerable, as the press reported in lurid detail how students were turning their backs on their traditional religious upbringing in favor of worldly pleasures like football games, jazz music, and petting parties. While secular critics expressed concern and mainline church denominations announced new programs to reach out to college students, Bryan urged that more be done about the problem, and fundamentalists began to rally around him. Beginning in 1920 they came together to cleanse and reform academia, confronting college presidents, investigating teachers and textbooks, and demanding (sometimes forcing) the resignation of professors. For fundamentalists, the campaign against the colleges provided a site where they could take their stand against the rising tide of secularity. It offered them a target: college professors whom they could hold responsible for destroying the faith of their students. It also gave them a leader. Although Bryan himself was not a fundamentalist, he soon became the most widely recognized voice of the new fundamentalist movement, delivering hundreds of speeches and publishing scores of articles and essays that reached millions of readers. Above all, the campaign gave them an issue, for it was in the colleges that students discovered Darwinism. From that time fundamentalism would become a movement increasingly committed to ending the teaching of evolution in the nation's schools.

Over the years, social movement theorists have shown a growing interest in how movements frame issues. According to Erving Goffman, who was one of the first to introduce the idea, frames are interpretive schemes that simplify and make sense of the world by locating and labeling events or experiences.[2] William Gamson and others have defined them as accentuating and punctuating devices, used to underscore the seriousness of a condition or to define as immoral or unjust situations that may previously have been regarded as unfortunate but tolerable.[3] But it was David Snow and Robert Benford who defined the concept most clearly. In their essay "Ideology, Frame Resonance, and Participant Mobilization," which has become something of a classic in social movement scholarship, Snow and Benford argue that frames must carry out three essential functions: (1) determining that a condition or situation is in need of alteration; (2) proposing solutions that specify what has to be done; and (3) providing a rationale for ameliorative action. In Snow and Benford's terms, these three tasks—*diagnostic, prognostic,* and *motivational*—are the core components of the framing process.[4] The tasks are interrelated (often overlapping); any one of them alone is not enough to provide meaning to a movement. When integrated, however, they can create a powerful template that allows activists to define what is wrong, how to fix it, and what they themselves can do. In addition to providing meaning, the three steps contribute to mobilization, since the framing process can have the effect of energizing movement followers, attracting the attention of bystanders, and embarrassing or even neutralizing enemies. Thus for social movements, frames inspire both a sense of agency and a commitment to action, "moving people," in the words of Snow and Benford, "from the balcony to the barricades."[5]

On the whole, previous studies have failed to address how evolution emerged as a fundamentalist issue. In his *History of Fundamentalism,* for example, Stewart Cole said little about evolution, preferring to treat fundamentalism primarily in theological and denominational terms. Ernest Sandeen, in *The Roots of Fundamentalism,* mentioned evolution almost as an afterthought, and then only to portray it as an anomaly, an issue that was incompatible with fundamentalism's true character as a millennialist movement. By contrast, Norman Furniss devoted most of *The Fundamentalist Controversy* to disputes over evolution but paid little attention to how or why the idea became controversial in the first place. Even in those histories that describe the development of the evolution fight, like George E. Webb's

The Evolution Controversy in America, the treatments seem too predictable, with fundamentalists moving easily, almost inexorably in the early 1920s from a concern about modernist theology into a full-scale campaign against evolutionary science.[6] In fact, the truth was more complicated, since most fundamentalists of the time saw modernism and evolutionism (along with atheism, agnosticism, and infidelity of all kinds) as bound together as part of a diffuse and mostly undifferentiated secularity. For evolution to emerge as an independent issue, it first had to be framed: that is, isolating it as a source of injustice, targeting those responsible, and motivating others to oppose it. In other words, the task taken up by Bryan and the phalanx of fundamentalist preachers who worked alongside him was to turn evolution from an idea into an issue.

Diagnosis

Framing begins with a diagnosis of the problem, a process that consists of identifying injustice and attributing blame. While most movements are inspired by the perception of some kind of injustice, it can be difficult for movement members to agree on the exact character or nature of the offense. Thus before problems can be corrected they must be defined: complaints must be collected, grievances filed, injuries investigated. Once the injustices are identified, cause or culpability must be determined, as someone or something is found to be at fault. The diagnostic process consists for the most part of collecting evidence.[7]

At the beginning of their campaign against the colleges, fundamentalists found the process to be fairly easy, since academia in America had already begun to attract widespread attention together with considerable criticism. With peace and prosperity, enrollments had increased sharply; by the end of the 1920s there were three times as many students in colleges and universities as before World War I. Church-related colleges had started to be surpassed by the expanding state universities, which grew steadily in number and size over the course of the decade. The character of higher education was changing too, especially in universities, where sectarian instruction was being replaced by more secular and scientific approaches to learning. Particularly striking were the students, who seemed unlike those of earlier generations: less serious, more skeptical, and decidedly more secular.[8] Academic critics noted the change, explaining that students of the time considered religion old-fashioned and out of date, and that they looked on it less with disdain than indifference.[9] Supporting this view, sociological studies showed a distinct decline in church attendance among students, as well as reduced participation in religious organizations such as the Young Men's Christian Association (YMCA) and Young Women's Christian Association (YWCA).[10] The leaders of the largest church denominations, expressing growing concern about the souls of America's students, announced efforts to expand their own denominational colleges and build student centers at state universities.[11] But for fundamentalists, many of them coming into contact with colleges for the first time, the situation required more than piecemeal reform. As early as 1917, in *The Menace of Modernism*, W. B. Riley had described their concern: "There are thousands of Christian parents in America who debate with the deepest anxiety the question 'To what college can we send our children and be sure the Bible will not be discredited in their presence, the deity of Christ denied, and their spiritual lives reduced if not wholly destroyed?' "[12]

In diagnosing the problem, fundamentalists were able to draw on revivalist precedents. For decades, evangelical preachers had warned of the dangers of secularity, perfecting the conventional trope of the wandering boy lost to the sins of the secular city. For preachers and revivalists, it was a standard tool of the trade, and appreciative audiences had come to expect the familiar format from popular orators. Among those who used it, William Jennings Bryan was a master. As America's most prolific speaker, he had traveled the Chautauqua circuit for thirty years, delivering an average of two hundred lectures a year; during the summers he was known to speak anywhere from 60 to 120 days in a row.[13] Reciting a well-worn repertoire of such crowd-pleasing orations as "The Value of an Ideal," "The Prince of Peace," and "The Price of a Soul," he would hone his words to perfection, capturing the precise phrasing that would leave his audiences captivated, if not mesmerized.[14] His lectures regularly attracted crowds of 5,000 or more, whom he nearly always addressed without artificial amplification. (On one occasion Bryan spoke to an audience of about 100,000 using no mechanical device, and it was reported that listeners could hear him clearly three blocks away.)[15] Bryan's speeches were often published in small-town newspapers and religious periodicals, as well as in his own monthly newspaper *The Commoner*. It has been estimated that his words, including his "Bryan's Bible Talks" and his syndicated columns (which by 1923 were carried by about 110 papers across the country), were regularly reaching twenty to twenty-five million people.[16]

Starting in 1920, Bryan brought his skills to bear on higher education, adapting the revivalist repertoire to create a standard litany of blameless childhood corrupted by the soulless university. In speech after speech, he began with the familiar invocation of childhood innocence and uncorrupted faith: "A boy is born into a Christian family; as soon as he is able to join words together into sentences his mother teaches him to lisp the child's prayer: 'Now I lay me down to sleep; I pray the Lord my soul to keep; if I should die before I wake, I pray the Lord my soul to take.' A little later the boy is taught the Lord's Prayer. . . . He talks with God. He goes to Sunday school. . . . he hears the preacher tell how precious our

William Jennings Bryan and the Bryan Bible Class, Royal Palm Park, Miami
(Courtesy Bryan College)

lives are in the sight of God." Then comes temptation. Arriving at college, the unsuspecting youth is confronted by the teachings of "a learned professor," armed with "a book 600 pages thick" whose lessons contain "no mention of religion, the only basis for morality; not a suggestion of a sense of responsibility to God—nothing but cold, clammy materialism." What followed inevitably was the fall, and with his voice rising in indignation, Bryan would describe how the insidious instructor, having indoctrinated the child with his secular teachings, "then SETS HIM ADRIFT, WITH INFINITE CAPACITY FOR GOOD OR EVIL BUT WITH NO LIGHT TO GUIDE HIM, NO COMPASS TO DIRECT HIM AND NO CHART OF THE SEA OF LIFE!" Finally, indignation having turned to outrage, he would single out those responsible, placing the blame squarely on academia: "And this is done in schools and colleges where the Bible cannot be taught, but where infidelity, agnosticism, and atheism are taught in the name of science and philosophy."[17]

Following what became a predictable pattern, Bryan turned next to an examination of the evidence, starting with the testimonies of students. In the campaign against the colleges, students played an essential role, as many stepped forward to give firsthand accounts of their struggles to maintain their faith while away at school. Bryan was well placed to receive their stories, since his cross-country speaking tours frequently brought him to college and university campuses. During his visits, students would crowd around to confide in him, confessing their doubts and complaining about classes and teachers. Afterward many would write to him, describing in painful detail the difficulty of keeping their faith in an atmosphere where their beliefs were derided or mocked by their teachers. According to Bryan, the letters came in large numbers, suggesting that the problem was widespread, reaching into Christian colleges as well as state universities and even into public high schools. "Even while I am putting on paper this part of the address," he would tell his audience, "a letter comes from a High School Senior in a small town in Illinois who says 'During my sophomore and junior years I became very skeptical in my religious belief, but . . . I have nearly overcome it. Others in the class are still agnostic.' "[18] In Bryan's speeches and writings of that time, student testimonies became common and expected. "Are you surprised," he would ask his listeners, "when I tell you that within a month I met a young man twenty-two years of age who said he had been made an atheist by two teachers in a Christian college?"[19]

Bryan was not the only one to make the case. By the early 1920s a growing cadre of college critics, many of them revival preachers, were regularly warning against the secularity of the university. Their sermons and writings included a veritable compendium of student complaints. Perhaps the most extensive collection was Alfred Fairhurst's *Atheism in Our Universities* (1923), an account based on the Kentucky preacher's frequent visits to college campuses. "I was told by a young woman there," he wrote of a recent visit to Ohio State, "who was ready to enter the Senior year, that three-fourths of the professors in that university were atheists, and that the other fourth were agnostics and Christians." A former student at "Missouri State University" described a three-year course in biology in which "60 per cent. of the students who take that course come out atheists." Still another student complained that at his university "the library on evolution contains two or three hundred volumes in favor of the theory and only two or three against it."[20] The criticisms went on and on. The most moving of them were related in letters, often written to hometown ministers, in which students confessed their confusion, doubt, and fear that they were losing their faith. Mississippi evangelist T. T. Martin described the desperate letter of "A Mother's Son," telling how college had challenged his faith and turned him into "a mental, spiritual, and physical wreck": "My soul is a starving skeleton; my heart a petrified rock; my mind is poisoned and as fickle as the wind, and my faith as unstable as water. I broke the heart of my mother, disappointed my friends. . . . I have run the gauntlet, I am at the end of the rope. Oh, wretched man that I am. There is no rest, happiness, or peace for me. I sometimes think I will jump overboard and end it all. I wish I had never seen a college."[21]

In most of these speeches and writings, parents were also a source of evidence. Continuing to draw from the revivalist repertoire, the critics depicted broken-hearted fathers and weeping mothers whose children had lost their faith at college. Throughout the early 1920s Bryan received a steady stream of letters from concerned parents. In a 1921 speech to the Moody Bible Institute entitled "The Bible and Its Enemies," he described their despair, citing case after case, like the Miami mother "who told me that her boy would not pray."[22] For years thereafter Bryan would embellish the theme, adding examples of anguished parents to an ever-expanding list: "A father (a Congressman) tells me that a daughter on her return from Wellesley told him that nobody believed in the Bible stories now. Another father (a Congressman) tells me of a son whose faith was undermined by this doctrine in a Divinity School. Three preachers told me of having their interest in the subject aroused by the return of their children from college with their faith shaken."[23]

Ministers furnished similar accounts. John Roach Straton, for one, told of his shock when his own son came home from high school "with theories in conflict with the Bible."[24] Some singled out specific classes or teachers. Fairhurst noted that a father had written to him "in great agony, saying that he has sent his son to Illinois State University; that when he sent him he was an excellent Christian worker in the church, but that a teacher of philosophy in that university had destroyed his son's faith."[25] Other clergy aimed their fire at doctrines or theories, with evolution beginning to emerge as a focus of special scorn. J. W. Porter wrote that after a sermon, no fewer than "three broken-hearted mothers" came forward to tell him how the teaching of evolutionary theory had contributed to "the wrecking of their children's faith."[26] T. T. Martin, who would later join with Porter to lead the Anti-Evolution League of America, supplied similar testimonies from parents, such as the Baptist mother who said that her son, a confirmed Christian, had listened to "an Evolutionist" lecture for one week, "and since then he seems to have no use for the Bible and takes no interest in the Lord's cause. It almost breaks my heart."[27] On the whole, however, the accounts of parents were relatively undifferentiated, centering less on specific teachers or theories than on the overall atmosphere of the college campus. Perhaps the most touching account of all came from parents who had received a recent letter from their daughter complaining of the teaching in her Bible class and begging them not to allow her younger brothers to attend the same college: "Oh, mother and daddy, for goodness sake, don't send the boys. . . . I was conceited enough to think that it wouldn't hurt me, and that I could sit through that stuff and come out unharmed, but oh, what a fool I was. As it is, it will take me some time to get over it. But please, oh, please, don't sent the boys."[28]

As the campaign took hold, reports of the damage being done in schools came from many sources. Bryan was particularly eager to provide as much evidence as possible, since he came in for considerable criticism, especially when speaking at colleges, from those who scoffed at his claims of rampant secularity. In one of his early speeches he had made the mistake of inventing a theatrical tale about a young woman who had fled from a classroom where the Bible was being criticized, weeping "like Mary Magdalene."[29] Challenged to name names, Bryan quickly backed away and from that time went out of his way to be more factual, or at least to cite his sources. The best evidence was of course his own, collected from his frequent visits to college campuses. "The head of the Department of Biology recently told a body of students, in my presence," he wrote, "that he did not pray; he said he did not believe in revealed religion."[30] Then there were the secondhand reports, admittedly hearsay but based on seemingly reliable sources, "informants," as Bryan called them, "whom I have reason to believe." These reports were more specific, with most of them referring to particular (albeit unnamed) teachers: "A teacher in Columbia University begins his lessons in geology by asking students to lay aside all that they have learned in Sunday-school; a professor at the University of Wisconsin tells his class that the Bible is a collection of myths; a professor at Ann Arbor occupies a Sunday evening explaining to an audience that Christianity is a state of mind." The descriptions sometimes seemed a bit strained: "A woman teacher in the public school in Indiana rebukes a boy for answering that Adam was the first man, explaining to him and the class that the 'tree man' was the first man." Furthermore, Bryan's evidence got shaky fast, especially when it consisted of third- and fourth-hand accounts: "A professor in Yale has the reputation of making atheists of all who come under his influence—this information was given by a boy whose brother has come under the influence of this teacher."[31] An article in the *Sunday School Times* alerted him to the Illinois professor who told of the great day "when a water puppy crawled up onto the land and decided to live there, and became man's first progenitor!" A "dispatch from Paris" provided information on a scientist who "recently talked to the soul of a dog and learned that the dog was happy."[32] With time, Bryan's evidence became increasingly suspect, as when he told a 1924 audience in Kentucky about the outlandish evolutionary theories of a Pennsylvania professor whom he had read about in the afternoon paper "two years ago last November."[33] Still, the anecdotal reports kept coming: "A professor in Bryn Mawr combats Christianity . . . a professor in a Christian college writes a book in which the virgin birth of Christ is disputed; one professor declares that life is merely a by-product . . . another says that the ingredients necessary to create life have already been brought together." And these were only the tip of the iceberg, Bryan would assure his audiences, "a few of the illustrations."[34]

As if all of these reports were not enough to show that colleges were destroying the religious faith of their students, confirmation was provided by the seemingly objective sources of contemporary social surveys. Although Bryan and his colleagues relied on data that were almost entirely anecdotal, they seemed fascinated by the surveys that were becoming popular in many social sciences of the time. Frequently they mentioned the findings of these studies, usually without attribution: "a considerable per cent.," "a large percentage," "sometimes as high as 75 per cent."[35] The surveys cited tended to be crude and simple, like this one of students at Carleton and Vassar Colleges: "Do you believe in the Virgin Birth of Christ? Yes, 14; No, 17."[36] Sometimes the critics made up their own surveys, like the one crafted by the energetic Alfred Fairhurst, who mailed standardized questionnaires to scores of college presidents and professors (as well as to superintendents of public instruction from selected states) in an effort to determine the extent of irreligious teaching in the schools.[37] But it was Bryan who really introduced social science to the antievolution cause, warning his audiences of James H. Leuba's findings in *The Belief in God and Immorality* (1921), which seemed to offer definitive proof that America's colleges were destroying the faith of their students. A Bryn Mawr psychologist and pioneer in the scientific study of religion, Leuba found in a 1916 survey that students at nine representative colleges were increasingly inclined to reject religion as they progressed through their academic programs: whereas only 15 percent of freshmen had discarded their Christian beliefs, 30 percent of juniors and 40 to 45 percent of graduates had abandoned their faith. Even more provocative were his findings concerning faculty members in the sciences and social sciences, more than half of whom admitted that they believed in neither God nor immortality.[38] Although Leuba saw his study as hopeful, suggesting that education encouraged people to become more informed and independent, Bryan considered it to be a sweeping indictment, showing clearly that students became less committed to Christianity the longer they stayed in school, and that it was their professors, especially those in the sciences, who were leading them astray. In his speeches before college audiences, he cited the findings repeatedly, emphasizing that they were objective and scientific. Of all the evidence presented, Leuba's was Bryan's trump card—incontrovertible proof that colleges were to blame for the secularity of the times. "Every Christian preacher should procure a copy of this book," he asserted, "and it should be in the hands of every Christian layman who is anxious to aid in the defense of the Bible against its enemies."[39]

Prognosis

Having diagnosed the problem, the framing process proceeds to prognosis, or the suggestion of solutions for fixing it. Here movements begin to identify targets and test out strategies and tactics that can be applied in righting wrongs. Although solutions are sometimes self-evident, more often they can be contentious, since even those who agree about a problem may disagree about how to approach solving it. In some cases, movements collapse before they are fully formed, as their members move off in different directions in search of solutions. Thus it is important for activists to agree at the start about targets and basic strategies.[40]

For the critics of the colleges, the prognosis was by no means self-evident. In the 1920s American higher education was changing dramatically. Inspired by the model of the German university, U.S. colleges and universities were being transformed, with classical and sectarian instruction giving way to newer kinds of applied and scientific training. Faculty roles were in flux, as teachers concentrated more on imparting information and less on ministering to the moral and spiritual needs of their students. Even in some church-sponsored schools, professors were being hired for their academic qualifications rather than their church affiliations or religious views. Most striking of all, students increasingly went to college to prepare for secular careers.[41] To Bryan and his colleagues, the changes seemed so sweeping—the problems so pervasive—that they hardly knew where to start in solving them. Writing in 1921 to decry the fact that colleges were no longer sending their students into the ministry (he pointed in particular to declining numbers from Oberlin, Yale, Princeton, Chicago, and Wesleyan), fundamentalist James M. Gray could offer no satisfactory explanation for the trends. "Is there any adequate answer," he asked almost plaintively, "except the present decline in faith, the apostasy in Christendom which the holy prophets foretold?"[42]

Thus beginning in 1920 critics of the colleges went looking for solutions. At the start, there was no clear candidate to serve as their target, no single factor that stood out as the cause of all the problems that plagued academia. In fact, most critics believed the campuses suffered from a broad spectrum of ills, consisting at a minimum (in Riley's words) of "Modernism, Skepticism, Agnosticism, Infidelity, and worldliness."[43] Of these, modernism came in for the most criticism. For years fundamentalists had been denouncing modernists, the liberal theologians (many of them associated with the University of Chicago) who championed biblical criticism and contended that Christianity should be brought into closer connection with modern culture, primarily through service and social reform. Throughout the early 1920s the attacks on the modernists continued, led by preachers such as Riley, Straton, and T. T. Shields, all of whom repeatedly warned in their sermons and speeches about the "the menace of modernism." As late as 1923, the World's Christian Fundamentals Association (WCFA) was passing resolutions censuring the presence of "modernism in malignant form" in many colleges and universities in the South.[44] But in the early days of the campaign, modernism was only one of many targets. Among the preachers in particular, atheism, agnosticism, and infidelity were regularly singled out as contributing to the loss of faith among students. Others blamed broader trends, including "naturalism," "materialism," and "skepticism."[45] A few ministers had simpler explanations: the decline of the colleges was the work of the devil. "My brethren," T. T. Shields told his congregation, "we had better face the facts. Some of the colleges are the Devil's instruments for the destruction of the souls of men. The colleges and the universities are the places where Satan's seat is."[46]

Then there was the theory of evolution. Even before the war, A. C. Dixon had attributed the problems in colleges to the teaching of evolution, but his warnings had attracted little attention. Alerted by Dixon to the threat, and alarmed by his reading of Benjamin Kidd's antievolutionary diatribe The Science of Power (1918), Bryan occasionally spoke out on the topic in speeches, also with little notice. In a 1920 address to the World Brotherhood Congress in Washington, D.C., however, he upped the ante. Surprising his audience, Bryan announced his "growing conviction" that "the doctrine, commonly known as the Darwinian theory" was "the most paralyzing influence with which civilization has had to contend during the last century." While impassioned and moving, the speech demonstrated little understanding of Darwinism, which Bryan seemed to confuse with Social Darwinism. Thus he argued, citing Kidd, that the greatest of all Darwinists was Nietzsche, the father of German militarism, who had "carried the Darwinian theory to its logical conclusion, and died in an insane asylum." Nevertheless, he made his point, depicting Darwinism as the root of virtually all existing evils, "a philosophy that condemned democracy as the refuge of the weakling, denounced Christianity as a system calculated to make degenerates out of men, denied the existence of God, overturned all standards of morality, eulogized war as both necessary and desirable, praised hatred because it leads to war, denied to sympathy and pity any rightful place in a manly heart and endeavored to substitute the worship of the superman for the worship of Jehovah."[47]

Aroused by Bryan, concern about evolution began to grow. Admittedly, few fundamentalists had ever heard of the theory. To many of those who had, the idea was complex and confusing, if not incomprehensible. As a prognosis for the problem of secularity, however, evolution had certain advantages over its competition. In contrast to modernism (and for that matter to atheism, agnosticism, and infidelity), evolutionary theory was not restricted to the realm of religion. While abstract and theoretical, it seemed somehow less philosophical and more specific than naturalism, materialism, or skepticism. Blaming Darwin may not have had the rhetorical power of blaming the devil, but in an increasingly secular society, it was more convincing to a lot of people. Besides, as Bryan showed, evolution was an expansive theory in that it could be held responsible for a host of evils—everything from heresy to immorality to war. All it lacked was someone who could translate an abstract, often unfathomable theory into terms that anyone could understand. The challenge was substantial, as J. Frank Norris showed in a 1921 article in The Searchlight, where he was reduced to relying on dictionary definitions to explain the term to his readers. "The doctrine of Evolution briefly stated, is as follows," he wrote:

That in some infinitely remote period in the past, how or from whence science does not affirm, there appeared matter and force; that within matter and in association with force there also appeared a primordial cell, how or from whence no man knoweth, in which there was a spark of life; and that from this cell all things animate have emerged, being controlled by certain laws variously stated by various evolutionists; that these laws in connection with the modifying influences of environment (surroundings—soil, climate, etc.) account for and explain the various species that have existed in the past and now exist upon earth, man included.[48]

With his famous lecture "The Menace of Darwinism," delivered first in the spring of 1921, then printed and reprinted as a pamphlet and in newspapers that reached readers in the tens of millions, Bryan rose to the task. For the anti-evolution movement, it was a defining document, providing in abbreviated and easily accessible form a compelling case against Darwin's theory, a case that would be cited, paraphrased, and copied for years afterward. Constructing his argument as if it were a legal brief, Bryan led his listeners though a laundry list of dangers posed by Darwinism, describing how it denied the existence of a personal and revealed God, destroyed human morality, and created a war of all against all. Introducing the theory itself, he proceeded to question its validity, calling it a "hypothesis" that was built "upon presumptions, probabilities and inferences," and insisting that it had no scientific standing, being "not science at all" but "guesses strung together." Here Bryan called on common sense, asking his audience whether it was conceivable that "natural selection, sexual selection or any other kind of selection" could "account for the countless differences we see around us." Although his command of the theory should not be overstated (at no point in his writings did he ever distinguish Darwinism from any other version of evolutionary theory, nor did he evince any serious knowledge of contemporary developments in evolutionary science), Bryan was able to demonstrate a respectable understanding of Darwinism in his speech, suggesting that he had been doing some studying. On occasion, he did retreat to simple stereotypes, as when he stated that the theory was based on the belief that "man is next of kin to the monkey." At other points he seemed unable to resist resorting to rhetoric, as when he uttered what would become antievolutionism's most famous sound bite, that "it is better to trust in the Rock of Ages than to know the age of the rocks." Even so, the speech was an impressive introduction to the theory, a primer and a popularization that for the first time brought the concept to the attention of a mass audience. With it, evolution became the centerpiece of the campaign against the colleges. In Bryan's words, it was "the duty of the moral, as well as the Christian, world to combat this influence in every possible way."[49]

In evolution, the critics had a big target. Unlike modernism, which was confined almost entirely to the seminaries, evolutionary theory could be found in church colleges, elite private institutions, and public universities. For that matter, evolutionists had even "wormed their way," as Bryan put it, "into a few of our theological seminaries."[50] Inside the colleges, it seemed to be everywhere, its influence radiating out from the sciences into almost every academic field of study. Indeed, writing in his 1921 essay "The Modern Arena," in which he compared colleges to ancient Roman coliseums where Christians were sacrificed, Bryan argued that evolutionary theory had become pervasive in the American university, "an arena in which a brutish doctrine tears to pieces the religious faith of young men and young women." For Bryan, whose own schooling had consisted of two years at a religious academy followed by four more at Illinois College, a piously Presbyterian church school, evolution was an explanation for almost everything that was wrong with the modern university. Darwinism had encouraged colleges to elevate science at the expense of religion. "Why," he asked, "are professors allowed to substitute Darwin's fictitious history of man, and his fanciful description of man's progress up through apehood, for the Bible's description of man's creation by special act of the Almighty, according to a divine plan and for a divine purpose?" In explaining the world, evolutionary theory emphasized the material over the spiritual, contributing to a conception of the college as a place where students received practical and technical training rather than moral and religious instruction. Taught to believe that things seen were somehow superior to those unseen, students forgot the simple fact that "the things that are seen are temporal; the things that are unseen are eternal." The theory also contributed to the academic attitude that education was an exclusively intellectual endeavor. Bryan firmly believed that colleges existed not only to cultivate the mind but also to build character and shape spiritual values. While an impressive intellectual tool, evolutionary theory was an educational failure, having proven itself incapable of providing a positive moral message. "Darwinism," he concluded, "when taken seriously, swells the head and shrivels the heart."[51]

At the same time, evolution provided a specific target: the teachers who taught it. In contrast to the modernist theologians, many of whom were well known and widely respected in their church denominations, most evolutionists were not prominent in their churches. Indeed, according to Leuba's study, many of those who taught Darwinism were actually atheists or agnostics. But there were other reasons for targeting the professors. For years, Bryan had been portraying them —especially those from eastern colleges and universities—as educated elitists who showed little sympathy for democratic values. Among his favorite quotations was Theodore Roosevelt's comment to Harvard law students that "there was scarcely a great conspiracy against the public welfare that did not have Harvard brains behind it."[52] Furthermore, he was suspicious of the growing tendency of college teachers to regard themselves as experts and specialists, hired on the basis of their academic credentials and qualifications. "The tests by which we select university instructors do not always give us the information most needed," he complained. "We get the measure of their brains, but that is no indication of the strength of the spiritual in their lives."[53] In the academic advocates of Darwinism, Bryan saw all of his concerns converging. Experts in their fields, protected in their professorial positions, more interested in their own theories than the well-being of their students, the evolution professors were extreme examples of a new kind of academic elitism. "Their minds are open to the most absurd hypotheses advanced in the name of science," he wrote, "but their hearts are closed to the plainest spiritual truths."[54]

Bryan was not the only one to target teachers. Among the fundamentalists who made up the bulk of the antievolution campaign, resentment against college professors was widespread. The fact that few knew any professors personally (or at least any at elite colleges or state universities) made the target even more tempting. For his part, Bryan was careful with his criticism, stressing that it was only "some of the teachers" who—"let us hope, unconsciously"—were undermining the faith of their students.[55] His fundamentalist followers, by contrast, were not so circumspect. Fairhurst characterized college professors as unbelievers, claiming that "a considerable per cent. of professor's chairs in our leading universities are occupied by agnostics and atheists."[56] Martin criticized them for their intellectualism, portraying them as educated elitists, or more simply, "a lot of high-brows." His descriptions reeked with sarcasm: "Their 'culture,' you know,—they are the 'intellectuals,' you know,—teaches them that there is no hell."[57] Norris preferred to put his criticism in class terms, as when he contrasted the high-toned theories of college professors to the solid common sense of ordinary people. "You know," he would tell his congregation, "if you want to find somebody that's got sense, don't always be looking for a fellow with pin whiskers sitting up in a professor's chair—don't do that. You go out and get some hard-handed, plain, God-fearing man."[58] On the whole, however, most of the attacks at least mentioned that the professors were indoctrinating their students in evolution. Here the criticism got personal, with the teachers being described as tempters who blithely stole the souls of their students. "But what do these evolutionists care for this?" wrote J. W. Porter of the fact that many of their students had lost their faith. "They will laugh and sneer at it. Having believed and taught that they have the blood of beasts in their veins, they now have the heart of a brute."[59]

The professors were not the only targets. For Bryan and most of the fundamentalist leaders who worked with him, the colleges were always the focus. But many of their followers were much more familiar with the high schools, and what they saw there had them worried. With the extension of compulsory education, American high schools were growing exponentially, with enrollment at well over four million students by the 1920s. As a result of state certification requirements, teachers were better trained, and many had attended at least some college, where they were usually introduced to evolutionary theory. As the selection of course curricula and textbooks came under the control of state education boards and textbook commissions, the theory was becoming more common in high school science classrooms across the country.[60] Although Bryan would change his view later, in the early 1920s he found it hard to believe that evolution was present to any appreciable extent in public high schools. But for Martin, the Blue Mountain, Mississippi, evangelist who would become a leader of the antievolution forces, it was not only present but spreading rapidly. In his *Hell and the High Schools* (1923), he told how college professors had passed the theory on to their students, many of whom became high school teachers. These young teachers in turn were indoctrinating their own pupils, so that "even down to the primary department" it was "being drilled into our boys and girls."[61]

As Martin saw it, high school teachers were more dangerous than college professors, for three reasons. First, they tended to be more successful, since they taught students "during the most susceptible, dangerous age of their lives." Second, they came into contact with more students. Bryan himself had estimated that only one in a hundred Americans graduated from a college or university. For Martin, the fact that so few went to college proved the point, since "vastly more" were "being poisoned and eternally damned in the High Schools than in the Universities." Third and most important, Martin insisted that it was in the high schools that evolution could be stopped. College professors were too well protected, "barricaded behind strong political influences and millions of money." High school teachers, by contrast, had to answer to local public officials: "Boards of Trustees of the public schools are absolute sovereigns; they can put in or put out whatever teacher they will."[62]

Having targeted the teachers, the critics turned to the question of what could be done about them. Here their concerns were essentially strategic. As before, Bryan took the lead in laying out a plan, arguing that steps could be taken to stop the teaching of evolution in its tracks. In a 1921 essay in *The Commoner* called "Back to God," he outlined the main points of his proposal. He began by stating that all teachers (he applied the same principle to ministers) should be required to make their views known and understood. As citizens, teachers had the inalienable right to their own opinions. At the same time, while they were employed as teachers, their employers had the right to know what they were teaching, in keeping with what he liked to call the "hired man" theory. He went on to apply the argument, asserting that only Christians should be allowed to teach in Christian colleges and schools. (Bryan would later broaden this claim to insist that "none but Christians in good standing and with a spiritual conception of life should be allowed to teach in Christian schools.")[63] He concluded by making his most important point, that educators in public schools must be neutral in teaching neither religion nor irreligion. Presupposing that teachers in secular schools were legally prohibited from advocating religion in their classrooms (an assumption that was constitutionally correct though widely violated at the time), Bryan allowed that fairness alone required that "the Bible should not be attacked where it cannot be defended." It followed, then, that public school teachers "should not be permitted to undermine the religious faith of their students."[64]

With the idea of neutrality, Bryan could develop a compelling strategy to be used against the teachers. No one was demanding that they teach religion: "The Christians are not asking that religion be taught in our public schools: they are protesting against the teaching of IRRELIGION in the public schools." No one was insisting that teachers give up any of their rights: "They are not asking that any man shall surrender his opinion or violate his conscience; they are only asking that teachers who are atheists and agnostics shall either obey their employers or else build schools of their own for the spread of unbelief." No one was preventing them from teaching evolution in their own schools, just as no one barred Christians from teaching Christianity in theirs: "Those who look to the jungle for their ancestry can teach this doctrine to their own children if they wish," Bryan concluded. All he asked was that they not be allowed to teach the theory to everyone else, "to make monkeys," as he put it, "out of all the children."[65]

The problem was how to put the strategy into practice. Activists could agree that the teaching of evolution in the schools must be stopped, but they sometimes disagreed about how to stop it. Though their tactics were sometimes complementary, they often took them in different directions. Among the critics, there were those who chose to work from within, relying on existing institutions to restrict the teaching of evolution. Many fundamentalist ministers, for example, preferred to work through their state denominational organizations, relying on them to initiate investigations, pass resolutions, and ultimately withhold contributions to the offending institutions. Some aimed their protests at boards of trustees, a tactic that worked particularly well at small religious colleges, where trustees often included the ministers themselves. In the early days of the campaign, a surprising number believed that college presidents were best positioned to eliminate the teaching of evolutionary theory from their schools. After all, said Fairhurst, the presidents "generally have it in their power to determine who the members of their Faculties will be. . . . It is their duty to know the characters of professors and the quality of what they teach."[66] Other detractors, less sanguine about working from within, suggested that it would be better to bring pressure from outside. Martin, for one, was convinced the best place to start in building a campaign against evolution was with the parents. "The Baptist, Catholic, Congregational, Disciple, Episcopalian, Lutheran, Methodist, Presbyterian and other fathers and mothers can, in twelve months," he wrote, "drive Evolution out of every tax-supported school in America and out of every denominational school."[67] But as the campaign progressed, and as it turned its attention to more state universities and public high schools, many activists contended that the best of all tactics was to rely on public pressure to bring down the teaching of evolution. As Bryan argued, it was taxpayers (he frequently used the term "Christian taxpayers") speaking through their school boards and state legislatures who were ultimately responsible for what was taught in public schools. "The right of the taxpayers to decide what shall be taught can hardly be disputed," he told readers of *The Commoner*. "The hand that writes the pay check rules the school; if not, to whom shall the right to decide such important matters be entrusted?"[68]

Motivation

Following prognosis, framing proceeds to its third and final task: motivation. Having suggested what needs to be done, movements must find ways to encourage their members to actually do it. Thus they have to provide a rationale for action or, more simply, a call to arms. In motivating, leaders try to formulate arguments that are convincing and persuasive: convincing their followers that something *can* be done and persuading them that something *has to* be done. Usually they tie their arguments to strategies and tactics, but they must be ready to shift them as conditions change. Above all, they need to convey a sense of urgency.[69]

For critics of higher education, this was their most difficult task. To all appearances, American colleges of the 1920s seemed increasingly beyond the reach of reform. State universities were becoming rapidly more secular; private colleges, encouraged by business benefactors, were growing away from their religious roots; even some church institutions were starting to seek more independence from their denominations. College professors had become more professional, protected in their freedom to teach and conduct research by sympathetic academic administrators and organizations like the American Association of University Professors. With the extension of compulsory education, even the high schools seemed to be beyond the control of local communities, answering instead to state administrators and education board members who chose their textbooks and set standards for their teachers.[70] Under the circumstances, the critics could be forgiven for being fatalistic. Even more troubling to them was that few seemed to be taking up the cause of removing evolution from the schools. Among fundamentalists, as Shields told his Toronto congregation, most had "not yet awakened to the perils of the hour." Many of those who had been alerted to the dangers of evolution were inclined to avoid the issue, since "they want peace and are prepared to pay any price for its possession." Hence they had to be motivated—convinced, persuaded, if necessary shamed—into seeing that the only way to deal with evolutionary theory was to join together to fight it. The time had come, suggested "T.N.T." Shields, to set off a little dynamite. "We are not organizing for a picnic," he told his flock, "but for war."[71]

In motivating the members of their movement, campaign leaders began by singling out specific targets. At least initially, these targets tended to be college presidents, individuals who were not only widely known but also well respected in their churches and communities. In confronting these formidable personages, the critics attracted immediate attention to their cause, while at the same time advertising its seriousness. As early as 1920, T. T. Martin had gone on the offensive against Wake Forest College president William Louis Poteat, a leading Southern Baptist who was also a German-trained zoologist and an articulate advocate of theistic evolution. In a series of articles published in the *Western Recorder* (and reprinted in several other fundamentalist newspapers), Martin used Poteat's prominence to warn Baptists across the South of evolution's growing influence. "Preachers trained in Wake Forest go to all parts of the South and West, and Wake Forest is not the only college that has been affected by President Poteat's teachings," he wrote.[72] Over the next several years he continued to hound Poteat, elevating his own role in the antievolution ranks while exhorting others to join the campaign and "make it a fight to the finish and to the death."[73]

Meanwhile, in the North, Bryan confronted Edward A. Birge, president of the University of Wisconsin, an outspoken advocate of evolution who was himself both a zoologist and a Congregationalist Sunday school teacher. Speaking in the university gymnasium in May 1921 with Birge on the stage, Bryan made a series of unsubstantiated claims about the teaching of evolution at Madison, provoking a face-to-face argument and weeks of charges and countercharges in state and national newspapers. By the fall, he was stumping the state, telling Wisconsinites that the president of their public university was an atheist who was determined to "undo the work of the Christian home and the Christian church, and set at naught the good work Christian mothers do with their little ones at their knees."[74] For months afterward Bryan continued to treat Birge as his principal target, advertising his argument with the president to audiences across the nation and baiting him in the columns of *The Commoner* for "hiding in the bushes."[75]

It was in the West, however, where J. Frank Norris electrified antievolution forces with his attacks on Baylor University and its thoroughly orthodox president Samuel P. Brooks, that the confrontations became most bitter and personal. Throughout the early 1920s Norris kept up a steady drumbeat of criticism, excoriating the respected and popular president for allowing evolution to fester within his faculty. "I am dead certain," he informed Brooks in one of a series of blistering letters published on the front page of The Searchlight, "that the Baptists of Texas are not going to stand for the teaching of evolution in their leading school and regardless of what you may think or how you may feel or what any other man may think or feel, it is the solemn duty of somebody to protest against this Bible-destroying and Deity-of-Christ denying teaching."[76]

Having confronted the college presidents, antievolution leaders challenged them to sign statements of faith. On its face, this maneuver might appear to be a sensible motivating tool. After all, many fundamentalists were members of churches in which the affirming of articles, creeds, declarations, and pledges was common practice. Moreover, pledge signing was one of the most successful tactics of the Prohibition movement, in which Bryan and many of his followers had been active. (As late as 1923, Bryan was calling on college administrators, faculty, and students to sign pledges to abstain from the consumption of intoxicating liquor; at the University of Florida, all of the faculty and 75 percent of the student body reportedly signed.)[77] Applying the convention, Bryan argued that all ministers and teachers should be required to issue statements revealing their beliefs about evolution. "Politicians make their campaigns for public support on written platforms defining their views," he explained; "preachers and professors who believe in evolution can hardly do less."[78]

But while the idea of pledge signing may have seemed sensible in theory, it proved unworkable in practice and sometimes actually backfired. For example, in the fall of 1921 Bryan challenged Wisconsin's President Birge to sign a statement avowing his belief in the Genesis account of creation, the Virgin Birth, the Resurrection, and other miracles. The statement was to include a promise to purge his faculty of any professors (read evolutionists) who in their teachings brought discredit on the Bible. In response, Birge declared not only that he embraced the faith of his parents but also that he had never experienced any conflict between religion and science. Taken aback, Bryan parried by upping the ante, offering one hundred dollars to the university president if he would sign a statement saying that he was descended from an ape. Birge rejected the ridiculous offer with high indignation, and he took the opportunity to issue a strong statement defending the academic freedom of his faculty and denouncing the "hired man" theory. Bested and embarrassed, Bryan pulled back, his efforts having provoked more derision than support. In a final blast at Birge, issued in The Commoner in May 1922, he was reduced to name-calling, crudely characterizing the distinguished educator as "a descendant of the ape."[79]

At about the same time, activists began to call for investigations of their own church colleges. In this effort, they turned to their denominations, working through local and state church organizations to look into rumors that evolutionary theory was being taught. Because their church structures tended to be decentralized and democratic, allowing fundamentalists more access, Baptist state conventions in particular stayed busy initiating such inquiries. For example, the Tennessee Baptist State Convention conducted an investigation of Union University, forcing its faculty to issue a statement repudiating all theories that were contrary to biblical accounts of creation.[80] The Georgia State Convention forced the resignation of a prominent biology professor at Mercer University.[81] In Texas, where the fiery Norris and his fundamentalist allies were strong in the Baptist General Association, a committee was established to examine the existence of evolutionary theory in the state's Baptist colleges. Yet among Texas Baptists the committee became rapidly mired in controversy, demonstrating the problems antievolutionists encountered in working within their state conventions, where powerful church leaders often acted to protect their colleges from their own investigators. Frustrated by how slowly the committee was proceeding, Norris accused state Baptist leaders of dragging their heels, initiating a power struggle that ended only when he was permanently removed from the Texas association in 1924.[82] Indeed, with state conventions usually controlled by moderates, fundamentalists were frequently outmaneuvered. Thus when his critics finally succeeded in requiring Wake Forest's President Poteat to respond to their charges at the 1922 meeting of the North Carolina Baptist State Convention, Poteat delivered a defense of his views that was so eloquent and sincere that even some of those who had come to censure him wound up voting for a resolution commending him for his work. Defeated and disillusioned, one conservative editor begrudgingly complimented Poteat on the victory he had won, describing it as "chloroforming his enemies." The president, he observed, had "played them for a bunch of monkeys."[83]

More successful were the direct exposés. Among fundamentalist preachers, many of whom had been active in antisaloon agitation, pulpit revelations were standard stock-in-trade. Norris was famous for the splashy sermons in which he revealed the corrupt practices of local saloon keepers, gamblers, and crooked politicians. A *Searchlight* headline from October 1921 announced this upcoming disclosure: "THE PASTOR WILL NAME, NEXT SUNDAY NIGHT, THE HIGH OFFICIAL WHO IS RESPONSIBLE FOR THE LARGE AMOUNT OF BOOTLEGGING NOW GOING ON IN FORT WORTH."[84] With the emergence of evolution as an issue, Norris shifted the spotlight to college professors, beginning with a series of sermons and published reports in which he examined the teachings of alleged evolutionists at Baylor and Southern Methodist University. In late 1921 he executed an end run around the state Baptist Convention by launching his own media campaign against Baylor's Professor G. S. Dow, describing Dow's introductory sociology textbook, which followed the development of society from lower to higher stages, as an insult to Adam and Eve. Bringing the book into the pulpit during a Sunday evening service, Norris proceeded to read aloud certain offending passages, while assuring his congregation that "the whole tenor of the book, from start to finish, is based on the theory of Evolution." Nor did he stop there, going on to assert that he "had it from reliable and most worthy sources" that there were "three other professors in Baylor who hold the same views he [Dow] does." Intimating that there may have been even more, he called for an investigation in which the college would be searched "from cellar to garret."[85]

For the next two years, Norris waged an unrelenting campaign against Dow and several other Baylor faculty members; he also attacked President Brooks, who defended them. Although Dow was forced to resign and others to endure repeated calls for their resignation, none was ever actually shown to be an evolutionist. The closest any came to heresy was when history professor Charles Fotergill admitted that he did have some doubts that Noah's Ark could have been large enough to transport two of every kind of animal.[86] Nevertheless, Norris was spectacularly successful in attracting attention to the evolution issue. Within days of his first attack on Baylor, publishers of Texas newspapers were expressing concern about the teaching of evolution in the state's public universities.[87] Across the South, fundamentalist papers carried reports of Norris's offensive, along with exhortations to extend it "without regard to State lines."[88] As far away as New England, where Norris (by this time dubbed the "Texas Tornado" by the Eastern press) made an extended tour in early 1922, audiences were reported to have been enthusiastic.[89] After every exposé, The Searchlight featured letters from readers begging for more. "The subscriptions," Norris crowed, "are simply coming in avalanches."[90]

The campaign may have experienced its most sensational moment at the 1923 meeting of the WCFA in Fort Worth, where activists staged a two-and-one-half hour show trial of Texas professors. Before a hushed audience of about three thousand in the auditorium of Norris's First Baptist Church, six students from Methodist colleges in Texas trooped to the stage to read from their class notebooks in an attempt to prove that their teachers had been instructing them in evolution. Testifying one by one, these witnesses personified the students that Bryan and his colleagues had been describing in speech after speech for the last two years—fresh-faced young Christians whose faith had been stolen by teachers in whom they had put their trust. In an unintended parody of a legal proceeding, "prosecutor" William E. Hawkins Jr., a youthful Methodist evangelist, led the

Texas students through their testimony, as described in a stenographer's report to *The Searchlight*:

REV. HAWKINS: Did you sign this affidavit?

MISS READ: I did.

REV. HAWKINS: This is the identical one?

MISS READ: That is it.

REV. HAWKINS: I want you now with this notebook in your hand just to read to this audience four or five statements—pick them out anywhere you want to—from your notebook. . . .

MISS READ: (*Reading from the notebook*): . . . "If you visit a hospital museum you can see the human animal in its early stages. It has a tail. Later, however, it disappears and forms the posterior of the spine. There are men in Australia at the present time who have tails." (*Laughter*).

The mock trial included no cross-examination, no defense, and no verdict. Its purpose was not legal, but political and psychological, to encourage the audience to take more aggressive action against evolutionists. On one occasion, an angry Hawkins cut short the testimony of a student to insert this pointed aside: "God grant that that teacher will repent before tomorrow or that scores of telegrams will be sent to the trustees and say, 'Out, and out in a hurry.' (*Applause*)." At another point, a student from Texas Women's College admonished the audience. "Now, what are you going to do about it?" she pleaded on concluding her testimony. "We can talk here for ten years and never do a thing. It is up to you."[91] In retrospect, the staged proceedings at Fort Worth can be seen as an eerie precursor of the Scopes trial, as well as a practice session for the scores of trials and public hearings on the teaching of evolution in the years to follow. At the time it sounded more like a call to arms, and by all accounts, as a motivating tool, it was a smashing success. According to one report, "the effect on the audience was tremendous."[92]

Of all the tactics used, however, the most successful were the public campaigns against state universities. All told, in the early 1920s small church colleges were not exactly teeming with evolutionary theory. Even where it existed, as at Wake Forest College, presidents and boards of trustees had proven to be surprisingly adept at protecting their teachers from outside pressures. In the state universities, by contrast, where evolution seemed more commonplace and administrators were less concerned about it, critics paradoxically found the going to be easier. In 1921 Bryan was already campaigning in states nationwide, using his stump speeches and newspaper columns to draw attention to the teaching of evolution in public colleges and universities, and calling for the creation of a "common sense commission" to protect the public against university presidents who were lacking in "moral enthusiasm" and "patriotism."[93] In Kentucky, J. W. Porter was working with the Baptist State Board of Missions to appoint a committee to investigate suspicious textbooks in use at the University of Kentucky.[94] In Minnesota, W. B. Riley was demanding the removal of texts on evolution and the investigation of teachers at the University of Minnesota.[95] In Texas, Norris had begun to turn his attention from Baylor and Southern Methodist to the University of Texas, where he singled out twelve professors as advocates of evolution.[96] Feeling the pressure, administrators began to carry out their own inquiries, often to fend off more serious attacks. At the University of Tennessee, for example, authorities dismissed Professor J. W. Sprowls for insisting on teaching from James Harvey Robinson's Mind in the Making, a widely used psychology text that expressed evolutionary views. In the protest that followed, six other faculty members were fired as well, in part for speaking out in his defense.[97] The protests were not confined to institutions of higher education: in cities and towns across America, state and local ministerial associations were drafting resolutions advocating the removal of textbooks on evolution from all public schools.[98] High schools had come under investigation. Teachers at Eastern High in Baltimore, for instance, were examined for their views on evolution after a local minister complained that "girl pupils" were being taught that Adam and Eve were "merely names of a couple of monkeys."[99] Most portentous of all, by 1923 Bryan and his fundamentalist colleagues had begun to lobby state legislatures, making the case for cutting off funds to any state-supported school where evolution was taught. "The professors say, 'let us have academic freedom,'" thundered Norris to a packed session of the Texas House of Representatives. "We have no objection to teaching or believing evolution, but don't ask us to pay the bills while they deny and destroy the faith in the fundamentals of our Bible."[100]

By 1923 Bryan and his fundamentalist allies had settled on the frame that would allow them to translate discontent into protest. In the theory of evolution, they had found the cause of the growing secularity of society. They had also identified the culprits: the professors and teachers who were responsible for indoctrinating their unsuspecting students in the theory. And they had conveyed a sense of urgency in their increasingly vitriolic attacks on the institutions they considered to be at fault. In the campaign against the colleges, they became antievolutionists. But before they could create a successful antievolution movement, they had to win additional popular support. Thus they began to reach beyond their own ranks to a wider public. In reaching out, they turned their cause into a crusade.

4 : Alignment

DEBATING DARWINISM

Zeno B. Metcalf had no idea what he was getting himself into. The small, soft-spoken, and bespectacled expert on winged insects at North Carolina State College had definitely not given it enough thought when colleagues prevailed on him to debate antievolution revivalist William Bell Riley over whether evolution could be considered a demonstrated fact. But as he entered Pullen Hall on the Raleigh campus that May afternoon in 1922, finding it filled to capacity with about two thousand boisterous students and townspeople who were whistling, yelling, and stamping their feet, he must have realized he had his hands full. Having opened the contest by reading from a carefully prepared text, Metcalf could only stand back and watch while a confident and smiling Riley, talking without notes, responded with a rapid-fire barrage of arguments, homey anecdotes, and sustained sarcasm, provoking outbursts of laughter and cheers from his supporters in the crowd. For the next hour Metcalf stood his ground, and news reports agreed that in the end neither side had completely carried the day, but the event had been a sensation. Moreover, it had started something, being the first of hundreds of similar debates that would take place throughout the 1920s and that would continue down even to today.[1]

In evolution, Riley and his followers had found the issue that would transform fundamentalism into a mass political movement. To carry out that transformation, however, they would need to bring it to a broader public, not only articulating their antievolution message but also aligning it—"tweaking" or "spinning" it (in today's parlance)—so that it would resonate with as many potential supporters as possible. Ironically, the fledgling antievolutionists were aided in the process by their evolutionist opponents, who began at this time to engage them in a series of spectacular confrontations. Some of these face-offs took place in the columns of magazines and newspapers. Starting in early 1922, for instance, the *New York Times* ran an extraordinary set of exchanges in its Sunday editorial section between William Jennings Bryan and several of America's leading scientists, including Henry Fairfield Osborn of the American Museum of Natural History and Edwin G. Conklin of Princeton University.[2] Other contests took the form of sermon and pamphlet wars like the ones that exploded when the outspoken modernist minister Harry Emerson Fosdick published his famous sermon "Shall the Fundamentalists Win?" and conservatives replied with a flurry of critical countersermons.[3] Attracting the most attention, however, were the stage debates that became increasingly popular from 1922 on, with speakers squaring off before unruly crowds that jammed auditoriums and music halls in cities and towns in every part of the country.[4] Taking advantage of these settings, activists aligned their antievolution frame, recasting their views in ways that would appeal to an ever-expanding audience. In debating Darwinism, they began to build a mass movement.

As described in social movement theory, framing is essentially a two-part process. In order to build movements, activists must be able to establish the frames that provide them with a common cause or purpose. Having created these frames, however, they must be able to apply them to attract supporters to their cause. In an often cited essay, David Snow and his collaborators have described this application process as "frame alignment," emphasizing that movements must constantly be recasting or refining their interpretation of issues so they "fit" or "resonate" with the views of potential supporters. According to Snow and his colleagues, the process can be seen as having four components: (1) *bridging*, the linking of two or more similar but previously unconnected interpretations of a particular issue or problem; (2) *amplification*, clarification of the beliefs and invigoration of the values that make an issue important to people; (3) *extension*, the broadening of the issue's boundaries to include other concerns and interests, thereby tapping more popular support; and (4) *transformation*, redefinition of existing understandings so the issue comes to be seen as more serious and threatening than ever before. Alignment can be a taxing process, testing the ability of activists to adapt to the changing currents of popular opinion. Building coalitions is challenging, since it requires defining issues in ways that will appeal to diverse groups of supporters. Maintaining these alliances can be even more difficult, particularly when they come under attack by countermovements. Nevertheless, if they are to consolidate and grow, movements must be able to align issues, convincing others of the importance of their cause and encouraging them to become part of it.[5]

Those who study the early antievolution movement have experienced some frustration (Ferenc Szasz has called it despair) in their attempts to describe how antievolutionists interpreted the evolution issue. The frustration is understandable, since activists viewed the issue in a bewildering variety of ways (one contemporary Baptist commentator saw "about fifty-seven" varieties). Thus whereas fundamentalists regarded evolution as a threat to revealed religion, those like Bryan were more concerned with the danger it posed to morality and democratic politics. Some activists opposed evolution because they considered it progressive, others because it smacked of Social Darwinism and was not progressive enough. Many held several conceptions of evolution at the same time, and some of these were contradictory or even at opposite poles. (There were surely also those among the rank and file who had no real understanding of evolution at all, except that they knew they were against it.) Present-day scholars have characterized the debates over evolution in still other ways, as being about the meaning of modernity, or the place of science in society, or the role of experts in a democracy. Even the best students of the movement have had to content themselves with the conclusion that evolution took on many meanings. "It is obvious in retrospect," as Szasz put it, "that the meaning of 'evolution' in the 1920s went far beyond the developmental theories of Darwin or Spencer. The word became a symbol for everything that was wrong with the nation in that decade."[6] What scholars have not done enough is to examine how those meanings were manipulated: how in aligning the evolution issue, antievolutionists turned it—debate by debate, essay by essay, sermon by sermon—into a tool for building their movement.

Bridging

For movements to grow, they must build coalitions, creating the connections that bring together discontented but otherwise disparate constituents. The first step is for activists to identify clusters of individuals and groups that share common grievances but lack ideological or institutional ties. Then they begin to build bridges, reaching out to these different pools of people and convincing them that they share concerns about a common issue. The process is carried out by activists who work through interpersonal or intergroup networks to connect congruent but previously disconnected framings of the issue or problem.[7]

For the founders of the antievolution movement, bridging meant connecting the diverse set of concerns about evolution that already existed. The truth is that for decades evolution had been targeted by a variety of critics in a variety of ways. Although almost all scientists of the early century agreed on the essential tenets of evolutionary theory, many expressed skepticism about the specifics, including such basic Darwinian doctrines as natural selection.[8] Although a few of the most prominent theologians proudly embraced evolution, most mainstream Protestant thinkers—even those who considered themselves theistic evolutionists—admitted that its materialism was troubling to them, while conservative evangelicals struggled to reconcile it with Scripture.[9] Bryan and other progressives had come to confound Darwinism with Social Darwinism, describing it as a theory based on the survival of the fittest and blaming it for the militarism and imperialism that had contributed to the onset of World War I.[10] More conservative moral reformers, concerned about what they regarded as a breakdown of conventional social roles, saw evolution as a threat to civilization and culture as they knew it.[11] Hard-boiled political conservatives were disturbed by the effect of evolutionary thinking on politics, fearing that it would lead to radicalism and political unrest.[12] For antievolutionists, the challenge was to connect all of these concerns, bringing diverse clusters of critics together into a broad-based coalition with evolution as the common enemy—"the only thing," as Bryan described it, "that has seriously menaced religion since the birth of Christ and it menaces all other religions as well as the Christian religion, and civilization as well as religion."[13]

The first bridge they began to build was to Christian evangelicals. The strategy was to reach beyond fundamentalism into the Protestant mainstream by contending that Darwinism was at odds with evangelical theology. To make the case, antievolutionists argued that the biblical account of the creation story was the basis of all Christian belief. To cast doubt on creation meant casting doubt on the fall from innocence, which meant denying the doctrine of the atonement, which meant eliminating any promise of salvation. Adventist scientist George McCready Price expressed it as a formula: "no Adam, no fall; no fall, no atonement; no atonement, no Savior."[14] The argument was important because it allowed antievolutionists to turn the debates over evolution away from the arcane aspects of Adam and Eve to the centrality of Christ and the Christian message of salvation. When carried to its logical conclusion, Bryan explained in an essay entitled "The Fundamentals," published in 1923 in the popular magazine The Forum, evolution "robs Christ of the glory of His virgin birth, of the majesty of His deity, and of the triumph of his resurrection; such a Christ is impotent to save."[15]

By shifting the spotlight from Adam to Christ, antievolutionists were able to position themselves at the center of Christianity, portraying themselves as the best of evangelical Christians. At the same time, and probably more important, it allowed them to cast doubt on the Christian credentials of theistic evolutionists. Thus A. C. Dixon contended that evolution had no place in early Christian thought, arising instead from pagan Greek philosophy.[16] J. W. Porter thought it was significant that theistic evolutionists chose to call themselves "theistic" rather than "Christian."[17] John Roach Straton went further, insisting in his famous New York City debates with Unitarian minister Charles Francis Potter that there was "no such thing as so-called 'theistic' or 'Christian' evolution. Such terms are misnomers."[18] Throughout the four Potter-Straton debates—three of which took place in Carnegie Hall—Straton stated the theme repeatedly, telling capacity crowds and others listening on the radio that those who believed in evolution were corrupt Christians, or simply not Christians at all. The terms "Christianity" and "evolution" were "mutually exclusive and self-contradictory," he summed up in the second debate. "If it is Christianity, then it is not evolution; and if it is evolution, then it is not Christianity."[19]

At about the same time, Bryan was building bridges to progressive reformers. Over the previous two decades Bryan had been active in successful campaigns for the progressive income tax, the direct election of U.S. senators, and woman suffrage. By the early 1920s, however, disillusioned by declining popular support for progressive policies (and the falling fortunes of his own political career), he had become increasingly convinced that political reform was collapsing and that evolutionary theory was at fault. Thus America's most famous democrat began to reach out to his followers by casting evolution as an antidemocratic doctrine. Although personally able to distinguish Darwinism from Social Darwinism, Bryan consistently collapsed the two in his speeches, emphasizing that the centerpiece of Darwin's theory was the doctrine of the survival of the fittest, "the cruel law," as he characterized it, "under which the strong kill off the weak." In his speeches he described how Darwin had discovered the essential elements of his theory in Thomas Malthus's contention that whereas food supply increased only arithmetically, population increased geometrically, requiring that the strong eliminate the weak in order to survive. He told of his astonishment at discovering how Darwin had argued in his *Descent of Man* that while smallpox vaccinations had saved thousands who would otherwise not have survived, it had in fact weakened society as a whole. It was an idea, he told his audiences, "at which I revolted." Bryan went on to argue that the doctrine had been passed on to the powerful and privileged of the modern world, who proceeded to use it as a weapon to oppress the poor. Adopted by the munitions makers of World War I, it had been instrumental in bringing about "the bloodiest war in history." In the hands of conservative industrialists of the postwar period, it had become "the basis of the gigantic class struggle that is now shaking society throughout the world." Indeed, he explained, it was the doctrine of evolution, inspiring class consciousness and eliminating sentiments of brotherhood and sympathy, that was "transforming the industrial world into a slaughter-house." Nor did it stop there, since Darwinian doctrine was present in the contemporary eugenics movement—led at the time by such prominent evolutionists as Henry Fairfield Osborn—whose "plan of operation is to improve the race by 'scientific breeding' on a purely physical basis." All told, evolution seemed to be afoot in every antidemocratic movement of the time. To Bryan, whose entire career had been dedicated to the cause of progressive reform, it was the ultimate enemy. Evolution, he concluded, "robs the reformer of hope."[20]

Others in the antievolution movement sought to build ties to more conservative cultural and social reformers. Throughout the early twentieth century, conservative commentators had expressed concern about the declining state of American society, as seen in everything from rising rates of alcoholism and divorce to the popularity of ballroom dancing and moving pictures. While sometimes working with progressives on Prohibition, these conservative reformers, whose ranks included many women, were more often found in church groups and women's clubs that advocated Sunday closing statutes and laws for the suppression of vice. In the early 1920s movement leaders like Straton reached out to them, exhorting their antievolutionist followers "to widen the scope of their work, because this subject has not only a religious bearing but a bearing on morals."[21] In reaching out, Straton began to describe evolution as one of the chief causes of cultural decline, leading inexorably, as he put it in one of his Carnegie Hall debates, to "the degradation of the modern dance, the sensualism of the modern theater, the glorification of the flesh in modern styles, the sex suggestion of modern literature, the substitution of dogs for babies, [and] the appalling divorce evil."[22] Focusing in particular on the family, antievolution preachers stressed how Darwinism endangered the home. "If the home is to be preserved as a sacred institution," Dixon wrote, "the Bible which teaches that marriage came down from God and not up from the beast must be believed. The jungle theory as to the origins of marriage is today keeping busy the divorce courts of the civilized world."[23] As Betty DeBerg points out, women—especially young women—were prominently featured in descriptions of evolutionary theory's contribution to this moral decline, with an unusual amount of attention given to their immodest dress, improper dancing, and immoral behaviors such as smoking, gambling, and swearing.[24] The teaching "that women are evoluted [sic] from lower animals," explained evangelist Mordecai Ham, "encourages them to act like animals."[25] But women were also presented as the theory's victims, as the ones who paid the price for the beastlike behavior of men. Orators took every opportunity to describe the antievolution movement as a defense of the home and, by extension, of women. North Carolina governor Cameron Morrison seems to have had this in mind when he warned that one of the state's biology textbooks posed a special threat to young women: "I don't want my daughter or anybody's daughter to have to study a book," he announced, "that prints pictures of a monkey and a man on the same page."[26]

Finally there were ties to be made to political conservatives. In the postwar period conservatism flourished, as business, civic, and patriotic organizations rallied against anarchists, immigrants, labor unions, and other enemies of the American Way. Though often overlapping with conservative cultural reformers, these political conservatives tended to take even more authoritarian and antidemocratic positions, while also being associated more often with nativist groups like the American Protective Association or the Ku Klux Klan. In the antievolution movement such sentiments could frequently be found. In movement newspapers like the *Western Recorder*, anti-Catholic and anti-immigrant agitation received prominent play, with Roman Catholics and other "unpatriotic Europeans" singled out for attempting to "exploit the American Sunday for the purposes of making money out of amusement."[27] Anti-Semitic strains were less prominent, though as early as 1921 W. B. Riley was warning of the growing influence of Jews in Germany and Russia.[28] While some leaders (like Straton) denounced the Klan, and others (like Bryan) offered only lukewarm support, many more (like Norris) worked actively with it.[29] Over time, the antievolution movement would become more reactionary, with anti-Catholicism coming to a head in the 1928 campaign against Al Smith and anti-Semitism peaking in the 1930s. But even in the early 1920s, right-wing rhetoric was a staple of many antievolution speeches. A classic example was Norris's 1923 address before the Texas legislature. "My friends, we are in a terrible hour," he told the lawmakers. "Wave after wave of crime is sweeping over the land, and the reign of lawlessness is engaging the best thought of our greatest statesmen. . . . Our penitentiaries are crowded, our jails are crowded and our juvenile courts are working overtime. Our crime used to be among men—mature men—but now it is committed by both men and women. It would be bad enough if confined to adults, but now we find it among the tender ages of 12, 14, and 16 years." Along with lawlessness came social disorder. "There is a wave of liberalism sweeping over this country," Norris continued:

> Marriage vows do not hold good any more. We are in the days of free-loveism. I can remember the time when a woman with a divorce was looked upon as a peculiar animal in society, but now if a woman has half a dozen divorces she has a passport to high society and becomes a moving picture star. I can remember the time when a man who deserted his wife and babies would not be allowed to put his face into decent company, and it was doubtful whether he would be allowed to live until the dawn of another day, but now he can desert half a dozen wives and leave his children upon the charity of a cold, merciless world.

The dangers were not only domestic but also included the growing threat of international instability: "The whole world is trembling in the balance. The war-clouds are dark. They hang low. Nothing is settled. If the hordes of Germany and Russia already in alliance should start west, France would not last until breakfast. We need not fool ourselves. We might just as well get ready. We are going in again." According to Norris, all of these problems could be attributed to the loss of authority that came with the acceptance of evolutionary theory. "Evolution means to deny authority," he summed up to the legislators. "Evolution rules God out of the life of men and out of the nation."[30]

In building conservative connections, antievolutionists made at least some use of racial prejudice. On the surface, references to race were few and far between in antievolution writings, and outright racism was rare. Yet the movement introduced race in more subtle ways. Although, for example, A. C. Dixon did not mention race in his speeches, it was common knowledge that he had been an early member of the Ku Klux Klan and that his brother, Thomas Dixon Jr., was the author of The Clansman. In the same way, Bryan avoided direct racial references, but his consistent refusal to criticize the Klan, many of whose members were among his strongest supporters, was well known. More important, Bryan probably managed to fan fears of race mixing among white audiences by his frequent references to evolution as being based on blood, or what he sometimes called "the blood of the brute."[31] Jeffrey Moran has suggested that such allusions had clear racial content, since white racists had for decades been equating Africans and African Americans with apes and describing them as bestial.[32] Norris made the connection explicit in his address to the Texas legislature: "My friends," he asked, "are you willing to admit that there is any brute blood whatsoever in your veins? Some men very bitterly resent the intimation of any negro blood, yet are willing to say we have the blood of a chimpanzee."[33] Especially in the South, antievolutionists intimated that any acceptance of evolution would encourage racial equality and the eventual mixing of the races. In his Mind of the South, W. J. Cash recalled from his youth how "one of the most stressed notions which went around was that evolution made a Negro as good as a white man."[34] Even bastions of southern progressivism such as the Atlanta Constitution issued dire warnings that evolutionists like H. G. Wells were calling for racial intermarriage as a strategy for improving the human race.[35] In the last analysis, however, it was usually enough to point out that evolution had the effect of placing people of different races in the same line of descent. As Texan J. T. Stroder put it, Darwinism was that "vicious and infamous doctrine . . . that mankind sprang from pollywog, to a frog, to an ape, to a monkey, to a baboon, to a Jap, to a negro, to a Chinaman, to a man."[36]

When all else failed, antievolutionists asserted that Darwinism was leading to political radicalism. At the end of the war, American conservatives were alarmed by the surge of labor unrest that accompanied demobilization. In 1919, however, with the Russian revolution, they bordered on hysteria as bolshevism assumed the status of a new national enemy. Throughout the early 1920s antievolutionists did their part in calling attention to the Soviet threat. Treating the Russian experience as a cautionary tale, they described in dramatic detail how that Christian country had been overcome by godless communism. "Look at Russia," Norris would tell his audiences. "On New Year's night in Russia the students—the students, mark you—led by their professors met in the streets of Moscow and in front of the Kremlin they burned God in effigy. Shocking! Blasphemous! Yes, they made a caricature of the Creator, marched around the public square, and then burned in effigy the One who gives life and breath to all creatures. Think of it! It is enough to make the world tremble."[37]

But the danger was not to Russia alone. Revolutionary radicalism appeared to be making its way everywhere in the world, including in the United States. Norris's sermons and speeches regularly contained firsthand reports of the labor and political protests that he had seen in American cities. "Last year I saw in New York a mob of 15,000 or 20,000 people," he told the Texas legislators. "They had the red flag on the lapel of their coats. They waved them in their hands. A man would harangue a while and then a woman. They were ready to overthrow this government. I saw the same thing happen in the public square of Philadelphia."[38] Antievolution orators drew the line at claiming that Darwin had directly inspired Marx and his communist minions. What they did say was that by advocating atheism and disrespect for the law, Darwinism had made it easier for bolshevism to flourish. The Moody Bible Institute's James M. Gray tied the theory to support for pacifism and the League of Nations, warning that sooner or later it would eventuate in "the red doctrines of the Third International of Moscow," along with "the overthrow of our government."[39] W. B. Riley told how evolutionists planned to "sovietize our schools as to make them hot-beds of Bolshevism."[40] By the mid-1920s, almost every antievolution orator was warning that evolution and revolution traveled in tandem. "You wonder why Russia is swept by bolshevism, why England and even your own country are swept by disruption," declared Mordecai Ham. "The day is not far distant when you will be in the grip of the Red Terror and your children will be taught free love by the damnable theory of evolution."[41]

Amplification

Next alignment turns to amplification, the process by which issues are put before the public to demonstrate their importance. As a practical matter, people generally find it difficult to see how issues may influence their own lives. Thus activists must be adept at convincing potential recruits why their particular issues or problems are more significant than any others. The process requires not only that those inside the movement accent and highlight their own stands, but also that they try to tie them to the beliefs and values of others on the outside.[42]

For antievolutionists, the challenge was to connect—really reconcile—their belief in the dangers of evolution with the widespread enthusiasm for science that existed at the time. Throughout the early postwar period, popular support for science was especially strong, as almost all Americans celebrated its contributions to winning the war, defeating disease, and producing material products from automobiles to X-rays.[43] At the same time, however, a certain amount of ambivalence could be detected in prevailing views of scientific progress. With advances in scientific thinking, exemplified by Einstein's theory of relativity, commonsense approaches to science had given way to arcane and highly theoretical understandings.[44] Professionalization and specialization had taken its practice beyond the reach of amateurs, creating a new class of scientific experts.[45] Perhaps most important, advancements in methods and standards had created the impression that science had lost all moral or spiritual purpose, as more and more practitioners engaged in "science for science's sake."[46] As antievolutionists saw it, their task was to claim and transform these views, acknowledging the contributions of science while distancing themselves from its more troubling developments, which could then be attributed to the insidious influence of evolution. Thus they set about recasting popular conceptions of science, redefining it in such a way that it would come to be linked in the public mind with biblical creation rather than evolution. In addition, while stressing the importance of science, they also tried to put it into perspective, reminding people that science was a means rather than an end and that it was only one of many ways to understand the world. As Bryan observed, "Man is infinitely more than science; science, as well as the Sabbath, was made for man."[47]

In reaching out to the public, antievolutionists had to align their message with the widespread respect that existed for all things scientific. The first step was to describe themselves as believers in science, albeit science of a certain kind. For at least a hundred years, as George Marsden has shown, American evangelicals had been embracing a Baconian brand of Scottish commonsense philosophy, according to which God's truths were revealed to all right-thinking and observant persons through both the Bible and the wonders of the natural world. As adopted by antievolutionists like A. C. Dixon, the theory suggested that Christianity and science were totally compatible. " 'Science is knowledge gained and verified by exact observation and correct thinking,' " said Dixon, citing the "best dictionaries" as the source of his definition, "and within the circle of this definition I am a Christian, because I am a scientist."[48] Because they saw Scripture as factual and science as an exercise in collecting and explaining facts, they assumed that the accounts of creation found in the Book of Genesis could be considered to have scientific validity. Writing in his 1920 pamphlet *The Scientific Accuracy of the Sacred Scriptures*, Riley made the case, arguing that careful study revealed "the most undreamed of agreement" between Scripture and science:

> First fact, in order—God created the heavens; second fact—"and the earth"; third—water; fourth—light; fifth—firmament; sixth—grass; seventh—herb; eighth—tree; ninth—appearance of heavenly bodies; tenth—fish; eleventh—moving things; twelfth—fowls; thirteenth—creeping things; fourteenth—cattle; fifteenth—man!

> Now, the latest science will consent to this order of creation. The heavens were certainly made first; the earth certainly made second; water certainly appeared third; light, fourth; firmament next; grass thereafter; the manifestation of sun and moon, ninth; the appearance of fish—tenth; moving things—eleventh; fowls—twelfth; creeping things—thirteenth; cattle, etc., fourteenth, and last—man.[49]

Moreover, because they believed that the world was created by a divinely intelligent deity, antievolutionists assumed it to be perfect and permanent, as exemplified by the timeless and unchanging division of nature into species, genera, and orders. Scientific observation confirmed the constancy of the orders, since plants and animals had been reproducing themselves according to the same predictable patterns—birds from birds, beasts from beasts, fish from fish—from the creation of the world down to the present day. "The truth of Genesis, we know," said Riley, "from the lowest form of grass to soulful man; everything is bringing forth 'after its kind.' We have seen that law executed tens of millions of times and in millions of forms." Riley had no illusion that the Bible somehow presupposed every discovery of modern science. The Scriptures did not address themselves, he averred, "to all subjects to which Science speaks." By the same token, he was equally clear that it conveyed truths that science could never imagine. "There are points in human experience where the microscope, the scalpel, the telescope tell us nothing," he noted.[50] The point, however, was that the Bible, and in particular the biblical version of creation, was superior on scientific grounds to any assumption of Darwinian science. As Bryan put it, "There is more science in the twenty-fourth verse of the first chapter of Genesis (And God said, let the earth bring forth the living creature after his kind, cattle and creeping things, and beast of the earth after his kind; and it was so.) than in all that Darwin wrote."[51]

In constructing their creationist version of science, antievolutionists consistently claimed that the best scientists believed in biblical creation and opposed evolutionary theory. Throughout the late nineteenth century, as the theory became commonplace in scientific circles, there had been continuing controversies over the exact nature of the evolutionary process. Although the basic idea of Darwinian descent went unchallenged, Darwin's concept of natural selection had been criticized, on many counts, by advocates of contending explanations that ran from Lamarckian ideas of acquired characteristics to germ plasm, orthogenesis, and saltation theories. Even after 1900, when advances in population genetics had ensured a central role for natural selection in evolution's emerging "modern synthesis," criticism of the concept persisted in certain scientific circles.[52] For antievolutionists, such statements were grist for their mill. Often mistaking, sometimes misrepresenting criticism for repudiation, they began to assemble rosters of scientists who at one time or another had expressed doubts about aspects of Darwinian theory. Their lists contained an odd assortment of critics, including such prominent scholars as Louis Agassiz, Arnold Guyot, and John William Dawson, along with numerous but little-known (and fairly dim) lesser lights.[53] Among those who constructed his own list was T. T. Martin, who in one of his early attacks on Wake Forest's President Poteat cited the support of no less than twenty-one critics of evolution who were also "really great scientists."[54] When Poteat replied that almost all of them were either dead, discredited, or not really scientists at all, Martin was unfazed: "Does the fact that they are dead prove that they were not great scientists?"[55]

More important than the lists was the singling out of contemporary scholars who occasionally expressed reservations—no matter how minor—about some aspect of evolutionary theory. The most celebrated of these was British biologist William Bateson, an outspoken advocate of mutation theory, who in a December 1921 address to the American Association for the Advancement of Science (AAAS) made the scientifically uncontroversial point that the process of natural selection had not been definitively demonstrated to be a satisfactory explanation for evolutionary development. Although Bateson strongly asserted his own belief in evolution, and encouraged other scientists to maintain their faith in it, antievolutionists selectively quoted and sometimes blatantly misquoted his remarks to provide one more proof, in Bryan's words, that "every effort to discover the origin of species has failed."[56] Bateson was only one of many such examples, as activists scoured the writings of reputable scientists searching for the smallest sign of criticism or doubt concerning any aspect of evolution, which they would then recast as a repudiation of the entire theory. In his 1922 pamphlet *Evolution and the Bible*, Canadian antievolution lecturer Arthur Brown demonstrated the strategy. Brown, who called Bateson "perhaps *the greatest living Biologist*," declared that his "revolutionary address" at Toronto had "*utterly repudiated Darwinism*" and "*denied that any new species had ever been formed from pre-existing species*." It did not seem to matter that none of these claims was true. After all, Brown wrote, almost as an afterthought, "other authorities might be quoted indefinitely to the same effect."[57]

In addition to claiming scientific credentials for themselves, antievolutionists contended that evolution was bad science. As a general rule, they evinced little understanding of evolutionary theory and with few exceptions lumped Darwinism with any and all schools of evolutionary thought. After all, Darwinists and their evolutionist critics were all still evolutionists. Besides, what all evolutionary science (Darwinian or otherwise) had in common was that it was theoretical. Being good Baconians, antievolutionists described science as a process of fact gathering, in which practitioners observed and organized the world. "Bacon insisted that we sit at the feet of nature and accept what she teaches," explained Dixon. "First learn the facts and then draw your deductions from them."[58] But evolution was based not on fact but on theory, and therefore, as J. W. Porter argued, it was "incapable of scientific demonstration," consisting of "sheer speculation."[59] Others were quick to pick up the theme. Arthur Brown believed that evolution was "nothing more than a theory." According to Baptist antievolutionist W. W. Everts, it could best be described as "mere guesses, and they are generally wrong."[60] For opponents of the theory, who attempted to convince onlookers that they themselves were the true scientists while the supporters of evolution were essentially frauds, it seemed like a reasonable case. "Those of us who deny the theory of evolution," observed Straton in the second Potter-Straton debate, "have no antagonism to true science. We only object to having that which is merely an hypothesis proclaimed dogmatically as though it were really fact."[61]

Among antievolutionists, Bryan was always the best at making this point. As he demonstrated in many of his writings, he had at least a rudimentary understanding of the hypothetical deductive method that had come to be accepted by most scientists of the time. In fact, on occasion he described it accurately and well. "Darwin does not use facts," he explained, more or less correctly, in an analysis of *The Descent of Man*; "he uses conclusions drawn from similarities. He builds upon presumptions, probabilities, and inferences, and asks the acceptance of his hypothesis 'notwithstanding the fact that connecting links have not hitherto been discovered.' "[62] Yet while he comprehended the basic character of the modern scientific method, Bryan did not accept it, and he went out of his way to criticize or mock everything about it. His favorite target was the term "hypothesis," which he described as a perfect symbol of evolutionary science, "euphonious, dignified and high sounding," while in truth "merely a scientific synonym for the old-fashioned word 'guess.' "[63] Repeatedly in his speeches he referred to evolution as "Darwin's guess," consisting of nothing more than "guesses strung together," "scientific guessing," or even "the wildest guesses."[64] He also liked to pass along the phony contention, as if repeating it made it true, that Darwin had used the phrase "we may well suppose" over eight hundred times in his two principal works alone. "The eminent scientist," he confidently concluded, "is guessing." Moreover, while Bryan personally delighted in satirizing science, his efforts were clearly self-conscious and strategic, aimed at convincing his audience of evolution's ultimate emptiness. "If Darwin had described his doctrine as a guess instead of calling it a hypothesis," he speculated, "it would not have lived a year."[65]

In attacking evolutionary theory, antievolutionists zeroed in on the idea of the transmutation of species. Assuming divine design, they held that observation showed that the world was orderly, with endless examples of animals and plants reproducing after their own kind. When evolutionists contended that organisms could change in such a way as to produce entirely new and different species, they insisted on seeing examples of these changing or transitional forms. "Surely, SURELY, we have a right to expect these," asserted Brown, "and they MUST exist if evolution be true. If the fish is changing into the reptile, and the reptile into the bird, the bird into the mammal, and the mammal into the man, we ought to have little difficulty in finding, at least, ONE instance. But we ask in vain for a glimpse of even a single specimen."[66] When evolutionists responded by characterizing transmutation as the product of continuous alterations and adaptations taking place over countless generations, antievolutionists found their answers easy to caricature. In speech after speech, Bryan parodied the process of natural selection. "The eye, for instance, according to evolutionists, was brought out by 'the light beating upon the skin' "; "the leg is the development of a wart that chanced to appear on the belly of an animal; and so the tommyrot runs on *ad infinitum*, and sensible people are asked to swallow it."[67] He also delighted in holding forth on the already largely discredited concept of sexual selection, depicting it as a process in which males evolved larger brains and less hair by fighting for females. It was a point, the balding Bryan would tell his listeners with mock seriousness, "that touches me deeply."[68]

In their sermons and speeches, antievolutionists treated transmutation as a target of endless satire. South Carolina evangelist "Cyclone Mack" McLendon, for instance, offered this fractured description of the evolutionary process:

In the beginning the amoeba begat earthworms; earth worms begat skull-less animals; these animals begat other kinds of animals; these other kind of animals begat some kind of fish, away back in the dateless date; and the fish away beyond the gates of morning begat some kind of gilled amphibian; and these begat tailed amphibians that lived away back when ages were but drifts of foam on the mighty sea of time; and these begat primeval amniota; and these begat mammals; and these begat kangaroos; and kangaroos begat apes; and apes begat gorillas; and gorillas, thank God, begat pin-whiskered, top-heavy college professors who draw their breath and salary and use great big jaw-breaking words, and talk about the Bible being allegorical, figurative, probable, inferential, and hypothetical.[69]

In response to arguments that adaptation operated over extended eras by means that remained unknown, they pointed derisively to the inability of evolutionists to agree among themselves on the exact nature of the evolutionary process. In his speech to the Texas legislature, Norris turned the subject into crude comedy:

Away back yonder some time, nobody knows when, six million, six hundred million, six hundred billion (one fellow put it at a quad-trillion, on the matter of time these fellows are very extravagant and a few billion years is immaterial with brains that deal in wild guesses)—away back yonder some time—when, nobody knows, something happened away back yonder somewhere—where, nobody knows, something happened away back yonder somehow, something happened, nobody knows how; away back yonder some time, somewhere, somehow, something moved—time, place and method nobody knows—a germ, a protoplasm, a cell, void and without form, and it moved again. What made it move nobody knows and whether interior or exterior force. It kept on moving somehow, somewhere, sometime, some way by some power—and this continual movement of this protoplasm, substance or something become elongated and grew and grew and grew—how, nobody knows, why, nobody knows, when nobody knows, where nobody knows.[70]

When evolutionists tried to be specific in estimating the length of life on the earth, the critics ridiculed their estimates as inexact and unscientific. "Exactness would seem immaterial," quipped Bryan, "when one scientist says twenty-four million and another three hundred and six million years."[71] Repeatedly he stressed the point that while evolutionary theory may have offered plausibility, it provided no proof. "To believe that natural selection, sexual selection or any other kind of selection can account for the countless differences we see about us," he summed up, "requires more faith in *chance* than a Christian is required to have in God."[72]

Finally, antievolutionists argued that evolution was an affront to common sense. Although the point seemed self-evident to them, it was not as obvious to most people. After all, every farmer and gardener knew that certain evolutionary principles were at work in such commonplace agricultural practices as hybridization and selective breeding. Therefore, antievolutionists had to convince their audiences that evolutionary theory went well beyond the boundaries of sensible applied science. "No one objects to an evolution defined, as growth, an unfolding, development, progress and cultivation," wrote Methodist minister Andrew Johnson in the *Pentecostal Herald*. "Our objection is not against involution, evolution, convolution, revolution but transvolution or the transmutation of species."[73] In describing the theory the critics focused almost exclusively on transmutation, insisting that the concept was inherently irrational. "If the evolutionists are correct," Bryan would say;

> if it is true that all that we see is the result of development from one or a few invisible germs of life, then, in plants as well as in animals there must be a line of descent connecting all the trees and vegetables and flowers with a common ancestry. Does it not strain the imagination to the breaking point to believe that the oak, the cedar, the pine and the palm are all the progeny of one ancient seed and that this seed was also the ancestor of wheat and corn, potato and tomato, onion and sugar beet, rose and violet, orchid and daisy, mountain flower and magnolia?[74]

Among those who made the argument, Mordecai Ham was especially effective. His famous "sermon on evolution," delivered to thousands at revivals throughout the South, portrayed the idea of natural selection as an insult to thinking people. In it, Ham would parody the evolutionary process, likening it to "a lot of iron ore that one day got to wiggling around and finally evolved of itself into a Ford automobile."[75] Sometimes relying on theatrical props to make his point, he would blow up a deflated balloon, demonstrating that "there has never been any development by resident force without assistance of outside forces." Then he would hold up an egg, asking which came first, the chicken or the egg, and declaring that evolutionists maintained that the egg had to come before the chicken. "Oh the fallacy, the folly, the folly, and the foolishness of a man who claims that everything has resident force!" With or without props, Ham's point was always the same, that evolution defied common sense: "There is nothing to prove that a horse is anything but a horse," he would conclude; "a cow anything but a cow; a fern anything but a fern; a monkey anything but a monkey and a man anything but a man and a fool."[76]

Extension

Of all the ways to build public support, frame extension may be the easiest and most efficient. If movements are to grow, they must be able to connect their causes to broader pools of public sentiment by defining their objectives in terms that resonate with a wide range of supporters. Although the process may require the adoption of new attitudes or values, more often it consists of presenting existing programs in more accessible and evocative terms. Often these terms are essentially symbolic, as activists make use of written or visual representations— catchphrases, exemplars, metaphors, or visual images—to translate complex concepts into simpler and more understandable ones.[77]

In searching for such symbols, antievolutionists did not have far to look. From the time of Darwin's *The Descent of Man*, with its suggestion that people were not uniquely and supernaturally created, but were descended from earlier hominids, antievolutionists had been describing Darwinism as a theory that somehow linked "men" to "monkeys." The fact that Darwin did not describe a direct line of descent, and that evolutionists repeatedly denied any biological connection between human beings and Old or New World monkeys (asserting only that humans and certain of the great apes may have shared a common anthropoidal ancestor), did not seem to matter. By the 1920s the idea had become a popular stereotype, with the term "monkey" being taken to include every possible kind of ape, baboon, chimp, or lemur. Scientists may have contributed to this misconception through a series of widely publicized primate studies that took place at the time. At the 1922 meeting of the AAAS, for example, papers were presented on the intelligence of "Soker" the chimp and "Rufus," an orangutan at the National Zoo. (Also reported at the same meeting was a study by British army officers on the behavior of chimpanzees, who were found to have the intelligence of "morons," along with "a disposition to get drunk whenever the officers left liquor around, but the gorillas were prohibitionists.")[78] Public interest seemed to peak in the early 1920s, sparked by reports on the death and postmortem examination of "John Daniel," a full-grown male gorilla owned by the Barnum and Bailey Circus, whose body was dissected and examined for weeks by surgeons and scientists at the Columbia College of Physicians.[79] Antievolutionists could not have asked for a more perfect metaphor. After all, complained social critic Lloyd

Douglas, "monkeys are very funny animals. A joke about a monkey is good for a hearty laugh anywhere. The very word 'monkey' will provoke a smile, even if nothing should be predicated of the subject."[80]

So as antievolutionists took to the podiums, the monkey metaphors began to fly and their audiences were primed for the performance. Bryan seemed to take particular pleasure in making use of the symbol, riddling his speeches with references to Darwinism as "the ape line of descent," calling evolutionists "tree men" and asserting that he for one had no known relatives who were part of the "simian tribe."[81] Although his references to monkeys and chimpanzees may have betrayed some misunderstanding of evolutionary theory, it is clear that his repeated use of the symbolism was strategic, to encourage the misconceptions of his listeners. "To put man in a class with the chimpanzee because of any resemblances that may be found," he observed, "is so unreasonable that the masses have never accepted it."[82] On occasion, he appeared to be quite serious about the use of the metaphor, as when he stated that evolution was blasphemous for implying that Christ had "an ape for his ancestor on his mother's side at least." More often, his allusion to monkeys seemed like good clean fun, intended to delight his audiences, as when he claimed that Darwin had traced human ancestry back through European apes. "He does not even allow us the patriotic pleasure," a comically indignant Bryan complained, "of descending from *American* apes."[83] But in whatever way it was used, the analogy seemed to work; almost every antievolutionist of the period managed to throw in a few passing references to apes, monkeys, or "hairy baboons," along with "orang-utans, now wagging friendly with their long tails, then fiercely fighting with claws and teeth."[84] If nothing else, for those struggling to come to terms with Darwin's complex scientific theory, the metaphor made everything seem so wonderfully simple. "Genesis 1:27 declares very plainly that God created man in his own image," said the Reverend George Fowler, a Minnesota Baptist. "Is the image of God that of an ape or gorilla God? Are we to worship an ape or gorilla God?"[85]

In applying the monkey metaphor, antievolutionists seemed to have a clear advantage over their evolutionist opponents. Debates on evolution were littered with satiric references to "monkey business," "monkeyshines," "monkeyfoolery," and the like. But while both sides made use of such phrases, antievolutionists used them more easily and effectively, particularly in casting derision at the alleged biological relationship between monkeys and humans.[86] Beginning with Bryan, antievolution speakers made a point of disclaiming any descent from ancient animals. "If only the evolutionists would stop with their own ancestors and leave mine alone," Bryan told a packed house at the Philadelphia Academy of Music. "They can't make a monkey out of me."[87] Norris liked to claim that certain of his forefathers had been put to death by hanging, "But I will tell you one thing, no matter how many were hung by the neck, I don't want anybody to ever say that any ancestor of mine ever hung by the tail from any tree (Applause.)."[88] Straton seems to have stolen Norris's joke, recycling it in one of his Carnegie Hall debates, where he admitted that "some of my remote ancestors hung by their necks, but I am willing to stake my life on the proposition that none of them ever hung by their tails!"[89]

Even when they were serious, antievolutionists consistently misrepresented evolutionary theory by describing a direct line of descent from monkeys to humans. "Darwinism stands for the descent of man from the monkey," insisted a solemn Andrew Johnson. "This is the crux of the whole question."[90] But most of the time they preferred to take the low road, creating cartoon caricatures of the evolutionary process, like Norris's slapstick version:

> . . . and the old male would set up in a tree and throw cocoanuts [sic] at his sweethearts, and the smaller ones got scared of the larger ones, and ran down to the caves, and having no further use for their tail, their eoudal [sic] appendages finally fell off; (laughter.) when they were down in the caves, they had no further use for their hair, and that's how the bald-headed men got their start, (laughter.) and one day one of these ape-men, or whatever they were, ran off and stole a suit of clothes, and became a professor in a chair of Biology. (Much laughter and applause.)[91]

In addition to being lots of fun, the satires served the more serious purpose of making evolution seem ridiculous. "If some of those fellows think they sprung from the monkey," wrote South Carolinian J. D. Croft to the Western Recorder, "they certainly did not get very far. . . . If I believed in such stuff the first old tramp I caught on the street corner with a string around a monkey's neck, with a cap on and playing a music-box and making the monkey dance, I would have arrested for making fun of his grandfather." Most of all, the monkey motif allowed antievolutionists to tap into popular skepticism about the biological connection between animals and humans. Certainly Croft spoke for many when he put the matter in its simplest terms: "Monkeys are not our kin folks."[92]

For their part, evolutionists appeared unable to respond. Denouncing the monkey metaphors seemed to make little difference. Introducing alternative concepts could be dangerous: any allusion to the "tree" of life, for example, could be counted on to elicit sarcastic comments about monkeys in its branches, with much hilarity all around. Even more hazardous was trying to cast the metaphor in their own terms. Thus when Princeton's Edwin Grant Conklin proposed what came to be known as the "monkey or mud" thesis, suggesting that on the whole it was better to be descended from living creatures than molded from lifeless earth (as was Adam in Genesis 2), Bryan announced that he for one considered the monkey inferior to the mud: "I prefer mud," he told an audience of about six thousand at New York City's Hippodrome. "Everything I eat comes from the mud. The flower grows from the mud. I know all about mud. What has the monkey ever done for Professor Conklin, that should cause so much affection for it?"[93] In fact, whenever evolutionists tried to turn the monkey metaphor back at their opponents, it almost always seemed to backfire, as when Charles Francis Potter, in a debate at Carnegie Hall, referred to Bryan's coccyx as proof that he was descended from animal ancestors. "And as for my opponent's references to Mr. Bryan's anatomy," countered John Roach Straton when it came time for his reply, "I must express my surprise that he assailed our great commoner after that fashion when he is not here to defend his own tail!"[94] (According to the New York Tribune, the audience "shrieked mirthfully at the mention of Mr. Bryan's member.")[95] Perhaps most frustrating was the response when evolutionists pointed out that Darwin did not say that present-day humans were in any way related to present-day monkeys, since they had branched off from the tree of life at some time after the ape. Antievolutionists took the explanation in stride. As Bryan liked to say, "cousin" ape was every bit as objectionable as "grandpa" ape.[96]

Finally, when the metaphors got old, antievolutionists brought on the monkeys themselves. In 1924 the New York Times reported that the Reverend S. Colin O'Farrell of Butte, Montana, had illustrated a recent sermon on the effects of evolution with a live monkey tied to a broomstick. While imitating the animal's antics, O'Farrell recited appropriate verse: "Turn backward, time, in your flight, / And make me a monkey just for tonight." After the monkey had jumped, turned flip-flops, and tried to pull the broomstick from the hands of O'Farrell's daughter, the somewhat embarrassed minister explained that "to save the world for God we all must use drastic means and methods."[97] Here at last there seemed to be limits, with O'Farrell being widely criticized in the national press for bringing an animal into the pulpit. "God's House is no place for the contortions of a flea-bitten ape," wrote the Providence (Rhode Island) News."[98]

In criticizing Darwinian explanations of human evolution, antievolutionists also found much to work with in the symbolism of the "missing link." Assuming that animals and humans had descended from a common ancient ancestor, it followed that there should be some archaeological evidence of a transitional species, an early hominid that was neither human nor simian but that shared characteristics of each. For decades, paleoanthropologists had been searching for this lost link, occasionally with spectacular results: such renowned finds as the fossils associated with Heidelberg, Neanderthal, Piltdown, and Trinil Man (also known as the "Java ape-man") had all been touted as definitive discoveries of the missing link.[99] Throughout the early 1920s the American Museum's Central Asiatic Expeditions reported that the fossilized remains of ancient hominids found in Mongolia and the Siwalik hills of northern India might well be examples of a transitional species.[100] At approximately the same time, Raymond Dart's discovery of a specimen of *Australopithecus africanus* in South Africa was being hailed as the last link between apes and humans.[101] At a 1924 conference at the American Museum, six scientists exhibited fragments of jawbones from *Dryopithecus*, the Asian forest ape, whom they declared to be "man's and the gorilla's lineal forefather, or else a first cousin of that forefather."[102] Then there was the team of adventurers led by Captain Edward Salisbury that had set out to explore the Malay Peninsula, following rumors of a tribe of wild men in the jungle with receding foreheads and short vestigial tails. (Finding no "ape men," the expedition spent most of its time in the Andaman Islands before its ship was wrecked in a storm and destroyed by an accident in an Italian dry dock.)[103] Antievolutionists could not have asked for a more effective indictment of evolution. "If anyone tells you that they have found the missing link," said Bryan, "tell him that there is a group of scientists in Africa now. They went from New York just a few months ago; they are to stay five years, using money supplied by some rich men. They are hunting for the missing link—and the longer they stay the better. It is far better to have them there than poisoning the minds of students in this country." The fact that the missing link was still missing provided irrefutable proof of evolution's fallacy. "If we have found the missing link," asked Bryan, "why hunt for it? If not, why not wait for it before believing in it?"[104]

At the same time, antievolutionists were casting doubt on the fossils themselves. For over fifty years, scientists working from fossil fragments had been attempting to reconstruct the skulls of early humanoids. Among these reconstructions, the most ambitious were those in the American Museum, where Henry Fairfield Osborn had commissioned an extensive collection of casts and reconstructions of early skulls. For several years, Bryan had been complaining about such exhibits, warning audiences to be wary of the creations of evolutionary scientists: "If you see these in museums, you may be misled. But do they look like the 'links' as they were when they were found? They find a piece of a skull, two teeth, and a bone of a leg: they don't know whether the teeth came out of the skull or whether the leg bone belongs to the teeth, but some man fixes the parts up according to his imagination and calls it a missing link. A man who can do this could take a keyhole and build a house around it."[105] In his 1922 opus *God—or Gorilla*, Catholic journalist Alfred Watterson McCann had presented a devastating critique of Osborn's reconstructions, insisting that for all his claims to have found "the intermediate forms, the transition types, the missing links, or whatever else the pedigree manufacturers may see fit to call them," they were "not to be found, they never existed."[106] Inspired by McCann, Arthur Brown continued the criticism in his 1923 pamphlet *Men, Monkeys, and Missing Links*, a study of six fossil specimens (Trinil, Heidelberg, Gibraltar, Neanderthal, Rhodesia, and Piltdown Man) that casts doubt on the methods used in finding and reconstructing all of them. According to Brown, these specimens were nothing more than "small pieces of bone" that had been creatively reconstructed into "purely hypothetical curiosities" that were also "wholly unscientific monstrosities."[107] But it was Straton who attracted the most attention in his second debate with Potter, when he described the discovery of *Pithecantropus erectus*, or the Java ape-man:

> There is a part of a skull, a part of a femur bone, and one molar tooth. The bones were not found at the same time or altogether in one place. The femur bone was found a year after the bit of skull was picked up. The bones were scattered far apart in a gravel pit on the bank of a rushing stream. The femur bone was fifty feet from where the skull was found. When Dr. [Eugene] Dubois discovered these pitiful bits of bones he announced his belief that they belonged to a being between the man apes and men.

His speech dripping with sarcasm, Straton concluded: "This, then, is the 'evidence,' so far as 'missing links' are concerned. I verily believe that if the little basketful of musty old bones and fossils, which have been found, after all these years of search in every part of the world, were brought together and presented as evidence of the evolution of man in any court of law, they would be thrown out of court with utmost scorn by judge and jury alike."[108]

Antievolutionists also were adept at claiming that certain fossils were fakes. Throughout its history, paleoanthropology, which relied on amateur archaeologists and fragmentary evidence, had been beset by some sensational hoaxes. Among these, the 1911 discovery of Piltdown Man, the fossil fragments found in a gravel pit in southern England that would soon come to be acclaimed as the Pleistocene "Dawn Man," would eventually prove to be the most embarrassing. Although not accepted as a forgery by the scientific community until 1953, Piltdown Man was suspect from the start, and antievolutionists were among its most active critics. In *God—or Gorilla*, McCann made an extensive case against the evidence, collecting the doubts of numerous scientists who believed (correctly, as it turned out) that the specimen consisted of nothing more than a human skull with a chimpanzee jaw. Brown continued the case in *Men, Monkeys, and Missing Links*, aiming his attack at Osborn, who was at the time one of the stoutest defenders of the Piltdown discovery. Straton too declared the discovery to be bogus in his Carnegie Hall debates:

> All they found in the gravel pit in Sussex, England, near Piltdown Common, were two or three bits of skull-bone, a piece of jaw-bone, and a canine tooth. And these few fragments were not found all together and at one time by the same person. They were scattered widely in the gravel pit, some of them were found by one person and others by another person, and some of them were found in one year and others in another year. With these few little scraps, that a juggler could conceal in the palm of one hand, and found under these loose conditions, the scientists "reconstructed" the "Piltdown man" and proclaimed it as a new genus.

For Straton, Piltdown Man was just one more proof that "the so-called 'ape men'" were nothing more than "figments of the heated and overly enthusiastic imagination of evolution's devotees."[109]

Antievolutionists scored again in 1922, when the American Museum's Osborn, responding to reports about the finding of a fossil tooth in northwestern Nebraska, announced the discovery of the so-called Nebraska Man, the first American anthropoid ape. Always aware of the power of public relations, a self-satisfied Osborn proposed that the animal be named *Bryopithecus*, "after the most distinguished Primate which the State of Nebraska has thus far produced."[110] Within a matter of months, however, he had stopped speaking of the discovery, having begun to have doubts about the tooth, which was later shown to have come from a pliocene pig. To his credit, Bryan treated the episode with bemusement, overlooking the insult while dismissing the fossil as yet another pathetic example of the failure to locate the missing link. The evolutionists, he concluded, "are frightened men in the dark, feeling around for something they can lean on."[111] Following final retractions in 1927, Straton chortled that the Nebraska tooth should be given the scientific label *Hesperopigdonefoolem osborniicuckoo* in honor of Osborn. The entire episode, he asserted shortly before his death in 1928, "justifies my assertion of some time ago that evolution is the most gigantic bluff in the history of the human mind."[112] For antievolutionists, the hoaxes were icing on the cake, providing still more proof that the missing link would always remain missing. As North Carolina's Governor Cameron Morrison reasoned, "If there were any such thing as a missing link, why don't they keep on making them?"[113]

Artistic depictions seemed to work to their benefit as well. On the whole, it can be said that, with the exception of a few limericks and some doggerel verses, antievolutionists were not particularly artistic. A fairly typical example was "Thoughts on Evolution," written by J. W. Butler, who would later draft the Tennessee antievolution bill. The poem included this stanza: "Tell me now, was your granddad an ape? / If so, have you ever changed your shape? / Tell me, did evolution ever fail / To rob a monkey of his tail."[114] The same applied to artistic depictions: except for E. J. Pace's striking "Christian cartoons," most of which were published in the *Sunday School Times*, antievolutionist art seemed to consist of crude caricatures.[115] Their evolutionist counterparts, on the other hand, tended to be quite aesthetically ambitious, creating an array of artistic celebrations of evolution that included painting, poetry, songs, and even statuary. More often than not, their works fueled antievolutionist fires. An excellent illustration was the celebration of "Evolution Day" at Potter's West Side Unitarian Church, featuring the unveiling of artist-naturalist Carl Akeley's *The Chrysalis*, a statue of a young man emerging from a gorilla.[116] After Potter delivered a sermon on the spiritual significance of evolution, and a church soloist, Miss Grace Leslie, provided a musical rendition of William Herbert Carruth's evolutionary poem "Each in His Own Tongue" ("Some call it Evolution, / And others call it God"), Akeley spoke briefly, stating that his purpose in creating the statue was not to depict humans as ascending from beasts, but rather to defend the gorilla and other animals against the charge that they were somehow "bestial."[117] Taking place in April 1924, only days before the fourth and final Potter-Straton debate, the event provided a prime opportunity for Straton, who did not miss a beat in turning the statue to his own purposes. Citing reports from the morning newspapers on the unveiling, the media-savvy preacher described it as "a man emerging from a gorilla" that was "supposed to give an artistic expression of man's alleged emergence from the brute." Observing that churches today needed statues of Christ and not "of men coming out of gorillas," he rebuked Potter for allowing *The Chrysalis* in his church, calling it a "desecration of the sanctuary." He also managed to turn Akeley's own words against him, recasting them as a critique of evolution itself:

> I noticed that both Mr. Akeley and my opponent . . . said at the unveiling of that statue that animals are not "bestial"—that "only man is bestial," etc. What becomes, then, of the theory of evolution? We thought that we were coming up all the while! We thought that "every day in every way we are getting better and better!" But if men are more "bestial" than the animals from which they are supposed to have come, then doesn't that, in itself, prove that we are a fallen race and that we need a divine Savior?[118]

Finally there were the images of early man. As Constance Areson Clark has shown, evolutionists of the 1920s were prolific in producing images—drawings,

"Another Pied Piper," E. J. Pace's widely reprinted editorial cartoon
(from William Jennings Bryan's Seven Questions in Dispute, 1924)

dioramas, museum displays—that purported to show the linear nature of the evolutionary process. Some of the most striking of these were the artistic reproductions of skeletons and skulls that paleontologists and their artist allies used to transform fragmentary fossil evidence into compelling depictions of the evolutionary connection between anthropoid apes and humans.[119] To antievolutionists, these images were red flags, and they missed few opportunities to condemn them as blatant misrepresentations. Straton initiated the most celebrated case early in 1924, when he lashed out at the American Museum's Hall of the Age of Man for "misspending taxpayers' money and poisoning the minds of school children by false and bestial theories of evolution."[120] At issue was a set of exhibits featuring skull reconstructions of various paleolithic hominids, along with zoologist J. Howard McGregor's full-scale sculptured busts of representatives of each group.[121] Although the display was designed to show that anthropoids had evolved separately from any species of hominids, Straton was convinced that the exhibit was nothing more than a transparent representation of the direct descent of monkeys into humans. He described what he saw when he visited the exhibit:

> The scene was interesting. There was the first showcase in the hall—a sort of synopsis of the whole theory. Down at one end of the line in that showcase they have the skull of a little monkey no bigger than one's fist. Next to it is the skull of an orang-outang, and then a chimpanzee, and then an old male gorilla, and then a young gorilla, and then the so-called "Java ape-man," and then a bronze model bust of that gentleman, and then the "Piltdown" skull, and then the "Neanderthal" skull, and then the "Talgai" skull, and then the "Cro Magnon" skull, and at last the skull of a modern white man.[122]

Recalling the scene in a sermon to his congregation, Straton told how groups of schoolchildren passed through the exhibit, progressing steadily along the line from monkeys to men, so that by the end they had reached the inescapable conclusion that one gave rise to the other. In closing, he affirmed: "It is treason to God Almighty and a libel against the human race to put into immature minds of little children the degrading idea that we have come up from the beasts."[123]

While museum officials dismissed his views as "rhetoric and rubbish," Straton insisted that his characterization of the exhibit was the correct one and continued to press the point in articles and interviews.[124] His charges eventually did their damage, as Osborn himself was forced to defend the exhibit and assure taxpayers that it had been paid for with private contributions rather than public money.[125] Yet at the end of the day, Straton was not completely victorious. When it came to contesting images, antievolutionists could score points, but they usually proved unable to offer much imagery of their own. When asked to suggest an alternative to the Hall of Man, Straton proposed that the "gruesome old bones" be moved to the side and other showcases be placed opposite them, featuring, among other icons, a display of Bibles, a diorama of the Pilgrims, and pictures of presidents at prayer, with the center of the first case reserved for "an open Bible, with a red line and a hand pointing (after the manner of the marking of the old bones) to the first verse of Genesis: 'In the beginning, God created the heavens and the earth.' "[126]

Transformation

For alignment to be complete, movements must be able to convince potential supporters to view the world in new and decidedly different ways. Conditions that were previously considered to be bothersome or troubling must come to be seen as inexcusable and intolerable; problems that were perceived as small must be recast as serious; situations that seemed inevitable must become capable of correction and reform. Blame must be externalized, with responsibility placed on outside enemies. Above all, any ambiguity or doubt must be banished, so that choices are presented as clear and simple, allowing no room for compromise.[127]

Ironically, in the antievolution movement this process of transformation was encouraged by the appearance of some fairly formidable enemies. Beginning in 1922, concerned scientists, liberal ministers, and academic leaders, realizing the threat posed by antievolutionism, had begun to band together into a loosely constructed countermovement. Taking the offensive—albeit belatedly—these individuals initiated an impressive campaign of public education, defending evolutionary science from podiums and pulpits, firing off letters to the editors of America's newspapers, and meeting antievolutionists in debates in cities across the country. Within a matter of months antievolution activists had started to strike back, defining themselves (and their opponents) in starker and more uncompromising terms than ever before. "We have a fight on our hands and I am on the defensive," Bryan told an audience at Nashville's Ryman Auditorium in January 1924, capturing the growing combativeness of the movement. "I have been on the defensive all my life; but when I am defending a thing I do not wait for the enemy to come and attack; when I find that there is to be an attack, I go over and do the fighting on the enemy's territory. . . . I shall not wait until he takes off his mask and comes out into the open, I shall shell him in the woods and make him come out."[128]

In transforming the evolution frame into a clear-cut confrontation between themselves and their enemies, antievolution activists started by singling out the scientists. Throughout the early 1920s most antievolutionists continued to show support for science, at least as it was practiced according to Baconian and Christian principles. At the same time, however, they expressed a growing suspicion of the scientific community, describing it as a collection of antidemocratic elitists who were conspiring to bring American science into the Darwinist camp. As proof, they pointed to the fact that growing numbers of scientists had become actively involved with the evolution issue. From 1922 on, a steady stream of science professionals were responding to antievolution attacks, challenging the academic credentials of their critics and declaring their views to be, in the words of one scholar, "ignorant and prejudiced."[129] In a 1923 speech, historian James Harvey Robinson urged members of the AAAS to respond to their antievolutionist critics by devising an educational campaign that would bring the case for evolution before the American public.[130] Within a year, science professionals across the country were answering Robinson's call, working through the AAAS and with state scientific societies and advocacy groups like the newly organized Science League of America to distribute information and lobby state and local officials.[131] For Bryan, the emergence of this countermovement confirmed his fears that a tiny elite—what he called a "scientific soviet"—was now "attempting to dictate what shall be taught in our schools and, in so doing, is attempting to mould [sic] the religion of the nation."[132]

Increasingly, Bryan portrayed the scientists in conspiratorial terms. Admittedly, he seemed uncertain about the size of the conspiracy, estimating it at anywhere from 11,000 (the membership of the AAAS, "and they have no examination"), to 5,500 (as listed in *American Men of Science*), to no more than 5,000 (as reported to Bryan by a Professor Steinmetz when he "met him on the train coming from the West").[133] Whatever the exact figure, the point was always the same: that American science had been hijacked by a small elite of evolutionists who were conspiring to control the curriculum of the public schools; unless defeated, they posed a danger to American democracy itself. Writing in response to the passage of a pro-evolution resolution at the AAAS's 1922 annual meeting, Bryan complained that in the past "it has been difficult to convince the Christian people that there is an organized effort to use the public schools for the overthrow of the Bible." He continued: "When the Bible was excluded from the schools—as it has been in many states—it was done on the ground that even the reading of it violated prohibition against the teaching of sectarianism. The public did not know that one of the real forces back of the exclusion was the atheism and agnosticism of those scientists who have substituted Darwinism for the Mosaic account of creation." Now, however, the passage of the AAAS resolution "makes the issue plain, and the forty million Christians can now decide whether a band of eleven thousand scientists can demand pay for undermining the Christian religion in our schools."[134] In later speeches Bryan contrasted this small group of scientists not only with all Christians, but also with all Americans. "I don't believe one in ten thousand should dictate to the rest of us," he would tell a Pennsylvania audience in 1925. "Can a handful of scientists rob your children of religion and turn them out atheists? We'll find 109,000,000 Americans on the other side. For the first time in my life I'm on the side of the majority."[135]

At about the same time, antievolutionists were accusing modernist ministers of conspiring with the advocates of evolution. For their part, at least some modernists gave every reason to believe that they had indeed gone over to the evolutionist camp. As early as 1920, Lloyd C. Douglas, writing in *Christian Century* magazine, the voice of American religious modernism, warned readers of Bryan's coming antievolution crusade, which he characterized as both ignorant and immoral.[136] In 1922, responding to an article by Bryan in the *New York Times*, Harry Emerson Fosdick took him to task for his "sincere but appalling obscurantism"; by associating Christianity with outmoded scientific opinions, Bryan was driving people, particularly young people, away from the church.[137] By 1925 Charles Francis Potter was calling from the pulpit for the creation of an alliance of evolutionists from both science and religion, with the forces of liberalism moving together as one. (Thinking in tactical terms, Potter suggested they undertake a campaign of public education in which modernists "take ten of the hundred reasons for doubting the Bible's literal truth and drop them from airplanes if necessary on centres in the South and West and in some parts of New York City.")[138] Although some modernists were ambivalent about the contest over evolution and many sought to avoid the issue altogether, antievolutionists portrayed all of them as card-carrying evolutionists. "When a modernist attacks the deity of Christ," Bryan wrote in his *Seven Questions in Dispute*, a 1924 collection of essays, "it is because the evolutionary hypothesis has no place for a Son of God." He explained: "Why is the Virgin Birth disputed? Because it is miraculous and involves the supernatural; it is, therefore, in conflict with the evolutionary hypothesis. On what ground do the modernists reject blood atonement? Because there is no place in the evolutionary hypothesis for the fall of man. . . . The bodily resurrection of Christ is denied by modernists because, if admitted, it would make a break in the slow and continuous development which the evolutionary hypothesis assumes."[139]

More important, by equating modernism and evolutionism, opponents could distinguish both from what they considered to be Christian orthodoxy. In his 1924 address at Nashville, Bryan made a sharp distinction between (evolutionary) modernism and (nonevolutionary) orthodoxy. Though well aware that millions of Christians believed in some form of evolution, he insisted on associating the idea with only a tiny minority of modernists. By the same logic, he contended that almost all Christians—what he called "the majority of the Christian church"—opposed evolutionary theory in any form. Bryan made it clear that he was speaking for this Christian majority, joking that he had "a bigger majority on my side on religion than I ever had in politics on any question." As for modernists, he maintained that they did not "have courage enough to come out and tell the people what they do believe, and let the people make their choice between the two kinds of religion." The Nashville speech, delivered in what many considered to be the home of southern religious modernism, sounded for all practical purposes like a declaration of war. In it, Bryan threw down the gauntlet, announcing that the time had come "to take the mask off," to reveal the modernists for what they really were—evolutionist enemies of true Christian faith—and to effectively expel them from the church. "There can be no unity and harmony," he concluded unequivocally, "between those who discard Christ and those who worship Him as their crucified and risen Lord."[140] Put simply, by 1924 Bryan was defining the antievolution campaign as a religious crusade. "It is time," he wrote in *Seven Questions*, "for the spiritual forces of the nation and the world to unite in opposing the teaching of evolution as a fact."[141]

Meanwhile, the campaign was becoming increasingly anti-intellectual. Although some of this hostility was apparent from the start, especially in the rhetoric of the revival preachers, antievolutionism did not begin as an assault on the educated. Bryan for one, while not above an occasional snide remark about "Harvard boys" or Chicago professors, was committed to the cause of higher education, and he avoided crude critiques of it. Over the course of the early twenties, however, antievolutionists waged a concerted campaign against what they saw as America's educational elite. To some extent the educators had been asking for it. In the wake of antievolution agitation in Kentucky in 1922, leaders of the National Education Association denounced Bryan for attempting to turn the clock back to the Dark Ages, implying that antievolutionists believed the earth was flat and the sun moved around it.[142] The following year, when Bryan took his campaign against evolution to Dartmouth College, faculty members described his performance in terms that ranged from ill-informed to pathetic. Malcolm Willey and Stuart Rice of the sociology department, who administered a questionnaire to members of the audience afterward, pronounced Bryan's speech a failure, predicting that the antievolution campaign would have the effect of influencing all Americans—first the educated classes and then the general public—to favor evolutionary theory.[143] Often the attacks on antievolutionists were personal, and Bryan took the brunt of them, as when renowned botanist Luther Burbank told a California audience that he had noticed that his old friend's skull displayed striking similarities to that of Neanderthal Man.[144] Bryan bristled at the criticism, calling attention to his own academic credentials—which consisted primarily of seven honorary doctoral degrees—and threatening ("if these fellows do not quit calling me an ignoramus") to print business cards with all of his degrees, running the letters up and down the card, "and then I will challenge any son of an ape to match cards with me."[145] Insults aside, Bryan crafted a case against his academic enemies on democratic grounds:

> If one must be educated to understand evolution, I am qualified, but it is not necessary that one shall graduate from college. Do you know that only about one in fifty of our boys and girls ever go to college or universities? Do you know that only about one in ten, taking the country over, goes to a high school? Do you mean to say, that nobody can understand where he came from unless he goes to college and gets a degree somewhere and calls himself a doctor of something? No, my friends, God was not so unkind to us as that.[146]

By arguing in such sweeping terms, Bryan found himself at odds not only with intellectuals, but also with intellectualism. Indeed, by 1924 he was describing education and faith as mutually exclusive, and he was making it clear that in choosing between them, education was less important than faith. Thus he concluded his speech at Nashville by distinctly separating the two. "There is not a Christian father and mother," he assured his audience, "who would not rather that the child should be without education than to come back with its faith destroyed."[147] It did not take long for the antievolution preachers to pick up the theme. "I would rather my boy would be in heaven without knowing one thing about bugs, lizards, apes or chimpanzees," Norris confided to his congregation, "than to be in hell with a basket full of degrees and a post-graduate in the sciences on earth."[148] For many in the movement, such sentiments tapped some deeply anti-intellectual roots. As one Texas fundamentalist boasted proudly, "We don't know anything about evolution and cherish no hope of ever learning anything about it."[149]

Before long, antievolutionists were extending their list of enemies to include political progressives as well. The movement had not begun with this in mind; in its earliest phase even fundamentalism had exhibited a strong commitment to social reform. Moreover, with the arrival of Bryan, whose credentials as a political reformer were unassailable, antievolutionism had become associated, albeit awkwardly, with his brand of progressive reformism. Yet over time it took on an increasingly reactionary tone. By 1924 Norris was regularly attacking Roman Catholics from the pulpit, declaring that Catholics were not real Americans.[150] The peripatetic Mordecai Ham was using his tent meetings to deliver anti-Semitic diatribes; his invectives reached a peak in 1924, when he accused Jewish philanthropist Julius Rosenwald of profiting from criminal activities including prostitution and white slavery.[151] At the Democratic National Convention that year, Bryan refused to condemn the Ku Klux Klan and successfully fought to block the presidential nomination of Catholic Al Smith.[152] While still calling himself a progressive, averred a *New York Times* editorial, America's greatest democrat had become "an irredeemable obscurantist and reactionary."[153] Contending that liberalism was the first step on the road to communism, a rising chorus of antievolutionists attacked progressives wherever they found them. Even more, they began to criticize the concept of progress itself. Thus by 1925 Bryan was making the argument, based on his recent reading of Edwin E. Slosson's *Creative Chemistry*, that there was no progressive force in the world, and that "the only active force discovered on this planet . . . is deterioration, decay, death."[154] He was not alone. In the minds of many antievolutionists, evolution had become synonymous with progress, and progress had come to be equated with all kinds of evil. "Man in his natural state," concluded the scholarly James Gray in a pamphlet called *Why a Christian Cannot Be an Evolutionist*, "does not represent an ascent but a descent . . . he is not an evolution but a devolution."[155]

Throughout the early 1920s, antievolution advocates had used the emerging debate over evolution to turn their fledgling movement into a broad-based popular protest. In aligning their antievolution frame—bridging, amplifying, extending, and transforming their opposition to evolution—they had been able to build coalitions, motivate followers, influence public opinion, and win over a growing number of supporters. What they had been unable to do was stop the spread of evolutionary theory. For this, they would have to enter the realm of public policy, crafting statutes to outlaw the teaching of evolution and persuading legislators to pass them. It was time to move from making speeches to making laws.

5 : Opportunities
STORMING THE STATE LEGISLATURES

Nicholas Murray Butler saw no need for concern. Alerted by the University of Kentucky's Frank McVey, who wrote in early 1922 to warn him that antievolutionists were moving their campaign against the colleges into the state legislatures, Columbia's patrician president advised against overreaction. The antievolution craze, he replied confidently, "will disappear within a few months. It is just one more of those waves of ignorance and fanaticism that sweep from time to time over the American people in whole or in part, apparently to remind us how far from being civilized we still are."[1]

Butler would soon eat his words. Throughout the mid-1920s an army of antievolution activists, lobbying lawmakers inside statehouses and bringing public pressure to bear on them from without, set off firestorms leading to the introduction of no fewer than forty-five antievolution bills in twenty-one states. Although efforts were made in every part of the country, they were most successful in the South, where the issue was fought and refought in every state legislature except Virginia's. In five southern states—Oklahoma, Florida, Tennessee, Mississippi, and Arkansas—antievolution bills would become law. In several more, they would be turned back by as little as a single vote, while in others they were defeated decisively.[2] In all of these states national personalities and organizations were present: William Jennings Bryan made frequent forays across the South to lobby old legislative friends and stir up popular support; J. W. Porter and T. T. Martin, working through the Anti-Evolution League, provided field organizers; popular revivalists like Billy Sunday, "Cyclone Mack" McLendon, and Mordecai Ham told raucous revival meetings that legislators had a Christian duty to end the evils of evolution. On the whole, however, the antievolution campaigns were home grown, consisting primarily of local preachers leading small but dedicated groups of grassroots activists. Statewide newspapers played a part, even when they themselves opposed antievolutionism, because they provided the activists with publicity and access to broader public audiences through op-ed columns and letters to the editor. In most cases, opponents of the antievolution campaigns organized as well, usually with some of the state's most respected educators in the forefront. Statehouses across the country saw scenes of legislative maneuvering, occasionally including dramatic debates, but more often consisting of backstage brokering by powerful local politicians. In the end, every state was different: in some, windows of opportunity opened that allowed antievolutionists to carry the day easily, while in others the windows stayed closed or shut so fast that their campaigns never really got off the ground.

In seeking to understand why social movements succeed or fail, investigators have shown increasing interest in the role of political opportunities. Over the last several decades, a growing body of American and European scholars—Peter K. Eisinger, William Gamson, Bert Klandermans, Hanspeter Kriesi, Doug McAdam, David S. Meyer, Dieter Rucht, Sidney Tarrow, Charles Tilly, and others—have argued that political systems contain "opportunity structures," complex configurations of institutions, ideologies, and elite interactions that provide openings that citizens and groups can use to exercise power and bring about reform. Although these structures may differ substantially from one situation to another, they have been found to be common components in a wide variety of contemporary social movements.[3] Indeed, Tarrow has lamented that the concept of political opportunity has been applied so broadly that it has become almost incoherent, "less a variable," as he described it, "than a cluster of variables."[4] In his *Power in Movement*, he sought to clarify the concept by delineating four dimensions: (1) *access*, the openness or closure of the institutionalized political system, (2) *alignments*, the stability or instability of elite interactions, (3) *availability of allies*, the presence or absence of elite allies, and (4) *cleavages or divisions among elites*, particularly those that affect the ability of the state to encourage or repress a political movement.[5] The assumption is that protesters will find favorable opportunities for their movements when institutional access opens, when alignments shift, when allies become available, and when conflicts emerge among elites. But as Tarrow pointed out, there is no reason to assume that these changes will take place together, since the different dimensions are independent and since windows of opportunity can close as fast as they can open. Thus opportunity structures will be diverse, demonstrating a variety of configurations (open and closed; stable and unstable; presence or absence of elites; divisions or nondivisions), and they will be dynamic in that these configurations will change over time. By understanding how the configurations change, scholars can better comprehend why movements sometimes succeed and why they so often fail.[6]

The antievolution campaigns that were endemic in the South of the 1920s offer a chance to study the structure of political opportunities in this more systematic way. For decades scholars have been describing the debates over the teaching of evolution that took place in the state legislatures of the time. On the whole, they have proceeded state by state, narrating a diverse set of stories, each with its own cast of characters, its own dramatic moments, its own idiosyncratic outcomes.[7] Many have concentrated on a single state. The best of these studies, like Willard Gatewood's *Preachers, Pedagogues and Politicians*, an analysis of the evolution struggles in North Carolina, are impressive works that provide a rich reservoir of historical detail.[8] Yet as a rule students of the antievolution campaigns have failed to consider the commonalities between these separate state stories, let alone make systematic or theoretical comparisons between them. In every state, activists faced a similar set of tasks: gaining access to the levers of power, taking advantage of existing political alignments while also attempting to build new ones, courting politically influential allies, and negotiating their way through the divisions among elites, especially those public officials who could either crush their cause or enlist the power of the state on their side. The question is how they managed to use the opportunities available to them and why some were so successful while others failed so miserably.

Access

From Tocqueville on, social theorists have argued that access to power is the first important incentive in inspiring any collective action. Movements tend to arise when access appears to be expanding, as emerging opportunities to influence existing institutions open up political systems to protest and reform. Thus for Tocqueville, aristocratic agitation against the French monarchy led to the opening of opportunities for political participation by the French Third Estate, eventually undermining the Old Regime. More recently, studies of democratizing states show that when citizens perceive even small possibilities for participation (as when authoritarian regimes begin to allow access to previously restricted sources of communication and information), they take advantage of them and demand more. In general, the assumption is that the best moment for movements to emerge is when expectations are rising and access has just begun to open.[9]

In the United States the early 1920s was such a time. At the end of World War I, inspired by isolationism and what they saw as the increasing influence of radical and socialist ideologies, conservative reformers had begun to search for ways to reassert patriotic and traditional values. In the public schools they found an abundance of openings, as expanding enrollment (attendance at public high schools almost doubled over the course of the decade) and growing state spending (expenditures for education more than doubled over the same period) provided new opportunities to exert control over public education.[10] As early as 1919, several states had passed laws to restrict the use of foreign languages in classrooms. In 1921, under the so-called Lusk laws, the state of New York required all public schoolteachers to receive a certificate from the commissioner of education stating that they had never advocated a form of government other than that of the United States. Other states moved to provide more religious instruction in their schools; by 1923 one survey found that daily Bible reading had been required by law in six states and permitted in thirty-two others. In most places such reforms were overwhelmingly popular, and educators, teacher's unions, and civil libertarians offered little or no resistance to them. It was in this context that antievolutionism arrived on the political scene as one of several similar conservative causes that Roger Baldwin of the American Civil Liberties Union (ACLU) characterized as "the drive to keep the schools safe for conservatism."[11]

The South was particularly receptive to such campaigns. With its deep rural roots and broad cultural commitment to religious and political orthodoxy, the region was historically predisposed to provide strong support for conservative and conformist causes ranging from Prohibition and Sabbatarianism to racial segregation and opposition to Roman Catholicism, immigration, and labor unions. But the South of the 1920s was in transition, moving from agrarianism to industry and from reactionary to moderately progressive politics. Much of the conservative moral reform of the time was a by-product of this process. In many southern states, populist and progressive governors like Jack C. Walton in Oklahoma, Cameron Morrison in North Carolina, and Austin Peay in Tennessee rose to power on platforms that promised administrative and tax reforms, expanded state highway systems, and support for education and more extensive social services.[12] State governments were for the first time beginning to invest in the region's poorly funded schools, and increased spending brought centralization and control to an educational system previously presided over by local school boards. With centralization came state standards, including compulsory education laws, standardized courses of study, and uniform pay scales for teachers, along with statewide administrative bodies and commissions to create curricula, set requirements for teacher training, and select textbooks. At the same time, the growing role of the state in the schools allowed access that had never before existed, opening new opportunities to insert patriotism and piety into the classroom. Thus as school reform brought evolutionary theory to the South, it also introduced the issue into its state legislatures, where members such as Tennessee farmer-legislator John Washington Butler would submit a steady stream of antievolution measures. "Ironically," explained Jeanette Keith in her *Country People in the New South*, "by creating a state system of education, reformers made it possible for people like Butler to influence education throughout the state and even the nation."[13]

Yet for antievolutionists in the South, access to the levers of power was by no means assured. The 1920s has been called the "classic period" of southern politics, an era of one-party dominance in which a far-flung county seat governing class was gradually making room for new business and professional groups.[14] Political participation was strictly limited through poll taxes and literacy tests, and southern elections consistently showed low voter turnouts, with scarcely more than one-fifth of adult southerners voting in either Democratic primaries or general elections, even after the enfranchisement of women.[15] In this closed and largely localized system, politics consisted of a confused multifactionalism in which party organizations were weak, factions tended to be loose and short-lived, and candidates ran campaigns on the basis of personality rather than issues or ideology—an arrangement that was ripe for all kinds of corruption.[16] Alignment of the electorate behind a prominent political family or a charismatic candidate sometimes provided an element of stability and structure, as in Texas, where either James E. Ferguson or his wife Miriam "Ma" Ferguson ran in every statewide election between 1914 and 1934. In general, however, though the system created some colorful characters, it produced little continuity or predictability. The institutions of government were ineffective: governors held office for two-year terms and in most states were prevented by law from succeeding themselves; citizen legislatures met in short biennial sessions, usually in the first few months of odd-numbered years; administrative agencies were understaffed and frequently riddled with patronage. As a result, access was easy but evanescent, opportunities seemed to open and close rapidly, and influence was inconsistent, with the ability to carry out reform being limited by the transient and unpredictable character of a politics that was, in Dewey Grantham's words, "essentially amorphous."[17]

In Oklahoma access seemed especially easy. It was there in 1923 that antievolutionists scored their first statewide success, appending legislation outlawing the treatment of evolution in state schoolbooks to a popular free textbook law. In the spring of 1922, activists in the state's Baptist associations had begun to agitate, sparking a series of resolutions condemning the teaching of evolution and warning that Darwinian textbooks were making their way into the public schools.[18] Textbooks were much on the minds of Oklahomans: for years, reformers had been advocating free books for schoolchildren, and new governor John C. Walton had called on the legislature to pass such a measure in its 1923 session. Thus when the bill was introduced early in the session, legislators sympathetic to the antievolution cause saw it as an opportunity to tap the strong support for free textbooks that existed in both parties and in the public at large. Seizing their chance, they presented an anti-Darwin amendment to the bill, apparently without warning, and called for an immediate vote. With the house sitting as a Committee of the Whole, a sympathetic chairman submitted the proposal at once, ignoring opponents who were clamoring to be recognized, and the amendment passed narrowly. When house majority leader Joseph P. Rossiter called for reconsideration, his argument for delay was met with howls of disapproval. "If you want to be a monkey, go out and be a monkey," shouted Representative J. L. Watson, "but I am for this amendment and will strike this infernal thing while I can!" What followed, according to news reports, was a "near riot," complete with threats of physical violence. ("If he wants to get personal," spouted one lawmaker, pointing at another, "let me take him! I'd like to do it.") Apparently surprised by the intensity aroused by the issue, and attempting to avoid any more fights on the floor, Rossiter withdrew his motion to reconsider and the amended bill passed by a vote of 87 to 2. "I am not against religion," the house leader explained lamely in withdrawing his motion. "I believe in the holy Bible!"[19]

In the state senate, where the bill went next, antievolutionists found the going even easier. Few Oklahomans could be found who took the evolution issue very seriously, at least at that time. While school administrators condemned the antievolution amendment, many citizens considered it to be an insignificant issue, far less important than the promise of free textbooks. Even some fundamentalists believed that the amendment was unnecessary. Thus when the textbook bill was introduced in the senate, it attracted little attention. Only two opponents spoke strongly against the measure, one of whom declared it "a throw-back to the middle ages." In response, its advocates alluded vaguely to widespread public support, with one senator assuring his colleagues that "practically all of the church members of this state are opposing the teachings of Darwinism and evolution in the public schools."[20] For most members, any concerns about evolution seemed to be eclipsed by more pressing political matters, primarily the question of whether the state could actually afford to distribute free textbooks to high schools as well as elementary schools. When one senator attempted to add another amendment barring evolutionary theory not only from textbooks but also from being taught in the public schools altogether, it was quickly tabled.[21] Approved on a voice vote, the bill went at once to Governor Walton, who signed it reluctantly into law. Although the populist chief executive believed the antievolution amendment to be the work of his enemies in the Ku Klux Klan, he supported the free textbook bill strongly enough to accept the bad with the good.[22] By the fall, free but censored textbooks were being distributed, and the State Textbook

Commission was scrutinizing texts to ensure that "nothing hinting at the Darwinian theory had been slipped into the wording" of any of Oklahoma's state-purchased schoolbooks.[23]

Yet while access came easily in Oklahoma, it carried certain costs, as anti-evolutionists found it difficult to achieve consistent or sustained support for their efforts. In linking the issue of evolution with the free textbook bill, they were in some ways forced to take half a loaf, for attempts to bar the teaching of evolution were passed over in favor of the less ambitious but more expedient approach of outlawing it only in state schoolbooks. Moreover, since the legislation was limited to grades one through eight and Darwinism almost never appeared in elementary school science books, it had little if any effect on actual classroom teaching.[24] When the erratic and increasingly unpopular Walton was subsequently impeached and removed from office, the free textbook cause lost its most ardent advocate. The books proved to be enormously expensive to purchase, popular opinion turned against the program, and the bill was repealed.[25] No additional antievolution legislation would ever make its way successfully through the legislature. Nevertheless, for antievolutionists Oklahoma was their first success, and Bryan set to work to build a bandwagon on it. "The State of Oklahoma has recently passed a law eliminating Darwinism from the text books of the public schools of the state," he wrote to New York's Mayor John F. Hylan, celebrating its passage even before he had read any of the provisions. "The question is up to other states and I beg to bring it to your attention for such action as you may deem proper to take."[26]

Alignments

Opportunities tend to open when alignments are changing. Especially at times of electoral instability, when political fortunes seem unpredictable, new coalitions are created as activists attempt to exercise marginal power and authorities try to shore up their standing by seeking public support. In their *Poor People's Movements*, Frances Fox Piven and Richard Cloward showed how the shifting electoral strength of twentieth-century American political parties encouraged workers, African Americans, and others to organize efforts to exercise political power by developing alliances of labor and civil rights groups. More recent studies demonstrate that even in authoritarian political systems, instability tends to inspire the formation of new coalitions and sometimes opens the system to popular protest such as urban insurrections or peasant uprisings.[27]

In the South of the 1920s, political systems were surprisingly unstable, as well as unusually open to the creation of such coalitions. In several states, including Oklahoma, Kentucky, North Carolina, and Tennessee, the post-Reconstruction party system, dominated by the Democratic Party, was under assault by an insurgent Republicanism. Even in states where Democrats remained solidly in control, such as Texas, competition within the party was increasing, with candidates proliferating in the all-important party primaries and long-standing alliances being replaced by shifting coalitions. More often than not, the result was even more instability, as seen in growing factionalism and high turnover in the legislatures. With parties so weak, politicians sought to build coalitions outside conventional party channels, seeking the support of newspaper editors, local business and civic clubs, and churches. In constructing these coalitions, they often turned to moral issues, campaigning on antivice or Prohibition platforms and aligning themselves with groups advocating such measures. What followed was a politics that seemed particularly welcoming to conservative moral campaigns, what Grantham has called "the politics of morality."[28]

In the Bible Belt South, churches emerged as powerful contributors to these new coalitions. Whereas parties concentrated on biennial election campaigns, denominational bodies and sometimes even local congregations exerted greater influence between elections, mobilizing their members to lobby legislatures during their brief every-other-year sessions and sustaining support for moral reform in the off years. The South was dominated by several large denominations—the Southern Presbyterian General Assembly, the Southern Baptist Convention, and the Southern Methodist General Conference—and these regional bodies played a significant political role by providing forums and foot soldiers for conservative reform causes.[29] By and large, however, mobilization took place within the states, where state synods and local church alliances were especially active. In Oklahoma, for example, it was the State Association of Missionary Baptist Churches that had set the stage for antievolution debates there by adopting a convention report stating that the public schools were "infested" with "false science."[30] The agitation in West Virginia was sparked by the state Conference of the United Brethren in Christ, an evangelical group, that resolved to support only candidates who openly pledged to defeat Darwinism.[31] The Minnesota antievolution campaign, which began a little later, was initiated by a statewide convention of pastors representing several denominations.[32] Churches and other religious bodies played similar roles in other states, producing a plethora of declarations, reports, resolutions, and memorials denouncing the teaching of evolution. Always attentive to churchgoing voters, shrewd politicians made regular rounds of Sunday morning services and Wednesday evening suppers, while also making themselves available to speak at congregational events. Some, like North Carolina's Governor Morrison, a leader in the Presbyterian Church, had no compunction about using the pulpit as a political platform. Thus he seized the occasion of his denomination's 1924 General Assembly to voice his opposition to evolution, declaring that "so-called scientists" had no right to "unsettle the minds of the youth" by making "a monkey out of Adam."[33]

Among the most active members of the coalitions were the revivalists. Independent and self-supporting, these Christian celebrities appeared in large numbers at this time, traveling from town to town along what came to be called the "sawdust trail." (A contemporary observer wrote that southern revivalists were "as thick and as thorough as crows in a Middle Tennessee cornfield.")[34] Bringing together believers from different churches and denominations, popular figures like Billy Sunday, Cyclone Mack McLendon, and Mordecai Ham attracted devoted followings with their soul-winning sermons, rousing hymn singing, and sometimes outrageous platform antics. Sunday was the most famous; in the 1920s the former professional baseball player took his traveling tabernacles into southern cities, where his crusades regularly drew audiences in the tens of thousands to listen to his spirited calls for moral revival and his animated attacks on an ever-changing set of enemies that included bolsheviks, Catholics, union members, and evolutionists.[35] McLendon, known as "Cyclone Mack" for his sweat-soaked gyrations onstage, concentrated more on the smaller cities and towns, where he pleased provincial audiences with the homey sayings he called "Mack-o-grams."[36] But the most successful, at least as far as antievolutionists were concerned, was Ham, whose revival sermons were by the mid-1920s concentrating more and more on the evils of evolution. Among his many admirers was Governor Morrison, who regularly attended his services and invited him to hold prayer meetings in the Executive Mansion in Raleigh.[37] Inspired by Ham's denunciations of evolution, Morrison became an early champion of the antievolution cause, directing the State Board of Education in early 1924 to reject two biology textbooks that contradicted the Genesis account of creation.[38] Ham in turn praised Morrison's action as "the greatest act that any Governor of any State ever did and one for which he will be remembered long after he is dead."[39]

In border state Kentucky, where the Democratic Party was deeply divided between reformers and conservatives, and where Republicans were strong enough to occasionally win statewide elections, the political system seemed especially porous, offering opportunities for outsiders to play a role in politics. The state was a Baptist stronghold, and among Kentucky Baptists fundamentalists were unusually well entrenched. Antievolution agitation had come early to Kentucky, due largely to the efforts of John W. Porter, the well-known pastor of the First Baptist Church of Lexington and sometime editor of the widely read Baptist periodical *The Western Recorder*. As early as 1921, Porter had invited William Bell Riley to the state, where he addressed no fewer than twenty-two meetings on

A street corner evangelist, thought to be T. T. Martin at Dayton, Tennessee, 1925
(Courtesy Bryan College)

the growing presence of evolution in the schools.[40] At the same time, working through the Baptist State Board of Missions, Porter had begun a public campaign against the teaching of evolution that soon attracted the attention of state legislators.[41] As bills began to make their way through both the senate and the house, William Jennings Bryan arrived in January 1922 to speak to large crowds in cities across central Kentucky, culminating in an address to a joint session of the legislature.[42] Activists at the local level took it from there; they were led by retired army officer Noel Gaines, of Frankfort, who showered the state with a steady stream of press releases attacking the University of Kentucky for harboring evolutionary teachers and textbooks. Writing as "a citizen and taxpayer," and using the American flag logo of his "Our Flag On Every Home" campaign, Gaines demonstrated the ability of a determined grassroots activist with a mimeograph machine to bring an issue to the general public.[43] Indeed, when the Kentucky House of Representatives took up debate on an antievolution statute in March 1922, Gaines appeared in person, invited by the bill's sponsor to address the house from its podium. As described in news reports, he proceeded to deliver a fiery denunciation of evolution in which he "ran up and down behind the clerk's desk scattering [zoology textbooks] about," drawing applause and cheers from lawmakers and spectators "as he waved his arms in emphatic gestures. Finally he threw one of the text books to the floor and trampled it under foot."[44]

With the legislature divided, opponents were able to take advantage of opening opportunities as well. As several antievolution bills made their way through the hearing process, skeptical legislators seemed to retreat, leaving it to others on the outside to speak out against the proposals. The state's largest newspapers, at first inclined to dismiss the campaign as unworthy of comment, soon realized the seriousness of the situation and began to publish critical editorials. (Notable among them was one in the Lexington Herald, entitled "Women and Evolution," which called on women to recognize antievolutionism as an antidemocratic and antiprogressive force that consigned women to the second-class status of having been created "out of Adam's rib.")[45] The annual council of the Episcopal Diocese of Kentucky weighed in with a strong resolution condemning efforts to restrict the teaching of evolution, insisting that the theory was not synonymous with atheism or agnosticism and reminding legislators that the choice of curricula and textbooks should be "left for those chosen and fitted for this purpose, namely, our educators themselves."[46] But the leading force in organizing the opposition was Frank McVey, who in late January 1922 became alarmed enough to fire off a barrage of telegrams to some fifty scientists, educators, and university presidents from across the country, alerting them to the situation and asking for their support.[47] Within days, they responded, as McVey began to receive notes and telegrams from scholars like Harvard's Charles W. Eliot, Yale's James R. Angell, and Columbia's Nicholas Murray Butler, as well as from representatives of the American Association of University Professors (AAUP), the Association of American Colleges, and the Federal Council of Churches. Admittedly, some found it impossible to take the threat seriously. Among the college presidents in particular, Butler was not alone in considering it a passing phase. "I remain of the opinion," wrote the eighty-eight-year-old Eliot, who at the time was universally considered to be the dean of American education, "that the best way to oppose such absurd legislation is to make fun of it."[48] Even so, strong statements from prominent figures poured in, and McVey quickly released them to the press. "Such an act," telegraphed the venerable Lyman Abbott, one of several church leaders who responded, "would be fatal to the best interests of pupils in any school on which it could be enforced."[49]

Meanwhile, a shrewd and serious McVey was mobilizing his own supporters within the state. For the next month he cleared his calendar and devoted his energies to defeating the pending antievolution statutes. Working both behind the scenes and through public pronouncements, he contacted sympathetic legislators, sent letters to alumni asking them to rally behind the university, and released a statement calling upon the people of Kentucky to stand up against this "attack upon the public schools of the state."[50] Even more important, McVey rallied church leaders. His most significant support came from E. Y. Mullins, president of the Southern Baptist Convention and perhaps the best-known Southern Baptist of his day. Conservative in doctrine but committed to the principle of separation of church and state, Mullins was determined to steer a middle course. Effectively forging an alliance with McVey and E. L. Powell, the respected pastor of Louisville's First Christian Church, Mullins proceeded to suggest a substitute proposal allowing the teaching of evolution but preventing teachers from seeking to destroy the religious views of their students. Offered as a bill in the state senate, the proposal seemed to confuse and divide the legislators, splitting antievolution supporters and slowing the progress of their efforts.[51] With Mullins at his side to divide Baptist opinion and deflect direct attacks from the fundamentalists, McVey survived the storm: the senate antievolution bill died in committee and the house bill was defeated by the narrowest of votes, 42 to 41. (Writing afterward to the "University men" in the legislature, a relieved McVey expressed his thanks for their support, confiding that if they "had not put your whole souls in the matter, the result would have been entirely different.")[52] As for the antievolutionists, they appeared to take the loss in stride. Alerted to the Kentucky defeat, Bryan at once declared it a moral victory, assuring J. W. Porter that the closeness of the vote made it even more certain that the movement would soon sweep the country and "drive Darwinism from our schools."[53]

Allies

Allies are an essential ingredient in establishing opportunities. Whether acting as friends, as mediators, or as protectors, allies provide the contacts and channels that connect movements to institutions, introducing activists and their issues to policy makers. For example, Sidney Tarrow suggests that the success of the United Farm Workers of the 1960s was made possible by allies that included liberal consumers, organized labor, and sympathetic administrators in the U.S. Department of Agriculture. In closed regimes allies become even more critical, as when the Catholic Church in Eastern Europe acted to protect activists during the protest movements of the 1980s. Although allies are always important, the more a movement is made up of outsiders, the more crucial it becomes to gain the support of those who have influence on the inside.[54]

In William Jennings Bryan, the antievolution crusade found the perfect ally, a crusader who shared their commitment but who also knew intimately the inner workings of American politics. For forty years, Bryan had been the nation's best-known Democrat. Over the course of his career he had traveled tens of thousands of miles and established connections with party activists and leaders in every part of the country. In the South, where his wing of the party was especially strong, he was revered, warmly welcomed by old comrades from earlier days as well as by young reformers who considered him to be a symbol of the party's populist past. Far from an anachronism, however, Bryan remained a forceful political figure, committed to using his extensive personal ties and still potent political skills to enact antievolution legislation. His mission, he told a friend in 1921, was "to deal with the questions which seem solvable in the immediate future or at least in my life time."[55]

For the antievolution campaign, Bryan was indispensable, bringing to it not only his name recognition and reputation, but also his astonishing energy. From 1921 on he crossed the country several times informing scores of audiences of the importance of the fight. Throughout that time he kept in close contact with allies in several state legislatures, particularly those in the South and West, encouraging them to introduce antievolution measures and making suggestions on their wording. In 1923 alone he was invited to speak to eight state legislatures in support of such bills.[56] In addition to these appearances, his written word reached millions through his books, pamphlets, and syndicated newspaper columns.[57] Nevertheless, antievolutionists bombarded him with requests to take on further responsibilities. In 1922 Riley asked him to assume a leadership role in the World's Christian Fundamentals Association (WCFA); the following year the WCFA elected him president without his agreement or even his knowledge. A year later Porter begged him to lead a national antievolution organization. J. Frank Norris was determined to bring him to Texas for the 1923 Fort Worth convention, telling Bryan that two of his speeches would deliver ten million new members to the cause. Overwhelmed by these and other offers, and concerned about his own health and that of his invalid wife Mary, Bryan repeatedly turned down the requests. Undeterred, Norris offered him a thousand dollars if he would reconsider his refusal to go to Fort Worth. "I am doing the best I can," replied a furious Bryan, who considered the offer an insult to his integrity, "and those who are not satisfied with the amount of work I am doing are, I hope, in a position to do more."[58]

Yet allies can also complicate movement politics. For antievolutionists, Bryan opened countless windows of opportunity that otherwise would have been closed to them. On the other hand, his own prominence could be problematic, at times confounding the agenda of the antievolution campaign. From the start, Bryan was an anomaly among antievolutionists. An advocate of the "day-age" theory of creation, he believed that the days described in Genesis could well have consisted of geological epochs lasting millions of years, a view that was shared by many theistic evolutionists of the day. In private, he confided to correspondents that he personally believed evolution to be true, at least for plants and animals, though not for human beings. Moreover, he always insisted that evolution should be taught in the schools, though as theory rather than fact, and alongside rather than instead of creationist accounts. At no time did he endorse serious penalties for violation of any antievolution law.[59] In addition, unlike most antievolutionists, Bryan was not a fundamentalist. Though deeply devout, he had no theological training and as a practical matter evinced no special interest in fundamentalism's doctrinal "five points." Unlike most fundamentalists, he was not a dispensationalist and probably did not know the meaning of the term. In many ways, it was even hard to call his brand of Christianity "conservative." He was active in the ecumenical Interchurch World Movement and the Federal Council of Churches, and his friends included left-leaning advocates of the social gospel such as Washington Gladden. On the whole, Bryan's approach to Christianity was surprisingly tolerant, and he was neither anti-Catholic nor anti-Semitic. In short, he was a curious choice to lead the antievolution movement, "a puzzling paradox," as Glenn Frank described him in his *Century* magazine, "a bundle of irreconcilable contradictions."[60]

Although Bryan brought assets to the antievolution campaign, he also came with liabilities. In any movement, allies present problems of control. Helpful to the cause but independent of it, they bring their own agendas and ultimately answer to themselves alone. In the case of Bryan, a man with a capacious appetite for causes, antievolutionists had difficulty keeping him on task. At the very least, they had to compete for Bryan's symbolic status, being repeatedly forced to share it with other organizations. In 1923, for example, with antievolution debates taking place in several state legislatures, he shifted his attention to the upcoming constitutional convention of the Young Men's Christian Association, where he actively opposed a provision eliminating membership in an evangelical church as a criterion for membership.[61] When campaigning, his other commitments could intrude, confusing or undercutting his message. In his antievolution speeches to lawmakers, for instance, Bryan often included at least some reference to other issues such as Prohibition or tax reform.[62] In the same way, his efforts to have evolution outlawed in the legislatures were sometimes complicated by his attempts to have it condemned in church denominational conventions. His disastrous showing in the 1923 Presbyterian General Assembly, where he not only failed to insert an antievolution plank into the assembly's platform but also lost his bid to become its moderator, was a blow to the antievolution campaign in the states, raising doubts about the popularity of his cause and his political abilities.[63] Bryan's antievolution efforts also may have suffered from his failures as a party politician, especially his awkward and impolitic performance at the 1924 Democratic National Convention, where his attempt to add a plank to the party platform in support of revealed religion brought boos from the delegates and led many to believe that he was becoming unbalanced.[64] The aging but ever optimistic Bryan hardly noticed these setbacks. "I think my defeat for Moderator was providential," he told his daughter Grace after failing to win the post. "I did far more from the floor than I could have done in the chair."[65]

Bryan's very visibility could sometimes be costly. During a lifetime in politics, he had made enemies as well as friends, and his willingness to commit himself to controversial causes had produced critics on many fronts. In embracing him, antievolutionists inherited many of his detractors.[66] Added to this, Bryan had a tendency to steal the show, diverting the issue away from evolution. That is to say, because his visibility made him an obvious target, his opponents often found it easier to attack him personally, questioning his intelligence and even his integrity, than to debate the principles at stake.[67] Bryan's prominence caused problems even among his friends, and more than once he found himself caught between feuding factions, as when Texas Baptists sought his support against the renegade Norris.[68] Then there was his tendency to attract controversy, which he seemed to relish: accusing professors of lying, criticizing college presidents and church leaders, denouncing organizations like the American Library Association as anti-Christian and antidemocratic. Already in 1923 his longtime editor Guy V. Viskniskki of the Republic Syndicate warned him that many newspapers were canceling his Bryan Bible Talks, concerned that his obsessive opposition to evolution was driving away readers.[69] Even Bryan was aware that he was becoming the issue: "The objection of the liberals is to me personally. They know that the fight is on and that I am the one conservative leader who can reach the public."[70]

It was in Florida that Bryan's role as an ally was most apparent. From 1912 on, he and his wife had lived for much of the year in Miami, where he acted as an unofficial ambassador, boosting the city's climate and its rapidly appreciating real estate.[71] His Sunday morning Bible class in Miami's Royal Palm Park drew audiences of thousands during the winter tourist season.[72] In 1921, the year he made Florida his legal residence, he embarked on an extensive tour of the state as part of a campaign to establish a religious activities building at the University of Florida. Bryan traveled from town to town making dozens of speeches, as well as hosting parties of five hundred or more at his Coconut Grove home.[73] By the spring of 1923 he had become a force in Florida politics, able to call upon friends in the legislature to introduce a resolution declaring it improper and subversive for any public school teacher to advocate atheism or teach Darwinism. Conferring closely with its sponsors, Bryan saw to it that the resolution was phrased in terms that would attract the most support possible by applying it only to the teaching of evolution "as fact" and making certain that it carried no legal penalties.[74] As the measure moved toward passage, he promoted it publicly and privately, addressing a joint session of the legislature and acting behind the scenes to prevent opposition from his close friend A. A. Murphree, president of the University of Florida, or from others in the educational community. Approved unanimously by both houses, the resulting concurrent resolution was in almost every way Bryan's bill, a triumph of personal politics. When it attracted little attention in the press, he set to work to publicize it, hailing the resolution as a model for other states. The Florida law, Bryan told the *Chicago Tribune*, was not only a vindication of his own views, but also of "the majority of all the church members of all the Christian churches, Catholic and Protestant alike."[75]

But Bryan's influence had its limits. In Florida, where he could personally oversee its passage, the antievolution measure sailed smoothly through the legislature. Elsewhere, even in those states where he was personally involved, such bills tended to founder and sink. In West Virginia, where Bryan delivered one of his most aggressive attacks on evolution to a joint session of the legislature, and where he spoke to enthusiastic supporters in cities throughout the state, all action on antievolution proposals was deferred and eventually died at the end of the 1923 session.[76] In Georgia, where he entered the chamber on crutches and addressed the lawmakers while seated because of a leg injury, the state house adopted a resolution thanking him for his interest in Georgia matters but avoided the antievolution issue by collectively affirming its belief in Christ's divinity.[77] Bryan encountered greater frustration in Tennessee, where a 1923 senate resolution inviting him to address the general assembly was tabled by the house of representatives, fearful that a debate on evolution would interfere with "important" legislation.[78] And in North Carolina, where he lectured to an estimated two thousand people in Raleigh's city auditorium in late April 1923, Bryan was not even invited to address the legislators who sat in session across town.[79]

In state after state, Bryan was extremely effective in attracting public attention, in bringing the antievolution issue before lawmakers, and in opening doors for local supporters. But his persuasiveness did not penetrate very far down the halls of legislatures, whose members tended to be concerned with more mundane issues and pressing political challenges. Moreover, what influence he had was short-lived, evaporating quickly as he moved on to the next state, leaving friendly local legislators to struggle with the specifics. Even in Florida, his greatest success, Bryan's victory was not particularly significant, since the legislature was willing to go on record as stating only its "sense" that it was improper to teach Darwinism as true, and since the resolution contained no force of law, provided no penalties, and had no noticeable impact on state policies. As far as teachers were concerned, the resolution had little if any effect, and a University of Florida biology professor could report a year later that "no effort has ever been made to influence in any way either the manner or the matter of teaching."[80]

Divisions among Elites

Finally, divisions among elites can have the effect of opening opportunities. With a divided elite, movement members are encouraged to take risks they would not have taken otherwise, and elites themselves may champion a cause to increase their own influence. According to Tarrow, such divisions can appear in almost every kind of political system. In relatively recent times, splits between hard-liners and reformers in authoritarian states (Spain in the 1970s) and state socialist ones (Poland in the 1980s) have been seen by insurgents as signals to mobilize. Although a unified elite can crush most movements, a divided one will often benefit and even promote them, extending the boundaries of the political system by providing outsiders with a chance to exercise at least some power.[81]

In the South of the 1920s, such divisions among elites could be found everywhere, as progressives fought traditionalists on a wide range of issues involving political and religious reform. The battles left communities divided and polarized; for every progressive reformer there seemed to be a conservative local leader who was committed to resisting reform and maintaining traditional ways. Public officials were left with little room for compromise or negotiation. Under the circumstances, they did the best they could, often seeking to avoid the most polarizing issues altogether, "flying quickly to cover," as Joseph Wood Krutch put it, lest they be compelled to sacrifice "some political advantage or some material gain."[82]

With the introduction of the antievolution issue, positions became further polarized. Throughout the early 1920s supporters and opponents staked out sides, determined to define the debate in the most dualistic and uncompromising terms. National organizations were active on each side, with the Anti-Evolution League and the WCFA providing support to antievolution's friends in the state legislatures, while the National Education Association, American Association for the Advancement of Science, and ACLU all aided its opponents.[83] Newspapers aligned themselves for and against the bills, with small town and rural weeklies generally supporting them while most big city and statewide daily papers were opposed.[84] Community organizations took positions, and local chambers of commerce, trade organizations, and parent-teacher associations could be found on both sides of the question.[85] Religious denominations were divided along the same lines, with Southern Baptists and Presbyterians tending to support antievolution efforts, while Northern Baptists, Congregationalists, Episcopalians, and Methodists often went on record to express their opposition.[86] But within the churches there were deep differences, as conservative and liberal factions engaged in pitched battles for control of several of the largest Protestant denominations during this time.[87] Even the most conservative denominations were split; among Southern Baptists, for example, where antievolutionists found many of their firmest friends, there were also powerful foes that included college presidents, seminary professors, and many editors of the denomination's statewide newspapers.[88] At the very least, some Baptists found the attention given to evolution to be a distraction from more important matters, "a poor thing," as the *Alabama Baptist* stated, "for Christian people to have a perpetual wrangle over."[89] Roman Catholics were divided as well. Some were sympathetic to the movement, sensing that evolution posed a threat to Catholic theology; others opposed it, not least out of an awareness of the anti-Catholicism that ran rampant among so many fundamentalists in the movement. But most Catholics avoided the issue altogether, assuming that it would have no effect on either church doctrine or parochial education.[90]

Despite the divisions, antievolutionists often had difficulty finding openings. Inside the legislatures, where party leaders had a stake in avoiding issues that would stir up controversy and threaten party unity, they found few friends. The powerful politicians who controlled the levers of the legislative process were adept at throwing up obstacles to measures that threatened their own prerogatives. Thus they often forced antievolution bills to run a bicameral gauntlet of hearings, floor debates, and conference committee meetings, all offering ample opportunity to amend, recommit, or eliminate provisions. In state after state, despite strong popular support for antievolution legislation, committee chairs refused to release proposed measures for full debate, killing them outright or retaining them for further discussion.[91] Bills were passed from committee to committee; house measures were killed when senate committees tabled them; in South Carolina, a senate proposal was scuttled when the house failed to concur and the bill was eliminated in joint conference committee.[92] On several occasions committee chairs used the calendar to prevent final votes from being taken, holding back their reports until the waning hours of the session.[93] In the biennial short sessions of the 1920s South, such delay was effectively the same as defeat. Antievolution supporters tried to bypass the committee structure wherever possible, preferring floor debates where balconies could be packed with supporters and requiring recorded votes that could be used in the next election campaign.[94] Legislative leaders, on the other hand, tended to resist open debates, which they saw as taking days or even weeks away from other business; even sympathetic lawmakers sometimes had little patience for such tactics.[95] For antievolution's opponents, time and the institutional intricacies of their state systems were their most effective resources, making it possible for them to avoid public votes in which they would be forced to "ape the monkey," in the words of one Florida legislator, "by voting like an ass."[96]

Added to this were the conflicts and divisions that existed among antievolution advocates themselves. For all the attention to Bryan, and despite the determined efforts of the WCFA, antievolutionism was never a centralized movement. States took up the issue separately, and there was surprisingly little contact from state to state between public officials who supported antievolution legislation. Although Bryan had attempted in Florida to frame a model bill that could be used by every state, few followed his lead. The result was a hopeless hodgepodge of legislation: over the course of the 1920s some forty-five amendments, bills, and resolutions were introduced in legislatures across the country, and each was different from every other one.[97] Bills were brought to outlaw the teaching of "Darwinism, Atheism, Agnosticism, or the Theory of Evolution" (Kentucky), the "creed" or "cult known as 'Darwinism'" (South Carolina), the "materialistic Conception of History" (Oklahoma), and even "disrespect for the Holy Bible" (District of Columbia).[98] Some measures focused on textbooks, others on teaching, and still others on both.[99] Bryan's plea that there be no penalties for violators notwithstanding, many proposals did contain penalties: one Kentucky bill required fines of "not less than fifty nor more than five thousand dollars" and/or confinement "to the county jail not less than ten days nor more than twelve months or both fined and imprisoned."[100] In some proposals teachers were to be fined or fired, in others the school boards or principals were held accountable, and in a few the schools themselves could lose appropriations or even their charters.[101] More often than not, antievolution proposals came from back benchers rather than legislative leaders. Most were written hastily and without much consultation. Sometimes several measures were introduced at more or less the same time. House bills differed from senate bills, senate bills from house bills. Occasionally, antievolutionists seemed ready to throw up their hands. "I am writing to you to know just what form of legislation you would suggest," one exasperated lawmaker appealed to Bryan. "Other members have ask [sic] me to write you for suggestions before the matters [sic] comes up for final passage. If necessary we can defer final action for a few days longer in order to have the benefit of your advice."[102]

North Carolina was the classic case in which antievolutionists proved unable to capitalize on the divisions that existed among elites. By all counts, the state should have been sympathetic. Beginning with his 1920 attack on Wake Forest president W. L. Poteat, T. T. Martin had continued to call upon Baptists to investigate the influence of evolutionary teaching in their schools. During the early 1920s, antievolution revivalists had been crisscrossing the state, led by Mordecai Ham, whose famous "evolution sermon" had become a favorite of thousands of North Carolinians. Bryan had made several visits as well. In addition, for some time critics at home had been leveling charges against the University of North Carolina, in Chapel Hill, where President Harry W. Chase and faculty members such as renowned sociologist Howard W. Odum had come under fire for being friendly to evolutionary theory and unsympathetic to orthodox religion. So it came as no surprise when in early 1925 first-term representative David Scott Poole, a conservative Presbyterian from rural Hoke County, introduced House Resolution Ten, declaring it injurious to the public welfare for any public school teacher "to teach or permit to be taught as a fact, either Darwinism or any other hypothesis that links man in blood relationship with any lower form of life."[103]

While popular opinion in North Carolina seemed broadly supportive, elites were sharply divided over the measure. In the General Assembly, the bill had the backing of powerful voices, including those of several key committee chairs. On the other side, however, were some formidable opponents, led by Representatives Henry Grove Connor, chair of the all-important Committee on Education, and Walter Murphy, who chaired the powerful Committee on Appropriations. Also opposed was young Sam Ervin Jr., later of Watergate fame, who worked against the bill on the house floor. Outside the legislature, Cameron Morrison had been succeeded in the Executive Mansion by Angus W. McClean, a business progressive whose main concern was centralized control over the state budget and who studiously avoided taking any position on the antievolution controversy. Newspapers in the state staked out positions on both sides of the Poole bill, with the *Charlotte Observer* editorializing in favor while Josephus Daniels's *Raleigh News and Observer* expressed strong views against it. Most important, however, was the role of the educational elite. Asked by Connor to coordinate opposition among the state's colleges, North Carolina State College's Eugene C. Brooks demurred in order to avoid jeopardizing his institution's pending funding requests. Battered by years of criticism and believing that the bill was more a matter for public than private colleges, Wake Forest's Poteat also begged off, promising only to attend committee hearings. Connor then turned, somewhat reluctantly, to Harry Chase, a Massachusetts-born Republican with little experience in the state capitol. With time running out, Chase threw himself into the fight, alerting influential allies of the university, sending "talking points" to friends in the legislature, organizing petitions from alumni and faculty, and personally rising from the back of the room to deliver a dramatic testimony before the house education committee. Advised that his stand could jeopardize state support for the university, Chase was said to have snapped: "If this University doesn't stand for anything but appropriations, I, for one, don't care to be connected with it."[104]

What followed was a flurry of lobbying by partisans from both sides. Antievolution advocates, led by ministerial groups like Charlotte's Presbyterian Ministers' Association, worked the statehouse halls in support of the Poole bill. Opponents countered by making their own contacts, with Poteat proving especially effective at lining up the votes of Wake Forest alumni among the lawmakers. For the next week proponents of each position sparred, making use of parliamentary maneuvers in an attempt to block the other side. While antievolutionists lost narrowly in committee (Connor breaking a tie vote), legislative rules allowed them to file a minority report, thereby sending the bill to the full house. As state newspapers continued to weigh in on both sides, the debate became a public sensation, attracting crowds so large and unruly that the first day's deliberations had to be canceled. When the house resumed deliberations the next day, Connor suggested a less intrusive substitute for the Poole resolution, and advocates from both camps were thrown into confusion, with the strongest advocates and opponents temporarily teaming up to defeat the compromise measure. Meanwhile, Murphy held his ground, taking the floor in the waning moments of the debate to assert that instead of fighting over issues that belonged outside the legislature, in the realm of personal religion, the lawmakers should work together to solve the political problems that actually could be solved inside it. In effect, the speech was a warning to his fellow elites that, by becoming divided, they ran the risk of losing control over state politics and ceding their power to an increasingly politicized public. Sensing that many of their colleagues were having second thoughts, antievolutionists quickly called the question, but the Poole bill was doomed, going down to defeat by twenty-one votes, a larger margin than anyone had expected.[105] Returning to Chapel Hill, Chase expressed relief at having survived the ordeal. "A man cannot argue with a cyclone," he wrote in a note of thanks to Murphy, "and my hope is that now that the cyclone is over folks will get their head back and two years from now things will look different."[106] However, well aware that Poole and his allies would be back in the next session, he quietly went about advising his faculty not to do anything that could stir up the issue again. The best strategy now, he would write, was for the university "to set back and saw wood."[107]

In Tennessee, by contrast, where events unfolded almost simultaneously with those in North Carolina, conflicts and divisions among elites worked in favor of the antievolution campaign, as opportunity came knocking at precisely the right moment. Antievolution agitation had been bubbling for some time in the state. In 1923, encouraged by the inroads made in neighboring Kentucky the year before, friendly legislators had introduced anti-Darwinist legislation in both houses only to see the bills wither and die in their education committees. But in early 1924 a more serious effort was sparked by Bryan's Nashville address. Published almost immediately in pamphlet form as *Is the Bible True?*, the speech was distributed across the state by antievolution supporters; an estimated five hundred copies went directly to the legislature.[108] By the time John W. Butler presented his own hand-crafted antievolution bill in the Tennessee House of Representatives, public opinion seemed to be so strongly favorable that he assumed his proposal would receive virtually no opposition. (A fellow legislator estimated at the time that no fewer than 95 percent of all Tennesseans opposed the teaching of evolution.)[109] Introduced during a two-hour session in which the house dealt with minor matters, the bill passed through almost unnoticed, "ground out of the hopper," reported the *Nashville Banner*, alongside "a local measure to prohibit suck-egg dogs from running at large in Cocke county."[110]

At this point, opposition did develop, but it was too little too late. While Tennessee newspapers seemed reluctant to take a stand, critics of the Butler bill blasted the legislature in biting letters to the editor. These were answered in turn by even stronger statements from the bill's supporters, including one letter writer who warned state senators that if the measure were not passed, the people would demand a public vote and would "snow it [the teaching of evolution in the public schools] under so deep it won't get out for years, neither will the senators that voted for it."[111] Modernist ministers took to their pulpits to condemn the legislation as a threat to religious and personal freedom, but their sermons were insignificant compared to the show put on by Billy Sunday, who arrived in Memphis in the midst of the debates to stage an eighteen-day crusade in which he regularly denounced "that Godforsaken gang of evolutionary cutthroats."[112] Most important, while a few academics led by Vanderbilt University's Edwin Mims attacked the Butler bill, much of the state's educational establishment was either supportive or silent. The Tennessee Academy of Sciences, for example, said nothing against the measure until after it had become law.[113] Tennessee educators were left largely leaderless when University of Tennessee president Harcourt Morgan refused to oppose the bill, fearing that he would lose support for a proposal pending in the legislature to significantly increase state support for the university.[114] "The subject of Evolution so intricately involves religious belief, which the University has no disposition to dictate," Morgan wrote Governor Austin Peay, "that the University declines to engage in the controversy."[115]

Moreover, in Tennessee legislative rules worked to the advantage of the antievolution forces. Arriving in the state senate, Butler's bill found a cordial reception from Speaker Lew D. Hill, of Sparta, an elder in the fundamentalist Churches of Christ, who acted to bar unfriendly amendments and personally intervened to prevent the Butler draft from being buried in committee. At one point he stepped down from the speaker's chair to make a personal appeal, claiming that he had been "petitioned by the women of the state and the teacher's association" to work for enactment of the law.[116] As newspaper editorials began to warn of the possibility of passage (even the arch-conservative *Memphis Commercial Appeal* expressed some reservations), and amid growing opposition in the senate, Hill was able to use his control of the calendar to delay consideration until after a scheduled four-week recess. The break seemed to revitalize the antievolutionists. With Billy Sunday pounding away at the issue in Memphis, drawing record crowds every evening (final attendance figures went above 200,000, approximately one-tenth of the state's population), activists used the time to lobby their legislators and rally their troops.[117] North Carolina's defeat of its antievolution bill, coming about two weeks into the recess, seemed to further galvanize supporters, who saw their efforts as the last chance for success in the 1925 legislative sessions. Returning from the recess, senators looked up to find their chamber galleries packed with expectant partisans. With the deadline for ending the session looming, amendments became impractical, and for once time worked in favor of the antievolution forces, as lukewarm lawmakers saw no alternative but to vote for the Butler bill, which passed by a comfortable margin.[118]

After passage the conflicts continued, with supporters and opponents turning their attention to Governor Peay. For more than a week the cautious Peay considered the issue, accepting petitions, meeting with delegations of ministers, and receiving a small flood (one biographer says "tens of thousands") of letters and telegrams urging him to sign or veto the measure.[119] While some believed that Peay privately opposed the bill, his own correspondence from the time strongly suggests that he was predisposed to sign it.[120] Although the governor received a few letters from business, trade, and church leaders who were against antievolution legislation, most were from those encouraging him to sign the measure and thanking him for supporting it. As one Nashville physician wrote: "I believe I can truthfully say that out of every hundred people that there is not more than three out of each hundred who oppose your action."[121] Whatever his personal inclination, Peay was eager to sign the bill to avoid further controversy, which he saw as threatening support for his own efforts to modernize Tennessee's public schools.[122] (That he may have had other political considerations in mind is suggested by Krutch, who reported that before signing the bill the governor was said to remark, "They've got their nerve to pass the buck to me when they know I want to be United States Senator.")[123] Ironically, Peay saw the bill as a way to avoid the division among elites that had allowed the legislation to proceed in the first place. Taking consolation that it would never be tested, the governor signed it into law, adding almost as an aside that "nobody believes that it is going to be an active statute."[124] Considering the extraordinary events that were about to follow, he could not have been more monumentally mistaken.

By 1925, antievolutionists had become familiar faces in the halls of many state capitols. Especially in the South, where political systems were porous and often poorly organized, they had become adept at taking advantage of political opportunities as they opened to them. Acting to gain access, build alliances, make use of allies, and benefit from divisions among elites, they had come to exercise political power with surprising speed, and in some cases with surprising success. In Tennessee, antievolution had become law. What remained to be seen was whether that law would stand if tested. Although antievolutionists were unaware of it at the time, that test was about to take place, and it would define the destiny of their movement.

6 : Staging

THE DRAMA AT DAYTON

John Scopes really could not remember if he had actually taught any evolution. The twenty-four-year-old teacher, who had just finished his first year at Dayton, Tennessee's tiny Rhea County Central High School, had been hired to coach the football team and take charge of general science courses, but the more advanced biology classes were the responsibility of someone else. That spring he had substituted for several days when the regular biology teacher was ill, though he had spent most of his time leading study sessions for upcoming examinations. But when local business leaders, who were considering bringing a test case against the newly minted Butler bill, called him over to Robinson's Drug Store to ask if he had taught the theory of evolution during that time, he confessed that he couldn't recall. "To tell the truth," he later wrote, "I wasn't sure."[1]

Not that it mattered, because the trial of John Thomas Scopes was more than a legal case, the prosecution of a Tennessee high school teacher for violation of the state's antievolution law. It was a public performance, a stage on which William Jennings Bryan and Clarence Darrow—two of the most celebrated and controversial figures of the era—confronted one another during two torrid weeks (10 July to 21 July 1925) in a courtroom drama that would captivate millions across the country and around the world. For the antievolution movement, the Scopes trial offered an unprecedented set of opportunities: to attract the attention of national and international media, to win extensive public support for its stand against the teaching of evolution in public schools, to confront and embarrass their evolutionist enemies, and to secure the Tennessee antievolution statute while encouraging the passage of similar ones nationwide. For fundamentalists in the movement, it was also a chance—perhaps the last chance—to rout their liberal and modernist religious rivals, return control of the churches to the forces of orthodoxy, and revive faith in the old-time religion. For Bryan, it was a way to reassert his role as a moral crusader, providing a fitting capstone to his illustrious career as a champion of popular causes. But antievolutionists realized that the Scopes case brought with it danger as well, since defeat could be devastating, stopping their movement in its tracks by overturning its most important victory. Thus they saw the trial as a portentous play in which much seemed to ride on the performance.

In recent years, scholars have become aware of the ability of movements not only to frame ideas and images, but also to present or "stage" them. Armed with agendas and convinced of the importance of their issues, activists often enter into the political system only to find themselves viewed with disinterest, suspicion, or hostility. In such unsympathetic settings, they turn to what sociologist Doug McAdam has called "strategic dramaturgy," creating and carrying out compelling dramas that convey the message of their movement in highly resonant ways. According to McAdam, the process requires activists to accomplish four ends: (1) *attracting and shaping media coverage*; (2) *winning the support of bystander publics*; (3) *constraining movement opponents*; and (4) *influencing state authorities and public policy*.[2] In a series of studies of the American civil rights movement, he showed how Martin Luther King Jr. and his followers in the Southern Christian Leadership Conference (SCLC) were able to use demonstrations and disruptive actions —boycotts, sit-ins, mass marches—to achieve these goals.[3] He also addressed the difficulties they had to overcome in doing so, suggesting that the process was particularly complex and challenging because it required tactics that provoked reactions from four separate constituent publics (the media, the sympathetic public, segregationists and other movement opponents, and federal and state officials), all more or less simultaneously. His analysis of the civil rights movement in the South, while stressing its victories, also cites some of its failures, instances in which activists were frustrated in carrying out their strategy by the tactical counter-responses of opponents and unsympathetic public officials.[4] Indeed, McAdam makes it clear that while the effective use of dramaturgy may be essential to the success of many movements, it is seldom easy and never totally predictable.

Almost all students of the Scopes trial have concluded that it was less a trial than a media event. This is not to say that it has been treated as inconsequential: from Ray Ginger's classic *Six Days or Forever?* to Edward J. Larson's Pulitzer Prize–winning *Summer for the Gods*, scholars have shown its significance, both legal and political, in defining the debates that have taken place over the teaching of evolution in the United States. Yet even among those who take the trial most seriously, there remains the sense that its larger meaning was in the way it dramatized these debates, capturing them as a confrontation between charismatic personalities.[5] The problem is that many historians, responding to the theatrical character of the trial, have gone on to dismiss it, with those like Martin

Marty describing it as nothing more than "a good show."[6] What few have seemed to realize is that one of the reasons the Scopes trial was so significant is precisely because it was such a good show, or more to the point, because it provided the setting for the dazzling use of strategic dramaturgy.[7] In preparing for it, Bryan and his colleagues consciously developed strategies for not only stating their case but also staging it in the most compelling way possible. Over the two weeks of the trial they courted the media, they spoke to bystanders on the streets and reached out to listeners and readers throughout America and in other parts of the world, they maneuvered to shape public perceptions of their opponents both within and outside of the courtroom, and at its conclusion they schemed to find ways to package the outcome of the case to have maximum effect on public policy. Of course, their evolutionist opponents were doing many of the same things at more or less the same time, creating a dynamic and sometimes improvised and unpredictable drama. In short, the Scopes trial was indeed a spectacular show, and its significance was by and large the result of its staging.

Attracting Media Attention

For almost all movements, media coverage is a pervasive concern. Activists lack access to the levers of power, so they must work to break down the boundaries of the political system, exerting pressure from the outside by influencing public opinion. In informing the public about issues, the mass media are important; for conveying the moral message of a movement, they are absolutely crucial. In his studies of the civil rights movement, McAdam showed how—from the time of the Montgomery bus boycott—Martin Luther King and the SCLC consciously choreographed protests with an eye to media presentation. The culmination of these efforts came in the 1963 Birmingham campaigns, in which defenseless demonstrators confronted unrestrained, violent police while news cameras rolled and reporters described the events to audiences at home and abroad. McAdam's point is that for movements to succeed, they must be seen, and to be seen, they must attract the attention of the media.[8]

So it is appropriate that the story of the Scopes trial begins with an attempt to attract media attention. Admittedly, George Rappleyea was not an antievolution activist, nor did he have the mass media in mind when, one afternoon in early May 1925, he read in the *Chattanooga Times* that the American Civil Liberties Union (ACLU) was seeking to test Tennessee's new antievolution law. A native New Yorker, Rappleyea was a relatively recent arrival to the small town of Dayton (population 1,800), where he managed the struggling Cumberland Coal and Iron Company for its northern owners. He was also a firm believer in evolution, having become familiar with the theory while earning a college degree in chemical engineering, and he wanted to see the law overturned on principle. But by the next day, when he sought to persuade local business leaders gathered at Robinson's soda fountain that Dayton should be the site for such a test, he was making his case on the grounds of publicity. For years the town's economy had been in decline, and business boosters were always on the alert for ways to attract investment to their ambitious and forward-looking community. Rappleyea did not have to argue much to convince the others. Even county school superintendent Walter White, who favored the antievolution law, realized that a controversial case of this kind, attracting attention from every part of the country, had the potential to "put Dayton on the map."[9]

The plan to stage a trial proved more successful than anyone could have ever imagined. Since court cases require defendants, the boosters sent at once for Scopes, the amiable young science teacher, hailing him to the drugstore from the high school tennis court. The fact that he was unsure whether he actually ever had taught any evolution theory seemed inconsequential to everyone there. After all, he had substituted in W. F. Ferguson's regular biology class that spring, and since Ferguson was not only a married man but also the school principal, he could hardly be expected to bring the case. Besides, in his review sessions with the students, Scopes had used Hunter's *Civic Biology*, an approved Tennessee science text that contained explanations of evolution and an evolutionary chart. Moreover, he firmly believed that biology could not be explained without some treatment of the theory, and as a teacher he opposed the new antievolution statute.[10] Having no reason to assume that the matter would attract much notice, he announced himself willing to stand trial and went back to his tennis game. The local boosters had other ideas; almost immediately they were telephoning the Chattanooga papers. By the next day newspapers across the state were running front-page stories that a Tennessee man had been arrested for teaching evolution and that a major court case was in the making. "Many witnesses will appear," announced the *Nashville Banner*, "and it is expected that the trial will be bitterly contested."[11]

The Associated Press immediately picked up the story, and within days it was appearing in papers nationwide. Hurrying to take advantage of the trial (and to keep it from being lured away by Chattanooga or Knoxville), the Dayton Progressive Club, a group of business and civic boosters, set up an arrangements committee to find facilities and housing for an anticipated onslaught of as many as ten thousand spectators.[12] Townspeople flew to work painting the main courtroom in the gloomy Rhea County Courthouse, building overflow seating on the courthouse lawn, setting up loudspeakers at public places across town, and cleaning up the county jail in preparation for an influx of pickpockets, bootleggers, and crooks.[13] Promotional brochures were prepared, complete with photographs of local banks and businesses. ("Dayton would be woefully remiss in her duty to herself not to grasp the hour of her lime-light incandescence," observed the authors of one brochure entitled *Why Dayton—of All Places?*, "and make of it an occasion for self-aggrandizement with some incontrovertible facts about her products and natural resources.")[14] Anticipating international interest, and seeking celebrities to increase it, trial promoters went so far as to invite British historian and science fiction writer H. G. Wells to town to make the case for evolution.[15] Put off by Dayton's desire to draw attention to itself, which at one point included staging a mock fistfight between evolution supporter Rappleyea and evolution opponent Thurlow Reed, a town barber, the Tennessee press warned that the town's penchant for publicity was getting out of hand. "Apparently the 'booster' element in Dayton have [sic] with questionable wisdom and taste, seized on this as an opportunity to get widespread publicity for their city," proclaimed the staid *Nashville Tennessean*, "evidently proceeding on the doubtful theory that it is good advertising to have people talking about you, regardless of what they are saying."[16]

It did not take long for antievolutionists to provide Dayton with a certified national celebrity to serve as the star of its show. Throughout the first week of May, the World's Christian Fundamentals Association (WCFA) had been holding its 1925 convention in Memphis, with William Jennings Bryan as the featured speaker. Arriving in Memphis at the same time were about ten thousand Baptist messengers from across the South, delegates to the annual assembly of the Southern Baptist Convention. Because Tennessee's antievolution law was still in the news, and since preliminary proceedings in the Scopes case were taking place even as they met, the two conventions were alive with evolution talk. In a series of rabble-rousing speeches, Bryan added to the buzz, commending the state for passing the statute and criticizing those who challenged it. Yet despite all of their rhetoric, antievolutionists were defeated in the Baptist Convention on a measure that would have added an antievolution article to the denomination's statement of faith. Taken aback by the defeat, and concerned that the case at Dayton might easily be lost by local attorneys, the WCFA decided to do something dramatic. "In order to secure for the state law a just and adequate hearing," the convention unanimously resolved, "We name as our attorney for this trial WILLIAM JENNINGS BRYAN and pledge to him whatever support is needful to secure equity and justice and to conserve the righteous law of the Commonwealth of Tennessee."[17]

For his part, Bryan was experiencing other setbacks as well, having moved on from Memphis to the annual meeting of the Presbyterian General Assembly at

Columbus, Ohio, where he not only watched another antievolution resolution go down to defeat, but also lost his post as assembly vice moderator. Searching for some sort of victory, he eagerly accepted the WCFA invitation—seconded a few days later by attorneys for the prosecution—despite the fact that he had not acted as a courtroom attorney in almost thirty years.[18] Antievolutionists were ecstatic, anticipating that the case would be less a courtroom discussion of legalities than a platform from which America's most eloquent enemy of evolution could make his case before a national audience, reasserting the issue and reinvigorating the movement. As J. Frank Norris told him, "It is the greatest opportunity ever presented to educate the public, and will accomplish more than ten years campaigning."[19] Indeed, Bryan's entry on the scene had a galvanizing effect: according to one news report, "people all over the county are becoming interested in the trial."[20]

The next day America's leading trial lawyer Clarence Darrow offered to defend Scopes, and the event became a sensation. The ACLU had envisioned a low-profile litigation, a cautious test of the law's constitutionality conducted by conservative and highly respected counsel. With the appearance of the controversial Darrow, who had made his name pleading the cause of unpopular defendants from labor radicals to society murderers, the ACLU lost control of its own suit.[21] Certain that the case would be tried less in the courtroom than in the press, Darrow conceived of it as a chance not only to test the constitutionality of a foolish state statute, but also to confront Bryan and derail the antievolution movement, which he considered a dangerous threat to individual liberty and free thought. Announcing the offer of his services, he set the tone for the trial by attacking Bryan personally, charging him with bigotry and closed-mindedness, and declaring that if those like Bryan had their way, people would still be persecuting witches and punishing those who believed that the earth was round.[22] As Edward Larson has suggested, Darrow's strategy was to substitute Bryan for Scopes as the accused, and he would pursue it relentlessly throughout the trial.[23] When Bryan responded by impugning Darrow as an atheist, the terms of the trial were set, for although Darrow insisted that he was an agnostic rather than an atheist, he was among the first to admit that his interest in the case was piqued by the irresistible invitation it offered to debunk Bryan's orthodox Christianity.[24] As the ACLU's Roger Baldwin later observed: "It was immediately apparent what kind of a trial it would be: the Good Book against Darwin, bigotry against science, or, as popularly put, God against monkeys. With Bryan for the prosecution, it was almost inevitable that Clarence Darrow should volunteer for the defense."[25] Bryan alone was a media event; Bryan and Darrow together would be a media extravaganza. In the words of the *Memphis Commercial Appeal*, their decision to meet at Dayton was "the opening move in a drama that will hold the attention of the world."[26]

As the trial date approached, it became clear that Dayton would provide the perfect setting for the show. A town created by the railroad and the influx of heavy industry into the emerging New South, Dayton was a progressive place. Its civic culture was dominated by the small-town bankers and businessmen who made up the local Progressive Club; its religious life was more Methodist than Baptist; and its race relations were comparatively congenial, at least to the extent that the town's two hundred African Americans lived without fear of the Ku Klux Klan, which had no local members.[27] Big-city newspaper reporters were disappointed that the town seemed more typically American than stereotypically southern. ("I expected to find a squalid Southern village," confessed the *Baltimore Evening Sun*'s acerbic H. L. Mencken in his first report from Dayton. "What I found was a country town full of charm and even beauty."[28]) As members of the media began to search for local color and human interest stories to fill the sidebars, they discovered Dayton to be endlessly obliging. Weeks before, the town had begun an advertising blitz. Local businesses like Robinson's Drug Store ("Where It All Began") took the lead in erecting banners and billboards to lure customers, while other shopkeepers decorated their stores ("We handle all kinds of meat except monkey," said a sign at the butcher shop) and set in supplies of picture postcards and monkey umbrellas. Portable refreshment stands selling hot dogs and ice cream cones appeared overnight around the courthouse square, with four of them doing business in a single block. Circus performers set up tent shows; musicians and singers entertained on the street corners. T. T. Martin arrived with a makeshift bookseller's stand, where he sold copies of Bryan's books and his own *Hell and the High Schools*. Itinerant preachers also staked out the street corners; white-whiskered prophets carried placards and passed out handbills announcing the end of the world; one professional atheist spoke to audiences at the corner of Main and Market Streets until he was arrested for disturbing the peace. Also arriving were a variety of performers, including a strange misshapen man, three and one-half feet tall with a receding forehead and protruding jaw, who labeled himself "The Missing Link." And, of course, there were monkeys, one of whom, carnival chimpanzee Joe Mendi, wore a houndstooth sport coat and bow tie, while another, Mindy the Monkey, carried his own set of golf clubs.[29] Although Dayton struggled to maintain decorum, it seemed unable to escape its instant image as a town like any other that for the moment had become what the *Memphis Commercial Appeal* called one of the "centers of the world's wonder."[30]

Bryan and Darrow had been doing advance publicity of their own. In the weeks leading up to the trial, as both prepared their cases, they spent much of their time giving interviews and staging impromptu press conferences. By early summer public attention was riveted on the two principal performers. Arriving at Nashville in June to confer with local lawyers, Bryan was met by enthusiastic state officials and exuberant crowds who followed him from the railroad station to the strains of "The Old Time Religion," "Onward Christian Soldiers," and "Christ the Royal Master" played by the Tennessee Industrial School Band.[31] Two weeks later Darrow staged his own pretrial visit to Dayton, addressing the Progressive Club and impressing local leaders less with his libertarian message than with his homespun humor and self-effacing style.[32] As for the defendant Scopes, following a whirlwind visit to New York City that included banquets, press conferences, and photo opportunities at the Statue of Liberty, he was largely forgotten, his presence overwhelmed by the personalities who had taken charge of his case.[33] With all eyes on Bryan and Darrow, observers compared the Dayton trial to a heavyweight prizefight: "The squared ring is ready," wrote John P. Fort of the *Chattanooga News*. "The chloroform bottle on hand. Seconds are prepared to do the rubbing: William Jennings Bryan, Clarence Darrow are in the ring; the rest are but shadows."[34] Other writers tried out other metaphors: "the big show," "the inquisition," "the crusade for God."[35] At least a few chose more cynical descriptions, like "the three ring circus."[36] However they saw it, all agreed that Bryan and Darrow were certain to put on a memorable performance. Fort wrote: "Science and religion, in the persons of Darrow and Bryan as their courtroom champions, are face to face. . . . And so the gong sounds. The battle is on."[37]

In attracting the mass media, trial planners succeeded beyond all expectations. Although exact numbers remain unknown, somewhere between 150 and 200 journalists descended on Dayton during the time the trial was in session. Among them were some of America's leading newspaper and magazine writers, including Philip Kinsley of the *Chicago Tribune*, Joseph Wood Krutch of *Nation* magazine, and of course Mencken, editor of the *American Mercury* and columnist for the *Baltimore Evening Sun*, who was already widely known as one of the nation's most brilliant and cynical iconoclasts. Crowding around courtroom press tables, then returning each evening to a makeshift dormitory above a hardware store, the reporters sent their publications an estimated 150,000 to 200,000 words per day. More than 2 million words were transmitted over the wires throughout the trial.[38] Western Union kept sixteen operators on duty, working from a sweltering storeroom in the back of a grocery store. Telegraph lines had been specially strung to the courthouse so the three major wire services could tap out their reports directly from the courtroom; a telephone switchboard that was installed could handle one hundred calls a day.[39] WGN radio broadcast the proceedings live, with announcer Quin Ryan's reports being carried by rented AT&T telephone cables to the station's transmitter in the Drake Hotel in Chicago, from where they were sent out across the Midwest.[40] (Three large microphones were placed in the courtroom, one directly in front of the judge's bench and the others at the tables of the opposing counsel; Ryan did his broadcast from a windowsill he sometimes shared with Mencken.) Newsreel and movie crews set up their cameras on desks just beyond the railing that separated participants from spectators, and at the end of each day their film was sent off in small aircraft from a specially prepared airstrip outside of town.[41] The deliberations made headlines in newspapers throughout America, as well as in Great Britain, Europe, and Japan. "Assuredly no other court proceeding in recorded history," the *Chattanooga News* would conclude, "has been so thoroughly 'covered' from a publicity point of view."[42]

Seeking Public Support

To attract the attention of the media is one thing; to use it is another. To be successful, movements must make use of the media to transform awareness into support. They do this by reaching out, both to the general public of interested but ill-informed onlookers and to more specific publics, bystander groups that seem most likely to be swayed by the right choice of arguments and tactics. In the civil rights movement, for example, King and the SCLC became adept at staging highly publicized protests to build sympathy for the movement, especially among northern liberals in the Democratic Party who would eventually ensure the electoral support needed to put pressure on Congress and the president. The challenge, as described by McAdam, is to keep the issue squarely before the general public while simultaneously building support among an expanding set of bystander groups.[43]

In the 1920s, before television or instant Internet connections, the task of crafting campaigns that could reach broad publics was at best daunting. For Bryan and his colleagues it was doubly difficult, since much of the mainstream media was unsympathetic to them. Antievolutionists were able to make their case in the conservative church papers, and they relied heavily on the fundamentalist press, which churned out a steady supply of books, pamphlets, and tracts. When it came to the popular press, however, especially the major metropolitan newspapers, their case appeared only rarely, often as a counterweight to the pro-evolution columns provided by Watson Davis and his Science Service news bureau. Although T. T. Martin, W. B. Riley, and others sent out frequent press releases, few papers took the space to run them. Even in Tennessee, only the *Memphis Commercial Appeal* offered consistent support. "To get the real facts of this case before the people, especially in the north, is going to be a difficult task," wrote Ira Hicks, a New Jersey fundamentalist pastor, to his brother, Dayton prosecutor Sue K. Hicks.[44]

To get their story out, antievolutionists turned to Bryan. Throughout late May and June he was on the road speaking to audiences of thousands, sometimes from train platforms in a style reminiscent of his barnstorming presidential campaigns. By early July, having crisscrossed the eastern part of the country a half-dozen times, he had become convinced that his message was getting through. "The wide publicity given evolution and religion," he told the Miami Kiwanis Club, "is focusing the attention of the world on a subject the people did not fully understand."[45] Yet Bryan faced obstacles in reaching the public, for while he was capable of creating headlines, he had few real friends in the press, being unpopular with most editors and writers, especially those from the eastern magazines and big-city newspapers.[46] Some of these could not contain their scorn. To Heywood Broun of the New York World, Bryan was "the Great Vulgarian."[47] Dudley Nichols, who wrote editorials for the World, called him "the apostle of the morons" and "The Great Realtor of Miami."[48] Then there was Mencken, who turned Bryan bashing into a spectator sport, describing him as a "buffoon," an "old buzzard," and a "poor clown," and depicting him to the delight of his Baltimore readers as "a tinpot pope in the coca-cola belt and a brother to the forlorn pastors who belabor half-wits in the galvanized iron tabernacles behind the railroad yards."[49] For Bryan—as well as for Darrow—the biggest challenge was to have the case taken seriously by a press that seemed determined to treat it as an opportunity to run monkey cartoons and tell monkey jokes. In pretrial speeches Bryan repeatedly assured his audiences of the importance of the antievolution issue, promising that the prosecution of Scopes would be carried out with full seriousness. "The newspapers that have treated the Tennessee law as a joke," he warned, "will find it no joking matter."[50]

On arriving in Dayton, Bryan began building public support, starting where he was most effective, at the grass roots. Although his skill as a speaker was legendary, his career as a political campaigner, to say nothing of his success on the summer Chautauqua circuit, had been based every bit as much on his ability to connect to people one by one, often thousands of them in a single week. In Dayton, he immediately put his powers of personal persuasion to work. Arriving from Miami three days before the trial was scheduled to begin, Bryan alighted from the Royal Palm Limited to the cheers of about 250 citizens, many of them members of welcoming committees organized by local churches. Wearing a large white tropical pith helmet, he plunged into the crowd, shaking hands and receiving gifts (among them a bag of radishes, to which he was known to be partial) before climbing into an automobile at the head of a parade that took him through town to the home where he was staying. Over the next few days, he courted the citizens of Dayton tirelessly, greeting admiring onlookers as he strolled or motored slowly through town, conferring with public officials and members of the school board, and addressing audiences on numerous occasions: at a banquet of the Progressive Club, in a mountaintop speech at the Morgan Springs Hotel outside of town, in sermons at churches, and in impromptu talks to thousands on the courthouse lawn. Daytonites responded warmly: "Mr. Bryan's manner with these people is most persuasive," reported the *New York Times*. "His voice seems to reach out and caress them with its gentle cadences; his arms stretch out over them as if they were those closest to his heart and he would gather them."[51] Defense lawyers later complained that Bryan was proceeding unfairly in attempting to influence the views of the community toward the case. Darrow himself took to the streets during breaks in the trial to undo the damage, winning considerable praise from the citizenry for his folksy congeniality.[52] But it was Bryan who captured the local constituency. Said Frank Kent, Mencken's colleague at the *Baltimore Sun*: "It is extraordinary how completely he fits into the town. Of all the lawyers, of all the visitors, he is the one man thoroughly at home. These are his people; he is their champion. They are his; he is theirs. The overwhelming sentiment is with him."[53]

While wooing Dayton, Bryan was also solidifying the support of Tennesseans statewide. As early as the first week of June, in a statement to the press made after meeting with lawyers at Nashville, he framed the case as a contest between Tennessee and its critics. Asserting that the issue was not free speech, but the constitutionality of state law, he scored the "Northern papers," especially the "New York newspapers," for waging an "attack on Tennessee law."[54] Tennessee had received considerable criticism in the weeks following the passage of the antievolution law, and state leaders had begun to answer back. "Tennessee needs no sympathy nor commiseration," Governor Austin Peay had written to Dayton school superintendent Walter White. "I have profound contempt for those who are throwing slurs at Tennessee for having this law."[55] Although not a Tennessean himself (a point that Darrow went out of his way to make during the trial), Bryan's strong ties to the state, combined with his long-standing suspicion of eastern elites and the northern big-city press, allowed him to cast himself as a defender of the state's honor. In his address to the Progressive Club, he lavished praise on the state, assuring his audience that he would "put the character of the people of Tennessee against that of the people of any state in the country."[56] Almost as soon as the trial commenced, he issued a press release criticizing defense plans to bring in experts on evolution from the North, stating that "no specialists from the outside are required to inform the parents of Tennessee as to what is harmful."[57] As the case proceeded, Bryan's colleagues on the prosecution team took up the torch, with local attorney Ben McKenzie pointedly referring to members of the defense as "foreigners" and "visitors" from Chicago and New York.[58] (Mencken added fuel to the fire with his famous reports, many of which were quoted or reprinted in full in Tennessee newspapers, in which he described Daytonites and their fellow Tennesseans as "hill billies," "peasants," and "yo-kels.")[59] Even before the trial would come to a close, Bryan was on the road to other towns in Tennessee, denouncing the defense as "those who have come from another state to speak of you as bigots."[60] For his part, he concluded, comparing himself to Christ standing before Pilate, "I esteem it a great privilege to come down to Tennessee and defend the rights of her people."[61]

In reaching out for support, Bryan also sought to expand his Christian constituency. The task was by no means as simple as it seemed, for some of the strongest critics of antievolutionism were liberal and modernist church leaders. Indeed, the trial was certain to provide a platform for these critics, since the defense had announced plans to bring a collection of theologians and scientists to Dayton to testify on the compatibility between Christianity and evolution. In a move to preempt their testimony, Bryan announced on the day of his arrival that the trial would pit Christianity against evolution in "a duel to the death." Anything that attacked the Bible attacked revealed religion, he argued, casting the conflict in apocalyptical terms as an Armageddon-like battle between faith and unbelief. "If evolution wins," he asserted at the Progressive Club banquet, "Christianity goes—not suddenly, of course, but gradually, for the two cannot stand together. They are as antagonistic as light and darkness; as antagonistic as good and evil." The statement was denounced by the defense team and caused consternation among those prosecution lawyers who were trying to confine the case to the constitutionality of the Tennessee law. But it made headlines across the country ("DUEL TO THE DEATH!") and set the stage for the coming confrontation. At Dayton, Bryan proclaimed, Christians "will fight evolution as their only great foe."[62]

He continued to emphasize this theme throughout the trial. On the first Sunday, after delivering the morning sermon at Dayton's Southern Methodist Church (with the presiding judge John T. Raulston and his family seated prominently in the front pew), he released a statement to the press deriding the defense strategy of relying on "so-called theistic evolutionists:"

They know that evolution has led many into atheism, like Nietzsche, for instance, but they will not call any atheists. They know that evolution has led a still greater number into agnosticism, like Darwin, for instance, but they will not call any agnostics. They will only call those who still cling to religion and try to harmonize evolution with it. They will thus present a very one-sided view of evolution and its results. A half truth is sometimes worse than a lie; and evolution as they want to represent it is less than half truth.[63]

In the middle of the week, Bryan told an interviewer that the Scopes case had uncovered "a concerted attack upon revealed religion" by "atheists, agnostics and unbelievers, aided by so-called theological evolutionists."[64] By the following weekend he was talking in terms of full-blown treachery, claiming in a press release that the case had revealed nothing less than a "conspiracy against Bible Christianity."[65] At every opportunity, he cast the trial as a conflict between Christianity and its enemies, calling upon all true Christians to stand at his side. "The Christian religion is revealed religion," he told an audience as the trial was coming to a close. "It is the Bible they are attacking."[66]

In presenting himself as a champion of Christianity, Bryan had plenty of help. The trial was in session over two Sundays, and on each of them ministers across the country took to their pulpits to comment on its meaning. Their sermons demonstrated a broad range of opinions, so much so that the Reverend Charles H. Beale, addressing a Massachusetts congregation that included the vacationing President Calvin Coolidge, could deride "the pitiful drama exemplifying the division among Christians."[67] But in church after church, from the smallest towns to the largest cities, conservative preachers marched to their pulpits to compare Bryan to Christ, depict Darrow as the devil, and portray the trial as a battle between good and evil. In his morning sermon at New York's Calvary Baptist, for example, John Roach Straton delivered a tribute to Bryan's sincerity and his service to the nation, describing him as "a true prophet of God." As for Darrow, who earlier in the week had created a sensation when he angrily objected to the practice of opening each session of the trial with a prayer, Straton showed nothing but scorn. Holding up a newspaper photograph taken during opening prayer, he described the Chicago lawyer as the embodiment of evil. "As I looked at these two figures in that picture, Mr. Bryan with his reverence and nobility of face on one side, and Mr. Darrow, with his sardonic sneer on the other, the two seemed to me to be almost as a human expression of Christ and the devil."[68] (The depiction of Darrow as the devil became a popular motif at the time. The previous Wednesday, following Darrow's objections to the courtroom prayers, the *Memphis Commercial Appeal* ran a front-page cartoon labeled "Darrow's Paradise!" in which he was pictured in hell perched on a mountain marked "Anti-Christ," presiding over a bleak set of images labeled "agnosticism," "anni-

DARROW'S PARADISE !

Editorial cartoon (from front page, Memphis Commercial Appeal, 15 July 1925)

hilation," and "spiritual despair.")[69] The trial, Straton concluded, was for the defense lawyers nothing more than an opportunity "to flaunt their agnosticism and sneering unbelief before the world."[70]

Most of all, Bryan sought the support of the American people. Over his thirty-year political career, he had consistently maintained an almost mystical conception of majority rule. Despite defeat in three bids for the presidency, he had come to increasingly identify with this mystical majority and to style himself as the voice of ordinary men and women. In his speech to the Dayton Progressive Club, he had concluded with what many regarded as a call for another constitutional amendment: "Who made the courts?" he asked rhetorically. "The people. Who made the Constitution? The people. The people can change the Constitution and if necessary they can change the decisions of the court."[71] At Morgan Springs, where he spoke to a crowd of common folk from the nearby mountain communities, he had elaborated on the theme of democratic decision making, assuring them that the case at hand would be decided not by educated experts but by the plain people who sat on the jury at Dayton. "According to our principles of government," he explained, "the people are interested in everything and can be trusted to decide every thing."[72] Afterward, amid stout denials that he was advocating a constitutional amendment outlawing the teaching of evolution, he had assured reporters that the issue was not the tyranny of the religious majority, but of the irreligious minority, "a little oligarchy of self-styled intellectuals" who were "attempting to force their views on the people through the public schools."[73] When Dean Henry H. Rusby of Columbia's College of Pharmacy created a stir by suggesting that universities like his own refuse to recognize the academic credentials of students from states that had passed antievolution laws, Bryan took it as an attack by an educational elitist on the less learned majority, whom he described as the "the ninety and nine."[74] Later in the trial he would drive over the mountain to the nearby town of Pikeville to address an open-air meeting, where he cast his remarks as a paean to ordinary people, those whose views were "representative of the best thought of the land."[75] For Bryan, the Scopes trial would be a success to the extent that it brought the issue of evolution before the public. The decision of the court mattered little, he had written to his friend Ed Howe. What mattered was the decision of the people, since "every question has to be settled at last by the public."[76]

To all appearances, Bryan's attempt at building public support was paying off. Throughout his career he had received a steady stream of letters and notes, many of them handwritten, some almost illegible with misspellings and poor grammar, expressing admiration for him and his work. As the time for the trial approached, however, the stream became a flood, as letters and telegrams poured in from every part of the country offering advice and wishing him well. "You are defending God's cause," wrote W. F. Brockman of Janesville, Wisconsin. "By thy direct connection with God Almighty the words which thou shalt use shall be placed in thy mouth by God himself," stated Coloradan C. J. Schnebly. "We want you to know we are praying to God to sustain you," Mrs. G. P. Cannon of Tampa, Florida, assured him. On rare occasions, the messages contained criticism. "This trial is silly and your reputed statement shows you to be either a fool or a faker," wrote Charles S. Wharton, a former Republican congressman from Illinois. But with few such exceptions, the notes were admiring and laudatory, and they came by the scores. Many telegrams were from church groups: "Two thousand men of the Strand Bible Class unanimously endorse your stand"; "In behalf of 15,000 organized Baptist young people . . . we affirm our faith in the whole Bible and pledge to you our sympathy and support"; "Ten thousand members of Angelus Temple with her millions of radio church membership send grateful appreciation." The well-wishers were women as well as men, African Americans as well as whites: "The Negroes of southeast Miss assembled in the 49th annual session of the Gulf Coast Missionary Baptist Association . . . thank God for your uncompromising defense of the Grand Old Book of the Ages." All told, Bryan had tapped a remarkably deep well of public support. "May our brother Bryan fight them evolutionists until hell freezes over," wrote an admiring Happy Gordon Mead from Smackover, Arkansas, "and then give them around [sic] on the ice."[77]

Constraining Opponents

With the attention of the media assured, and having recruited and rallied supporters, movements turn to the matter of curbing the influence of their adversaries. It is a troublesome task, since the ability to check the actions of opponents is always limited, and since clever opponents can devise strategies to counter the constraint. Thus Doug McAdam has shown how SCLC protests were in large part dependent on the response of southern segregationists. He contrasts the success of protests in Birmingham, Alabama, where police led by Commissioner Eugene "Bull" Connor attacked demonstrators with dogs and fire hoses, with their failure in Albany, Georgia, where police chief Laurie Pritchett, aware that such atrocities could backfire, ordered arrests but avoided violence, thereby denying the movement the support of sympathetic onlookers. McAdam argues that activists and their opponents often find themselves engaged in a complex set of actions and reactions, creating strategies and counterstrategies, in which both sides are constantly mindful of how they will be perceived by the public. Put simply, strategic staging is a game that two must play.[78]

The Scopes trial was just this kind of game, in which each side simultaneously sought to limit the options of the other through their tactics inside and outside the courtroom. In fact, the trial was two separate games taking place simultaneously: one about the prosecution of the case, the other about the managing of public perceptions of it. Moreover, the two were to some extent at odds. "I have no doubt about the outcome of the case," Ira Hicks told his brother. "What I fear is that the news papers will color everything to look like a victory for evolution as their sympathy is there."[79]

The prosecution seemed to have a strategy. Admittedly, the group was an unlikely assortment of allies. Ably led by the sensible and soft-spoken A. T. "Tom" Stewart, attorney general for the circuit that covered eastern Tennessee, the bulk of the team consisted of local lawyers (the folksy father-son duo of Ben G. and Gordon McKenzie, brothers Herbert and Sue Hicks, and recent law school graduate Wallace Haggard). Bryan had argued for a more cosmopolitan group, suggesting that the prosecution be expanded to include corporate lawyer Samuel Untermyer, of New York, a close friend and president of the American Jewish Congress, and Senator Thomas J. Walsh, of Montana, a Roman Catholic. When the local attorneys bridled at asking these two, contending that the presence of a Jew and a Catholic as part of the prosecution might not play well with a Tennessee jury, Bryan had to settle for bringing along his son William Jennings Bryan Jr., a shy and self-effacing man who practiced civil law in Los Angeles. Nevertheless, at least at the beginning everyone seemed to be on the same page. Chief prosecutor Tom Stewart was determined to seek a speedy trial, arguing that the only legal issue was the right of the Tennessee legislature to control the curriculum of the state's public schools. More than anything else, Stewart wanted to avoid turning the trial into a debate on evolution, since the defense had already announced an expansive and multisided strategy that would challenge the law's constitutionality not only because of the limits it placed on personal liberty, but also because of its unreasonable assumption that evolutionary science was by definition in conflict with Christian faith. The Dayton lawyers, unprepared to argue constitutional points, let alone philosophical or scientific ones, appeared to agree. Even Bryan seemed acquiescent: "The real issue in the Scopes case," he observed in late May, in his first statement to the press after entering the case, "is not the teaching of evolution, but who shall control our schools and determine what shall be taught."[80]

Yet Bryan had other plans as well. Never one to avoid a fight, let alone be long out of the limelight, he clearly intended to turn the trial into more than an argument over legal niceties. Even as he announced his agreement with Stewart's strategy, he was privately preparing for a much more ambitious prosecution, in which the doctrine of evolution would itself be placed on trial. Following a final planning meeting in Atlanta, he issued no statement but sent word through other sources that he considered the case to be "one in which an assault was being made upon the precepts of Jesus Christ."[81] Although it is uncertain whether Stewart was aware of Bryan's plans, at least one other member of the prosecution team knew of them, describing the strategy in confidential correspondence: "It is part of our plan to keep the defense thinking that we are going to restrict the case to the right of the legislature to control," explained Sue Hicks in a June letter to his brother Ira, "but when the trial comes on we can gain a moral victory by opening out the field to our evidence."[82] Meanwhile, all agreed on a two-track attack in which Stewart would make the case inside the courtroom while Bryan took on evolution outside, in speeches and statements to the press. In effect, the tactic was to argue one case in court and a different one outside, in the court of public opinion. The strategy was complicated and risky, testing the ability of the prosecution to argue both cases at once while maintaining some kind of boundary between them. Nevertheless, with Bryan on the team there seemed to be no other option, since he was determined to take the case to the public. "I have been quoted as saying that I think the decision of this case will be of importance," he told reporters at the opening of the trial. "It is not the decision but the discussion which will follow that I consider important. It will bring the issue before the attention of the world."[83]

The prosecution's first task was to prevent the testimony of expert witnesses. The defense lawyers believed that expert evidence was essential to their case since it allowed them to strike at the heart of the Tennessee statute, contesting its constitutionality by arguing that it was both indefinite and unreasonable. They planned to send to the stand a carefully selected collection of highly reputed scientists and theologians—all of them theistic evolutionists—who would testify that there was no conflict between evolution and the Bible, let alone between evolution and religion.[84] Throughout June, Darrow's team regularly released the names of prominent scientists, including respected horticulturist Luther Burbank, whom it would supposedly call to testify at the trial. Prosecutors were clearly worried and set to work to discredit the experts, while at the same time quietly inviting their own.[85] Bryan bore the brunt of the effort, contacting every sympathetic scientist he knew or had heard of, as well as a long list of fundamentalist preachers to testify about the Bible, but he found few who were willing to go to Dayton. Among the scientists, several informed him that they actually believed in evolution, and another, the combative Alfred McCann, who had ridiculed evolution in his God or Gorilla, blasted Bryan for attempting to use legal means to inhibit the free flow of ideas and assured him that "I disapprove of the entire procedure from beginning to end."[86] As for the preachers, although several responded that they were eager to testify, including W. B. Riley, John Straton, and J. Frank Norris, in the end only T. T. Martin made the trip.[87] One potential witness, the Adventist geologist George McCready Price, wrote from abroad that the best of all experts would be Bryan himself, since "it is not a time to argue about the scientific or unscientific character of the evolution theory, but to show its . . . essentially anti-Christian implications and tendencies. This you are very capable of doing; I do not know of any one more capable."[88] As the list of defense experts grew, and as a deeply disappointed Bryan found himself with none of his own, he became even more determined to keep the defense experts off the stand. "If we can shut out the expert testimony," he told his friend W. B. Marr as the trial date approached, "we will be through in a short time. I have no doubt of our final victory, but don't know how much we will have to go through before we reach the end."[89]

In preventing expert testimony, the prosecution was actually attempting to define the terms of the trial. Specifically, Bryan and his colleagues had concluded that by avoiding the testimony of the academic experts, all of whom were certain to stress their own Christian credentials, they could cast evolution as a doctrine completely at odds with Christianity. In truth, Bryan knew all too well that evolution was not necessarily incompatible with Christian views of creation. Indeed, as he explained to Johns Hopkins professor Howard A. Kelly in late June, he himself believed not only that the days of Genesis may have been of indefinite length, but also that evolution may have taken place throughout them, at least "before man." Nevertheless, he confided to Kelly, to allow such a concession could be strategically catastrophic in the courtroom, since it "furnishes our opponents with an argument which they are quick to use."[90] Besides, the state statute seemed self-evident, defining evolution as "any theory that denies the story of Divine Creation of man as taught in the Bible."[91] All considered, the surest strategy would be the simplest one: to stick to the statute, to assume a creation of seven days, and to portray evolution as unbiblical and therefore unchristian. "All the facts needed for the trial of this case are at hand," he said in a statement to the press, "and can be furnished without any resort to so-called 'expert testimony.' We have the statute which is perfectly clear, we have the textbook which Prof. Scopes used in his teaching, and we have the evidence of what he taught. The defense have Mr. Scopes with his knowledge of science and his passion for scientific truth. What more do they want?"[92]

The second part of the prosecution plan was to try the defense team rather than the defendant. From the beginning, the state took little interest in John Scopes, whose earnest and unassuming personality, along with his almost complete conventionality, made him a popular and sympathetic figure. Besides, it had never been clear to anyone that Scopes had actually taught evolution, and prosecutors worried that if he were put on the stand under oath, he might admit as much, collapsing their case against him and rendering the whole trial pointless.[93] By contrast, they turned their attention to the big-city lawyers who had come to represent him. As if Darrow were not controversial enough, his colleagues at the defense table also made easy targets: Dudley Field Malone was a New York divorce lawyer, as well as an Irish-American Catholic with a feminist wife; Arthur Garfield Hays, another New Yorker, was a corporate attorney of Jewish heritage with left-leaning political sympathies; and John Randolph Neal, the team's principal local representative, was an eccentric law professor who claimed to have been dismissed from the University of Tennessee for protesting the firing of four faculty members who had taught evolution.[94] The prosecutors avoided attacking the rumpled Neal, presumably out of deference to his Tennessee ties ("the home folk insist that he has just fallen into bad company," wrote *Chattanooga Times* correspondent Robert T. Small, "and will be all right when the contaminators get away"). But the cosmopolitan credentials of the others left them fair game. "The prosecution for days has been whaling the life out of Darrow, Malone, and Hays," Small went on, "their views, their beliefs, their modes of life, the things they have done and the things they have left undone, until all the countryside is convinced there is no health in the trio and that they ought to be placed in the hoosegow for life for the good of the public morals and religions."[95]

From the first, the lawyers for the state had viewed Darrow as their principal target. After the third morning in court, when he protested the opening prayer, he became for all practical purposes their only target. With popular indignation rising both in Dayton and beyond, the prosecution saw its advantage and Tom Stewart took the lead in disparaging "the agnostic counsel for the defense."[96] But it was Bryan who pursued this line of attack, his onslaughts in the press mounting and becoming more personal; by the end of the first full week of the trial he was describing Darrow, the "avowed agnostic," as an enemy to "all those who believe in Orthodox Christianity"[97]

But maligning attorneys was a game that both sides could play, and Bryan made an enticing target, especially since for the first several days he sat silently, having agreed to allow others to present the technical aspects of the state's case. Day after day Darrow and his colleagues set their sights on him, blaming him for the antievolution law, criticizing his brand of Christianity, even quoting his earlier writings on religious liberty. On Wednesday, the fourth day in court, when Stewart objected to the barrage of criticism, Bryan overrode him, saying that he needed no protection. But by the next day an agitated Bryan had apparently had enough. When he finally rose to speak, he began by complaining that the defense was trying to make him the defendant by portraying him as the "arch-conspirator" behind the antievolution law as well as the leader of the forces of "ignorance and bigotry."[98] Attempting to turn attention back to Darrow, he proceeded to launch an awkward and ultimately counterproductive attack on his character. Bryan quoted from the transcript of the infamous Leopold-Loeb trial, in which Darrow had successfully defended two child murderers, only to be interrupted and corrected by an offended Darrow and lectured at length by an incensed Malone. But the defense would save its sharpest cut until Friday, at the end of an exhausting week, when Judge Raulston finally announced his decision to bar all expert testimony. Defeated in the most critical move of the case, Darrow lashed out at Bryan in a blistering statement to the press in which he derided him for his unwillingness to allow his opinions to be tested in open court against the testimony of scientists and theologians. Unable to attract reputable witnesses of his own, Bryan had "fled from the issue," he explained, "and sought the protection of technicalities." As Bryan weakly defended the decision of the judge, Darrow concluded with a devastating thrust: "Bryan who blew loud trumpet calls for a 'battle to the death,' has fled from the field, his forces disorganized and his pretentions exposed."[99]

The third main point of the prosecution strategy was to cast its case as a defense of revealed religion. For his part, Bryan was deeply disquieted by his role as prosecutor. As he saw it, his entire career had been spent defending democratic principles and the common people. Moreover, he had only the most solicitous feelings toward the actual defendant, the mild-mannered Scopes.[100] Thus he was strongly predisposed to present himself not as prosecuting anyone at all, but as defending Christianity against its evolutionist enemies. So it was that when Bryan addressed the court on Thursday afternoon, in what would be his only long speech at the trial, he immediately turned the tables, casting the real issue of the case as a conflict between religion and science (or "religion and irreligion," as he put it). Evolution, he insisted, denied the transcendent truths of the Atonement, the Resurrection, and the Virgin Birth; the entire purpose of the defense was to discredit the Bible and the one true faith. "The Bible is the Word of God," he thundered; "the Bible is the only expression of man's hope for salvation. The Bible, the record of the Son of God, the Savior of the world, born of the virgin Mary, crucified and risen again. That Bible is not going to be driven out of this court by experts." As for the other side, he concluded to a great round of applause, its intention all along had been "to banish from the hearts of the people the Word of God as revealed." When Dudley Field Malone responded by contrasting the open scientific mind to the closed theological one, ending his speech with a ringing plea for academic freedom that brought cheers from the crowd and a standing ovation from the press, the crux of the case became clear. Even the cautious Stewart, apparently carried away by the day's florid oratory, concluded that the trial had come down to "a battle between religion and science." Stretching his arms heavenward, he made it clear to everyone "that I am on the side of religion."[101]

The prosecution's trump card was Bryan himself. The plan was to hold him back until the end, building suspense until the final summations, when he could at last unleash his legendary skill as a public speaker in what was certain to be a show-stopping closing argument to the jury. Everyone at the trial knew it was coming and seemed to be awaiting it expectantly. The defense, however, had a plan of its own. Well aware of Bryan's persuasive powers, it had devised a strategy to preempt any final performance by calling him to the stand as an expert on the Bible. Darrow knew that he could hobble Bryan's soaring oratory by insisting that he limit himself to answering questions. Moreover, the canny courtroom lawyer knew how to interrogate witnesses, a skill he had honed through decades of practice as a defense attorney. As to what he would ask, Darrow was ready. Two years earlier, addressing Bryan in a public letter appearing in the *Chicago Tribune*, he had posed a long list of questions concerning the Bible's literal truth. ("Is the account of the creation of the earth and all life in Genesis literally true. . . ? Was the earth made in six literal days. . . ? Was Eve literally made from the rib of Adam?")[102] Although Bryan had never responded, Darrow still had his questions. Over the weekend he had prepared for the coming interrogation, practicing with Harvard geologist Kirtley Mather, who played the role of Bryan. By Sunday, reporters had begun to suspect that something was up. "Rumors go about that the defense is preparing to spring a coup d'etat," wrote the *Nashville Banner*'s Ralph Perry.[103]

Of course, Bryan still had to agree to take the stand. On Monday, the seventh day of the trial, attempting to escape the stifling heat inside the courthouse and fearing that the second-story courtroom might collapse from the weight of the crowds that continued to fill the chamber, Judge Raulston convened the afternoon session outside on the courthouse lawn. With the principals seated on an elevated platform and several thousand people looking on, the setting seemed more fitting for an afternoon oration than a courtroom cross-examination. Bryan was in his element. Thus when defense counsel Arthur Hays suddenly called him as an expert witness, he seemed surprisingly acquiescent. Everyone knew that an attorney had no right to examine counsel from the other side. Moreover, the previous Friday all expert testimony had been foreclosed and removed from the record. Nevertheless, Bryan was willing, even eager to testify. Forced to sit for several days in silence, taunted by the defense at every turn, upstaged in his one

*Darrow interrogating Bryan on the side lawn of the courthouse at Dayton, 20 July 1925
(Courtesy Bryan College)*

substantial speech, he had found the trial to be a frustrating experience. For weeks his attempts to introduce his own team of experts had been met with a train of excuses and outright refusals. Besides, after years of speaking and writing on Christian topics, he considered himself as much an expert on the Scriptures as anyone. Additionally, Bryan assumed that by taking the stand he could confront the defense directly, on his own terms, since he had agreed to be questioned only on the condition that he could in turn examine Darrow, Malone, and Hays. ("Not at once?" quipped Darrow). All told, Bryan seemed supremely confident. "These gentlemen have not had much chance," he blithely told the court. "They did not come here to try this case. They came here to try revealed religion. I am here to defend it and they can ask me any questions they please."[104]

What followed would come to be considered the trial's climax. At the time, it appeared distinctly anticlimactic, even boring to the spectators who watched from the lawn. The examination went on for two hours, turning into a desultory debate in which Darrow asked increasingly tedious questions about the size of Jonah's whale and whether Joshua could command the sun to stand still. Afraid of being trapped, Bryan avoided specific responses wherever possible. On occasion the bobbing and weaving became comedic, as in this exchange on the dating of Noah's flood:

Q [Darrow]—You believe the story of the flood to be a literal interpretation?
A [Bryan]—Yes, sir.
Q—When was that flood?
A—I would not attempt to fix the date. The date is fixed, as suggested this morning.
Q—About 4004 B.C.?
A—That has been the estimate of a man that is accepted today. I would not say it is accurate.
Q—That estimate is printed in the Bible?
A—Everyone knows, at least, I think that most of the people know, that was the estimate given.
Q—But what do you think that the Bible, itself, says? Don't you know how it was arrived at?
A—I never made a calculation.
Q—A calculation from what?
A—I could not say.
Q—From the generations of man?
A—I would not want to say that.
Q—What do you think?

A—I do not think about things I don't think about.

Q—Do you think about things you do think about?

A—Well, sometimes.

(*Laughter in the courtyard.*)

Bryan was already in trouble. At a minimum, he had confused Bishop Ussher's date for the creation of the world (4004 B.C.) with the biblically assigned date of Noah's flood (2348 B.C.). But things did not get any better. At least a dozen times the prosecution rose to object, but each time Bryan insisted that the interrogation continue. At one point the combatants wandered off into an apparently pointless argument over the teachings of Buddha and Confucius. But when Darrow returned to the age of the earth, Bryan was cornered. All along, the prosecution strategy had been to argue that the biblical account of creation was self-evident, that the world had been created in seven days. The defense, by contrast, was determined to show that the creation story was open to interpretation, thereby raising questions about both the meaning and the reasonableness of the Tennessee antievolution law. Thus when Bryan admitted that he did not believe that the earth had been created in seven actual, literal, twenty-four–hour days, he seemed to be contradicting himself, while also playing into Darrow's hand:

Q—Would you say that the earth was only 4,000 years old?

A—Oh no; I think it is much older than that.

Q—How much?

A—I couldn't say.

Q—Do you say whether the Bible itself says it is older than that?

A—I don't think the Bible says itself whether it is older or not.

Q—Do you think the earth was made in six days.

A—Not six days of twenty-four hours.

Q—Doesn't it say so?

A—No, sir.

Aware of what was happening, Bryan tried to recast the issue, arguing that the real question was the authority of the Bible, not its literal meaning. The purpose of the defense's examination, he blustered, was "to cast ridicule on everybody who believes in the Bible." ("We have the purpose," Darrow shot back, "of preventing bigots and ignoramuses from controlling the education of the United States and you know it, and that is all.") Forging on, Bryan attempted to turn the issue back on Darrow by casting him as an enemy of Christianity. "I am simply trying to protect the word of God against the greatest atheist or agnostic in the United States," he went on, eliciting prolonged applause from the spectators. "I want the papers to know that I am not afraid to get on the stand in front of him and let him do his worst. I want the world to know." By this time Darrow had realized his advantage and was relentless in adding to it. For several minutes more he pressed on, grilling Bryan with questions about Adam's rib and Cain's wife. With both men apparently approaching exhaustion, the examination soon devolved into an exchange of insults. "The only purpose Mr. Darrow has is to slur at the Bible," Bryan sputtered before Raulston abruptly adjourned court for the day. "I object to your statement," replied Darrow. "I am exempting [sic] you on your fool ideas that no intelligent Christian on earth believes."[105]

At the end of the day, few of those who had been there were willing to describe the confrontation as decisive. Predictably, both sides insisted that the interrogation had worked to their advantage. "Mr. Bryan made a monkey out of Mr. Darrow, said the fundamentalists who were present," reported the *Chattanooga Times* in its evening edition. "Mr. Darrow made a monkey out of Mr. Bryan, say the evolutionists who were present. Perhaps a ringside decision would call it a draw."[106] Most historians have characterized Bryan's testimony as a serious miscalculation, emphasizing the damage done to his reputation among fundamentalists by his admission that he did not believe in a seven-day creation. Ron Numbers has recently confounded these claims, arguing that few fundamentalists expressed either surprise or disappointment with Bryan's views. Contemporary news reports suggest that Numbers is right. All that mattered to Bryan's followers, an insightful Philip Kinsley wrote that evening, was that he had placed Darrow in the untenable position of opposing the Bible. "They number millions and they will applaud him in this struggle," wrote Kinsley. "He will be a brave figure to them after today. He emerged as a hero."[107] Ultimately, however, the most important fact of that fateful afternoon would be Bryan's treatment by Darrow. In attempting to constrain opponents, there is always a danger of going too far, as constraint can backfire into public sympathy for one's foes. Although Bryan had hardly intended it, the grilling he took on the stand— Darrow's tenaciousness, Bryan's own defensiveness and uncertainty—had made him a more sympathetic figure to many. "You felt the cruelty of it," wrote Chattanooga's Dr. W. S. Keese, who was himself at best ambivalent about Bryan. "The hearts of many of us ache—they almost bleed."[108]

Influencing Public Policy

In the end, the success of strategic staging must be judged by its ability to influence public policy. For any movement, the final goal must be to inspire authorities to take action, reshaping policies and rewriting laws. This can be the most difficult part of the staging process. Although public officials can occasionally move swiftly in implementing policies, much of the time the process is painfully slow, and more often than not activists end up with little to show for their efforts. As King and the SCLC discovered, it took the atrocities of Birmingham and Selma, beamed nightly by television into the nation's living rooms, to evoke the public outcry that led to the passage of the Civil Rights Act of 1964 and the Voting Rights Act of 1965. After that time, as the civil rights movement proceeded to address more complex forms of racism in the North, it became increasingly divided, while previously supportive public officials, distracted by other policy concerns, eventually lost interest in the issue. The lesson is that activists must continue to make their case, sustaining the pressure on policy makers, or see their goal slip beyond their grasp.[109]

With the Scopes trial coming to a close, antievolutionists found themselves in the same position, facing the challenge of transforming the trial into a springboard for further political action. The end of the trial, said John Roach Straton, would be the beginning of the next phase of the antievolution movement, with bills being introduced into legislatures across the country. Speaking to reporters in New York City, he confidently predicted that "the southern states would be first to put such laws on their statute books; that the western states would follow, and that the movement would eventually reach the north and east."[110]

On Tuesday morning, the eighth day, the trial came suddenly to a close. With court reconvened inside because of a welcome rain, Judge Raulston put an end to the confrontation between Bryan and Darrow, declaring that Darrow's interrogation had contributed nothing substantive to the case and ordering it expunged from the record. The defense, already planning its appeal to a higher court (and still determined to prevent Bryan from taking the floor for a final summation), at once threw in the towel, asking that the jury be instructed to convict the defendant. It took the twelve Tennessee jurors exactly nine minutes to declare Scopes guilty, the only point of contention coming when Raulston himself imposed the minimum $100 fine, in keeping with local practice, instead of allowing the jury to set the penalty. Following a short statement by Scopes, in which he called the antievolution law unjust and promised to continue fighting it, there were speeches by the attorneys and representatives of the press thanking the court and the Dayton community. Predictably, Bryan's address ran longer than the others. Already at work interpreting the meaning of the trial, he used his final statement to encourage antievolutionists to continue their efforts. In itself, he told the court, the case of the small-town schoolteacher meant little. But it illustrated how people could be drawn into prominence by attaching themselves to a great cause, since "causes stir the world." The importance of the trial was not in the individuals involved, but in the issue it raised. "Human beings are mighty small, your honor," he continued, becoming more eloquent as he spoke. "We are apt to magnify the personal element and we sometimes become inflated with our importance, but the world little cares for man as an individual. He is born, he works, he dies, but causes go on forever, and we who participated in this case may congratulate ourselves that we have attached ourselves to a mighty issue." Because of the trial, he observed, the conflict between biblical creation and evolution would be discussed, debated, and eventually decided. In the end, he assured the court, "the people will determine this issue."[111]

No sooner had the trial ended than antievolutionists were declaring victory. In truth, the outcome had been a foregone conclusion, and all concerned considered the case to be little more than a preliminary hearing in preparation for appeals to higher courts. Yet with Bryan taking the lead, antievolutionists proclaimed the outcome of the trial as a significant triumph, as well as a turning point for their cause. Within hours of Judge Raulston's dismissal, Bryan had issued a statement in which he declared that his only purpose in Dayton had been to counter "an attack upon the authority of the Bible" that was "organized, deliberate and malignant, and had only to be uncovered to be understood."[112] Appearing to still be arguing the case, and reminding the world that he had been promised the opportunity to cross-examine Hays, Malone, and Darrow, he directed a series of nine questions to the defense, quizzing them on their beliefs in God, Christ, and immortality.[113] Darrow was singled out for special scorn: he had "slurred the Bible, insulted the court, and shown his contempt for everything Christian and everybody identified with Christianity."[114] By the next day Bryan had begun to talk about his own performance on the stand. Admitting for the first time that his answers could have been better, he told reporters on Wednesday evening that Darrow had taken advantage of his lack of technical knowledge in such scientific specialties as paleontology, archaeology, and philology. Clearly smarting from Darrow's insults, he found himself defending his own intelligence, dusting off his college degrees and pointing out that his life had been spent in the study of society and politics rather than science. "In all my varied experience before intelligent people in many lands as well as in every state in the Union, I was never called 'ignorant' or an 'ignoramus,' so far as I know, by any one except an evolutionist," he declared.[115] Above all, Bryan prepared his closing statement, never delivered in the abbreviated trial, to be published in the newspapers and delivered as a stump speech to audiences all over the country. "The unexpected termination of the trial," he told reporters on Friday evening, "while a surprise, was very gratifying to me because it gave me a chance to publish the speech as I prepared it without interruption and without having to make extemporaneous replies to preceding speeches."[116] The statement, he would later say, would be his "supreme effort."[117]

Over the weekend Bryan continued to declare victory. On Saturday he crossed the mountain again to speak in Tom Stewart's hometown of Winchester, Tennessee, where a record crowd of six thousand treated him like a conquering hero, interrupting him repeatedly with applause and cheers. Describing the trial as a kind of exposé, he said that at Dayton the evolutionists' attacks against him, long made in the dark, had been finally brought to light. In closing, Bryan called on the crowd to join him in a "crusade for the enlightenment of the people."[118] Critics began to issue warnings about his intentions. Robert Small, writing for the *Chattanooga Times*, reported on the general opinion that Bryan would try to write fundamentalism into the platform at the next Democratic National Convention.[119] Doris Stevens, the feminist writer and wife of Dudley Field Malone, wrote from Dayton of her fears that Bryan would use the issue of evolution to solidify a political base among conservative Christians in the South and West, turning his next political campaign into a "gigantic national revival."[120] The editors of the *New Republic* went so far as to warn that if Bryan and his fundamentalist followers could make religion the central issue in the next election, they might "succeed in breaking party lines and securing a majority of the popular vote in a large number of states."[121] Furthermore, Bryan reportedly was drawing up plans for new anti-evolution campaigns and preparing to take them into seven states over the next two years.[122] According to observers he seemed energetic and enthusiastic, "in the best of health and spirits," as one report described him, the trial having "left little mark upon him."[123] His supporters were encouraged as well. "As a result of the Scopes trial under your splendid leadership," wealthy Florida fundamentalist George F. Washburn wrote to Bryan, "I believe that Legislative bills will be introduced in the Legislatures of many states."[124] According to another admirer: "The outcome of the Dayton case makes you the Christian leader of the world."[125] Returning by train from Winchester to Dayton, Bryan spoke to crowds at each stop along the way, addressing an estimated fifty thousand people in scenes that recalled his 1896 campaign. The conviction of Scopes, the aging warrior assured the cheering throngs, had been "a great victory for the cause of Christianity, and a staggering blow for the forces of darkness."[126]

On Sunday, after attending church, Bryan enjoyed a leisurely lunch with his wife, made a few telephone calls, and stretched out to take a nap before another evening speech. He never awoke, dying peacefully in his sleep. His death was attributed to apoplexy compounded by cerebral hemorrhage, but its underlying cause was Bryan's diabetes mellitus, which he had struggled unsuccessfully to control for years.[127] Coming five days after the close of the trial, his passing was immediately seen as its product, as friends and supporters speculated—entirely without evidence—that he must have suffered not only from the heat and fatigue, but also from the psychological beating he had taken on the stand. "For days he sat under a terrific bludgeoning by Darrow and the defense," according to one report, which totally misrepresented the facts; then came the "duel with Darrow, and at least to many who watched it, the blow that brought his death."[128] Others further embellished the confrontation. Writing in *Outlook* shortly after the trial, Bryan's old friend George F. Milton called it "a thing of immense cruelty." The humiliation, he observed, had "cut Bryan to the quick." Even four days after the interrogation, Milton reported, when they had talked shortly before his death, Bryan had been "quivering with hurt at the epithets which had been applied to him. He was a crushed and broken man."[129] The fact that other reports had described Bryan as appearing fit and optimistic after Darrow's examination, that he had been energetic and upbeat in his stump speeches over the ensuing weekend, and that even that Sunday at lunch—hours before his death—he had told his wife he had never felt better, could not counter the influence of this interpretation of events. Within a week, reported the *Independent*, a "legend" had already been created, of "Darrow the cruel, godless inquisitor" and "Bryan the martyr."[130]

Others described the outcome at Dayton in very different terms. Throughout the post-trial period, the members of the defense team remained upbeat, assuring the press that they were happy with the verdict since it allowed them to appeal the case to higher courts. Although none claimed victory, the irrepressible Malone, back in New York City, did describe the verdict in an extemporaneous speech at the Ziegfeld Follies as a "victorious defeat."[131] While less effusive, Darrow also found a silver lining: "Today in Dayton," he said in a statement to the press a few days after the trial, "they are selling more books on evolution than any other kind and the bookshops in Chattanooga and other cities of the state are hardly able to supply the demand for works on evolution. The trial has at least started people to thinking."[132] Even among members of the prosecution there were worries about how the outcome would be perceived by the public. Herbert Hicks told his brother Ira: "We gave the atheist Jew Arthur Garfield Hays, the agnostic Clarence Darrow, and the ostracized Catholic Dudley Field Malone, a sound licking although the papers are prejudiced against us and may not say so."[133] His concern was well founded: unable to decide exactly who had won, many magazine and newspaper writers pronounced the contest a draw. A few suggested that both sides had actually lost, since, as the *San Francisco Bulletin* put it, the trial had "settled nothing and unsettled everything."[134] One thing was clear: the town of Dayton had definitely come out a loser. Although a few businesses and local residents showed a profit, the expected tens of thousands of visitors never appeared, the spectators were mostly farmers from the nearby mountains, and the concessionaires left unhappy, since "no one in the business has made any money."[135] Stung by the biting criticism of the national and international press, Tennesseans mixed resentment with relief that the trial was over, while state officials led by Governor Peay began to look forward impatiently to the final resolution of the case. Returning home from the Michigan sanitorium where he had been treated for a chronic illness, the tired chief executive seemed determined to move beyond the trial. "I haven't had time to talk politics," he told a group of reporters. "Let's settle this evolution business."[136]

The trial over, interest in the Scopes case began to wane. Headline stories that had dominated the news for two weeks disappeared, replaced by minor notices in the back pages. Commenting on the change, cynics began to dismiss the proceedings as nothing more than a publicity stunt, "a chance to sir up 'reader interest' in the jaded, dog-day newspaper public."[137] As the appeal filed by the defense slowly wended its way to the Tennessee Supreme Court, political leaders busied themselves with local and state issues, trying their best to keep the case from having an effect on the next year's election. In May 1926 many of the principals were present to argue the appeal before the state supreme court in Nashville, but the absence of Bryan, combined with the more controlled, dignified setting, assured that the case attracted little public attention. The court seemed determined to take its time, issuing an opinion only in January 1927, eighteen months after the original trial had ended. In its convoluted verdict, which confounded the case even more, the court found the Tennessee antievolution law constitutional but overturned the conviction of Scopes on the grounds that the trial judge rather than the jury had set the fine. Urging the state attorney general to dismiss the prosecution by entering a judgment of nolle prosequi, the court effectively brought an end to what it called "this bizarre case," thereby ensuring "the peace and dignity of the state."[138] Amid protests from both sides, the case was unceremoniously closed. The Literary Digest captured the inconclusive character of the decision: "A victory for both sides, with everybody dissatisfied."[139]

Even so, with the Scopes trial antievolutionists had transformed their movement. In staging the proceeding, they had used the media to attract the attention of onlookers around the world. Depicting events in the most dramatic terms, they had raised the stakes, turning their cause into a conflict between irreconcilable enemies: Bryan and Darrow, creation and evolution, religion and science. In the end, they went away convinced that they had won and that their victory would secure the success of their movement. What they did not seem to realize was that their evolutionist opponents considered themselves to be winners as well and were equally certain that their side would prevail. Thus as Dayton's stage was being dismantled, others were being set for the next phase of protest. The Scopes trial, as J. W. Butler would declare in 1927, had been only "the first skirmish."[140]

7 : Climax

COMPLETING THE CYCLE OF CONTENTION

Clarence Darrow could have been excused for thinking that he had put the Scopes case behind him. But even as the Southern Railway Pullman car that carried the remains of William Jennings Bryan made its way slowly across the Upper South on its way to Washington, D.C., the growing crowds suggested that the followers who had filled the ranks of his last crusade would continue to march on. They came all day and throughout the night, gathering at the country crossroads and lining the tracks for miles to pray, sing hymns, and pay their last sorrowful respects. At Washington's New York Avenue Presbyterian Church, where the body lay in state, more than twenty thousand silent mourners filed past the closed casket. Thousands more, unable to come in person, sent cards, letters, and telegrams conveying their condolences and promising to carry on his work. "Bryan is gone," lamented *The Searchlight* days after his death. "He is in heaven with his Lord, but—THE FIGHT MUST GO ON."[1]

In the wake of the Scopes trial, antievolution activity would not only continue but also come to a climax, culminating in a period of extraordinary activity and organization. Inspired by the trial's outcome, which upheld the constitutionality of Tennessee's Butler bill, activists went on the offensive, introducing more than twenty antievolution statutes over the next several years in state legislatures across the country. Following Bryan's death, new leaders rose to prominence, new organizations were created, and new members were brought into the movement, especially in the South and West. Mississippi soon joined Tennessee in removing the teaching of evolutionary theory from its public schools. Given these inroads, advocates and critics alike forecast additional victories for the movement, while its enemies worked feverishly to slow the pace of its success. As late as 1928, Arkansas voters overwhelmingly approved a statewide initiative to ban the teaching of evolution. Yet as the decade wore on, the movement seemed to lose steam, beset by incompetent leaders, organizational infighting, and declining popular support. Their commitment flagging, activists turned their attention increasingly to other causes, including a revived push to defend Prohibition and a determined effort to defeat Al Smith in the 1928 presidential election. Even before the economic collapse of 1929, contributions were declining. By the end of the decade, things were in a state of shambles, the antievolution movement having fallen from public prominence almost as rapidly as it had risen.

Surprisingly, scholars have shown little interest in how social movements come to their culmination, let alone how they decline and fall. On the whole, most have been more concerned with mobilization than with demobilization, finding the study of how movements begin not only more interesting but also somehow more important than how they end. Moreover, because they have tended to concentrate on individual organizations, and to study them at one place and time, they have often overlooked the broader patterns that define the life of movements over longer periods. Among the few exceptions is Sidney Tarrow, who has argued that political movements change over time according to a cyclical pattern—what he calls a "cycle of contention"—in which they rise and fall, proceeding through a series of stages from mobilization to demobilization. In his *Power in Movement*, Tarrow describes the cycle, suggesting that while its exact configuration and timing may vary, several elements will always be present: (1) the *acceleration and diffusion of conflict* across the social system; (2) the creation of *new frames and repertoires* of protest; (3) the development of *new organizations*, leading to *competition with old ones*; and (4) the *intensification of interaction between activists in the movement and authorities of the state*.[2] These elements contribute to the creation of a cyclical dynamic that can propel movements to the peak of protest and then push them past that peak into decline and eventual collapse. Implicit in the concept is an important and often overlooked insight: that movements rise and fall for many of the same reasons, and as part of the same political process.

The story of the antievolution movement following the Scopes trial is by no means simple or straightforward. Predictably, it has provoked considerable controversy among historians. For years those like Norman Furniss, who hold what can be called the orthodox view, have contended that the Scopes trial represents a high point in the history of the movement, after which it declined in intensity, became increasingly marginalized, and "precipitously lost its strength."[3] More recently revisionists like Ferenc Morton Szasz have described a decidedly different process, arguing that the case had the effect of energizing the movement, inspiring what would become not only its most active but also its most successful period of protest. "Far from representing the culmination of the antievolution crusade in America," writes Szasz, "the Dayton proceedings marked the beginning of the most active period of the controversy."[4] To all appearances, these explanations appear to be mutually exclusive. But when considered in cyclical terms, as components of a single cycle of contention, they may be more complementary than they seem. For in the post-trial period the antievolution movement was coming to culmination, climbing rapidly toward its highest point of protest and then declining precipitously in its wake. Moreover, these seemingly incommensurate trends were taking place for many of the same reasons. To put it simply, antievolutionism reached its peak at this time and also fell from it, and both are part of the same story.

Acceleration and Diffusion of Conflict

According to Tarrow, cycles of contention appear when conflict becomes contagious, increasing in intensity and spreading out from the center to the periphery. As the message of the movement begins to resonate, new activists and groups arise, adopting and extending the agenda of older organizations while also creating the potential for cooperation and the construction of broader coalitions. Action moves from mobilized to less mobilized sectors, the pace of protest picks up, and anything seems possible, as if the world were waiting to be transformed.[5]

For antievolutionists, the Scopes trial served as a catalyst for one such cycle, initiating a period of unprecedented protest. The decision at Dayton was itself an incitement, in that it not only ensured the survival of the Tennessee law, but also made it easier for similar statutes to be passed in other states. Within days of its announcement, antievolutionists had already introduced legislation in Georgia, one of the few states where the legislature was sitting at the time.[6] In several other states, committees formed to frame bills in anticipation of the next legislative session.[7] On Capitol Hill, sympathetic members of Congress let it be known that they would propose federal measures to outlaw the teaching of evolution in the District of Columbia.[8] Congressman William D. Upshaw, a Democrat from Georgia and an old friend of Bryan, went even further, announcing that he was seriously considering introducing a bill in the House of Representatives that would prohibit the teaching of evolution "in any schools in the United States."[9] With popular support for such measures apparently on the rise, critics began to predict the worst. "The success at Dayton has surprised even them," wrote an alarmed *Nation* magazine of the antievolution crusaders, "and the next year will see a flood of bills introduced into the legislatures of every State in the Union."[10]

Even more than the Scopes verdict, however, it was Bryan's death that inspired new heights of protest. For weeks following the funeral, the eulogies continued, as even old enemies saluted his principles and mourned his passing. But for antievolutionists, his death had special significance. Having fallen in the fight against evolution, Bryan had become a martyr to the movement, being elevated by his followers to the status of secular sainthood, what one would call a "new Saint of Fundamentalism."[11] All things considered, he made an excellent martyr. The day after his death, the closing statement that he had been unable to give at the trial was released through the United Press and printed by newspapers throughout the nation. The 15,000-word text, which was essentially a synopsis of many years of speeches, attacked evolution, defended revealed religion, and closed triumphantly with the well-worn lines from a popular hymn (itself a celebration of Christian martyrdom): "Faith of our fathers, living still. . . . We will be true to thee till death!"[12] Delivered now, the message took on a transcendent quality, as if Bryan's spirit was calling to his followers from the grave "to take up the battle in the midst of which the flesh had died."[13] Determined that he should not have died in vain, activists across the country dedicated themselves to continuing the fight of their fallen leader. "Mr. Bryan has fought the good fight, he has kept the faith, he has finished his course," wrote the *Watchman-Examiner*. "May the devotion of those of us who are left be increased, and may our diligence be as constant as his."[14] Everywhere antievolutionists set to work with renewed purpose. As one British observer put it, an "almost fanatical faith has been set ablaze by the dramatic death of Mr. Bryan."[15]

At the same time, Bryan's death had the immediate effect of leaving the movement leaderless. Although he never held an official position, and despite the fact that his own views were considerably less doctrinaire than many of his fundamentalist disciples, Bryan had been antievolutionism's symbolic leader. His loss left an enormous vacancy, and realistically one that could never be filled. Nevertheless, self-appointed successors soon began to position themselves to take his place. John Roach Straton was first to announce himself available, the ambitious and media-savvy New Yorker telling reporters that "everywhere I have been I have been urged to take up Mr. Bryan's work."[16] Although still recovering from a serious automobile accident suffered a year earlier, the indefatigable William Bell Riley made it known that he was the most qualified candidate.[17] Others presented their own credentials, such as preacher Paul Rood, of Turlock, California, founder of the Bryan Bible League; Rood claimed to have had a vision from God naming him Bryan's successor.[18] A more serious contender was George Washburn, the Boston businessman who had made a fortune investing in Florida apartments, hotels, and real estate. Describing himself as divinely commissioned to succeed his old friend Bryan, he stepped forward in the fall of 1925 to create the Bible Crusaders of America, underwriting the organization with a pledge of $200,000, establishing a national newspaper called the *Crusaders' Champion*, and making plans to recruit eighty million foot soldiers for the antievolution cause.[19] Yet for all the claims of the would-be successors, none began to approach Bryan's personal stature or public visibility. Riley observed: "Our judgment is that it will take a number of us, and at our best, to fill the place vacated by the fall of this magnificent thinker and leader." Bryan, he concluded with some understatement, had been a leader "greater than any organization or any board."[20]

With new leaders came new organizations. From its earliest days, antievolutionism had been an uneasy alliance of charismatic figures and diverse groups. Bryan had given meaning to the whole, holding the parts together by the power of his reputation and receptive personality. In his absence, established leaders like Straton, Riley, and Kentucky's J. W. Porter reasserted their roles, while newer stars like Rood and Washburn—and even for a brief time the Los Angeles faith healer Aimee Semple McPherson—rose alongside them. Older organizations such as the World's Christian Fundamentals Association (WCFA) continued to claim preeminence, but new ones appeared as well. Washburn's Bible Crusaders was the most ambitious and best organized of these, a small army formed along military lines, with Washburn serving as "Commander General," Straton as "Director General of Discussion," and T. T. Martin, revived by his visit to Dayton, as "Director General of Campaigns."[21] In Kansas, preacher-publicist Gerald B. Winrod established the Defenders of the Christian Faith, known for its squadrons of speakers, the so-called Flying Defenders, which beginning in 1926 conducted hundreds of antievolution meetings in the Midwest.[22] Within a year over 2,500 followers had paid two dollars apiece to join the group, and its newspaper claimed some five thousand subscribers.[23] Also appearing on the scene was the so-called Supreme Kingdom, the creation of Edward Young Clarke, an erstwhile advertising agent at one time associated with the Ku Klux Klan. The Kingdom was a Klan-like organization featuring dukes, earls, and princes, along with elaborate classification schemes to encourage donations and membership benefits that included health and life insurance policies.[24] Meanwhile in Arkansas, an obscure Baptist minister named Ben M. Bogard was establishing the Little Rock–based American Anti-Evolution Association, promising to organize activists in every county of every state, as well as in school districts "clear down to the corners."[25]

In every part of the country state and local antievolution societies appeared almost overnight. Many of these were chapters of larger organizations, created as the most ambitious ones reached out regionally to build new networks: the Metropolitan Evangelist Association in the Northeast, the Bible Crusaders and Supreme Kingdom in the South, Winrod's Defenders in the Midwest, and others, including the Bryan Bible League in the West. With independent groups surfacing as well, organizations began to overlap, creating a cacophony of antievolution voices. For example, California was home not only to Rood's Bryan Bible League but also to Harry Rimmer's Research Science Bureau, "Fighting Bob" Shuler's Defenders of Science vs. Speculation, and the short-lived American-False-Science-League-and-Home-Church-State-Protective-Association.[26] Some groups with curious names seemed to have their own specialties, such as the School-bag Gospel League, which fought evolutionary theory by distributing copies of selected books of the Bible to children. Also active in the antievolution movement were allied groups like the National Reform Association, which advocated a constitutional amendment to make the United States a Christian nation.[27] Smaller societies sprang up at the local level, often begun by preachers who had admired or known Bryan. Individual churches also jumped onto the antievolution bandwagon. Commenting on the proliferation of new organizations, a worried H. L. Mencken observed that Bryan's death had "started something that it will not be easy to stop."[28]

What followed was an explosion of antievolution activity. Within state legislatures, antievolution bills were introduced in every part of the country. Over the next five years, from the time of the Scopes trial to the end of the decade, about twenty-four bills would be debated.[29] In 1926 Martin and a squadron of speakers from the Bible Crusaders descended on the Mississippi state capitol, where they announced mass meetings and threatened to take their message to every county in the state. Within days, an antievolution bill had been passed by both houses of the legislature. The American Civil Liberties Union (ACLU) appealed at once to Mississippi teachers and taxpayers to test the constitutionality of the bill in court, but not a single citizen was willing to bring the case.[30] Elsewhere sympathetic candidates announced campaigns for the next legislature. In North Carolina, scores of supporters ran in the spring primaries on platforms promising to reintroduce the Poole antievolution bill—"shelling the woods," as the Greensboro Daily News put it, "on evolution."[31] In the peak year of 1927 alone, eighteen different antievolution statues were introduced in fourteen states.[32] Admittedly, most of these efforts did not succeed. (An extreme case was in Delaware, where a proposed measure to prohibit public schools from teaching that humans evolved from a lower order of animals was referred to the Committee on Fish, Game, and Oysters, where, chuckled the Literary Digest, "it was drowned.")[33] But even when legislators balked, activists were often able to work around them, as they did in Florida where they circumvented the established committee system by introducing concurrent resolutions calling for the investigation of teachers and establishing new committees to recommend textbooks.[34] With every victory, movement leaders predicted others. "Within twelve months," announced a confident William Bell Riley, "every State in the Union will be thoroughly organized." The

Supreme Kingdom's E. Y. Clarke was more specific: "We are laying our plans carefully for the Presidential election two years hence. We will have an organization in every political precinct in the United States by that time. Our financial backers now number about 500 outstanding American citizens in twenty-odd States. The radio will be our most powerful weapon."[35]

Outside of the legislatures, antievolution activity was increasing in other ways as well. From the early 1920s, activists had been busy cultivating the support of sympathetic state executives and their appointees on state administrative boards. As early as 1924, their efforts had begun to pay off when North Carolina's Governor Cameron Morrison, acting through his State Board of Education, had eliminated books that even mentioned evolution from the list of acceptable high school biology texts.[36] A year later, responding to resolutions drafted by fundamentalist clergy, the California State Board of Education had gone on record as favoring the teaching of evolution only "as theory."[37] But in 1926 the antievolution movement scored one of its most significant victories when Governor Miriam "Ma" Ferguson directed the Texas Textbook Commission to remove references to evolution from all high school science books used in the state. Acting through the commission's Subcommittee for the Modification of Textbooks on Biology, state education officials used the state's formidable purchasing power to arrange contracts with national publishers Henry Holt, Macmillan, and others that required changes and deletions in their science textbooks, including the elimination of references to evolutionary theory, the substitution of terms such as "change over time" or "development" for evolution, and the removal of charts and diagrams that showed humans as part of an evolutionary process. Inspired by Ferguson, Louisiana's superintendent of schools took similar action, demanding the removal of six pages on evolution from Hunter's *Civic Biology*, the textbook that Scopes had been convicted for using. The publisher complied willingly; in the 1927 edition there were no charts depicting evolutionary development, ideas about natural selection were identified as scientific suggestions rather than facts, and all explicit references to human evolution had been excised.[38] Anticipating similar problems, other publishers began to advise their own authors to omit all discussion of evolution, and some began to publish two editions of science textbooks, one covering evolution and the other omitting it.[39] Governor Ferguson was exultant: "I'm a Christian mother who believes Jesus Christ died to save humanity," she told her supporters, "and I'm not going to let that kind of rot go into Texas text-books."[40]

Also at this time antievolutionists were attracting growing audiences to the public debates they staged with their evolutionist opponents. From 1922 on, when Riley and Zeno Metcalf had gone toe-to-toe, such debates had become increasingly popular, attracting large audiences and sometimes being broadcast by local radio stations. The Charles Potter–John Roach Straton debates of 1923–24 had made the front page of most of the nation's leading newspapers. But it was after 1925 that debates over evolution became most important to the movement, as antievolution speakers took on scientists, modernist ministers, and sometimes atheists and freethinkers before packed houses more than a hundred times in the last half of the decade.[41] Riley alone debated twenty times against opponents such as Maynard Shipley of the Science League of America, Edward Adams Cantrell of the ACLU, and Charles C. Smith of the American Association for the Advancement of Atheism (AAAA). Debate details were worked out in advance, often requiring extensive negotiations.[42] Although judges sometimes were present, the winner was usually declared by a vote based on the applause of the audience.[43] Riley was defeated only once—in a 1926 debate at the University of Chicago—after which he took pains to see that large numbers of supporters were present each time he went on the stage.[44] Other antievolutionists became debaters as well, including the peripatetic T. T. Martin, who took his show on the road, teaming up with Howell England of the AAAA (England sometimes arrived with a trained monkey named "Genesis" in tow) to stage florid debates before raucous crowds in towns across the South.[45] As the crowds got bigger, they sometimes became more unruly. In North Carolina in 1927, Martin and England were able to complete only two of their scheduled series of debates because of angry local reaction and the Ku Klux Klan's announcement that it opposed allowing atheists to appear in public. The following year in Arkansas, debates between Riley and Charles Smith of the AAAA were suspended after Smith announced that he wanted to convert Arkansans to atheism; Smith was promptly thrown in jail on a minor charge.[46] Bested in a series of California debates with Riley, Shipley warned that antievolutionists were using these events to build a mass movement. "If evolution has had cause to fear the power of Bryan's name and his silver tongue," he told the Los Angeles Herald after one of his defeats, "it has more cause to fear Riley, for he is not only eloquent and magnetic, but he has a genius for leadership."[47]

Finally, there was growing activity at the grass roots. Frustrated by the ponderous pace of state politics, many antievolutionists turned their attention to the local level. There they achieved some of their most significant victories, bringing popular pressure to bear on school boards (including those in Atlanta and Charlotte, North Carolina) and individual school administrators to ban books, censor curricula, and fire educators who advocated the teaching of evolution.[48] In public schools across the country, teachers were forced out or not reappointed because they believed in the theory, or because parents had accused them of

Another Big Debate on Evolution!

Municipal Auditorium Theatre

Oakland

Sunday, June 21, 8 p.m. sharp

For Evolution:
MAYNARD SHIPLEY
President Science League of America

Against Evolution:
REV. W. B. RILEY
Exec. Sec. Christian Fundamentals Assn.

Admission Free

Pass this on to an East Bay Friend

Another Big Debate on Evolution!

Debate handbill, Riley-Shipley debate, 1925
(Rare Book Room, University of North Carolina Library, Chapel Hill)

teaching it. Among those who lost their job was John Scopes's sister Lela, a mathematics teacher in Paducah, Kentucky, who refused to renounce her brother's views on the teaching of evolution.[49] Organizing at the grass roots, activists like the ones in the Florida Purity League ran public advertisement campaigns vowing to rid all libraries of objectionable books and all schools of "dangerous teachers."[50] In some places, parents took matters into their own hands. In one Kansas county they voted to burn *The Book of Knowledge*, bought for classroom use, because it contained a discussion of evolution.[51] When all else failed there were spontaneous demonstrations, usually presided over by local preachers, such as the one in Tennessee where fundamentalist college students burned biology books at the stake, along with "lip sticks, rouge, novels, questionable pictures, jazz music and cigarets [sic]."[52] As the pace of protest picked up, the movement seemed unstoppable. "In another two years," boasted E. Y. Clarke in 1926, "from Maine to California and from the Great Lakes to the Gulf, there will be lighted in this country countless bonfires, devouring those damnable and detestable books on evolution."[53]

New Frames and Repertoires

In Tarrow's cycle of contention, conflict begets innovation, as new actors and groups introduce new ideas and revise old ways of operating. Particularly important in this process is the adoption of new frames to give meaning to the movement and new protest repertoires to carry them out. Tarrow suggests that while frames and repertoires are constantly being created, tested, and refined, the process accelerates significantly as the cycle approaches its peak.[54]

So it was that after 1925, as protests intensified, antievolutionists began to define evolution in broader and more politically potent ways. Especially for fundamentalists in the movement, evolution was always one of many fronts in a larger campaign against modernism in the churches and liberalism and socialism in the political world. As early as August 1925, a bitter Curtis Lee Laws complained in the pages of his *Watchman-Examiner* that by concentrating so closely on the teaching of evolution in the schools, fundamentalism had been distracted from its bigger and more critical task of reforming American religion.[55] Billy Sunday soon seconded the thought, declaring in his inimitable way that evolutionary theory—"this evolution hokum"—was only one of many evils confronting the country, including "this gland bunk, this protoplasm chop suey, this ice water religion, this mental-disease crime stuff, this mortal-thought-instead-of-sin blah."[56] Kentucky fundamentalist Andrew Johnson saw the solution to such problems in revival religion, arguing that although combating evolutionary theory was important, it was "absolutely secondary to the main line work of intense, soul-saving evangelism."[57] Others favored different political strategies, proposing statutes to make Bible reading compulsory in the public schools or to prevent atheists and agnostics from becoming teachers. (In 1926 no fewer than eleven states made Bible reading compulsory in their public schools.)[58] The issue of evolution did not decline in importance, but many activists began to recast their struggle as a more ambitious attack, not only on evolutionists, but also on what one group of Mississippi state legislators called "infidels, agnostics, modernists, and all the mongrel forces that tend to destroy virtue, truth, and the institutions that have held together and promoted the welfare of the human race."[59]

In expanding the movement, activists sought to redefine its regional identity. As antievolutionism spread, it followed a classic course of diffusion from center to periphery, moving from the cities of the North to the rural areas of the South and West. The Scopes trial had contributed to the change, and Mencken and other northern newspaper writers, drawing heavily on the crudest southern stereotypes, persisted in describing antievolutionism as a southern phenomenon.[60] While some southerners expressed concern that the continuing debate over evolution could only bring derision on their region, others were defiant, casting themselves increasingly as defenders of the South and its conservative cultural values. The Scopes trial, wrote the *Manufacturers' Record*, a southern business weekly, "will ultimately prove to be an advertisement of immeasurable value to the South":

> There are millions of people in other parts of the United States who do not want to raise their children in an atmosphere of agnosticism and atheism . . ., where the alien foreign element is so dominant, and who, having learned as a result of this trial that there is a section in this country where religion pure and undefiled still holds sway, will turn their eyes longingly to that land of Promise, hoping that in the South they may be able to have their children raised in an atmosphere of Christianity rather than an atmosphere of anti-Christianity.

Far from an embarrassment, the *Manufacturers' Record* concluded, the trial would actually work to the advantage of the region, standing as "one of the South's supremest advertisements, and an advertisement which will do boundless good."[61] Quoting the article approvingly, Bishop Warren A. Candler argued in Methodist publications that the publicity surrounding the trial would bring "devout men and women" to the South, where they could avoid becoming "infected with liberalism."[62] The trial was also embraced by southern intellectuals like Donald Davidson, John Crowe Ransom, and others associated with the emerging Southern Agrarian School, who described it as a defense of traditional values against the dehumanizing forces of modernity and science.[63] But above all, it was antievolutionists who were most vocal in casting themselves as defenders of the South and its conservative cultural values. "It is claimed that the law will bring on Mississippi the ridicule and abuse from the North that have been heaped upon Tennessee," T. T. Martin told lawmakers in the state's house of representatives:

> Reply: Shall the legislature of Mississippi barter the faith of the children of Mississippi in God's word and in the Savior for the fulsome praise of a paganized press? Go back to your homes and face your constituents and tell them that you bartered the faith of your children for gold; go back to the fathers and mothers of Mississippi and tell them that because you could not face the ridicule and scorn and abuse of Bolshevists and Anarchists and Atheists and Agnostics and their co-workers, you turned their children over to a teaching that God's word is a tissue of lies and that the Savior who said it was God's word was only the illegitimate son of a Jewish fallen woman.[64]

Over the course of the post-trial period, antievolution advocates continued to develop the theme, drawing on southern resentment and regional pride to forge a consciously created southern strategy. Even the Yankees among them did their part, like the cosmopolitan New Yorker Straton, who in his speeches made a point of describing the South as a place "where women are still honored, where men are still chivalric, where laws are still respected, where home life is still sweet, where the marriage vow is still sacred, and where man is still regarded, not as a descendant of the slime and beasts of the jungle, but as a child of God."[65]

While they played on regional resentments, antievolutionists also tapped concerns about class and status. Throughout the early 1920s, as fundamentalism had moved into the South and West, the character of its constituency had been changing. By 1925 what had begun as an elite, educated group consisting mostly of big-city ministers had been effectively transformed into a mass movement of small-town and rural churchgoers. The Scopes trial captured the change, as Mencken and other critics had insisted on portraying Bryan's followers as backwoods illiterates and village rustics. Although Mencken's descriptions had a distinctly southern cast, he was the first to admit that antievolution sentiment was not confined to the small-town South. ("Heave an egg out of a Pullman window," he famously wrote in his scathing memorial of Bryan, "and you will hit a Fundamentalist almost anywhere in the United States to-day.")[66] In the post-trial period, leaders of the movement seized on the rural stereotypes to cast their cause in more populist terms. Addressing themselves to audiences of small-town Protestants, they began to characterize antievolutionism as a crusade of what George Milton called "simple, faithful folk."[67] Contrasting country with city and posing poorly schooled people against educated elites, they left little doubt where they stood. In Mississippi, antievolutionists claimed to speak for "every man, woman and child in the place."[68] In North Carolina, they styled themselves as Jeffersonian democrats who were carrying out the will of the people.[69] In Arkansas, they described their efforts as a campaign to show "that the PEOPLE are not dead and that they can be aroused and when aroused woe be unto the exalted high brows who seek to control."[70] Everywhere they sided with the many against the few, the plain against the pretentious. In introducing an antievolution bill in the Georgia house, Representative Paul Lindsay told his colleagues: "I don't want any smart Aleck trying to teach my child that man descended from a tadpole or a monkey."[71]

Before long the movement was turning to nativism and nationalism. In the rapidly modernizing 1920s, anxieties about the loss of traditional values ran deep among small-town Americans. Tapping those anxieties, antievolutionists peppered their speeches with strident strains of prejudice. Evolution, they argued, was an anti-American idea, the product of foreigners and outsiders. Gerald Winrod blamed atheists, Catholics, and Jews for preventing passage of an antievolution bill in California.[72] W. B. Riley published exposés purporting to show that southern colleges and universities had been taken over by communists and socialists.[73] George Washburn pointed to the influence of shadowy anti-Christian conspiracies, including a "deep, devilish, and premeditated plan of propaganda," presumably the work of socialists and Jews, "to discard the Bible, discredit Christ and destroy the Church."[74] Adopting a strategy of creating coalitions with other cultural conservatives, movement activists began to ally themselves not only with conservative civic and patriotic groups, but also with reactionary and racist ones in a common campaign to protect the status quo. With membership in the Ku Klux Klan cresting, Straton appeared at chapter meetings across the South, where he voiced his approval of Klan principles and encouraged members to join the campaign against evolution.[75] Antievolutionists in Virginia participated in the Patriotic Welfare Committee, a coalition of representatives of the Klan and other nativist groups. In addition to introducing an antievolution bill into the legislature, the committee announced that in the next session it would bring up a "Bible bill" providing that "a certain number of verses from the Bible be read by each school-teacher to her class every day."[76] Across the country, antievolution campaigners, seeking to build a wide base of support, began to wrap themselves in the flag, describing their crusade as a defense of the nation against its enemies. "The time is coming," declared Straton, "when the American people . . . are going to wake up to the fact that this fight goes even deeper and is not merely religious, but is patriotic."[77] To those like Riley, whose libertarian leanings made him deeply suspicious of the American state, the adoption of such patriotic rhetoric did not come easily. Even so, he began at this time to conclude his mass meetings with the singing of "America." Indeed, speaking at the University of Minnesota in 1926, he presented antievolutionism as part of an American civic religion, concluding with a ringing call for his audience to stand together in "our fight for the faith of our American fathers."[78]

New Organizations and Old Ones

As movements proceed along Tarrow's cycle of contention, old groups tend to revive and new ones proliferate, creating tensions between them. In several studies, Tarrow has analyzed the conflicts between established movement organizations, or what he calls "early risers," and newer ones, the latecomers who appear on the scene as protest begins to peak. In competing for scarce resources and support, the older organizations often are forced to adopt the more aggressive public positions of the upstarts, leading to a spiral of radicalization and a more militant movement.[79]

For the WCFA, the first and most formidable antievolution organization, the post-trial period seemed to be especially plagued with these tensions. Within weeks of Bryan's death, it had taken the lead in announcing an ambitious national campaign advocating the establishment of a Bryan memorial university, calling for the introduction of state antievolution statutes nationwide, and declaring that the time was ripe for a million fundamentalists to provide a million dollars to send fifty preachers into the field "to sweep America for fundamentalism."[80] Yet as new groups proliferated, each with ambitious intentions, the organization found itself competing with the upstarts for membership and money. Already by late 1925 William Bell Riley, acting in his capacity as WCFA president, had become alarmed enough to call upon state antievolution groups to reconstitute themselves as state chapters of the national organization and send 40 percent of their membership dues to its national office.[81] When his suggestion was met with deafening silence, Riley regrouped, trying again the next year to shore up the organization by reconstituting it along coalitional lines. In the spring of 1926 he staged a show of unity at the association's annual meeting in Toronto, inviting the leaders of many of the fledgling groups to address the convention and recruiting several of them, including Paul Rood of the Bryan Bible League and Harry Rimmer of the Research Science Bureau, to become paid officials of the group.[82] The following year, at its 1927 convention at Atlanta, the WCFA attempted to assert its authority by adopting proposals to establish a uniform antievolution bill to be introduced into state legislatures and calling on all allied groups to clear their campaign plans with the association in advance.[83] Nothing seemed to work. For all practical purposes, the antievolution movement had become an awkward alliance of headstrong local leaders with independent followings who insisted on pursuing their own agendas with their own separate strategies. Struggling to reassert control, Riley pleaded for more centralized power, insisting that in order to succeed "coordination is to be a primary essential."[84]

With no dominant organization able to contain the energies let loose in the post-trial period, the antievolution movement followed a course of division and discord. The trend should not have been surprising, since many movement activists were affiliated with dissenter and separatist denominations. But the divisions had other explanations as well. As always personalities played a role, exaggerated in the post-trial period by the question of Bryan's succession. Thus in 1927 when Frank Norris changed the name of his newspaper from *The Searchlight* to *The Fundamentalist*, Riley concluded that it was a grab for power on the Texan's part, and he proceeded to angrily break off relations with him.[85] Regional and local loyalties were also a factor. For example, plans for a Bryan Memorial University became an early bone of contention, with Riley advocating that it be located in Chicago, Washburn supporting the efforts of local business leaders to establish it in Dayton, Tennessee, and others making the case for their own sites, including Miami and Dallas.[86] Denominational differences also led to divisions, both between denominations and within them. The fact that Baptists dominated many regional and state antievolution societies was often cause for resentment, particularly among Methodist and Presbyterian partisans.[87] Among fundamentalists, conflicts were common between those who chose to work within their denominations, remaining loyal while seeking to turn them in more conservative directions, and those who broke away to form interdenominational fundamentalist fellowships. On this point, the conflicts among Baptists were intense, as seen in the sharp divisions that erupted between denominational diehards like Riley and J. W. Porter and secessionist renegades such as Norris.[88] Finally, differences of belief and style separated moderate conservatives from radical ones, leading to monumental struggles like that at Des Moines University, where Baptist conservatives fought fiercely to prevent the takeover of the college by a faction led by T. T. Shields and his fundamentalist firebrands.[89] "We have done our best through the years to unite fundamentalists," wrote a discouraged Riley in the summer of 1929, "and we grieve a guerilla method of warfare."[90]

What followed was a spiral of radicalization, as groups competed for attention by adopting more extreme positions and increasingly sensationalistic tactics. From its beginnings antievolutionism had flirted with extreme forms of conservatism, and strains of anti-Catholicism and anti-socialism had always been present. After 1925, however, as activists became more aggressive in their campaigns, the movement took on an even more reactionary tone. In Arkansas, Baptist elder

J. R. Clark maintained that evolution was a Catholic plot, the product of plans set in motion by "the Italian organ-grinder, the Pope of Rome."[91] In Oklahoma, the irrepressible Mordecai Ham assured audiences that "Red" money from the Soviet Union was financing the teaching of evolution at the University of Oklahoma.[92] Barnstorming across the Midwest, Gerald Winrod warned of the coming apocalypse, insisting that the spread of evolution was one of the signs of the end times.[93] Anti-Semitic conspiracy theories began to percolate among the rank and file, encouraged by Henry Ford's publication of the *Protocols of the Learned Elders of Zion*, the notorious forgery that claimed to show how a Jewish cabal had been working to destroy Christian civilization.[94] Meanwhile, Frank Norris continued to attract media attention with his reckless rhetoric and angry attacks on his opponents. In 1926 he shot and killed an unarmed man in an argument in his church office. Acquitted by a Texas jury, which found him innocent by reason of self-defense, Norris told a Fort Worth, Texas, crowd of some eight thousand well-wishers gathered to meet him on his return from Austin that the trial was the result of persecution by his enemies.[95] When Canadian newspapers condemned T. T. Shields and his Toronto fundamentalists for their extreme views, Shields fired back that they were proud to be called "fanatics."[96] As for Riley, while always aware of the dangers of radicalism in the ranks, he was committed to maintaining the movement, even at the risk of encouraging extremism. Unable to control his more aggressive followers, he began more and more to applaud and encourage them, advising them to "stand like Spartans at Thermopolae, with the courage of St. Paul, to resist the invasion of the enemy."[97]

But radicalization also created problems within the movement. The post-trial period saw growing animosity between the militants demanding more aggressive strategies and moderates seeking to consolidate gains. Ambitious newcomers found themselves frustrated by existing efforts, while more cautious movement regulars resented the intrusion of the upstarts. Occasionally there was friction between locals and the outsiders who tended to descend at the last minute in anticipation of a legislative vote. In 1926 in North Carolina, tensions reached the breaking point. To all appearances, the state seemed to be next in line to turn an antievolution bill into state law, having missed by a handful of votes on the ill-fated Poole bill of the previous year. During the Scopes trial, Martin, then field secretary of the Anti-Evolution League, had confided that his organization would move into North Carolina next. With statewide primaries set for June 1926, and with public opinion lining up with the antievolutionists, candidates embraced the issue as a sure winner. Wake County's Sherwood Upchurch, for example, flooded his district with handbills decorated with photographs of himself and a monkey. "I Did Not Come from Him," said the broadside. "Neither Did

Did Not Come From HIM ☞

NEITHER DID YOU!

I May Look Like Him, But
I Refuse to Claim Kin

On This I Stand!

J. Sherwood Upchurch

They are Going to Talk About Him in the Next

LEGISLATURE

So They Say

I WANT TO BE THERE!

For House of Representatives

DEMOCRATIC PRIMARY
SATURDAY, JUNE 5TH

If you will vote for me, in return I will give you action. 14 years Member Board of Aldermen; 2 years City Auditor; 3 years in charge of Sanitary Department, City of Raleigh. During the 14 years as Alderman I never cast one vote against the people. I will thank you for your support.

J. Sherwood Upchurch

P.S.—I am positively against the Salary and Stave Commission.

Mitchell Printing Co., Raleigh, N. C.

P 13195

North Carolina primary campaign advertisement, 1926

(North Carolina Collection, University of North Carolina Library, Chapel Hill)

You! I May Look Like Him, but I Refuse to Claim Kin. On This I Stand!"[98] Political observers sensed a smashing victory in the making. "The feeling is strong in the state about the evolution question," commented one politician on the upcoming primary. "If a candidate came out for the teaching of evolution he wouldn't have as much chance as a Catholic."[99]

Yet for North Carolina antievolutionists, the 1926 campaign was an unmitigated disaster—one almost entirely of their own making. At the outset everything seemed to be going right. Antievolution forces announced the creation of a statewide organization, the Charlotte-based "Committee of One Hundred," so named because it included representatives from each of the state's one hundred counties. Outside organizations had been contacted for support, and Martin, acting as director-general of campaigns for the Bible Crusaders, had agreed to bring a team of organizers into the state. A convention was called, and three hundred activists prepared to descend on Charlotte to plan a strategy for the primaries. Then the disagreements began. Some of the divisions were denominational, such as those between bumptious Baptists and the powerful Presbyterians who controlled the committee. Others were more institutional and political, as seen in the conflicts that soon developed with Martin's Crusaders. Although Martin himself was well known in the state, some of his speakers (from as far away as Texas and New Jersey) were not, and locals worried that the outsiders would be seen as interlopers attempting to influence a state election. When Martin attempted to coordinate all campaign efforts, he was roundly rebuffed by those who had come to consider him and his troops less an asset than a liability. Meanwhile, the Committee of One Hundred itself was hobbled by infighting. At its May 1926 convention, held at the Second Presbyterian Church in Charlotte, disputes exploded into near pandemonium when a Methodist minister threw off his coat, doubled up his fists, and attempted to attack a more moderate speaker at the podium.[100] Battered by unfavorable publicity, and with some of its most prominent members resigning as a result of the proceedings, the committee saw its public support evaporating. An embarrassed Martin rapidly withdrew his forces from the state. The following month antievolutionists failed dismally at the polls. Among others, Wake's Sherwood Upchurch was easily defeated, despite the vigorous efforts of antievolutionist supporters.[101] Even the *Charlotte Observer*, a sympathetic supporter of the antievolution cause, admitted that "the State has had enough of the monkey business for quite a spell."[102]

Interaction between Activists and Authorities

In the final stage of Tarrow's cycle, as protest reaches its peak, interactions between activists and authorities are expected to increase in frequency and intensity. With conflicts creating deep cleavages in society, public officials are forced to play a more prominent role. Alliances begin to form against and around them, and these alliances compete to become part of governing coalitions, sometimes succeeding and sometimes failing in the attempt to achieve public power.[103]

In the post-trial period, antievolutionism followed the predicted pattern. The Scopes case had redefined relationships between activists and state and local authorities, flooding the media with information, polarizing popular opinion, and forcing civic leaders and public officials to take more decisive stands. In addition to energizing the antievolution forces, it had alarmed and inspired their opponents: the AAAS, the Science League of America, and numerous other national and state science associations, teachers' groups, and liberal church bodies stepped up their efforts at this time. Adopting some of the same techniques that antievolutionists had used so successfully, advocates of the teaching of evolutionary theory constructed an unprecedented campaign to bring their message to the public. Taking the lead was the Science Service news syndicate, which lobbied newspapers for more coverage of science, issued press releases on the contributions of evolutionary theory to modern agriculture and business, and syndicated its *Science News of the Week* programs over radio stations throughout the country. Activists brought evolution into the schools as well, sponsoring seminars for teachers, organizing essay contests for students, and producing films to show in science classrooms. Science writers introduced evolution to popular readers, with Henshaw Ward's *Evolution for John Doe* selling briskly throughout the post-trial period.[104] Stunned by the counterpunch of their opponents, antievolutionists realized that they had a serious fight on their hands. The debate over evolution had become "a nation-wide battle in which every voter must, in veritable self-defense, take sides," observed the Science League's Maynard Shipley. "And the fight has just begun."[105]

As public opinion polarized, politicians found themselves caught in the middle. Although antievolutionism had always had its champions, many public officials who supported it had been somewhat wary of the movement, seeing it as a force that had to be taken seriously even when it was not entirely welcome. But as the critics began to score points, some officeholders stepped back, lest they be tied too closely with the cause. With Mencken and others like him continuing their drumbeat of disparagement, antievolutionism was repeatedly portrayed in the popular press as a benighted and foolish cause. Antievolutionists did not exactly help their image with a series of spectacular scandals—Norris's murder trial, Aimee Semple McPherson's mysterious disappearance and allegations of romantic escapades, E. Y. Clarke's embezzlement of funds from the Supreme Kingdom—that began to turn mainstream public opinion against them.[106] Across the country, politicians quietly backed away from antievolution measures, citing worries that they might tarnish the reputation of their states.[107] But even in those areas where public opinion remained strongly supportive, antievolutionism proved to be a difficult issue for public officials to negotiate. Thus Tennessee's Austin Peay found himself in a bruising 1926 primary battle with an opponent whose main contention was that the governor had been lax in enforcing the state's antievolution law.[108] For Peay, the Scopes trial had ironically become a political liability. "The greatest problem," wrote one local attorney in reference to the Peay campaign, "has been in keeping the case out of politics."[109]

As the politicians retreated, movement activists took steps to increase the public pressure on them. With bills appearing in state legislatures nationwide, Riley and other antievolution leaders drew up a strategy that concentrated on those states where they saw the most chance for success. High on the list was Minnesota, an early bastion of antievolution sentiment and Riley's home state. Working under the aegis of the WCFA, Rimmer, Winrod, and a small legion of lesser-known operatives arrived in 1927, determined to bring about a mass mobilization of popular support for the antievolution bill that had been introduced in that year's legislative session. Riley himself spoke approximately sixty-five times, addressing audiences in the thousands, and Rimmer and Winrod made appearances in about two hundred towns between them. While the antievolution forces mobilized at the grass roots, their opponents concentrated on informing and influencing elites, organizing strong opposition among educators, newspaper editors, and church leaders. Although generally cool toward evolutionary theory, Lutheran leaders led the opposition, in part due to their distrust of Riley and his fundamentalists. Before the campaign was over, both of the state's conferences of Lutheran pastors, along with the presidents of every major Lutheran college, had come out against the bill. Similar stands were taken by Congregationalist, Methodist, Episcopal, and other church groups. Most important, while antievolutionists brought pressure from outside, their opponents worked the legislature from within. In its final floor vote in the Minnesota senate, the antievolution bill was defeated by a wide margin.[110] "The fundamentalists did their work in the state with the voters and won," observed an exasperated Riley. "The evolutionists did their work at St. Paul with the senators and representatives and won." Nevertheless, Riley saw no need to reconsider political strategy. Certain that the strength of the antievolution movement lay in its ability to mobilize popular support, he assured his followers that the victory of their enemies in Minnesota "is temporary and that the voters will in the course of time, reverse the decision."[111]

In Arkansas, the strategy was carried to its logical conclusion. After an antievolution bill narrowly went down to defeat in the 1927 legislature, a coalition of ministers led by Ben Bogard launched a church-based campaign to have the bill enacted through a statewide initiative. Using the columns of the *Baptist and Commoner* to announce the drive, the group proceeded to gather over 19,000 signatures in a matter of months. "You can take the petition to church and read it and ask every voter to sign it right there," Bogard instructed his troops. "ANYBODY WHO CAN READ AND WRITE can circulate the petition among the negroes and at the churches. Get every voter of all denominations and no denominations to sign."[112] Led by the *Arkansas Gazette*, the state's largest newspaper, opponents mounted a strong offensive against the initiative, arguing that by passing the measure Arkansas would be opening itself to the same ridicule that Tennessee had experienced following the Scopes trial. Bogard and his allies blithely dismissed their concerns. "The *Gazette* and Russian Bolsheviks laughed at Tennessee," read an election-week broadside that appeared in Arkansas newspapers. "True, and that sort will laugh at Arkansas. Who cares?"[113] On election day citizens overwhelmingly approved Initiated Act 1 by a vote of 108,991 to 63,406.[114] Celebrating back home in Minnesota, Riley declared the outcome a victory for democracy and asserted that initiative and referendum votes would be the focus of future antievolution campaigns. "There are nineteen states in the union that have a referendum law," he commented in congratulating the Arkansas antievolution forces. "It is our confident expectation that when we can get to it, every single one of these states will pass an anti-evolution law."[115]

Nevertheless, the Arkansas vote conveyed a mixed message. By any measure, it was an impressive showing for antievolutionism, winning the approval of voters in sixty-eight of seventy-five counties and receiving over 63 percent of the ballot statewide. In a close analysis, political scientist Virginia Gray found that while voters in rural counties were slightly more supportive, a broad-based majority of Arkansans—defying stereotypical assumptions that antievolutionists consisted only of illiterate fundamentalists—turned out to assure the measure an easy victory.[116] But the Arkansas ballot also demonstrated some of the difficulties that antievolutionists faced in their attempt to exercise public power. At the beginning of the initiative campaign, Bogard had promised to defeat all of the representatives and senators who had voted against the original antievolution bill. Predictably, his plan met with only limited success. In the 1928 primaries, several candidates for governor, including the popular incumbent Harvey Parnell, insisted that evolution should not be a campaign issue at all. Representative A. L. Rotenberry, the strongest antievolution supporter in the legislature and sponsor of the original bill, was soundly defeated in his primary contest to become the state's attorney general, suggesting that evolution—no matter how important—was only

Help Us Put Evolution Out of Our Public Schools

My Dear Friend:

On November 6 everybody will be called upon to vote either for or against evolution. It will be on the ballot and surely all of us should have the moral courage to vote to put evolution out of our free schools.

Well knowing that very few will stay in the voting booth long enough to read the long laws and amendments that will be on the ballot I want to explain to you that Act No. 1 is all you need to remember. Vote FOR Act No. 1 and you will be voting against evolution.

If all who believe the Bible will go to the polls and vote there will be no trouble in passing the law. Remember we pass the law by our votes. We should rejoice that we can go to the polls and pass any law we please. The governor can't veto a law passed by the people at the polls, and if Act No. 1 carries at the polls it will be the law and those who teach evolution in our free schools will pay a fine for it and it will also prohibit text books being used in the schools that teach evolution.

Please explain to your friends that they should vote FOR Act No. 1. That is all that we need to remember.

Will you please copy this letter and write exactly these words to at least five of your friends no matter where they may live in Arkansas? If you will do this and they in turn will write to five of their friends it will produce an endless chain that will cover the entire state. But be sure and sign your name to the letter. Anonimous letters are always wrong. Let us all get busy and help pass Act No. 1.

Sincerely against evolution,

Note: If a thousand of the brethren and sisters will copy this letter and send it to five of their friends and sign your own names to it and then the ones they write will copy and send to five of their friends it will win the election against evolution with ease. You can write MORE than five letters if you will. The more the better.

B. M. B.

Open letter from Ben W. Bogard on Act 1, the Arkansas Antievolution Initiative
(from The Baptist and Commoner, 10 October 1928)

one of many concerns on the minds of voters. In the general election that year, political considerations became even more complex, with the antievolution initiative sharing ballot space not only with statewide races but also with the closely fought Hoover-Smith presidential contest. (In Arkansas, the presidential race was further complicated by the presence on the ticket of favorite son Senator Joe T. Robinson as Smith's running mate.) With Al Smith presenting the serious possibility of a Roman Catholic president who would repeal Prohibition, even the most ardent antievolutionists had to divide their energies between supporting Act 1 and opposing Smith. Bogard, for one, told his readers: "No Christian and no red blooded American can support him."[117]

The election of 1928 complicated antievolution efforts in other ways as well. At the beginning of the campaign, activists rejoiced, viewing Al Smith's favorable stance toward evolution as an opportunity to recoup recent losses and revitalize their movement. In addition, because Smith was not only an evolutionist but also a New Yorker, a Catholic, and a "wet," many in the movement believed that they could increase their influence by constructing coalitions with other Smith opponents, including mainstream Protestant church leaders and Republican politicians. In the South especially, support for Prohibition was the common thread that united independent fundamentalist preachers with Southern Methodist bishops, Baptist and Presbyterian seminary presidents, and church leaders from virtually every Protestant denomination.[118] Thus antievolution leaders began to forge alliances with Prohibition forces, denouncing those southern Democrats who supported what the *Western Recorder* called "a soaking wet presidential candidate."[119] In correspondence, J. Frank Norris sounded less like an antievolutionist than a Prohibitionist, advising his allies not only to emphasize Smith's opposition to Prohibition but also to confront him on his own drinking habits. "If he ignores it everybody will call attention to it," he wrote to Mordecai Ham, "and if he undertakes to answer it he will have to evade or admit that he drinks."[120] But even beyond the South, movement leaders saw an opportunity to advance their cause by riding piggyback on the popularity of Prohibition. After all, observed Riley, "the United States by an overwhelming majority has voted dry."[121]

The attempt to build coalitions did not stop there. Even as antievolutionists adopted prohibitionist arguments, they also raised the specter of Smith's Roman Catholicism, warning of insidious popish plots to overthrow the U.S. Constitution and subordinate the president to the Vatican. Among anti-Catholic agitators, Norris took the lead, attacking Smith's Catholic faith in more than a hundred speeches in thirty cities during the three and a half months leading up to the election. He also published scurrilous reports in *The Fundamentalist* about sex-crazed priests and secret plans to move the Papacy to Washington, D.C.[122] Ham railed regularly against the Catholic Church in his Sunday sermons, boasting that his congregation would applaud every time he "took a swing at the Catholics."[123] Ben Bogard ran special editions of his *Baptist and Commoner* on "Rum and Romanism," where he declared that any "Protestant politician" who would support Smith's candidacy was "either an ignoramus or a political dupe."[124] Bogard also collaborated with the Klan in the campaign against Smith, printing a letter from the Grand Dragon of the Knights of the Ku Klux Klan calling upon readers to join a common campaign against the Catholic Church. "The cause of Protestantism is now appealing to Protestants to rally for the cause," he wrote, "and without regard to sectarian Protestant belief." Appearing alongside the appeal in the *Baptist and Commoner* was Bogard's own editorial endorsement, praising the Klan for its efforts and declaring that he was "glad there is an organization with thousands of members ready to present an organized front against RUM and ROMANISM as represented by Al Smith."[125]

Some antievolutionists supplemented anti-Catholicism with racism. As a general rule, the movement avoided references to race. Even in the South, where racist attitudes tended to be expressed more frequently in public, the remarks of movement leaders like Norris were surprisingly free of blatant racial prejudice.[126] Yet as the 1928 campaign intensified, southern antievolutionists turned to racism in order to attract white voters. In the late summer, Mississippi's *Baptist Record* commenced a full-scale smear campaign against Smith by running a story based on the claim of a Catholic priest—"if the word of a Catholic priest can be believed"—that "the negroes of Mississippi are being organized by the Catholic hierarchy to vote for Smith."[127] Over the next several months, the *Record* printed rumors that Democrats were attempting to attract black voters by promising to give them jobs in the federal government. Confirming all rumors, the paper insisted that its own "investigation" had found "that Mr. Smith has employed negroes and shows every favor to them that he can."[128] In articles tying Smith to the Tammany political organization, the *Record* confounded themes of corruption and racial privilege, noting Tammany's "thousands of negro members, its scores of negroes with white wives, its 'exclusive' negro clubs, its negro political bosses." Among other examples, the "Smith-Tammany civil service commissioner for New York, Ferdinan Q. Morton is a negro, with a $10,000.00 job, passing upon applications of white men."[129] Even worse, the same commissioner Morton had been placed in charge of white female employees. Three weeks before election day, the *Baptist and Commoner* ran a story with a photograph of Morton seated at his desk with his white female stenographer. Pointing to the "disgusting picture," and warning that the election of Smith would place other "negro bucks" in authority over white women, an outraged Bogard observed that "it is enough to make the blood of any true southern white man boil with indignation." Voting for Smith, he concluded, was "voting for negro equality," a prospect that would be resisted by "the great majority of southern white men." As for himself, Bogart's intentions were clear and unqualified: "I intend to vote for the Lily White Republican, Herbert Hoover."[130]

Yet for the antievolution movement, the 1928 election was a Pyrrhic victory. Herbert Hoover was elected easily, his margin of victory over Al Smith made more comfortable by Protestant voters who crossed over in large numbers, especially in the South, to carry traditionally Democratic states for the Republican Party. On election night his antievolutionist supporters celebrated in rallies like the one at Norris's First Baptist Church in Fort Worth, where the preacher received an engraved watch for his efforts from the campaign manager of the state's anti-Smith Democratic forces.[131] Their triumph was a costly one, however, in that antievolutionists had allowed their message to be recast as one among many campaign issues, a plank in a party platform. In addition, by throwing their support to the Republican Party they had incurred the animosity of powerful Democratic politicians. Virginia's Senator Carter Glass, for one, denounced Southern Methodist bishops—he called them "Methodist popes"—for trying to lead the church "into the camp of a political party whose crimes have shocked the nation."[132] At the same time the movement had managed to alienate many sympathizers, mainstream moderate and conservative churchgoers who saw their ministers crossing the line into partisan electoral politics. These "political parsons," wrote one critic in a letter to the *Memphis Commercial Appeal*, had not only "cheapened their calling and profession" but also "cheapened their churches and . . . even cheapened themselves."[133] Above all, in attempting to build the broadest coalition, antievolutionists had antagonized those in their own ranks who regarded the adoption of partisan politics as a threat to the harmony and integrity of their churches. The election of 1928 thus had the effect of turning many congregants away from the antievolution movement altogether, lest it encourage what one group of Methodist lay leaders called "the dragging of our beloved church into politics."[134]

Within a matter of months, antievolutionists had come to see their actions in the 1928 campaign as even more of a mistake. Before the election, their hopes had been unusually high, in large part because it appeared to be their last best chance to exercise political power. Afterward, having won, they seemed unsure that they had gained anything at all. Indeed, as Kenneth Bailey argued, when the Hoover administration made no clear changes in public policy, it appeared as if they had been used, leaving many activists disillusioned and increasingly alienated from the movement.[135] Attendance fell off sharply at meetings.[136] The turnout at debates declined markedly, at one point forcing Riley and Rimmer to debate one another over the issue of whether the days of Genesis were literal or representational.[137] Competing groups continued to carp among themselves, so much so that Riley was compelled to remind them that "back biting is not a Christian virtue."[138] Some leaders lost interest, turning their attention to other issues: Norris announced a new crusade to confront the growing Catholic influence in politics, Riley and Winrod began issuing anti-Semitic diatribes. As for the antievolutionist rank and file, large numbers began to abandon politics altogether. Embarrassed by the behavior of some of their leaders, ground down by the infighting between moderates and radicals, alienated by their ill-fated venture into electoral politics, many retreated into a more pietistic practice of evangelical religion. In 1929 Riley passed the presidency of the WCFA to Paul Rood, who announced that the future of the organization lay not in political reform but in personal revival. "The time is short," Rood told the WCFA's 1929 convention. "The need is urgent. Souls are perishing. Christ is coming. . . . Let us give ourselves unto the Lord in a new whole-hearted surrender and go forth energized by the Holy Spirit to finish our task of evangelizing the world."[139]

The stock market collapse of 1929 was the final blow. The Great Depression would be devastating for the antievolution movement, depriving it of resources that had been scarce in the best of times. But even before the crash, antievolutionism had arrived at what Tarrow calls the "tipping point," beyond which decline led irreversibly to demobilization.[140] Months before the crash, money had already become scarce. Most movement organizations operated on bare-bones budgets backed by the small but regular contributions of loyal members. With the proliferation of protest groups, contributors had been asked to give more, dividing and diluting their giving, and forcing antievolution groups to compete and sometimes cooperate in order to stay solvent.[141] By 1929 the newer organizations in particular were in serious financial straits: Washburn's Bible Crusaders, reeling after the collapse of the Florida real estate boom, had to close down publication of the *Crusaders' Champion*; Winrod's Defenders were reduced to running advertisements begging readers to scrape up the seven hundred dollars needed to hold their annual convention; Clarke's Supreme Kingdom, damaged by reports of accounting irregularities, was almost bankrupt.[142] Even the venerable WCFA was strapped. Bombarded with requests for support from state and local groups, Riley lamented that he had nothing to give them but good wishes: "and we often wish that we had enough money to lend these Christian men and women aid in their fight against this false and bestial philosophy."[143]

As the 1920s closed, the antievolution movement appeared to have come to an end. From 1925 on, the movement had culminated in a spectacular show of popular protest and an equally spectacular series of failures. By the end of the decade it seemed a dead letter. Yet though antievolutionism declined, it did not disappear. Indeed, its culmination at the close of the 1920s was as much a beginning as an end.

8 : Renewal

THE CONTINUING RE-CREATION OF CREATIONISM

The always ebullient William Bell Riley was discouraged. Hit hard by the Great Depression, the World's Christian Fundamentals Association (WCFA) had fallen deeply in debt, unable at times to pay the salaries of its own secretaries. Over the course of the early 1930s Riley had been reduced to a painful ritual of pleading, writing one letter after another in which he begged WCFA members for "any amount you can send to me."[1] Although a few responded with small sums, most were unable to keep up with their dues, and membership had been shrinking steadily. Now the organization seemed close to collapse: "I even I," he lamented in 1935, "only am left."[2]

To all appearances, the antievolution movement had come and gone. Yet despite its obvious decline, Riley and antievolutionist leaders like him were not ready to admit defeat. Instead, they began to carry out a process of retreat in order to regroup and revitalize. Over the next several decades they would create an institutional infrastructure that allowed them to maintain their movement for the rest of the century and into the next one. Building from their base in fundamentalist churches, schools, and seminaries, they constructed an intricate network of antievolution activists and organizations. Movement organizers provided continuity, with many from the 1920s remaining active for decades, during which they inspired a new generation of leaders to take their place. Passing on protest strategies while preserving basic ideas and core identities, activists at the local level kept the cause alive at a time when few seemed interested in the issue. As a result of their efforts, antievolutionism would continue through periods of retrenchment and resurgence, emerging periodically into public view with the advent of the creation science of the 1960s, the alliance with the New Christian Right (NCR) in the 1980s, and the advocacy of "intelligent design" (sometimes called simply "ID") in our own time. Combining change and continuity, the movement has proven remarkably resilient. Yet even as it has changed, it has been constrained by its past, carrying along popular perceptions—many of them the work of the 1920s—that have continued to define it. Thus the antievolution movement has remained a product of its past, existing even today in the shadow of the Scopes trial.

It is only relatively recently that scholars have begun to seriously consider how social movements operate over the course of their lifetimes. For much of the early twentieth century, social theorists from Max Weber to Robert Michels conceptualized the lives of movements in linear terms, describing them as moving steadily through stages of birth, maturity, and decay, with popular protest and charismatic leadership inevitably giving way to accommodation and oligarchy. By the 1960s sociologists led by Mayer Zald and Roberta Ash had begun to suggest a more fluid interpretation, arguing that far from following a rigid pattern, movements tend to ebb and flow in response to sentiment in the larger society.[3] In a series of studies, Joseph R. Gusfield applied the insight to several social reforms movements, demonstrating how they avoided accommodation and decay by adapting and transforming themselves, by saving their strength during difficult times, and by regrouping and redefining their missions.[4] More recently, a growing group of social movement scholars has sought to explain the remarkable endurance of the American women's movement: how it has survived and thrived since its origins in the nineteenth century. Analyzing different aspects of the movement, studies by Anne Costain, Debra Minkoff, Leila Rupp, Suzanne Staggenborg, Verta Taylor, and Nancy Whittier have shown how activists have maintained continuity in the movement, preserving it through times of retreat and retrenchment, reviving it during periods of protest, and passing on its core character to future generations.[5] The studies also suggest some of the means by which activists have managed to adapt to changing circumstances, including (1) the construction of institutions, or the forming of new groups and transforming of older ones; (2) the development of issues, especially critical concerns that can initiate a resurgence of protest and solidarity; (3) the establishment of overlapping connections between movements, in which they penetrate or "spill over" into other ones; and (4) the introduction of new strategies and goals that allow them to respond to changes in the political and social climate.[6] Admittedly, the studies show that combining continuity with change can be a challenge, and that within the women's movement there frequently have been tensions between those concerned with maintaining the movement and those bent on transforming it. Nevertheless, all agree on the importance of attending to both, and that in order for movements to continue, they must constantly be re-creating themselves.

Among those who study antievolutionism there has been a difference of opinion on the extent of continuity and change within the movement. On the whole, all see certain similarities between early antievolutionists and more recent ones,

most of whom prefer to call themselves "creationists." At the same time all acknowledge that over the past century antievolutionism has taken different forms
and been recast in a variety of ways. In his *The Evolution Controversy*, George E.
Webb stresses the similarities among evolution's opponents, tracing the persistence of similar themes from Darwin's time to today and insisting that throughout that time continuity has been "obvious."[7] By contrast, in *The Creationists*, Ron
Numbers gives a detailed account of the differences that have divided antievolutionists over the last century, emphasizing the divisions between theological and
scientific creationism, and stressing the shift that took place, beginning in the
1960s, from orthodox theories to more contemporary forms of creation science.[8]
Yet in their various descriptions, the authors agree more often than they disagree, suggesting that antievolutionism has been marked by both continuity and
change. Indeed, in considering the enduring character of antievolutionism from
the 1930s until today, it is tempting to say that the more the movement has
changed, the more it has stayed the same.

Institutions

To survive over long periods, movements must be able to maintain themselves
through trying times. Changes in political climate often require strategic retreat,
in which movement members save their strength while preparing for the next
wave of protest. In their study of the American women's movement, Verta Taylor
and Leila J. Rupp showed how activists created and sustained personal and
professional networks and organizations to maintain a committed feminist community during the "doldrums" of the post–World War II period. By creating
these "abeyance structures," feminists built a bridge between suffrage and the
equal rights amendment, keeping traditions alive, passing on experience, and
recruiting activists of the next generation.[9]

Antievolutionists of the 1930s found themselves in a similar situation. To all
appearances, the antievolution movement was dead. After 1929, when a bill failed
to move out of committee in the Texas house, there would not be another antievolution statute introduced into an American state legislature for thirty years.[10]
In the three states where antievolution laws remained on the books, public
prosecutors made clear that they had no intention of enforcing them.[11] Unable to
find anyone willing to bring suit, the American Civil Liberties Union (ACLU)
announced in 1932 that it would no longer attempt to challenge their constitutionality.[12] As interest in evolution waned, movement leaders continued to take
up other causes. In the 1930s both Riley and Gerald Winrod pursued campaigns
in which they pointed to communist propaganda in the public schools, warned of
conspiracies being carried out by Jewish cabals, and eventually flirted with fas-

cism.[13] Meanwhile, growing numbers of activists were turning away from politics and embracing a more personal brand of conservative religion.[14] As the depression deepened, the antievolution movement fell into abeyance: "The tide of affairs," admitted Riley, "is against us."[15]

In response, antievolutionists retreated in order to regroup. From its beginning, the antievolution movement had been closely associated with fundamentalism, with most of its rank and file coming from fundamentalist churches. In the 1930s, as they retreated to their churches, these fundamentalists began to build from the bottom, reconstructing the movement as it had been constructed in the first place, from fundamentalist foundations. Over the next several decades, continuing to separate from their denominations, they would create an increasingly intricate network of associations, fellowships, and independent churches.[16] In the 1930s alone the number of fundamentalist Bible camps and conferences more than doubled, with more than two hundred of them meeting at over fifty sites, and with most providing special programs for young people.[17] During the same decade fundamentalist publishing houses expanded and new ones were established. While respected periodicals like *Moody Monthly*, *The King's Business*, and *The Sunday School Times* continued to be published, splashy tabloids like John R. Rice's *The Sword of the Lord* appeared alongside them, eventually reaching circulations in the hundreds of thousands.[18] With the growth of commercial broadcasting, fundamentalist radio ministries multiplied and attracted large audiences. By the mid-1940s the Reverend Charles E. Fuller's "Old Fashioned Revival Hour," carried by over 450 stations nationwide, would be the most popular program on the air.[19] Training schools, Bible colleges, and seminaries expanded their enrollments, and new colleges, including the fledgling William Jennings Bryan University (located finally after years of disagreement in Dayton, Tennessee) were launched.[20] Although antievolutionism was only one aspect of fundamentalism, it remained an important ingredient of the infrastructure. "During the 1930s and 1940s," wrote Joel Carpenter, "fundamentalists continued to challenge evolution wherever they could assemble an audience. The fact that after the Scopes trial they had trouble getting a hearing outside their own ranks did not deter them, for their antievolutionary arguments were meant to encourage the faithful as much as win a hearing in the larger world."[21]

While working within fundamentalist institutions, antievolutionists built their own as well. The core of the movement consisted primarily of preachers and speakers. Among the ministers, Riley, Frank Norris, and T. T. Shields were the most prominent; although their activism became less pronounced after 1930, they continued to talk about the topic for many years. Antievolution speakers followed the same pattern, with George McCready Price, Arthur Brown, and Harry Rimmer all continuing to make regular lecture rounds at churches, summer Bible conferences, and youth camps. Among these, Rimmer was the most visible. A Presbyterian minister and self-styled "research scientist," Rimmer was educated at a homeopathic medical school, worked from a small laboratory he built in the backyard of his Los Angeles home, and legally incorporated himself as the Research Science Bureau. During the 1930s and early 1940s he delivered thousands of lectures, spending up to six months each year on the road.[22] While the speakers were never able to reach much beyond fundamentalist ranks, they found receptive audiences there, inspiring protégés such as Henry Morris, the young student of flood geology whose reading of Price, Brown, and Rimmer introduced him to creationist thinking long before he himself would become known as a founder of modern creation science.[23] In addition, a small but steadily growing body of scientists, many of them Seventh-Day Adventists, established their own creationist scientific societies, including the Religion and Science Association, Deluge Geology Society, and American Scientific Affiliation (ASA).[24] Admittedly, such groups attracted little attention from the public and no support from the established scientific community. But they were a start. "During the heady days of the 1920s, when their activities made front-page headlines, creationists dreamed of converting the world," observed Ron Numbers; "a decade later, rejected and forgotten by the establishment, they turned their energies inward and began creating an institutional base of their own."[25]

In the same way, activists passed on their repertoires to a new generation of movement members. For the most part, antievolution activity changed slowly after the 1920s, with speakers continuing to troop from church to church and local ministers delivering occasional antievolution sermons. But even while strategies remained essentially the same, they were regularly updated to take advantage of new technologies. Thus the stage debates of the 1920s served as prototypes for hundreds of similar contests that would continue for decades, reaching a peak in the 1970s.[26] The rapid growth of religious radio, introduced on local stations in the 1920s by fundamentalist preachers like Paul Rader and John Roach Straton, paved the way for antievolutionists of the 1930s such as Herbert W. Armstrong to launch national programs that would eventually reach audiences in the tens of millions.[27] Motion pictures also opened new opportunities for conveying the antievolutionist message. As early as 1939 the crowd-pleasing lecturer Irwin Moon, famous for his spectacular stage demonstrations in which he sent charges of electrical energy running though his body, was commissioned by the Moody Bible Institute to produce a motion picture series of his "Sermons from Science."[28] Arriving later on the scene, television would play a major part after World War II, with antievolutionists being featured on the popular TV programs hosted by televangelists Jerry Falwell and Tim LaHaye, both of whom had long associations with Henry Morris.[29] Admittedly, the antievolution cause remained very much on the margins. But by passing on the lessons they had learned, antievolutionists of the mid-twentieth century helped to "bridge the gap," as Morris put it, "between the creationist revival preceding the Scopes trial and the modern creationist movement."[30]

In building an institutional infrastructure, antievolutionists faced some serious obstacles. Among these were the divisions that arose among themselves. By 1930 the antievolution movement had already devolved into an amalgamation of small, self-contained groups populated primarily by self-educated science writers, itinerant evangelists, and at least a few crackpots. While some were Adventists, most in the movement were members of independent fundamentalist congregations and small sectarian fellowships. In the 1930s and 1940s they were frequently at odds with one another. ("When they were not fighting modernists, Catholics, and evolutionists," as Louis Gasper described them, "they fought among themselves.")[31] Activists divided not only along denominational lines but also along theological and scientific ones, quarreling repeatedly over biblical and scientific interpretation. Creation scientists, a small cadre at the best of times, advocated competing theories, with day-age, gap, and young-earth interpretations being the most common, so that the first creationist scientific societies were soon dividing and disintegrating, to be superceded by other equally fractious organizations.[32] Even the ASA, an ambitious attempt to bring together antievolutionists of various views, foundered on the same rocks, as militant young-earth creationists found themselves increasingly at odds with more moderate advocates of old-earth and progressive creationism. By the 1940s, observed Numbers, "a split appeared inevitable."[33]

At the same time, antievolutionists had to deal with declining interest in the issue itself. As Americans struggled through the Depression, the battle over evolution seemed suddenly less important than it had been before the crash. Capturing the change was Frederick Lewis Allen's 1931 best seller *Only Yesterday*, a popular history of the 1920s, in which the antievolution movement was depicted as a product of the past, a throwback to Victorian tradition that had been anachronistic even at its peak. Allen's lively narrative drew heavily on the Scopes trial, which he portrayed as a symbolic struggle between William Jennings Bryan's old-time religion and Clarence Darrow's faith in modern progress. Edward J. Larson has argued that this characterization of the trial, cartoonlike in its simplicity, had an enormous effect on mainstream public opinion, creating the perception that the antievolution cause had effectively ended when Bryan was bested by Darrow on the stand at Dayton.[34] Yet surprisingly, as Larson has shown, antievolutionists chose not to contest this characterization, which began to be adopted by many social critics and historians, taking on the status of a Scopes legend. Instead, most ignored it, neither knowing nor caring what secular writers thought about them or their movement. Some may have found a certain comfort in the interpretation, regarding the fallen figure of Bryan as a symbol of their own failure to slow the growing secularity of the time. A few, like George McCready Price, the young-earth creationist, actually embraced the revised reading of the trial, seeing it as a way to break with the past, distancing the movement from Bryan's more moderate day-age creationism, as well as from his political activism and populism. In fact, Price contributed to the retelling of the trial, describing in the 1940s how he had advised Bryan to put the evolutionists on the defensive at Dayton by contending that the Flood of Noah was the cause of the fossil record. In essence, Price accepted antievolution's failure and blamed Bryan for it. Had Bryan taken his advice, he conjectured, "the history of the trial would certainly have been different."[35]

The truth, however, was that antievolutionists had not failed. After 1930 the debates over evolution disappeared from the headlines. In state legislatures, where dealing with the Depression had become paramount, the issue was almost immediately forgotten. Comforted by a tendentious retelling of the Scopes trial, evolutionists returned to their colleges and mainstream scientific societies secure in the assumption that the evolution controversy had been settled.[36] Yet what they assumed was an illusion: although the antievolution movement had indeed suffered setbacks, a committed core continued to carry on the cause. In the same way that they began to create institutions from the ground up, these activists focused on the grass roots, especially in America's small towns and rural schools, where they would stay active for decades.[37] Avoiding attention and going for the most part unnoticed, they developed campaigns encouraging publishers, school officials, and teachers to remove all references to evolution from books, curricula, and classrooms. More often than not, they were successful. Attempting to fend off persistent complaints from antievolutionists, textbook publishers concerned about their profits continued to systematically reduce or remove discussions of evolution from biology books.[38] By 1933 authors Arthur O. Baker and Lewis H. Mills had relegated evolution to the last two pages of their popular textbook Dynamic Biology, concluding with the comment that Darwin's theory, "like that of Lamarck, is no longer generally accepted."[39] At the same time, state and local school officials, fearing the same controversies that had plagued Tennessee, developed curricula that studiously avoided discussions of evolution. By 1942 a national survey of high school biology teachers, funded by the Carnegie Foundation, found that less than half of them were treating the topic at all.[40] As for teachers, while some avoided the subject of evolution because of their personal beliefs, others were clearly cowed by the power of community pressure, so much so that one study of the time would conclude that in much of the nation, teachers "dare not even mention the word."[41] Thus even while rebuilding, the antievolution movement remained remarkably successful, exercising influence over public policies well into the 1950s. Because of their efforts, wrote sociologist Dorothy Nelkin, even one hundred years after Charles Darwin evolution was "still not an integral part of the public school curriculum."[42]

Issues

To move from abeyance to action, movements need issues. Institutions can provide support, but activists tend to mobilize around issues, or even better, around what Suzanne Staggenborg has called "burning issues." Analyzing the ability of the women's movement to sustain itself over many decades, Staggenborg found that many local groups relied on critical events—instances of injustice usually brought on by political authorities or economic elites—to inspire collective action campaigns. Such instances, she argues, acted as catalysts, allowing activists to transform events into issues, while also sparking those surges of urgency that drive movements out of somnolence into active protest.[43]

In the early 1960s the antievolution movement experienced one such surge when evolution reappeared in the public schools. With the Cold War at its peak, and amid acute concern about the state of science in the United States following the successful launch of the Soviet space satellite Sputnik, American public education began to come in for criticism. Special scrutiny was given to teaching in the natural sciences.[44] Using federal funds made available through the National Defense Education Act, the National Science Foundation (NSF) sponsored a series of systematic reviews of science education, including the Biological Science Curriculum Study (BSCS), a five-year program leading to the publication of textbooks, films, and other instructional materials for high school students. Written by professional scientists, endorsed by national education groups, and funded with strong federal support that allowed the study to avoid the influence of local interests as well as ties to the textbook market, BSCS materials were expressly intended to take on controversial topics, including evolution. When they appeared in 1963, they were widely adopted and eventually made their way into almost half of all American high schools.[45] At about the same time, in part because of the adoption of the BSCS curriculum, teachers began to challenge existing antievolution laws, culminating in the 1968 Supreme Court case of *Epperson v. Arkansas*, in which that state's 1928 law was found to be unconstitutional for imposing a religious restriction on the teaching of evolution.[46] For antievolutionists, the changes were a double whammy, inserting evolution into the schools while at the same time removing laws protecting children from it. With state power and public opinion combining against them, they found themselves suddenly on the defensive, forced to fight, in Larson's words, "a rearguard action."[47]

Amid a growing sense of alarm, activists took up the cause. Almost as soon as the BSCS curriculum appeared in the schools, parents began to protest. Alerted by their concerns, school officials in several states took steps against BSCS books, refusing to purchase them, requesting revisions, and in some cases simply blacking out offending passages. In New Mexico, the state board of education decided that the inside covers of all BSCS texts should be stamped with a statement declaring its own official view that evolution was a "theory" rather than a "fact." Similarly in Texas, the Reverend Reuel Lemmons, a fundamentalist minister, initiated a campaign against the books, calling them "pure evolution from cover to cover," eventually persuading the state board of education to remove or revise much of their evolutionary content.[48] Realizing the extent of the protests, BSCS officials began to make their own revisions. In its 1961 edition, one high school biology text contained these sentences: "The fossil evidence dramatically shows that life has been gradually changing over millions of years from one form to another. There is no longer any reasonable doubt that evolution occurs." By 1963, as science educator Gerald Skoog later noted, the phrase "dramatically shows" had been replaced by "suggests," and in subsequent editions the second sentence would be dropped altogether.[49] But the revisions were too little too late. The antievolution movement was back in business, and critics were coming out of the woodwork. In a letter to Governor John Connally of Texas, one detractor attributed the assassination of President John F. Kennedy and the attempt on Connally's own life to "the atheistic teaching of evolutionary theory."[50]

Along with the popular protests, however, antievolutionism experienced an intellectual revival in the 1960s. At issue—the issue—was science. With science receiving unprecedented public support, antievolutionists saw no choice but to embrace it. The task fell to Henry Morris, a professor of civil engineering at Virginia Polytechnic Institute (VPI) and a born-again conservative evangelical, who for years had been quietly building a case for what he termed "creation science." Morris argued that biblically based explanations of creation could be confirmed by evidence gathered though the strictest scientific observation and research. The concept was not new: throughout the early 1920s antievolutionists like A. C. Dixon and W. B. Riley had insisted that biblical truths had been repeatedly proven by archaeological and geological research, and that Scripture and science were in complete conformity. Since the 1920s advocates of young-earth creationism led by Price had been using the science of flood geology to argue for a seven-day catastrophic creation, as described in Genesis, and for a geological and fossil record that was best explained as the product of an ancient Noachian Deluge, or Noah's Flood.[51] Adopting and updating these assumptions, Morris and theologian John Whitcomb teamed up to present their case in the 1961 book *The Genesis Flood*. Here they combined biblical interpretation and flood geology to argue that the world was about ten thousand years old, that dinosaurs and humans had coexisted, and that evolutionary explanations for an ancient earth were based not on facts but on flawed science.[52] Although theologians and scientists—including most evangelical ones—roundly rejected the book's basic tenets, lay readers were more receptive, and it became a surprising success, selling tens of thousands of copies over its first ten years in print. For antievolutionists of the 1960s, it was exactly what they needed, a theory that seemed thoroughly scientific, in keeping with the tenor of the times.[53] Activists immediately recognized its political potential: "Sell more SCIENCE," the *Bible-Science Newsletter*, a monthly creationist magazine, would advise its activist readers. "Who can object to teaching more science?"[54]

Morris sold creation science better than anyone could have imagined. In the early 1960s, buoyed by his book's popularity, he began to travel extensively, introducing his ideas to growing audiences at conservative churches and Christian colleges. While continuing to teach civil engineering, he wrote articles and books, along with a series of Sunday school lessons, all of which advocated his version of young-earth creationism over the more popular day-age and gap theories. More important, he began to build networks among creation science supporters. In 1970, giving up his academic appointment at VPI, he took a position at Tim LaHaye's fledgling Christian Heritage College in San Diego. According to Morris, it was "the first college in modern times formed in order to provide a liberal arts education based specifically on strict Biblical creationism."[55] At about the same time, working with Nell and Kelly Segraves, a mother-son team of Southern California antievolution activists, he also established the Creation-Science Research Center (C-SRC), an organization that would not only support scientific research on Noah's Flood, but also reach out to the public by preparing creationist educational materials and encouraging schools to adopt them.[56] Following disagreements over the center's direction, the Segraveses broke away, taking the C-SRC name with them and leaving Morris to reorganize the remaining staff into the Institute for Creation Research (ICR).[57] In the 1970s the ICR grew rapidly, building its own team of over two dozen creation scientists and becoming increasingly independent from the Christian Heritage College.[58] It also gained notoriety by sponsoring creation-evolution debates in which Morris and his protégé Duane Gish, a onetime Michigan biochemist, teamed up to take on various evolutionists no fewer than 136 times during the decade, appearing before live audiences totaling over 100,000 people and radio listeners and TV viewers estimated at over 5 million more.[59] By the 1980s the ICR had become the flagship of creation science, publishing a steady stream of books, pamphlets, and a monthly newsletter called *Acts & Facts*, which eventually generated a mailing list of approximately 75,000 readers. It also provided summer seminars and flood geology tours of such sites as the Grand Canyon and Mount St. Helens, as well as a Museum of Creation and Earth History where visitors could see a scale model of Noah's Ark.[60] As the ICR grew, it reached out to creationist groups across the country, offering its speakers to "to any who wish to sponsor local creation seminars or similar meetings in their own areas."[61]

During the same period creationism was proving its political potential. Early on, Morris had resisted applying the idea politically—indeed, one of the reasons for his break with the C-SRC was his insistence on the importance of research and education as opposed to legislation and litigation. In the 1970s, however, as activists began to adopt his conception of creation science, Morris changed his view. As early as 1963, Nell Segraves and her friend Jean Sumrall, assisted by the newly established Creation Research Society, had petitioned the California Board of Higher Education to mandate the addition of creationism to the biology curriculum in public schools. Citing the Supreme Court's 1963 decision on school prayer in *Abington School District v. Shempp*, they argued that since the state had been required in that case to remain neutral on all issues involving religion, the teaching of evolution (promoting atheism) without an alternative based on biblical creation (promoting Christianity) could be considered to have violated the principle of neutrality.[62] Following the same logic, activists in Arizona began to call for more balanced treatment of evolution and divine creation, adopting the concept of "equal time" from regulatory rules covering political broadcasts that had recently been announced by the Federal Communications Commission (FCC).[63] Antievolutionists across the country began to take up the idea, and in 1973 it became state law when Russell Artist, a biology professor at Nashville's David Lipscomb College and the author of a creationist textbook, successfully sought a bill in the Tennessee legislature allowing equal time for the teaching of creationism in science classes.[64] Over the course of the decade, two dozen similar bills were introduced in twelve state legislatures, state agencies and boards of education approved the use of creationist texts in at least six states, and local school boards in many parts of the nation passed resolutions supporting equal time for the teaching of creationism.[65] By 1981 even Henry Morris had become a believer, celebrating the coming of equal time for creationism, declaring the

1970s to be the "decade of creation," and predicting that the term "may well apply even more to the decade of the eighties."[66]

As bills providing equal time for creationism appeared in the legislatures, creation science began to make its way through the courts. Following World War II, federal courts became more active in extending First Amendment freedoms to the states, and political movements of all kinds came to rely on them in claiming rights and seeking protection against unconstitutional state statutes. Although antievolutionists had no reason to regard the judiciary as especially friendly, court rulings in a series of freedom-of-religion cases running from *Everson v. Board of Education* (1947) to *Lemon v. Kurzman* (1971) suggested a reading of the First Amendment that required public agencies to practice strict religious neutrality while allowing individuals more freedom of religious expression. As early as 1970, Leona Wilson, the mother of Houston high school student Rita Wright, had tested the waters. In a suit against the city's school system, Wilson argued that the teaching of evolution not only constituted state establishment of a secular religion but also denied her daughter's right to express her own religious views by insisting that her creationist beliefs were wrong.[67] Although eventually dismissed, the case of *Wright v. Houston Independent District* encouraged other legal challenges, among them actions brought by citizens against the National Science Foundation for funding the BSCS program and the Smithsonian Institution for sponsoring an evolutionary educational exhibit called "The Emergence of Man."[68] Nevertheless, these suits were almost always unsuccessful, as plaintiffs were unable to convince courts that the teaching of evolution either established a state religion or prevented the free exercise of their own faith. At the heart of the issue was the scientific status of evolution. With science enjoying strong cultural support, courts consistently sided with scientists and science educators who argued that instruction in evolutionary theory was in no way religious. It followed that since evolution could not be claimed as religion, creationism would have to be cast as science. "As long as the teaching of creationism is done strictly in a scientific context," Morris counseled teachers in a 1974 newsletter, "without reference to the Bible or other religious literature, such teaching is perfectly constitutional, legal and proper."[69]

Activists were ready for a new approach. After all, every time state and local statutes providing for the teaching of creationism had been enacted, they were almost immediately challenged by groups led by the ACLU and the National Association of Biology Teachers. In case after case, biblically based creationism had failed to pass the so-called Lemon test set in *Lemon v. Kurzman*, by which courts required all state-sponsored programs to have a secular purpose, to neither advance nor inhibit religious practice, and to avoid excessive entanglement between church and state. Thus in 1975, when Tennessee's equal time law was pronounced unconstitutional, creationists adopted Morris's advice: stressing religion less and science more, they began to attack evolution as bad science, while building up creation science as an acceptable scientific alternative.[70] By 1978 the argument had become a full-fledged legal strategy, spelled out by creationist law student Wendell Bird. In an article in the *Yale Law Journal*, Bird contended that creation science could be taught entirely as science, therefore not running afoul of constitutional restrictions on teaching religion. (Not teaching it, he argued in the same article, would violate the rights of creationist students to the free exercise of their religion.)[71] When Paul Ellwanger, a South Carolina respiratory therapist and head of the creationist group Citizens for Fairness in Education, shaped Bird's suggestions into a model state statute, activists believed that they had found a "balanced treatment" bill that could stand up to constitutional scrutiny. As copies circulated throughout the country, the proposed statute was introduced in eight state legislatures in 1980 and in fifteen more in 1981.[72] Lawmakers in Arkansas soon adopted a version of the statute by a lopsided margin, and creationists celebrated its passage, declaring balanced treatment to be "an idea," in the words of North Little Rock's Reverend A. A. Blount, "whose time has come."[73]

In arguing for balanced treatment, however, creationists had to contend with the legal legacy of the Scopes case. Edward Larson has shown how the Scopes legend continued to flourish in the 1960s, with its misinterpretations of Bryan and Darrow becoming mainstream history. In *Epperson v. Arkansas*, Larson argues, the legend was written into law. Drafted by Justice Abe Fortas, who had followed the case closely as a Memphis high school student in 1925, the majority opinion in *Epperson* referred repeatedly to the forty-year-old trial, both beginning and ending with references to it. Determined to correct the errors of earlier courts, Fortas found the 1928 Arkansas law to be unconstitutional (and, by implication, the 1925 Tennessee law along with it) because it violated the First Amendment prohibition against the establishment of religion. Accepting the argument that Arkansas had a religious purpose in outlawing evolution, Fortas went on to declare that in order to ensure due process, all states had to remain strictly neutral toward religion.[74] While the decision was a clear defeat for the creationist cause, a few creationists were actually heartened by its insistence on strict state neutrality. After all, with the widespread reintroduction of evolution in the public schools in the 1960s, the tables had been turned, so that creationists were now the ones barred from the classroom, in a situation similar to evolutionists forty years earlier. Adopting the premise that states must assume an attitude of neutrality toward alternative theories of origins, they began to call for balanced treatment of competing explanations, insisting that teachers be free to teach creationism as well as evolution. In essence, they found themselves making almost the same case as Clarence Darrow, whom they began to cite frequently (if incorrectly) as having stated at the Scopes trial that it was "bigotry for public schools to teach only one theory of origins."[75] Indeed, creationists discovered not only a new friend in Darrow, but also a new hero in—of all people—John Scopes. As creationist theologian Norman Geisler put it, "John Scopes summed it up well when he said, 'If you limit a teacher to only one side of anything the whole country will eventually have only one thought, be one individual.' "[76]

But creationists could not entirely escape the legacy of the trial. When Arkansas's "Balanced Treatment Bill" was challenged by a coalition of liberal clergy and the ACLU, provoking the 1982 action of *McLean v. Arkansas Board of Education*, the case was at once dubbed "Scopes II." Convinced that the trial would be a media spectacle, reporters from seventy-five news organizations converged on Little Rock to cover the proceedings.[77] In the absence of charismatic personalities such as Bryan and Darrow, however, or a sympathetic schoolteacher like Scopes to stand in the dock as defendant (it being a civil rather than a criminal proceeding), the case lacked the drama of the original trial and left the media without a sensational story. In contrast to the Scopes trial, the court allowed testimony from expert witnesses for both sides. The appearance of figures such as Harvard paleontologist Stephen Jay Gould inspired little popular interest, however, and news reports consistently treated the testimony of the specialists as arcane and insignificant.[78] At times the creationist experts did attract attention, as when Geisler, a professor of theology at Dallas Theological Seminary, speculated on the stand about his belief that Satan was behind the presence of UFOs.[79] (In general the creationist experts were unprepared and disorganized, unable to agree among themselves on the character or purpose of creation science, let alone point to any of its accomplishments. In fact, one of the state's best witnesses, British astrophysicist Chandra N. Wickramasinghe, who testified to the inability of Darwinian theory to explain the origins of life, also offered his personal view that creation science was "claptrap.")[80] But for the most part, reporters paid no attention to the testimony, treating the trial instead in stereotypical terms, less as a sequel to Scopes than a rerun. In fact, in her study of media coverage of the Arkansas trial, science writer Marcel La Follette found that John Scopes was mentioned more often than any of the actual witnesses. She concluded that "if the readers learned anything, we may assume it was the details of the Scopes trial."[81]

For creationists, *McLean* was a decisive defeat. In a detailed and sweeping opinion, Judge William Overton completely denied the case for balanced treatment. More important, Overton not only found the Arkansas law unconstitutional, but also declared unequivocally that evolution was not religion and creation science was not science.[82] As if that were not enough, the case reinforced Scopes stereotypes, adding to the common perception of creationists as dogmatic fundamentalists, while allowing evolutionists to continue playing the more popular role of defenders of free speech and open inquiry. Trapped by such impressions, creationists struggled unsuccessfully to free themselves from the Scopes myth. "The 'Fundamentalists' of the 1920's were categorically opposed to teaching evolution and for teaching only the Genesis account of Creation," explained Geisler in a sharply worded criticism of the McLean decision, in which he tried to divorce contemporary creationism from the earlier antievolution movement. Again citing (and misquoting) Darrow, he reiterated the claim that the sides had been switched and that creationists now played the part of Scopes: "And if it was bigotry when the creationists were trying to keep the evolutionists out, it is still bigotry when evolutionism attempts to exclude creationism."[83] The argument was convoluted and ultimately unconvincing. With McLean, the case for balanced treatment collapsed, confounded by legal precedents and public perceptions of events that had taken place more than five decades earlier. Nevertheless, the opponents of evolution were not about to surrender. Stopped short by the judges, they turned once again to the jury of public opinion, where they had experienced so much success in the past. "When you consider what I was trying to do, we've been victorious," commented state senator James L. Holsted, the original sponsor of the Arkansas bill, after the court ruling. "I feel like we really won because people are talking about it, kids will be asking about it. Teachers will have to talk about creation-science. There'll be more debates on college campuses. In fact, it's just starting."[84]

Connections

Among the ways that movements maintain themselves over long periods is by connecting to other movements. As David Meyer and Nancy Whittier have shown, movements exist within constellations of overlapping organizations, networks, and individuals. Thus activists can participate in multiple movements, moving back and forth across easily penetrable boundaries to work in tandem with others who share their general goals and values. Meyer and Whittier have called the phenomenon "spillover," and in a study of the interaction between feminists and peace activists in the 1980s, they showed how it worked to revitalize both of these left-leaning movements.[85] Coincidentally, at almost exactly the same time a similar example of spillover was taking place on the right.

With the rise of the New Christian Right, the creationist movement saw the potential to exercise unprecedented political power. In television evangelists Jerry Falwell, Pat Robertson, and Tim LaHaye they found old friends and strong supporters, as well as access to their millions of viewers. Through politicians such as Senator Jesse Helms of North Carolina, they were introduced to conservative leaders and policy makers. In the political operatives of the NCR—Gary Bauer, Ralph Reed, Richard Viguerie, Paul Weyrich—they met seasoned professionals who could counsel them how to build their movement and expand its influence. Moreover, with the post-Watergate realignment taking place in American party politics, antievolutionists had begun to find common cause with conservatives in the Republican Party. One who seemed especially sympathetic was presidential candidate Ronald Reagan, who in his 1980 campaign described his doubts about evolution to a group of conservative religious leaders, calling it a "theory only" and saying that "I have a great many questions about [evolution]. I think that recent discoveries down through the years have pointed up great flaws in it."[86]

To cement their connections to the NCR, creationists turned to the concept of "secular humanism." Over the course of the 1980s, the term would become commonplace among conservative commentators. But it began as a creationist concept, introduced in a 1978 article in the *Texas Tech Law Review* by conservative legal theorist John Whitehead, who was attempting to argue that the First Amendment's establishment clause could be brought to bear against the teaching of evolution. Searching for possible precedents and making use of an obscure footnote to the 1961 case of *Torcaso v. Watkins*, Whitehead contended that, in seeking to prevent the establishment of a theistic state religion, the Supreme Court had in fact created an atheistic one, the religion of "secular humanism."[87] As legal strategy, the concept was weak from the start, since courts had been consistent in declaring evolution a secular and scientific principle rather than a religious one. As a political tool, however, the idea had potential. Adopted by LaHaye in his book *The Battle for the Mind*, it soon became a rallying cry for the NCR: everything from abortion and homosexuality to the loss of the Panama Canal was attributed to a conspiracy of secular humanists centered in organizations like the American Humanist Association and extending its influence into government, the media, and the public schools.[88] Almost immediately secular humanism became a bond between creationism and the NCR, introducing creationists to a more extensive set of cultural issues while simultaneously instructing a broad cross section of Christian conservatives on evolution's role in inspiring so much of the immorality of the times. For their part, creationist writers began to cast their arguments in broader terms. Writing in the ICR's newsletter *Impact*, creation scientist Jerry Bergman argued that creationism was only one of many issues that secular humanists had conspired to banish from the public schools. "Rarely do students hear an objective and effective presentation of the case against abortion, homosexuality or fornication," observed Bergman in 1980. "Again, one side of these issues tends to be labeled *non-religious* and therefore a topic teachers are permitted to discuss, but the other side tends to be labeled *religious*, and off limits in the school. The facts are that, for whatever reason, teachers often indoctrinate their students in *one* side, and many times it is the secular humanist position."[89]

Creationists had no trouble adopting the argument against secular humanism. Among antievolutionists, the assumption of a connection between evolution and immorality was an old one, reaching back to Bryan's condemnation of Social Darwinism. As early as the 1960s, Henry Morris had claimed that evolutionary principles provided the starting point for every false ideology of the modern age; it was "at the foundation of communism, Fascism, Freudianism, social Darwinism, behaviourism, Kinseyism, materialism, atheism and, in the religious world, modernism and Neo-orthodoxy."[90] Similar statements were made a decade later by the C-SRC's Nell Segraves, who claimed to have conducted social scientific studies demonstrating a cause-and-effect relationship between evolutionary theory and social breakdown, especially "divorce, abortion, and rampant venereal disease."[91] By 1980 activists like Bergman were blaming it not only for abortion, homosexuality, and fornication, but also for "bondage, sadomasochism, pedophilia, and incest."[92] Writing in his *God's Own Scientists*, a study of creationism in the 1980s, cultural anthropologist Christopher Toumey argued insightfully that creationists had come to assume that the principal danger of evolutionism was not determinism, the fact that it allowed no free will, but rather randomness, the implication that it led inevitably to disorder and immorality. Whereas earlier antievolutionists (like Bryan and his colleagues of the 1920s) had been most concerned about the notion of natural selection, contending that it turned people into prisoners of their biological history, creationists now worried more about random mutation, charging that if people saw themselves as the product of disorderly events, they would act in disorderly ways. Thus they saw connections between evolutionism and every imaginable evil. Moreover, in combating those evils, they found common cause with conservative activists who were fighting a host of political enemies. As one North Carolinian told Toumey: "The homosexual gay rights movement is very evolutionary. The women's movement is very evolutionary. The civil rights movement is very evolutionary. All these things have their roots in evolution."[93]

By collaborating with the NCR, creationists were able to bring their message to growing numbers. From the 1930s on, antievolutionism had been a small and self-contained—almost sectarian—movement. Even in the 1960s, with the growing influence of creation science, creationist groups had given little attention to building a mass membership. Now, however, with conservative religion and conservative politics both on the rise, creationists saw the chance to enlist countless new recruits in their cause. Across America, sympathetic televangelists were introducing creationism to millions of viewers, sometimes preaching it themselves, more often hosting its speakers, promoting its literature, and sponsoring its films and television specials.[94] Mass membership organizations like Tim LaHaye's American Coalition for Traditional Values, Beverly LaHaye's Concerned Women for America, Phyllis Schlafly's Eagle Forum, and Jerry Falwell's Moral Majority had made antievolution a part of their conservative agendas. Advocacy organizations such as the Rutherford Institute began to offer legal assistance to students and their parents who brought cases opposing the teaching of evolution in their schools to the courts.[95] Grassroots groups like Mel and Norma Gabler's Educational Research Analysts, Robert Simonds's Committee for Excellence in Education/National Association of Christian Educators, and Donald Wildmon's American Family Association created home-grown campaigns to remove evolution, sex education, and liberal teaching techniques from public schools.[96] Public sentiment seemed to be swinging to the creationist side, as polls in the 1980s consistently showed surprisingly strong support—often as high as 75 percent—for teaching creationism alongside or in place of evolution in the public schools.[97] Encouraged by these polls, Henry Morris predicted even greater growth. "Whatever the future may hold for the present complex of creationist organizations," he wrote in 1984, "we can be sure that things will not go back like they were before. Creation will continue to be recognized by multitudes as a truly viable model of origins."[98]

Creationists took heart even in the courts. After *McLean*, with its ringing declaration that evolution was not religion and creation science was not science, the legal strategists seemed stymied, uncertain as to how to proceed. Nevertheless, they continued to make their case. On the question of whether evolution theory constituted a religion, the concept of secular humanism appeared to provide some possibilities. In his 1987 decision in *Smith v. Mobile*, Alabama federal district judge W. Brevard Hand accepted the argument that secular humanism was an atheistic religion, but his finding was soon overturned on appeal, leaving creationists at an apparent dead end.[99] At roughly the same time, the issue of creation science's scientific credentials remained very much alive in a complex series of Louisiana cases that culminated in the Supreme Court's 1987 ruling in *Edwards v. Aguillard*. In this case, creationist lawyers led by Wendell Bird sought court sanction for Louisiana's Act 590, arguing that the bill's predominant purpose was scientific (allowing an alternative scientific view in the classroom) and secular (promoting fairness and academic freedom). Writing for the Court's majority, Justice William Brennan rejected these claims, deeming the act an unconstitutional attempt at religious establishment while also finding that creation science was more religious than scientific.[100] On the announcement of the verdict, evolutionists were ecstatic, believing that creationism was no longer a threat. ("Somewhere in heaven John Scopes is smiling," declared the ACLU's Ira Glasser.)[101] Yet Brennan's decision had left a door open, allowing that a more clearly scientific brand of creation science might be constitutional, especially if it were "done with the clear secular intent of enhancing the effectiveness of science instruction."[102] Moreover, in a minority decision, Justice Antonin Scalia, a recent appointment to the Court, made a strong case that the citizens of Louisiana, including Christian fundamentalists, were entitled "as a secular matter" to have "whatever scientific evidence there may be against evolution presented in their schools, just as Mr. Scopes was entitled to present whatever scientific evidence there was for it."[103] Even in defeat, then, creationists could claim a certain victory, confident that future courts, especially those containing more conservative appointees, might well allow for scientific alternatives to evolution. Indeed, for some the defeat itself had a silver lining. Preparing his 1988 campaign for president, Pat Robertson declared himself delighted on learning of the Louisiana ruling: "Everyone in America who believes he or she was created by God will be outraged," he told the press. "This is going to help my position wonderfully."[104]

For all its high hopes, however, creationism seemed to come up short in the 1980s. Following a flurry of activity in state legislatures in 1981 and 1982, most of it in response to the *McLean* decision, creationist initiatives became few and far between. As for the alliance with the New Christian Right, it soon proved to have its problems. In making connections to the NCR, creationists were suddenly required to compete with other issues and interests, distracting attention from evolution and diverting resources to other conservative causes. As one in a constellation of concerns, evolution was often shunted to the side in favor of more pressing issues like abortion, homosexuality, or school prayer. Occasionally creationists would find their allies in the NCR deserting them, as when Falwell, threatened by the loss of accreditation for his Liberty University, appeared to backtrack on his support for the teaching of creation science there.[105] But as Toumey has shown, even when the alliance was working there were certain costs. For instance, whenever Falwell made the case for creationism, many of those who opposed his views on other matters came to distrust the creationist cause as well. In the process, creationists were caught in a kind of whipsaw, alienating potential supporters while at the same time diluting their own message by casting it as part of a larger collection of conservative concerns.[106] Added to this was the fact that many creationists had never been predisposed to engage in politics in the first place, preferring to work within their churches. Related as well was the extraordinary growth in Christian schools at this time, along with the parallel increase in home schooling among Christian conservatives. For parents of children in these schools, almost all of whom used standardized curricula in which creation science was the exclusive explanation of human origins, the teaching of evolution in public schools was no longer much of a concern.[107] Most important, however, was the growing realization that in making connections to other conservative groups, creationists had gained little. Abandoned by their allies, abused by the Republican politicians who had courted their votes but failed to deliver on their concerns, they increasingly seemed to pull back from politics. Having had its "day in the sun" in the early 1980s, wrote Toumey, creationism "receded to the lesser ranks."[108]

But there were other reasons for the creationist movement's failure to thrive. Perhaps most important of these was the inability to overcome stereotypes. Here as before, the legend of the Scopes trial figured prominently, especially as it was embodied in a dramatic retelling that would shape public perceptions of the movement for decades. In *Inherit the Wind*, Jerome Lawrence and Robert E. Lee's 1955 stage play, history was transformed into theater, and the events of the trial took on mythic meaning. The play was set not in Dayton, Tennessee, in 1925, but in the fictional southern town of "Hillsboro" at an indeterminate date "not too long ago." While featuring Bryan, Darrow, and Scopes, it portrayed them in stylized and highly stereotypical terms, as Bryan became the bombastic Matthew Harrison Brady, Darrow the folksy Henry Drummond, and Scopes the principled Bertram Cates. Other characters were added for effect, including a bigoted fundamentalist preacher and his troubled and torn daughter, who was portrayed in the play as Cates's fiancée. While the plot roughly traced events of the trial, it provided a decidedly more dramatic depiction, featuring a furious confrontation between Brady and Drummond in which Brady is clearly bested, left pathetically babbling out the names of the books of the Bible. (In the last act he dies of a stroke, falling face first onto the courtroom floor as he attempts to give his final summation.) Originally written as a response to the abuse of power by McCarthy-era politicians, the play is a paean to academic freedom and scientific progress. It is also a thinly veiled attack on creationism, which is presented as the product of fundamentalist fanaticism. Whereas critics blasted the play as a caricature, audiences loved it, and it soon became a staple of the American theater, enjoying some eight hundred successive showings on Broadway and inspiring thousands of performances by professional, school, and community theater troupes. In Stanley Kramer's 1960 Hollywood movie version, featuring memorable performances by Frederic March and Spencer Tracy, the play took on iconic status, effectively replacing history with myth. By 1967 journalist Joseph Wood Krutch could write that "most people who have any notions about the trial get them from the play . . . or from the movie."[109]

For creationists, *Inherit the Wind* posed insurmountable problems. The movie version was particularly troublesome, having introduced millions of moviegoers to the possibility that the biblical account of creation might be contradictory and inconsistent. Additionally, in its stereotypical treatment of Bryan and his fundamentalist followers, it confirmed popular preconceptions that creationism was based on biblical literalism rather than scientific study. Though creationists cried foul, their attempts to counter the inaccuracies of the movies met with little success. Henry Morris recounted how the movie version haunted him during a speaking tour of New Zealand in the early 1970s, as it appeared on public TV stations in city after city during or immediately after his visit.[110] Throughout the 1980s activists continued to criticize the film, and students at Bryan College went so far as to write an alternative play, entitled *Destiny in Dayton*, based more closely on the transcripts of the trial.[111] Nevertheless, creationists seemed unable to undo the damage that had been done by *Inherit the Wind*, in part because they could not decide exactly how to tell their version of the story. In his syndicated TV special "The Case for Creation," filmed partially in the same Rhea County courtroom where Scopes had stood trial, television evangelist D. James Kennedy spoke for many of them in trying to take both sides at once, denouncing Darrow for his attacks on Bryan and biblical Christianity, but embracing his supposed support for allowing alternative views into the classroom. In closing, Kennedy was reduced to parroting what was rapidly becoming a time-honored misquotation: "Remember, Clarence Darrow was right," he intoned solemnly. "It is the height of bigotry to teach only one view of origins. That bigotry needs to end."[112]

Unable to create a mass movement because of continuing popular perceptions, creationists took another path. With the failure of Pat Robertson's 1988 presidential primary campaign, Christian conservative operatives suggested an alternative approach to politics, putting aside national ambitions in favor of local successes. In particular, Christian Coalition executive director Ralph Reed began to advise Christian conservative candidates on how to win lower-level elections, encouraging them to seek the support of secular and moderate voters by downplaying their religious credentials and controversial political views. This so-called stealth strategy seemed tailor-made for creationist candidates, especially those running in local school board elections where easy entry and low visibility was a distinct advantage.[113] The election of 1992 appeared to signal the success of the strategy, as candidates backed by the Christian Coalition and the California-based Citizens for Excellence in Education won control of school boards in Texas, California, Florida, and several other states.[114] The most visible of the victories was in California, where conservative candidates (one of whom was an employee of the ICR) captured a majority of seats on San Diego County's Vista Unified School Board of Trustees. In keeping with the stealth strategy, the victorious candidates waited until after their election to announce an agenda that featured introducing creationism to the curriculum, limiting access to questionable library books, and revising sex education to include warnings against abortion and homosexuality.[115] What followed were two years of rancorous meetings, along with a recall campaign and a mobilization of determined moderates who regained majority control in the next election. For creationists, the reversal was another setback, demonstrating not only the failure of the stealth strategy, but also the difficulty of overcoming popular perceptions, even at the local level. As one of the Vista moderates put it, "People get very upset when one group takes the position that they speak for God."[116]

Strategies and Goals

For movements to endure they must be flexible. Changing circumstances require an ability to adopt new strategies and sometimes even entirely new goals, "bending with the wind," as sociologist Debra Minkoff has put it, in order to survive. In a study of organizational change in almost nine hundred American minority and women's organizations from 1955 to 1985, Minkoff found a surprising amount of adaptability, as groups responded to changing political conditions by revising organizational objectives and on occasion even instituting new collective identities for themselves. While the study suggested that adaptability has its limitations as well as its risks, it found that those groups that are equipped to be the most flexible are the ones that are most likely to survive.[117]

It was a lesson that creationists came to learn in the 1990s. At the beginning of the decade, their movement was in political trouble, with the NCR in retreat and conservative supporters going down to defeat in elections at every level. Efforts on the legal front had been frustrating as well, as following *Edwards v. Aguillard* federal courts consistently continued to deem creationist efforts unconstitutional.[118] Even at the grass roots the movement seemed to be at a standstill. Thus activists adapted: led by Phillip E. Johnson, a born-again evangelical and professor at Berkeley's Boalt Hall Law School, a diverse coalition of evolution opponents came together to recast short-term strategies and redefine long-term goals. In a series of books, beginning with his best-selling *Darwin on Trial*, Johnson laid out a plan. For decades creationists had been on the defensive, contending that creation science could be shown to be scientific and therefore constitutional.

After *Edwards*, it was clear to everyone that they had failed, that creation science was too entangled in its religious roots to ever claim constitutionality. It was time to take another tack. Since creationists could no longer defend creation science, argued Johnson, a onetime criminal prosecutor, they should instead put evolution on the stand. After all, courts had consistently allowed that arguments against evolution could be presented in the classroom as long as they were secular and scientific. By picking away at evolution, piece by piece, like a trial lawyer breaking down a recalcitrant witness, creationists could cast doubt on its scientific status, eventually discrediting not only its mechanisms but also its presuppositions, meaning the methodological materialism on which it was premised. Adopting a less legalistic metaphor, Johnson claimed that by finding cracks in the theory, then applying persistent pressure on them, pounding away little by little, creationists could eventually split the entire trunk of the tree that was naturalistic science. He called the new strategy "the wedge."[119]

Its centerpiece was the idea of intelligent design. Introduced by chemist-historian Charles B. Thaxton in the 1980s, the concept claimed that certain living organisms were so complex that they could not have come into being by evolutionary means. In his 1996 book *Darwin's Black Box*, biochemist Michael Behe maintained that recent scientific advances, especially in cell biology and genetics, had made clear that certain intracellular processes and structures—the biochemical cascades that produce blood clotting, the molecular motor of a bacterial flagellum—were too irreducibly intricate to be explained by random mutation; they could only have been created by some intelligent source. William Dembski, a mathematician and philosopher, added to the argument, insisting that complex but specific patterns in nature, like the sequencing of amino acids in proteins, could be shown to be so mathematically improbable that they could not be the product of a random process, requiring instead deliberate design.[120] As to the identity of the designer, both Behe and Dembski were agnostic, insisting that intelligent design did not require a theistic creator. (In fact, neither writer completely denied the existence of evolution, since ID did not preclude processes such as natural selection.) That said, most of the early ID proponents were, like Thaxton, conservative evangelicals as well as creationists. The concept received strong support from old-earth creationists, and some of the first gatherings of ID scholars were sponsored by old-earth creationist groups such as John Buell's Texas-based Foundation for Thought and Ethics. But intelligent design soon began to attract the attention of a broadening circle of creationists, including even some of the young-earth variety, who saw it as an alternative to the materialistic naturalism of evolutionary theory.[121] Indeed, in 1990 Phillip Johnson was already asserting that ID had the potential to bring together creationists of almost every conceivable kind. "The important thing is not whether God created all at once or in stages, or whether the process of creation required a greater or lesser period of time. Anyone who thinks that the biological world is the product of a pre-existing intelligence," he explained, "and that its development up to and including mankind occurred in furtherance of a divine purpose, is a creationist in the most important sense of the term."[122]

For contemporary creationists, intelligent design was an unusually useful tool. As theory, the concept was controversial; many critics argued that it was theoretically vague and scientifically untestable. Even its strongest supporters, like Dembski, had to admit that the theory was undeveloped and that, as far as testing it was concerned, its advocates had "our work cut out for us."[123] In practice, however, it was a brilliant tactical tool. By adopting it, creationists could break the connection to biblical literalism that had dominated scientific creationism for decades. In freeing themselves from literalism, they could begin to overturn the general understanding of creationism as a fundamentalist movement. In court, they could make a credible case that because ID was not an inherently religious notion, it could offer a constitutionally acceptable alternative to the teaching of evolution.[124] Outside the courts—as when addressing audiences of conservative evangelicals—they could just as easily argue the opposite, stressing the idea's religious implications. (Dembski would tell the National Religious Broadcasters that "Intelligent Design opens the whole possibility of us being created in the image of a benevolent God.").[125] By remaining open to different descriptions of the character of design, they could avoid doctrinal divisions among themselves, escaping the internecine conflict that had plagued creationism for so much of its past.[126] There were other practical advantages as well. The adoption of ID bought the creationist movement a certain degree of scientific legitimacy, because for the first time creationists could point to the support of a small but noticeable number of scientists, some with credible scientific credentials and positions at secular universities.[127] It also offered growing financial and organizational support from groups like the Seattle-based Discovery Institute, a conservative think tank whose Center for the Renewal of Science and Culture (CRSC) was created to sponsor ID research, inform the public about it, and introduce it to the public schools.[128] Above all, by replacing God with "intelligent cause" and creation with "abrupt appearance" or "initial complexity," creationists believed that they could recast creationism as a mainstream movement. "By this broader definition," boasted Johnson, "at least eighty percent of Americans, including me, are creationists."[129]

Throughout the 1990s, activists applied the new approach. In contrast to earlier advocates of creation science, with their elaborate explanations of creation based on flood geology, these new-style creationists came with no full-blown theories of their own. Instead, they described themselves as critics and questioners, emphasizing gaps in the evidence and pointing out problems with existing explanations of evolution. Using terminology like "alternative theories," "evidence against evolution," or simply "other views," they began to argue that teachers should be allowed to present all sides of the evolution issue, bringing to bear the best scientific evidence both for and against the theory. In Alabama, at the urging of Governor Fob James, the State Board of Education required that biology textbooks include a disclaimer on the inside cover warning students that since "no one was present when life first appeared on earth," any statement of its origins "should be considered as theory, not fact."[130] (Concerned that the disclaimer was not enough, and frustrated by the continuing presence of evolutionary theory in Alabama classrooms, James used public money to send a copy of Johnson's *Darwin on Trial* to every high school biology teacher in the state.)[131] In Georgia and Ohio, bills were introduced requiring that "evidence against evolution" be taught in the public schools.[132] But the biggest controversies came as a result of federal "Goals 2000" legislation that required regular review of state educational standards, inspiring activists to initiate campaigns to exclude evolution from elementary and secondary school science standards in as many as one-third of the states.[133] The most visible of these campaigns was in Kansas, where in 1999 the State Board of Education, acting at the urging of several newly elected conservative members, removed all references to "macro-evolution" (meaning change from one species to another) from state science standards, leaving local schools the option of teaching it while also ensuring that it would not be included on statewide assessment tests. Kansas science teacher Harry McDonald explained the significance of removing evolution from the tests: "Many districts, not with any particular agenda, will leave out evolution because, obviously, it must not be important. Why spend our time teaching something that isn't going to be assessed?"[134]

In many of these controversies, intelligent design figured prominently. As early as 1990, activists petitioned state and local school boards to adopt *Of Pandas and People*, the high school biology textbook commissioned by John Buel's Foundation for Thought and Ethics to bring the concept into the high school classroom.[135] Throughout the mid-1990s discussions of the teaching of ID surfaced in state legislatures, with bills calling for its introduction in over a dozen states.[136] By the end of the decade, as attention turned to revising state science standards, ID had become a watchword of the new creationism. Beginning in Kansas, where the Discovery Institute took the lead in lobbying, creationists used the idea to build bridges between evangelicals, conservative mainline Protestants,

A MESSAGE FROM THE ALABAMA STATE BOARD OF EDUCATION

This textbook discusses evolution, a controversial theory some scientists present as a scientific explanation for the origin of living things, such as plants, animals and humans.

No one was present when life first appeared on earth. Therefore, any statement about life's origins should be considered as theory, not fact.

The word "evolution" may refer to many types of change. Evolution describes changes that occur within a species. (White moths, for example, may "evolve" into gray moths.) This process is microevolution, which can be observed and described as fact. Evolution may also refer to the change of one living thing to another, such as reptiles into birds. This process, called macroevolution, has never been observed and should be considered a theory. Evolution also refers to the unproven belief that random, undirected forces produced a world of living things.

There are many unanswered questions about the origin of life which are not mentioned in your textbook, including:

- Why did the major groups of animals suddenly appear in the fossil record (known as the "Cambrian Explosion")?
- Why have no new major groups of living things appeared in the fossil record for a long time?
- Why do major groups of plants and animals have no transitional forms in the fossil record?
- How did you and all living things come to possess such a complete and complex set of "Instructions" for building a living body?

Study hard and keep an open mind. Someday, you may contribute to the theories of how living things appeared on earth.

Alabama textbook warning label, 1996–2001

and Catholics like those in the state Catholic Conference who announced their support for the revised science standards.[137] In Pennsylvania, biblical creationists teamed up with design theorists to convince state education officials to allow ID as an alternative to evolution.[138] In several states, Republican Party organizations added their support, and in 2001 Senator Rick Santorum (R-Pa.) attempted to insert language supporting its teaching into federal "No Child Left Behind" legislation.[139] In communities nationwide, parents lobbied teachers and school boards to add ID to the science curriculum, while students discussed the concept in home-grown "creation clubs."[140] And in a national survey released in 2001, Zogby International found that 71 percent of a random sample of American adults approved teaching both Darwinian evolution and the evidence against it in the public schools, while an even higher percentage favored providing students with "evidence that points to an intelligent design of life."[141]

In spite of its apparent success, intelligent design faced some serious challenges. To continue to flourish, movements must be flexible, adopting tactics that allow them to respond to changes in their environment. As Minkoff has shown, many movements are unable to adapt, since changes can be costly and disruptive, and since they can leave supporters questioning their group's legitimacy.[142] Applied to the creationism of the 1990s, her findings suggest that short-term successes can conceal longer-term problems. Thus the greatest strength of intelligent design theory, its intellectual inclusiveness, soon began to seem like its greatest weakness. By choosing to put aside differences, ID theorists avoided disagreements, but they also begged questions, covered over conflicts, and limited their ability to act politically. "All you do is attack evolution," young-earth paleontologist Kurt Wise complained to Johnson. "You do not propose an alternative. This is a wimp's way out."[143] ID advocates with varying views began to speculate that the origins of life could be in anything from a biblical God to extraterrestrial intelligence, inanimate life forces, and meteor seedings.[144] Predictably, there were tensions when fundamentalists found themselves allied with agnostics, Orthodox Jews, Muslim fundamentalists, and, at one point in Kansas, a group of Hare Krishnas who showed up at a meeting on state standards wearing their saffron robes.[145] Alliances with Republican politicians also could be complicated. In Kansas, for example, evolution opponents became entangled in a factional struggle for control of the state Republican Party between moderate Governor Bill Graves and the party's right wing.[146] Finally, even when creationists were successful, their achievement was transitory. A year after Kansas revised its state science standards, and following protracted debates over the new policies, Republican primary voters ousted three of the four State Board of Education members who had voted to limit the treatment of evolution in state science standards. The new board soon reversed the previous policy. As one sympathetic observer commented, "on the topic of evolution, elected creationists cannot survive a public controversy."[147]

As before, creationism continued to be dogged by its past. Contemporary creationists insisted that their arguments represented a break with the past and avoided the problems associated with scientific creationism. But critics were quick to point out that many of their claims, including the criticism of transitional forms, increasing complexity, and radiometric dating, sounded suspiciously like the scientific creationism of the 1960s, and, for that matter, like the antievolution rhetoric of the 1920s.[148] "Creationism by any other name," observed Randy Moore, editor of The American Biology Teacher, "remains creationism."[149] Even more important were the public perceptions that continued to be shaped by the legacy of the Scopes trial. In 1996 a Tennessee attempt to introduce a bill penalizing teachers who presented evolution "as a fact" was buried amid front-page stories that consistently referred to the Scopes trial and called the statute a new "monkey" bill.[150] On the eve of the 2000 Republican primary in Kansas, People for the American Way sponsored a presentation of Origins, a play starring actor Ed Asner based on transcripts from the Scopes trial. Three thousand people attended, including Governor Graves.[151] Creationists like Nancy Pearcey continued to try to claim the trial for themselves, describing the controversy in Kansas as "Scopes in reverse." But the legacy of the trial continued to haunt them. While Pearcey pointed out that members of the Kansas audience had been prompted with cue cards saying "hiss" and "hubbub," she also had to admit that they repeatedly had gone beyond the instructions, breaking in to boo Bryan and cheer Darrow, making clear their support for evolution with "eager cheers and applause."[152]

Nevertheless, at the beginning of the twenty-first century creationism was thriving. Despite a series of setbacks, activists continued to be committed to their cause. Indeed, armed with intelligent design, they appeared to be more sure of themselves than at any time in the recent past. As Phillip Johnson put it in 2001, "the Wedge is lodged securely in the crack."[153] Betraying his fondness for military metaphors, Johnson compared recent campaigns against the teaching of evolution to the earliest battles of the American Revolution, reminding readers of his "Wedge Report" that their cause was a revolution too and that revolution required sustained struggle. Like the American patriots at Bunker Hill, they had suffered early defeats. But by continuing to make their case, even against overwhelming odds, they would eventually win the war. Evolution's enemies, he predicted confidently, were "on the way to eventual victory."[154]

From the 1930s on, the antievolution movement had endured. Adapting to a constantly changing environment, antievolutionists had proved remarkably resilient in constructing institutions, developing issues, establishing connections to other movements, and introducing tactics that allowed their movement to survive. At the same time, they had managed to combine change with continuity, maintaining identity, sustaining networks and organizations, and passing on the repertoires of protest and sustenance that had allowed them to retain the core character of their movement. The continuity came at a cost, in that antievolutionism had been continually constrained by its past, struggling to free itself from popular perceptions, many of them created as a result of the Scopes trial. Nevertheless, it had become a persistent feature of American politics in the twentieth century. And it seemed certain to continue into the twenty-first.

Conclusion

"*If you believe in evolution*," the science teacher told my son when he had asked about the relationship between gorillas and humans. After writing this book, I am no longer so surprised at her answer, nor at the ability of antievolutionists to influence what our children are being taught in their science classes. This book has described how they have done it. Between the close of World War I and the coming of the Great Depression, antievolutionists created a political movement. Coming together out of their shared fundamentalist faith, mobilizing through networks of ministers and their congregations, they seized on the theory of evolution as an explanation for the growing secularity of their time and proceeded to transform it from an idea into an issue. Over the course of the 1920s, armed with an uncompromising certainty in the rightness of their cause, they debated evolutionists, lobbied state legislators, and made unprecedented use of the media to bring their message to growing numbers of supporters. At the famous Scopes trial of 1925, they cheered William Jennings Bryan when he described their crusade as a symbolic struggle between the faith of their fathers and the forces of modern science. Afterward, encouraged by the court's decision and determined to carry on Bryan's campaign after his death, they intensified their protests, taking them into every part of the country. As conflict accelerated, the movement became dispersed and divided, beset with ideological and organizational infighting; by the end of the decade antievolutionism was in disarray. Nevertheless, since then several generations of activists have managed to maintain and renew the movement, which has continued through periods of retreat and revival over the rest of the twentieth century and into the twenty-first. With today's creationism, antievolution remains a force in our politics. Indeed, by most counts it is stronger now than at any time since the 1920s.

So what is the influence of the antievolution movement today, and what will it be in the coming decades? At its core, the identity of the movement remains Christian and conservative, solidly based on an abiding belief in the authority of the Bible and its transcendent truths. Since the appearance of The Fundamentals, antievolution's strongest supporters have been conservative evangelicals and fundamentalists, for whom evolution stands as a threat to the scriptural truths that provide the building blocks of their faith. Yet over the last century the movement has grown beyond its central core, expanding steadily as a result of the rise in evangelical church membership in the late twentieth century, while also reaching out to more mainline congregants. For several decades, national opinion surveys have consistently shown that almost half of all Americans believe that God created humans in their present form sometime in the last ten thousand years. In addition, about two-thirds of those asked in such surveys say that creation should be taught alongside evolution in the public schools.[1] Although these numbers have remained stable for some time, there is potential for them to increase even more. For while support for creationism has probably peaked in conservative churches, recent reports suggest that doubts about evolution may be growing within some of the more moderate mainline ones. Most portentous in this regard are changes taking place within the Roman Catholic Church, where conservative theologians have begun to reconsider Catholicism's long-standing position of qualified support for evolutionary theory.[2] In addition, a recent Pew Forum survey found that one-third of all members of mainline Protestant churches believe that life on earth has existed in its present form since the beginning of time.[3] Even some seculars—people who claim no religious affiliation or views—have begun to express their own concerns about evolution, often citing postmodernist arguments about the inherent subjectivity of science.[4] Finally, it should be remembered that while the creation movement is American in origin, its advocates have been exporting it for decades. Today there are active creationist groups not only in England, Canada, and Australia, but also in Europe, Latin America, and parts of Africa and the Middle East.[5]

As in the past, the antievolution movement of today consists primarily of networks of activist preachers and their grassroots followers, together with a small but dedicated cohort of creation scientists. Organized locally in churches and nationally in creationist ministries and research institutes, the movement is supported by the contributions of a few large donors and many small ones. Though the names are different—William Bell Riley has given way to Phillip Johnson; George McCready Price, to Henry Morris, Michael Behe, and William Dembski; the World's Christian Fundamentals Association, to the Discovery Institute—the movement remains organizationally much the same as in the 1920s. What has changed is its size and scope. In recent years, the annual budgets of organizations like Ken Ham's creationist ministry Answers in Genesis, Morris's Institute for Creation Research, and the Discovery Institute's Center for the Renewal of Science and Culture (recently renamed the Center for Science and Culture) have each been in the several millions of dollars.[6] These and similar smaller organizations have produced a steady stream of books, newsletters, pamphlets, journals, magazines, videos, and radio and television programs, while also sponsoring conferences, seminars, and creation safaris. For groups like Answers in

Genesis, Ham's Kentucky-based ministry, creationism has become big business; the organization has brought in profits of well over a million dollars yearly through the sale of merchandise such as baseball caps, mouse pads, coffee cups, and T-shirts.[7] Moreover, Ham has announced plans for a 25-million-dollar Creation Museum and Family Discovery Center, complete with dioramas of Adam and Eve being pursued by dinosaurs, a reconstruction of the interior of Noah's Ark ("You will hear the water lapping, feel the Ark rocking and perhaps even hear people outside screaming," explained Ham), and a planetarium designed to demonstrate how God created the world in six days.[8] Advocates of intelligent design (ID) have been especially skillful in networking and organizing. Over the last ten years, they have created think tanks like the Center for Science and Culture, which boasts a media-savvy staff and some forty fellows, including scientists, philosophers, and experts in public policy. They have constructed a growing network of associations, conferences, and research groups such as the International Society for Complexity, Information, and Design, which, among other activities, publishes its own online scholarly journal. In addition, they have generated new outreach organizations like the Access Research Network, which provides regular ID updates for a popular audience.[9] All told, today's antievolutionists, bound together by an intricate maze of instant messaging devices, listservs, podcasts, and weblogs, are more closely connected and instantly informed than any in the past.

The movement's message has remained remarkably consistent. From the 1920s on, antievolutionists have developed an elaborate critique of evolutionary theory, attacking it with an arsenal of theological, philosophical, and scientific arguments. (In the late 1970s, one creationist writer already was able to collect no fewer than 148 separate criticisms.)[10] As Raymond Eve and Francis Harrold have pointed out, however, almost all of the arguments boil down to basic themes that appear repeatedly in creationist literature. Thus from Bryan's time to our own, antievolutionists have insisted on adopting a vernacular version of the word "theory" that allows them to imply that the theory of evolution, far from consisting of a systematically tested explanation of facts, is nothing more than conjecture, an untested hypothesis, or ultimately just a good guess. They have cited the work of scientists—William Bateson in the 1920s, Stephen Jay Gould and Niles Eldredge in the 1970s and 1980s—who have been critical of any aspect or mechanism of evolution, embracing their criticisms to characterize the theory as bankrupt, flawed, or (at the very least) controversial. Pointing to the absence of a definitive "missing link," they have contended that discoveries from Java Man to "Lucy" have been either apes or modern humans, but not transitional forms. (When asked to state whether selected specimens are either apes or humans, creationists frequently disagree among themselves.)[11] Some antievolutionists insist that most fossil hominids are either mistakes or outright hoaxes. Others deny the validity of radiometric dating, speculating that the decay rates of radioactive isotopes may have been faster in the past. Still others reject the fossil record altogether, preferring cataclysmic explanations.[12] Today's advocates of intelligent design have introduced sophisticated concepts of complexity, probability, and specification, but the argument that evolution cannot explain complex organisms like the human eye has been commonplace among antievolutionists for generations, going back to Darwin's time.[13] Above all, the sophistication of contemporary creationism notwithstanding, many critics of evolution continue to resort to crude but always popular caricatures, describing evolution as a theory, as one creationist lecturer recently put it, whose purpose is to "make a monkey out of man."[14]

In debating Darwinism, antievolutionists have become masters at bringing their message to the public. In the 1920s they captured the attention of the country with their barnstorming tours, radio broadcasts, and high-profile stage debates, culminating in the media spectacle of the Scopes trial. Since that time they have continued to focus their efforts on reaching out to the general public, taking advantage of the new technologies of television, satellite broadcasting, and the World Wide Web. Today more than ever, creationists seem at home with modern media, making their case in op-ed pieces, on talk shows, and through constantly expanding Internet sources. Aware of the authority of science in modern mainstream culture, they state their case in scientific terms and point to the academic affiliations of the scientists who support them. Appealing to common sense and essential fairness, they ask for balanced treatment and equal time. When challenged on their claims or credentials, they appeal to populist sentiments, insisting that an elitist scientific establishment has prevented them from publishing their findings. Along the way, they have convinced many that their position represents not only a credible critique of evolution, but also an acceptable alternative to it. "I'm not a Ph.D. in biology," as Columbus lawyer Michael Cochran, an elected member of the Ohio State Board of Education put it. "But when I have X number of Ph.D. experts telling me this, and X number telling me the opposite, the answer is probably somewhere between the two."[15] Above all, today's creationists have attempted to put the Scopes trial behind them, depicting their case as a defense of academic freedom in which they are supporting the right of teachers to teach alternatives to evolutionary theory. "The greatest irony," wrote the Discovery Institute's Bruce Chapman and Jay Richards on the seventy-fifth anniversary of the trial, "is that Darwinists often invoke the Scopes Trial even while trying to prevent any evidence against Darwinism from being heard in the classroom. They've turned the lesson of Scopes entirely on its head."[16]

Translating theory into practice, antievolutionists also have continued to influence American politics, especially at the state and local levels. In the 1920s activists showed surprising political acumen in attracting allies, lobbying legislators, and exerting pressure on local school boards and teachers. Today they draw on many of the same skills. Although no one can replace Bryan, contemporary creationists have found powerful friends in the political world. In recent times, House majority leader Tom DeLay (R-Tex.) denounced evolution from the floor of Congress, at one point intimating that the theory was a reason for the 1999 high school shootings in Columbine, Colorado.[17] Senate majority leader Bill Frist (R-Tenn.) also expressed support for the teaching of intelligent design, joining Rick Santorum (R-Pa.), Sam Brownback (R-Kans.), and other sympathetic senators.[18] In a 2005 statement that attracted extensive media attention, President George W. Bush appeared to advocate equal treatment for evolution and ID in public schools.[19] That same year ten bills concerning the teaching of evolution were introduced in state legislatures, calling for equal time for scientific creationism (Mississippi), allowing or requiring the teaching of intelligent design (Arkansas and Pennsylvania), investigating alternatives to evolution (South Carolina), covering scientific evidence inconsistent with evolution (Georgia), and requiring that students be shown the full range of scientific views on the question (Alabama, Kansas, and Missouri).[20] Between 2000 and 2005, according to one count, activists raised the evolution issue in legislatures, state boards of education, and local school districts in no fewer than forty-three states.[21] Over the same time, state school boards in Minnesota, Ohio, and New Mexico adopted science standards that allowed more critical treatment of evolutionary theory. The Discovery Institute was particularly active in providing information and expert testimony to these and other state education agencies and boards. ("Personally, I believe in the Genesis account of God's creation," confessed Kansas school board member Connie Morris, who had relied on documents provided by the Discovery Institute in making arguments against evolution to the board. "But as a policymaker looking at science standards, I rely mostly on research and expert documentation.")[22] Meanwhile, local school boards have debated the issue in at least twenty states, and the controversy shows no sign of subsiding.[23] "My worry," said Ohio biologist Steve Edinger, "is that we're going to have to fight this school district by school district."[24]

Antievolutionists have been especially successful at the local level. In many places, they continue to rely on the same tactics used by their predecessors in the

1920s: agitating against evolution before local school boards, encouraging principals to revise curricula and remove textbooks that treat the topic, pressuring teachers not to cover it in their classes. Today, however, activists often find it easier to make their case. In confronting school boards, creationist parents receive support from national organizations like the Thomas More Law Center, a Michigan-based conservative legal foundation that provides advice and legal services to those who challenge school officials on the teaching of evolution.[25] Textbook publishers have become more receptive in responding to protests in local school districts. In 1996 Georgia's Cobb County school district asked Macmillan/McGraw-Hill to remove a chapter called "Birth of the Earth" from the fourth-grade textbook *Changing Earth*, following complaints from parents who objected to the absence of any reference to creation in the book. With electronic publishing, removing the seventeen-page chapter was easy and inexpensive, and the publisher willingly complied with the request. According to William Bennetta, president of the Textbook League, a textbook watchdog group, custom publishing of this kind "may mean that publishers will do less self-censorship in designing their basic books, but will censor particular versions of the books afterward to pander to particular factions in particular places."[26] In addition, many school administrators, under pressure from parents or local ministers, encourage their teachers to avoid the topic whenever possible. "Their principals tell them, 'We just don't have time to teach everything,' " complains the National Center for Science Education's (NCSE) Eugenie Scott, " 'so let's leave out the things that will cause us problems.' "[27]

It should come as no surprise that evolution is not taught in a significant number of schools. In some cases, its absence is the product of state policy. Here statewide curriculum standards play an increasingly important role. In a 2000 study of these standards, the Thomas B. Fordham Foundation found that nineteen states did a "weak-to-reprehensible" job of dealing with evolution, that eight states included creationist principles in their standards, and that four states avoided teaching evolution altogether.[28] But standards are not always the issue, since many teachers simply ignore them. In Indiana, for example, where the Fordham report ranked standards for teaching evolution among the top ten in the nation, studies have shown that 43 percent of high school biology teachers avoid or only briefly mention the theory, 33 percent spend less than three class days on it, and at least 20 percent either do not accept or are undecided about its scientific validity.[29] In many of these classrooms, field trips or science fairs take the place of evolution units, or other topics such as personal hygiene are treated instead. Often evolution may be mentioned but not seriously studied. "The most common remark that I've heard from teachers," stated John R. Christy, a climatologist and a member of Alabama's curriculum review board, "was that the chapter on evolution was assigned as reading but that virtually no discussion in class was taken."[30] Sometimes teachers avoid any treatment of the theory, as Randy Moore reported, by simply "not quite getting around" to it.[31] (The long-standing convention of including chapters on evolution at or near the end of science textbooks tends to encourage the practice.) Somewhat more surprising are those teachers who actually introduce creationism in their classrooms. Over the last two decades a score of studies have found that anywhere from one-fifth to one-third of science teachers in America include some treatment of creationism in their classes, and that even more endorse creationism and would like to include it.[32] Recent research suggests that these numbers are growing.[33] The result is that in many places there may actually be less teaching of evolution today than in the 1920s. At Rhea County High School in Dayton, Tennessee, for example, no one on the science faculty teaches the theory. Department head Joe Wiley does not teach creationism, but he believes that it would not "hurt a thing" to teach intelligent design. He sums up the views of his staff: "We all basically believe in the God of creation."[34]

Teachers avoid evolution for several reasons. Many admit that they do not feel competent to teach the subject. In Louisiana, for example, one study found that more than one-quarter of high school biology teachers thought that their academic training had left them unqualified to teach evolution, and 15 percent said that they did not recall ever hearing the word in any of their college biology courses.[35] More often, they mention pressure not to introduce the topic. In a study of Minnesota science teachers, Randy Moore and Karen Kramer found that the number reporting such constraint increased from 19 percent in 1994 to 48 percent in 2003.[36] In other states, particularly in the South and West, anecdotal evidence suggests that the influence of administrators, parents, and community members can be overwhelming. "You can imagine how difficult it would be," said Dr. John Frandsen, a zoologist and former chair of the committee on science and public policy of the Alabama Academy of Science, "to teach evolution as the standards prescribe in ever so many little towns, not only in Alabama but in the rest of the South, the Midwest—all over."[37] Furthermore, with increasing frequency teachers report resistance from their students. More often than in the past, students come to class with their minds already made up about evolution, having discussed the issue in their churches and with their families. "I see the same thing I saw five years ago, except now students think they're informed without having ever really read anything," noted Salina, Kansas, biology teacher John Wachholz. "Because it's been discussed in the home and other places, they think they know, [and] they're more outspoken. . . . They'll say, 'I don't believe a word you're saying.' "[38] Other teachers report that their students are more informed about their own creationist views, sometimes coming to school with creationist books, DVDs, or lists of "10 Questions to Ask Your Biology Teacher."[39] Brad Williamson, another Kansas science teacher, sees the hand of creationist organizations in the attitudes of some students. "Today there are many more arguments that kids bring to class," he observed, "a whole fleet of arguments, and they're all drawn out of the efforts by different groups." Yet although such students are sometimes willing to argue their case, more often they seem closed to other views. When evolution comes up, said Wachholz, they tune out: "They'll put their heads on their desks and pretend they don't hear a word you say."[40]

In spite of its growing impact, however, creationism's influence will continue to be limited. In the 1920s the antievolution movement followed a cyclical course in which peaks of protest culminated in division and eventual disarray. While today's creationism is in many ways different from in the past, it may well follow a similar cyclical pattern. At the very least, there continue to be factors that are certain to check the movement's progress. First among these will be the role of the courts. Over the last century, antievolutionist attempts to overcome the constitutional problems posed by the First Amendment's establishment clause have consistently ended in frustration and failure. In intelligent design, contemporary creationists have seen a possible solution. Yet in *Kitzmiller et al. v. Dover Area School District* (2005), the first federal court case to test ID's legal merits, Judge John E. Jones III dashed many of their hopes, pronouncing the Dover, Pennsylvania, School Board policy of encouraging its teaching to be unconstitutional. In a sweeping judgment, Jones not only discounted the claims of local school board members that they had adopted the theory for strictly scientific reasons, but also went on to declare that intelligent design was not science; rather, it was a "relabeled" creationism whose purpose was to advance "a particular version of Christianity."[41] In response, ID advocates characterized the decision as judicial censorship and committed themselves to continuing its teaching. "Anyone who thinks a court ruling is going to kill off interest in intelligent design is living in another world," declared the Discovery Institute's John West. "Americans don't like to be told there is some idea that they aren't permitted to learn about."[42] Nevertheless, since *Kitzmiller* even its strongest supporters have few illusions about the theory making much headway in the courts. As for ID, observed Discovery Institute attorney Casey Luskin, its ultimate validity will be determined "not by the courts but by the scientific evidence pointing to design."[43]

Then there are the political problems. From the 1920s on, antievolutionists have struggled to construct electoral majorities. Even when they have been elected, as during the days of the stealth strategy of the 1980s, these victories have tended to be temporary, with creation supporters frequently turned out of office in the next election. The reasons for their failure are several. First, while evolution has its critics, it still can elicit sizable popular support. Although public opinion surveys consistently show that almost half of the respondents express creationist views, they also reveal that about the same percentage believe in evolution, with substantial numbers (38 percent in a 2004 Gallup poll) supporting the proposition that God has guided the evolutionary process.[44] Moreover, with few exceptions, creationism has had little appeal to voters. In general elections, creationist candidates tend to have a polarizing effect, attracting attention, intensifying the issue, and mobilizing voters on the other side. In such cases, critics of creationism have been particularly successful in raising concerns about how others will view the election results. Invariably, complained Phillip Johnson, creationism's enemies have been able to create the impression that "people are laughing at us, people think we're rubes, industry doesn't want to come here anymore."[45] Scopes stereotypes continue to feed this perception. As final arguments were being made in the Kitzmiller case, for instance, a local theater troupe was opening a production of Inherit the Wind in an arts center only a block from the courthouse.[46] Perhaps most important, the issue itself tends to alienate mainstream voters who prefer less polarizing politics. On election day 2005, four days after the Kitzmiller trial ended, Dover voters turned out all eight school board members who were up for reelection, replacing them with a slate of candidates who campaigned against the decision to allow the teaching of ID in local schools. "I think voters were tired of the trial," said Bernadette Reinking, one of the winners, "they were tired of intelligent design, they were tired of everything that this school board brought about."[47]

A related problem is that creationism has a coalitional character, in that to win elections creationists must be able to build alliances, primarily with those supporting other conservative causes. More often than not, these alliances have been evanescent, with other conservatives proving to be fickle friends, eager to encourage creationists but ultimately more interested in their own agendas. When Pennsylvania's Senator Santorum found himself facing a hard fight for reelection in 2006, for example, he hurriedly backed away from his previous support for the teaching of ID, insisting in a National Public Radio interview that he was "not comfortable with intelligent design being taught in the science classroom."[48] Recently other conservatives have begun to distance themselves from the issue as well, warning about the dangers of getting too close to creationists lest they be seen as irrationally opposed to science. Intelligent design, observed conservative commentator Ross Douthat in the New Republic, has the potential to make conservatives "look like crackpots."[49] Sometimes creationism's friends have proved as harmful as their enemies. An angry Pat Robertson invited ridicule when, in response to the anticreationist vote in November 2005, he warned Dover's citizens that they should not bother seeking God's help in a disaster since "you just voted God out of your city."[50]

Equally difficult are the divisions that exist within creationism itself. From its inception, the antievolution movement has been an awkward amalgam of young-earth, old-earth, and progressive creationists. In recent years, with contemporary creationism's "big tent" philosophy, the movement has become more diverse. It now includes not only Protestant evangelicals and Catholic traditionalists, but also assorted sectarians such as Jonathan Wells, a member of the Unification Church, who has said that the words of the Reverend Sun Myung Moon were instrumental in convincing him that he "should devote my life to destroying Darwinism."[51] With diversity comes disagreement. Activists associated with both Answers in Genesis and the Institute for Creation Research have criticized ID advocates for their unwillingness to identify God as the original designer. For that matter, some moderate evangelicals have been critical of the claims of ID proponents that they are not talking about God or religion. "I just think we ought to quit playing games," commented Derek Davis, head of church-state studies at Texas's Baylor University. "It's a religious worldview that's being advanced."[52] Furthermore, even among those who agree on the short-term strategy of avoiding biblical arguments and stressing scientific ones, there is no consensus on long-term goals. If creationists succeeded in introducing alternative approaches to evolution into public school science classrooms, the arguments over alternatives would only begin again. For in the last analysis, as Henry Morris has repeatedly insisted, most creationists believe that design is simply not enough. "Even if one becomes a believer in intelligent design," he wrote in a 2005 review, "he is still unsaved until he receives—by faith—God in Christ as His personal Designer, Creator, and Redeemer."[53]

A still bigger problem is that evolution has considerable support of its own. Even in Bryan's day some form of evolutionary theory was almost universally accepted by scientists, and its teaching was widespread in the public schools. Today, despite eighty years of antievolution agitation, the situation remains much the same. Within the scientific community, evolutionary theory continues to be accepted by huge majorities. A 1998 study of natural and physical scientists showed that 95 percent were evolutionists, with 55 percent describing themselves as naturalistic evolutionists and another 40 percent, theistic evolutionists.[54] In a smaller but more detailed survey of five hundred Ohio scientists conducted at Case Western Reserve University in 2002, 93 percent expressed unqualified support for evolutionary theory, and 92 percent endorsed its inclusion in the high school science curriculum. (The survey also found that 84 percent of the scientists stated that they thought evolution was compatible with belief in God.)[55] In science classrooms, evolution continues to be the rule: the same studies of high school science teachers that found small but growing numbers including creationism in their courses also revealed that, in some states, as many as 88 percent of the sample taught evolutionary theory. Moreover, one recent study reports that this percentage is increasing and that teachers are devoting more time to discussing evolution.[56] Indeed, while recent surveys show strong public support for including creationism alongside evolution in science classes, they also suggest that most people see it as supplementing rather than replacing evolutionary theory. In a 2000 Yankelovich survey, one of the few to ask specific questions about the place of creation and evolution in the classroom, two-thirds of the respondents agreed that evolution should be taught in the public schools.[57] Other national surveys have found similar if slightly smaller numbers. In a 2005 Gallup poll, for example, 61 percent of respondents stated that evolution should be taught, while only 20 percent said that it should not be taught at all. "Despite the fact that fewer than half of Americans personally believe in evolution," add the authors of a 2005 Pew Forum survey, which reported similar findings, "a solid majority over the past 20 years has supported the teaching of alternative accounts of the origins of life, including evolution."[58]

Evolutionists are determined to defend the theory. In the 1920s, groups like the American Civil Liberties Union and the American Association for the Advancement of Science (AAAS) were instrumental in slowing the antievolution bandwagon. Today, these and other organizations are more active than ever in resisting contemporary creationism. In the courts especially, these defenders of evolution continue to be a force, filing amicus briefs, arranging for expert testimony, and providing legal support to parents. Attorneys advocating for creationist clients have been candid about the success of such groups. Having installed evolution as the law of the land, observed Thomas More Foundation attorney Dick Thompson, evolution advocates can be counted on to do "everything they can to suppress any effort to challenge it."[59] Beyond the courtroom, evolutionists have been more visible as well. For example, in an attempt to counter the classic tactic of developing lists of scientists who oppose evolution, the NCSE has launched "Project Steve," a petition supporting evolution that is limited to scientists named "Steve" (Stephen, Stefan, Esteban, and other variations, including Stephanie, are accepted). The project, which honors the late Stephen Jay Gould, contrasts the small cohort of scientists who oppose the theory (most lists contain several hundred names) to the larger number named Steve alone (estimated to comprise 1 percent of the tens of thousands of all scientists) who have already signed the petition supporting it.[60] In a March 2005 letter to members of the National Academy of Sciences, academy president Bruce Alberts warned of creationism's growing threat to science education, calling on members to use their influence to counter it when it "arrives at your doorstep."[61] And at a 2006 meeting of the AAAS, the *Chronicle of Higher Education* reported, middle-school science teachers lectured leaders of America's scientific establishment on the need to support the teaching of evolution in schools in their own communities. According to the NCSE's Eugenie Scott, the audience seemed to be listening. "What is new is that it's finally trickling down," she commented after the meeting. "These scientists are saying, 'I've got to do something.' "[62]

Nevertheless, creationists continue to make their case. Starting in the 1920s, antievolutionists have constantly renewed their movement, introducing innovative strategies and tactics in an unceasing attempt to end the teaching of evolution. What distinguishes them today is not only their continuing commitment but also their ability to act incrementally while never losing sight of their ultimate goal. In testimony before the Ohio Board of Education in 2002, Stephen Meyer of the Discovery Institute advised activists that their best strategy would be to avoid advocating alternative theories, including intelligent design, but instead support the less ambitious requirement that teachers lay out the main arguments for and against evolutionary theory by "teaching the controversy."[63] Since then, Meyer and his colleagues have also advised the adoption of policies like that of the Cobb County, Georgia, School Board, which declares evolution to be a "disputed view," calling on teachers to discuss the concept in the interests of "balanced education," "critical thinking," and "tolerance and acceptance of diversity of opinion."[64] In addition, although Meyer has been personally unenthusiastic, many of his allies have supported the Cobb County board's decision to paste antievolution disclaimers, or "warning labels," in science textbooks alerting students that their book "contains material on evolution," that "evolution is a theory, not a fact," and that it should be "approached with an open mind, studied carefully, and critically considered."[65] Following *Kitzmiller*, the strategy of avoiding alternatives while continuing to criticize evolution has become more commonplace. In fact, in a statement made shortly after the decision, Phillip Johnson himself said that it was never his intention to incorporate ID in the public school curriculum, but rather only to provoke discussion among educators and scientists.[66] Intelligent design has by no means been banished, though in the future advocates can be counted on to be more careful in its use, including it as part of a larger critique of evolution while making sure to emphasize the scientific character of its claims.[67] At present activists seem content to proceed slowly, avoiding major constitutional challenges and buying time to perfect alternative theories. "The strategy this time is not to go for the whole enchilada," confessed Wichita, Kansas, pastor Terry Fox. "We're trying to be a little more subtle." For now, he continued, it is enough to sow doubts about evolution, concentrating on the means, while assuming that the ends will follow in good time. "We're in it for the long haul."[68]

Meanwhile, the conflict continues. With each success, creationists are emboldened; with every failure, they reassert themselves anew. The same can be said for their enemies: whenever the creationists succeed, their evolutionist counterparts seem to double their efforts. So it was that in 2005, following the elections of the previous year, the Kansas Board of Education was debating evolution once again, this time with a new conservative majority voting to adopt state standards not only calling upon schools to teach scientific criticism of evolution, but also recasting the definition of science itself, expanding it to include more than "natural explanations."[69] As soon as the new standards were announced, evolution supporters were again organizing, and less than a year later Kansas voters once again ousted several of the board's critics of evolution, ensuring a return to more evolution-friendly standards. While the victors exulted, few believed that the conflict had been resolved. "In the seesawing of Kansas politics on this issue," wrote the *Washington Post*, "it is too early to declare victory."[70]

Yet even as the conflict continues, antievolutionists remain sure of its outcome. The issue of evolution, William Jennings Bryan told the court in his closing speech at Dayton, "will some day be settled right, whether it is settled on our side or the other side. It is going to be settled right."[71] Today's creationists agree that the issue will be settled and that it will be settled right. They are also absolutely certain that their side is right and will eventually win. The antievolution movement is entering its second century. For those who march behind its banner, the fight is only beginning.

Notes

ABBREVIATIONS

Bryan Papers	William Jennings Bryan Papers, Manuscript Division, Library of Congress, Washington, D.C.
CF in S&C	*Christian Fundamentals in School and Church*
CN	*Chattanooga News*
CT	*Chattanooga Times*
Hicks Papers	Judge Sue K. Hicks Papers, Special Collections and Archives, University of Tennessee-Knoxville
McVey Papers	Frank L. McVey Papers, University of Kentucky Archives, Lexington
MCA	*Memphis Commercial Appeal*
NB	*Nashville Banner*
Norris Papers	J. Frank Norris Papers, Southern Baptist Historical Library and Archives, Nashville, Tenn.
NT	*Nashville Tennessean*
NYT	*New York Times*
Peay Papers	Governor Austin Peay Papers, Tennessee State Library and Archives, Nashville
Riley Papers	William Bell Riley Papers, Haburn Hovda Archives, Northwestern College, Roseville, Minn.
S&C	*School and Church*
UNC Papers	University of North Carolina Papers, University Archives, Chapel Hill

INTRODUCTION

1. On the status of creationism in the 1980s, see Edward J. Larson, *Trial and Error: The American Controversy over Creation and Evolution*, 3rd ed. (Oxford: Oxford University Press, 2003), 156–84. See also Dorothy Nelkin, *The Creation Controversy: Science or Scripture in the Schools* (New York: Norton, 1982), 93–103; Raymond A. Eve and Francis B. Harrold, *The Creationist Movement in Modern America* (Boston: Twayne Publishers, 1991), 1–29.

2. Norman F. Furniss, *The Fundamentalist Controversy, 1918–1931* (New Haven: Yale University Press, 1954).

3. George M. Marsden, *Fundamentalism and American Culture: The Shaping of Twentieth-Century Evangelicalism, 1870–1925* (Oxford: Oxford University Press, 1980); Ronald L. Numbers, *The Creationists: The Evolution of Scientific Creationism* (Berkeley: University of California Press, 1992); Larson, *Trial and Error*.

4. On antievolution's intellectual roots, see Michael Ruse, *The Darwinian Revolution: Science Red in Tooth and Claw* (Chicago: University of Chicago Press, 1979); James R. Moore, *The Post-Darwinian*

Controversies: A Study of the Protestant Struggle to Come to Terms with Darwin in Great Britain and America, 1870–1900 (Cambridge: Cambridge University Press, 1979); Jon H. Roberts, Darwinism and the Divine in America: Protestant Intellectuals and Organic Evolution, 1859–1900 (Madison: University of Wisconsin Press, 1988); and Paul K. Conkin, When All the Gods Trembled: Darwinism, Scopes, and American Intellectuals (Lanham, Md.: Rowman and Littlefield Publishers, Inc., 1998). Studies by anthropologists and sociologists include Nelkin, Creation Controversy; Eve and Harrold, Creationist Movement; and Christopher P. Toumey, God's Own Scientists: Creationists in a Secular World (New Brunswick, N.J.: Rutgers University Press, 1994). The best study by a political scientist is Virginia Gray, "Anti-Evolution Sentiment and Behavior: The Case of Arkansas," Journal of American History 57 (1970): 352–66.

5. See Randy Moore, Evolution in the Courtroom: A Reference Guide (Santa Barbara, Calif.: ABC-CLIO, Inc., 2002).

6. The best of these is Larry A. Witham, Where Darwin Meets the Bible: Creationists and Evolutionists in America (New York: Oxford University Press, 2002).

7. For hundreds of examples, see James L. Hayward, The Creation/Evolution Controversy: An Annotated Bibliography (Lanham, Md.: Scarecrow Press, Inc., 1998).

8. On this point, see the best book on the Scopes trial: Edward J. Larson, Summer for the Gods: The Scopes Trial and America's Continuing Debate over Science and Religion (New York: BasicBooks, 1997), 225–46.

9. Ronald L. Numbers, Darwinism Comes to America (Cambridge: Harvard University Press, 1998), 23, 76.

10. For an introduction to "new social movement" theory, see Nick Crossley, Making Sense of Social Movements (Buckingham, England: Open University Press, 2002), 149–67. See also Alberto Melucci, "New Social Movements: A Theoretical Approach," Social Science Information 19 (1980): 199–226; Alain Touraine, "An Introduction to the Study of Social Movements," Social Research 52 (1985): 749–87; and Jean L. Cohen, "Strategy or Identity: New Theoretical Paradigms and Contemporary Social Movements," Social Research 52 (1985): 663–716.

11. For the "political process" model, see Crossley, Making Sense of Social Movements, 105–26. Among the most important early examples were Charles Tilly, From Mobilization to Revolution (Reading, Mass.: Addison-Wesley, 1978); Doug McAdam, Political Process and the Development of Black Insurgency (Chicago: University of Chicago Press, 1982); and Sidney Tarrow, Power in Movement: Social Movements and Contentious Politics (Cambridge: Cambridge University Press, 1994).

12. See Elisabeth S. Clemens, "Organizational Repertoires and Institutional Change: Women's Groups and the Transformation of American Politics, 1890–1920," American Journal of Sociology 98 (1993): 755–98; Craig Calhoun, " 'New Social Movements' of the Early Nineteenth Century," in Mark Traugott, ed., Repertoires and Cycles of Collective Action (Durham, N.C.: Duke University Press, 1995), 173–215; and Ann-Marie E. Szymanski, Pathways to Prohibition: Radicals, Moderates, and Social Movement Outcomes (Durham, N.C.: Duke University Press, 2003).

13. See Rebecca E. Klatch, "The Development of Individual Identity and Consciousness among Movements of the Left and Right," in David S. Meyer, Nancy Whittier, and Belinda Robnett, eds., Social Movements: Identity, Culture, and the State (New York: Oxford University Press, 2002), 185–201. See also Rebecca E. Klatch, Women of the New Right (Philadelphia: Temple University Press, 1987).

14. See Rhys H. Williams, "From the 'Beloved Community' to 'Family Values': Religious Lan-

guage, Symbolic Repertoires, and Democratic Culture," in Meyer, Whittier, and Robnett, *Social Movements*, 247–65. See also Charles Kurzman, *The Unthinkable Revolution in Iran* (Cambridge: Harvard University Press, 2004).

15. See Claus Offe, "New Social Movements: Challenging the Boundaries of Institutional Politics," *Social Research* 52 (1985): 817–68. For examples, see the essays in Enrique Larana, Hank Johnston, and Joseph R. Gusfield, eds., *New Social Movements: From Ideology to Identity* (Philadelphia: Temple University Press, 1994).

16. For examples, see the essays in Bert Klandermans, Hanspeter Kriesi, and Sidney Tarrow, eds., *From Structure to Action: Comparing Social Movement Research across Cultures* (Greenwich, Conn.: JAI Press, 1988).

17. On these differences, see David S. Meyer, "Opportunities and Identities: Bridge-Building in the Study of Social Movements," in Meyer, Whittier, and Robnett, *Social Movements*, 3–7.

18. For examples, see the essays in Aldon D. Morris and Carol McClurg Mueller, eds., *Frontiers in Social Movement Theory* (New Haven: Yale University Press, 1992).

19. See Mary Bernstein, "Celebration and Suppression: The Strategic Uses of Identity by the Lesbian and Gay Movement," *American Journal of Sociology* 103 (1997): 31–65. See also Manisha Desai, "Multiple Mediations: The State and the Women's Movements in India," in Meyer, Whittier, and Robnett, *Social Movements*, 66–84.

20. See Sidney Tarrow, *Power in Movement: Social Movements and Contentious Politics*, 2nd. ed. (Cambridge: Cambridge University Press, 1998). See also the essays in Doug McAdam, John D. McCarthy, and Mayer Zald, eds., *Comparative Perspectives on Social Movements: Political Opportunities, Mobilizing Structures, and Cultural Framings* (Cambridge: Cambridge University Press, 1996).

21. See Nancy Whittier, "Meaning and Structure in Social Movements," in Meyer, Whittier, and Robnett, *Social Movements*, 289–307.

22. Meyer, "Opportunities and Identities," 4.

23. William Gamson, "Political Discourse and Collective Action," *International Social Movement Research* 1 (1988): 219–44.

24. Robert Wuthnow, *Communities of Discourse: Ideology and Social Structure in the Reformation, the Enlightenment, and European Socialism* (Cambridge: Harvard University Press, 1988).

25. See Ann Swidler, "Culture in Action: Symbols and Strategies," *American Sociological Review* 51 (1986): 273–86; Michael Billig, "Rhetorical Psychology, Ideological Thinking, and Imagining Nationhood," in Hank Johnson and Bert Klandermans, eds., *Social Movements and Culture* (Minneapolis: University of Minnesota Press, 1995), 64–81; Gary Alan Fine, "Public Narration and Group Culture: Discerning Discourse in Social Movements," in Johnson and Klandermans, *Social Movements and Culture*, 127–43; and Stephen Ellington, "Understanding the Dialectic of Discourse and Collective Action: Public Debate and Rioting in Antebellum Cincinnati," *American Journal of Sociology* 101 (1995): 100–144.

CHAPTER ONE

1. For background on Stewart and his project, see Ernest R. Sandeen, *The Roots of Fundamentalism: British and American Millenarianism, 1800–1930* (Chicago: University of Chicago Press, 1970), 188–207.

2. Alberto Melucci, "New Social Movements: A Theoretical Approach," *Social Science Information* 19 (1980): 218. See also Melucci, *Nomads of the Present: Social Movements and Individual Needs in Contemporary Society* (Philadelphia: Temple University Press, 1989), 30–36.

3. On this constructivist approach, see Alain Touraine, "An Introduction to the Study of Social Movements," *Social Research* 52 (1985): 749–87; Jean L. Cohen, "Strategy or Identity: New Theoretical Paradigms and Contemporary Social Movements," *Social Research* 52 (1985): 663–716; and Hank Johnston, Enrique Larana, and Joseph R. Gusfield, "Identities, Grievances and New Social Movements," in Larana, Johnston, and Gusfield, eds., *New Social Movements: From Ideology to Identity* (Philadelphia: Temple University Press, 1994), 3–35.

4. Verta Taylor and Nancy Whittier, "Collective Identity in Social Movement Communities: Lesbian Feminist Mobilization," in Aldon D. Morris and Carol McClurg Mueller, eds., *Frontiers in Social Movement Theory* (New Haven: Yale University Press, 1992), 104–29. See also Karen A. Cerulo, "Identity Construction: New Issues, New Directions," *Annual Review of Sociology* 23 (1997): 388.

5. See Norman F. Furniss, *The Fundamentalist Controversy, 1918–1931* (New Haven: Yale University Press, 1954), 13; Stewart G. Cole, *The History of Fundamentalism* (Hamden, Conn.: Archon Books, 1963), 34; and Milton L. Rudnick, *Fundamentalism and the Missouri Synod: A Historical Study of Their Interaction and Mutual Influence* (St. Louis: Concordia Publishing House, 1966), 48. For a brief history of the "five points," see George M. Marsden, *Fundamentalism and American Culture: The Shaping of Twentieth-Century Evangelicalism, 1870–1925* (Oxford: Oxford University Press, 1980), 117.

6. On the creation of collective consciousness, see Taylor and Whittier, "Collective Identity," 114–17.

7. Quoted in Ferenc Morton Szasz, *The Divided Mind of Protestant America, 1880–1930* (University, Ala.: University of Alabama Press, 1982), 78. For more on *The Fundamentals*, see Sandeen, *Roots of Fundamentalism*, 188–207; Marsden, *Fundamentalism and American Culture*, 118–23; Rudnick, *Fundamentalism and the Missouri Synod*, 37–46; and Szasz, *Divided Mind*, 68–83.

8. Foreword to *The Fundamentals: A Testimony to the Truth*, 12 vols. (Chicago: Testimony Publishing Co., [1910–15]), 1:1. On the editors and authors, see Sandeen, *Roots of Fundamentalism*, 194–201.

9. On Hodge and the idea of biblical inerrancy, see Marsden, *Fundamentalism and American Culture*, 109–18. See also Charles Hodge, *What Is Darwinism? And Other Writings on Science and Scripture*, ed. Mark A. Noll and David N. Livingstone (Grand Rapids, Mich.: Baker Books, 1994); Ronald L. Numbers, "Charles Hodge and the Beauties and Deformities of Science," in John W. Stewart and James H. Moorhead, eds., *Charles Hodge Revisited: A Critical Appraisal of His Life and Work* (Grand Rapids, Mich.: Eerdmans, 2002), 77–101; and Jonathan Wells, *Charles Hodge's Critique of Darwinism: An Historical-Critical Analysis of Concepts Basic to the Nineteenth-Century Debate* (Lewiston, N.Y.: Edwin Mellen Press, 1988). Nancy Ammerman writes: "One should not look for the ideas behind the words; truth is contained in the words themselves, words whose meanings are true and changeless, words that have the power to change lives." Ammerman, "North American Protestant Fundamentalism," in Martin E. Marty and R. Scott Appleby, eds., *Fundamentalisms Observed* (Chicago: University of Chicago Press, 1991), 15.

10. James Orr, "The Virgin Birth of Christ," *Fundamentals* [1910], 1:10, 14, 16.

11. Benjamin B. Warfield, "The Deity of Christ," ibid. [1910], 1:21. See also Ammerman, "North American Protestant Fundamentalism," 16. On Warfield's views of inerrantism, see David N.

Livingstone and Mark A. Noll, "B. B. Warfield (1851–1921): A Biblical Inerrantist as Evolutionist," *Isis* 91 (2000): 283–304.

12. Dyson Hague, "History of the Higher Criticism," *Fundamentals* [1910], 1:105, 111, 120.

13. On Moody and urban revivalism, see William G. McLoughlin, *Modern Revivalism: Charles Grandison Finney to Billy Graham* (New York: Ronald Press, 1959), 217–81. See also Ammerman, "North American Protestant Fundamentalism," 18–20.

14. Reuben A. Torrey, "The Personality and Deity of the Holy Scripture," *Fundamentals* [1910], 1:60–61, 65. See also Arthur T. Pierson, "The Proof of the Living God," ibid. [1910], 1:86. For background on Torrey, see McLoughlin, *Modern Revivalism*, 366–74.

15. Philip Mauro, "A Personal Testimony," *Fundamentals* [1911], 4:107, 108, 109, 112, 114. In his essay "Life in the Word" (ibid., 5:66), Mauro went on to describe Christian conversion as an antidote for the psychological problems of "millions of anxious souls." He wrote: "The startling increase in the number of suicides adds to its forcible testimony; and the frequency with which one encounters cases of mental depression, insomnia, melancholia, and other nervous disorders, tells of wide-spread and insidious foes which attack the seat of reason, and which call for methods and means of defense and repair which are beyond the resources of medicine." Other testimonies are Pierson, "The Proof of the Living God," ibid., 1:70–86; Howard A. Kelly, "A Personal Testimony," *Fundamentals* [1910], 1:123–26; Charles T. Studd, "The Personal Testimony of Charles T. Studd," ibid., 3:119–26; and H. W. Webb-Peploe, "A Personal Testimony," ibid. [1911], 5:120–24.

16. See Sandeen, *Roots of Fundamentalism*, 208–32. On dispensationalism, see Timothy P. Weber, *Living in the Shadow of the Second Coming* (Chicago: University of Chicago Press, 1987), 13–42. On Darby and Scofield, see Paul Boyer, *When Time Shall Be No More: Prophecy Belief in Modern American Culture* (Cambridge: Harvard University Press, 1992), 86–100. See also Ammerman, "North American Protestant Fundamentalism," 16–17.

17. G. Campbell Morgan, "Purposes of the Incarnation," *Fundamentals* [1910], 1:49, 49–50, 54.

18. Hague, "History of the Higher Criticism," 1:115.

19. On boundaries, see Taylor and Whittier, "Collective Identity," 111–14.

20. Rudnick, *Fundamentalism and the Missouri Synod*, 39–40.

21. "The suggestion has come to us that a Circle of Prayer be organized for the express purpose of making this entire movement an object of definite prayer—that God will guide in *every detail* and entirely fulfill His purpose in the existence of the movement." "Publisher's Notice," *Fundamentals* [1910], 3:128.

22. Foreword, ibid., 3:i.

23. Hague, "History of the Higher Criticism," 1:88, 106, 111. On the higher criticism, see also Szasz, *Divided Mind*, 15–41.

24. Hague, "History of the Higher Criticism," 1:115, 117, 117–18, 119, 118.

25. J. J. Reeve, "My Personal Experience with the Higher Criticism," *Fundamentals* [1910], 3:105.

26. F. Bettex, "The Bible and Modern Criticism," ibid. [1911], 4:86. See also Franklin Johnson, "Fallacies of the Higher Criticism," ibid. [1910], 2:67, and R. A. Torrey, "The Certainty and Importance of the Bodily Resurrection of Jesus Christ from the Dead," ibid. [1911], 5:105.

27. Reeve, "Personal Experience," 3:110, 111. See also Robert Anderson, "Christ and Criticism," *Fundamentals* [1910], 2:84.

28. William Caven, "The Testimony of Christ to the Old Testament," ibid. [1911], 4:70.

29. Reeve, "Personal Experience," 3:112.

30. Philip Mauro, "Modern Philosophy," *Fundamentals* [1910], 2:89, 98, 100, 105.

31. See "Tributes to Christ and the Bible by Brainy Men Not Known as Active Christians," ibid. [1910], 2:120–25.

32. E. Y. Mullins, "The Testimony of Christian Experience," ibid. [1910], 3:79, 84, 79. On Mullins, see William E. Ellis, *"A Man of Books and a Man of the People": E. Y. Mullins and the Crisis of Moderate Southern Baptist Leadership* (Macon, Ga.: Mercer University Press, 1985).

33. James Orr, "Science and Christian Faith," *Fundamentals* [1911], 4:91, 93, 98.

34. George Frederick Wright, "The Testimony of the Monuments to the Truth of the Scriptures," ibid. [1910], 2:28. Writing in the same volume, biblical archaeologist M. G. Kyle pointed to recent discoveries by Clermont-Ganneau, Macalister, Winckler, Schumacker, Sellin, Hilprecht, Glaser, Petrie, and Reisner, in addition to himself. See Kyle, "The Recent Testimony of Archaeology to the Scriptures," ibid., 2:41–42. See also David Heagle, "The Tabernacle in the Wilderness: Did It Exist?," ibid. [1911], 4:18. On Wright, see Ronald L. Numbers, *The Creationists: The Evolution of Scientific Creationism* (Berkeley: University of California Press, 1992), 20–36.

35. Reeve, "Personal Experience," 3:103. See also Johnson, "Fallacies of the Higher Criticism," 2:55. For background on turn-of-the-century scientific critics of Darwin, see Peter J. Bowler, *The Eclipse of Darwinism: Anti-Darwinian Evolution Theories in the Decades around 1900* (Baltimore: Johns Hopkins University Press, 1983). On Orr, see David N. Livingstone, *Darwin's Forgotten Defenders: The Encounter between Evangelical Theology and Evolutionary Thought* (Grand Rapids, Mich.: Eerdmans, 1987), 149–50.

36. Orr, "Science and Christian Faith," 4:101, 103, 104, 103. See also James Orr, "The Early Narratives of Genesis," *Fundamentals* [1911], 6:96.

37. "Words of Appreciation," *Fundamentals* [1911], 5:127, 127–28, 128.

38. See Taylor and Whittier, "Collective Identity," 117–21. On the concept of collective agency, see Cerulo, "Identity Construction," 393.

39. See Marsden, *Fundamentalism and American Culture*, 124–38.

40. Foreword, *Fundamentals* [1911], 6:i.

41. See George L. Robinson, "One Isaiah," ibid. [1912], 7:70–87; Joseph D. Wilson, "The Book of Daniel," ibid., 7:88–100; and Andrew Craig Robinson, "Three Peculiarities of the Pentateuch Which Are Incompatible with the Graf-Wellhausen Theories of Its Composition," ibid., 7:101–5. See also Dyson Hague, "The Doctrinal Value of the First Chapters of Genesis," ibid., 8:75.

42. George S. Bishop, "The Testimony of Scriptures to Themselves," ibid. [1912], 7:43. For an earlier statement of the theory, see James M. Gray, "The Inspiration of the Bible—Definition, Extent, and Proof," ibid. [1910], 3:14–15.

43. See W. H. Griffith Thomas, "Old Testament Criticism and New Testament Christianity," ibid. [1912], 8:23. See also James Orr, "Holy Scripture and Modern Negations," ibid., 9:31–47.

44. Howard Crosby, "Preach the Word," ibid. [1912], 8:108. The piece by Crosby (1826–91), a leading Presbyterian preacher of his day, was one of several essays in *The Fundamentals* that had been written earlier and reprinted from other sources.

45. R. G. McNiece, "Mormonism: Its Origin, Characteristics, and Doctrines," *Fundamentals*

[1912], 8:113–14; Maurice E. Wilson, "Eddyism, Commonly Called 'Christian Science,' " ibid., 9:127; William G. Moorehead, "Millennial Dawn: A Counterfeit of Christianity," ibid., 7:125; Algernon J. Pollock, "Modern Spiritualism Briefly Tested by Scripture," ibid. [1915], 10:125. Adam Laats has traced the efforts of early fundamentalists to distinguish themselves from Adventists, Pentecostals, and other groups. See his "Constructing Fundamentalism: Orthodox Christianity or Heretical Cult?," unpublished paper.

46. T. W. Medhurst, "Is Romanism Christianity?," *Fundamentals* [1915], 11:100. Medhurst wrote: "'No peace with Rome,' must be on our lips, and be in our lives" (p. 110). See also J. M. Foster, "Rome: The Antagonist of the Nation," ibid., 11:113–26.

47. J. C. Ryle, "The True Church," *Fundamentals* [1912], 9:9. Written by the late Anglican Bishop John Charles Ryle (1816–1900), "The True Church" was originally an 1858 sermon, versions of which had been circulating in America for decades.

48. Thomas Spurgeon, "Salvation By Grace," *Fundamentals* [1912], 9:48.

49. A. W. Pitzer, "The Wisdom of This World," ibid. [1912], 9:29, 28.

50. George F. Pentecost, "What the Bible Contains for the Believer," ibid. [1915], 10:104.

51. Robert E. Speer, "Foreign Missions or World-Wide Evangelism," ibid. [1915], 12:74.

52. Daniel Hoffman Martin, "Why Save the Lord's Day?," ibid. [1915], 10:17.

53. Charles R. Erdman, "The Church and Socialism," ibid. [1915], 12:112. According to Erdman, the church consisted of rich and poor alike. Its purpose was not to obliterate class distinctions. Indeed, its commitment to brotherhood and communitarian concern flew in the face of socialism's declaration of class hatred, which "unless controlled, will result in violence and anarchy and universal disaster" (p. 114).

54. Martin, "Why Save the Lord's Day?," 10:16, 4.

55. Pitzer, "The Wisdom of This World," 9:23, 24, 24–25.

56. Crosby, "Preach the Word," 8:108, 108-9, 109.

57. See George Frederick Wright, "The Passing of Evolution," *Fundamentals* [1912], 7:12, 17, 20. On Wright's conception of the relationship between creationism and evolution, and especially on his ability to reconcile them, see Numbers, *Creationists*, 32–36.

58. Dyson Hague, "Doctrinal Value," 8:82–84. See Alexander Patterson, *The Other Side of Evolution: Its Effects and Fallacy* (Chicago: Bible Institute Colportage Assn., 1903); E. Dennert, *At the Deathbed of Darwinism* (Burlington, Iowa: German Literary Board, 1904); and Luther T. Townsend, *Collapse of Evolution* (Boston: National Magazine Co. and American Bible League, 1905). These sources are reprinted in Ronald L. Numbers, ed., *Antievolutionism before World War I* (New York; Garland Publishing, Inc., 1995). For an extensive discussion of turn-of-the-century debates on Darwinism among Protestant intellectuals, see Numbers, *Creationists*, 37–38; Jon H. Roberts, *Darwinism and the Divine in America: Protestant Intellectuals and Organic Evolution, 1859–1900* (Madison: University of Wisconsin Press, 1988), 209–31; and James R. Moore, *The Post-Darwinian Controversies: A Study of the Protestant Struggle to Come to Terms with Darwin in Great Britain and America, 1870–1900* (Cambridge: Cambridge University Press, 1979), 193–216.

59. An Occupant of the Pew, "Evolutionism in the Pulpit," *Fundamentals* [1912], 8:30, 27, 29, 31. This essay was reprinted from the *Herald and Presbyter*, 22 November 1911. Bryan (incorrectly) cited the article as his source for the claim. See William Jennings Bryan, *In His Image* (New York: Flem-

ing H. Revell Co., 1922), 91. David Livingstone believes that the author of the essay was Frank Allen, a Reformed Presbyterian minister from Winnipeg, Canada, who would continue to publish anti-evolution essays into the 1920s. See Livingstone, *Darwin's Forgotten Defenders*, 161–62. An online word search shows that the phrase "we may well suppose" does not appear in either of Darwin's major works: *On the Origin of Species by Means of Natural Selection* (1859) or *The Descent of Man* (1871). Variations on the phrase, including "we may suppose," "we must suppose," "let us suppose," or simply "we suppose" appear forty times in *Origins* and ten times in *Descent*. By contrast, in *Descent* alone, variations on the phrase "we cannot suppose," ("we have no reason to suppose," "it cannot be supposed," "no one supposes," etc.) appear twenty-nine times.

60. An Occupant of the Pew, "Evolutionism in the Pulpit," 8:33–34.

61. Henry Beach, "The Decadence of Darwinism," *Fundamentals* [1912], 8:36, 41, 45, 44, 46, 48.

62. Numbers, *Creationists*, 39. See also ibid., 38–39; Livingstone, *Darwin's Forgotten Defenders*, 150–51; and Marsden, *Fundamentalism and American Culture*, 122–23.

63. Arno C. Gaebelein, "Fulfilled Prophecy a Potent Argument for the Bible," *Fundamentals* [1915], 11:86. His essay included an extensive flowchart that traced the fulfillment of Daniel's prophecies from the invasion of Greece in 480 B.C. through Alexander the Great to the reign of Antiochus Epiphanes and the Maccabean revolt. See ibid., 11:78–86. See also Weber, *Living in the Shadow*, 105–27.

64. Pentecost, "What the Bible Contains," 10:105; Henry W. Frost, "What Missionary Motives Should Prevail?" *Fundamentals* [1915], 12:92; Jessie Penn-Lewis, "Satan and His Kingdom," ibid. [1915], 10:92; George W. Lasher, "Regeneration—Conversion—Reformation," ibid. [1915], 10:38; R. A. Torrey, "The Place of Prayer in Evangelism," ibid. [1915], 12:107. On the influence of World War I on fundamentalist thinking and rhetoric, see Marsden, *Fundamentalism and American Culture*, 141–53; Elvin Keith Mattison, *A Movement Study of Fundamentalism between 1900 and 1960* (Ann Arbor, Mich.: Xerox University Microfilms, 1983), 38–77; and Szasz, *Divided Mind*, 85–86.

65. See, e.g., John Timothy Stone, "Pastoral and Personal Experience, or Winning Men to Christ One by One," *Fundamentals* [1915], 12:24–44. The turn is part of the larger transformation that David Moberg calls the "Great Reversal," the early twentieth-century subordination of evangelical social reform to personalized religious revivalism and conservative political attitudes. Moberg, *The Great Reversal: Evangelism and Social Concern* (Philadelphia: Lippincott, 1972), 2–45.

66. Charles Gallaudet Trumbull, "The Sunday School's True Evangelism," *Fundamentals* [1915], 12:61. Trumbull preferred that social reform take place through personal revival, which he believed to be practiced in its most perfect form by conservative evangelist Billy Sunday: "Sunday preaches the individual Gospel of the apostolic church. He says little about social service." Nevertheless, Trumbull claimed that "the community results where Sunday's evangelism has had an opportunity are revolutionizing. There is no social service worker in America whose work can compare, in the very results for which the social service program aims, with that of Sunday's" (pp. 61–62).

67. Speer, "Foreign Missions," 12:84. In the early 1920s, during battles over control of the Northern Presbyterian Church, Speer would disassociate himself from the fundamentalist ranks. For several decades afterward he served as secretary of the Board of Foreign Missions of the Presbyterian Church, U.S.A., often coming in for criticism by later fundamentalists.

68. Pentecost, "What the Bible Contains," 10:105.

CHAPTER TWO

1. William B. Riley, "The Great Divide, or Christ and the Present Crisis," in *God Hath Spoken: Twenty-five Addresses Delivered at the World Conference on Christian Fundamentals* (Philadelphia: Bible Conference Committee, 1919), 27.

2. For the first use of the term, see Curtis Lee Laws, "Convention Side Lights," *Watchman-Examiner* 8, 28 (1920): 834.

3. See "The Fundamentals Movement," CF in S&C 3, 2 (1921): 19.

4. William Bell Riley, "The Christian Fundamentals Movement: Its Battles, Its Achievements, Its Certain Victory," CF in S&C 5, 1 (1922): 4–14. See also "The Fifth Annual Convention of the Christian Fundamentals Association," CF in S&C 5, 4 (1923): 16.

5. On resource mobilization theory, see Anthony Oberschall, *Social Conflict and Social Movements* (Englewood Cliffs, N.J.: Prentice-Hall, 1973); John D. McCarthy and Mayer N. Zald, "Resource Mobilization and Social Movements: A Partial Theory," *American Journal of Sociology* 82 (1977): 1212–41; and J. Craig Jenkins, "Resource Mobilization Theory and the Study of Social Movements," *Annual Review of Sociology* 9 (1983): 527–53.

6. For discussions of these critiques, see Bert Klandermans and Sidney Tarrow, "Mobilization into Social Movements: Synthesizing European and American Approaches," *International Social Movement Research* 1 (1988): 1–38.

7. See Mario Diani, "Social Movements, Contentious Actions, and Social Networks: 'From Metaphor to Substance?,'" in Mario Diani and Doug McAdam, eds., *Social Movements and Networks: Relational Approaches to Collective Action* (Oxford: Oxford University Press, 2003), 1–20.

8. See Bert Klandermans and Dirk Oegema, "Potentials, Networks, Motivations, and Barriers: Steps towards Participation in Social Movements," *American Sociological Review* 52 (1987): 519–31. See also Klandermans, "Mobilization and Participation: Social Psychological Expansions of Resource Mobilization Theory," *American Sociological Review* 49 (1984): 583–600; Klandermans, "The Formation and Mobilization of Consensus," *International Social Movement Research* 1 (1988): 173–96; and Klandermans and Tarrow, "Mobilization into Social Movements," 10–14.

9. See Norman F. Furniss, *The Fundamentalist Controversy, 1918–1931* (New Haven: Yale University Press, 1954), 30.

10. See H. Richard Niebuhr, "Fundamentalism," *Encyclopedia of Social Sciences* (New York: Macmillan, 1937), 4:526–27. The theme was adopted by William E. Leuchtenberg, *The Perils of Prosperity, 1914–32* (Chicago: University of Chicago Press, 1958), 222–23.

11. See Richard Hofstadter, *Anti-Intellectualism in American Life* (New York: Knopf, 1963), 17–36.

12. Klandermans, "Formation and Mobilization of Consensus," 174. For the role of social networks in mobilization potential, see Hanspeter Kriesi, "Local Mobilization for the People's Social Petition of the Dutch Peace Movement," *International Social Movement Research* 1 (1988): 41–46.

13. On Bible schools, see Virginia Lieson Brereton, *Training God's Army: The American Bible School, 1880–1940* (Bloomington: Indiana University Press, 1990).

14. On Bible conferences, see Ferenc Morton Szasz, *The Divided Mind of Protestant America, 1880–1930* (University, Ala.: University of Alabama Press, 1982), 73–75.

15. See Joel Carpenter, *Revive Us Again: The Reawakening of American Fundamentalism* (New York: Oxford University Press, 1997), 25–27.

16. William Bell Riley, "The World Premillennial Conference vs. the Coming Confederacy," S&C 2, 8 (1919): 95. Founded by Riley in 1918, S&C was published quarterly in Minneapolis in association with his Northwestern Bible and Missionary Training School. With Riley as editor, it became the voice of the WCFA in 1919 and remained the organization's official outlet until the publication's demise in 1932. In 1921 its name was changed to Christian Fundamentals in School and Church and in 1928 to The Christian Fundamentalist.

17. For background on the ministers, see David O. Beale, In Pursuit of Purity: American Fundamentalism since 1850 (Greenville, S.C.: Unusual Publications, 1986), 97–109.

18. On Norris, Riley, and Straton, see C. Allyn Russell, Voices of American Fundamentalism: Seven Biographical Studies (Philadelphia: Westminster Press, 1976), 20–106. For more detailed discussions, see William Vance Trollinger Jr., God's Empire: William Bell Riley and Midwestern Fundamentalism (Madison: University of Wisconsin Press, 1990); Ferenc M. Szasz, "John Roach Straton: Baptist Fundamentalist in an Age of Change, 1875–1929," The Quarterly Review: A Survey of Southern Baptist Progress 34 (April–June 1974): 59–71; and Barry Hankins, God's Rascal: J. Frank Norris and the Beginnings of Southern Fundamentalism (Lexington: University Press of Kentucky, 1996). On Shields, see Leslie K. Tarr, Shields of Canada (Grand Rapids, Mich.: Baker Book House, 1967).

19. Riley, "World Premillennial Conference," 95.

20. See Furniss, Fundamentalist Controversy, 35–45. For a rebuttal, see George M. Marsden, Fundamentalism and American Culture: The Shaping of Twentieth-Century Evangelicalism, 1870–1925 (Oxford: Oxford University Press, 1980), 199–205.

21. On fundamentalism's view of women, see Margaret Lamberts Bendroth, Fundamentalism and Gender, 1875 to the Present (New Haven: Yale University Press, 1993), esp. 63–64, and Betty A. DeBerg, Ungodly Women: Gender and the First Wave of American Fundamentalism (Minneapolis, Minn.: Fortress Press, 1990), esp. 75–98. See also Jeffrey P. Moran, The Scopes Trial: A Brief History with Documents (Boston: Bedford/St. Martin's, 2002), 70–72. The estimate that 70 percent of fundamentalists were women was by Rollin Lynde Hartt, "What Lies Beyond Dayton," Nation 121 (1925): 111.

22. See Jeffrey P. Moran, "The Scopes Trial and Southern Fundamentalism in Black and White: Race, Region, and Religion," Journal of Southern History 70 (2004): 95–120. On African American responses to scientific racism, see Moran, "Reading Race into the Scopes Trial: African American Elites, Science, and Fundamentalism," Journal of American History 90 (2003): esp. 903–7. On the role of evolutionists such as Henry Fairfield Osborn in promoting scientific racism and the eugenics movement, see Constance Areson Clark, "Evolution for John Doe: Pictures, the Public, and the Scopes Trial Debate," Journal of American History 87 (2001): 1275–1303. See also Moran, Scopes Trial, 66–69.

23. Quoted from Baltimore Afro-American, 4 July 1925, 17, in Moran, "Scopes Trial and Southern Fundamentalism," 101. The case against evolution was also made in church publications. See, e.g., Charles H. Wesley, "Does the First Chapter of Genesis Teach Evolution?," A.M.E. Church Review 2, 158 (1923): 75–76; John W. Norris, "Evolution Not a Fact—The Bible a Fact," A.M.E. Church Review 2, 166 (1925): 323–25; and J. W. Sanders, "Evolution—Its Weak Spots," A.M.E. Church Review 2, 168 (1925): 440–45.

24. Quoted in T. W. Callaway, "Monkey Is Kin Only in Court," CT, 17 July 1925. Sandefur went

on: "It is true that we have followed the white race, for good and evil, from Africa on through the centuries to the present, but if they are going after the modern evolution business, here is where we part."

25. See Moran, "Scopes Trial and Southern Fundamentalism," 113. For the reasons for the failure of black and white fundamentalists to forge an alliance, see ibid., 113–20.

26. "The New York Prophetic Bible Conference," S&C 2, 8 (1919): 97.

27. See Trollinger, God's Empire, 10–32.

28. Szasz, Divided Mind, 89–90.

29. "World Conference on the Fundamentals of the Faith," S&C 2, 9 (1919): 131.

30. Riley to J. D. Adams, 5 April 1919, Riley Papers.

31. Riley to J. D. Adams, 28 April 1919, ibid.

32. See "The Northwestern Premillennial Association," S&C 2,8 (1919): 97–98.

33. Riley to J. D. Adams, 28 April 1919.

34. Riley, "Report of Committee on Correlation of Bible Conferences," God Hath Spoken, 22. See also Trollinger, God's Empire, 38–39.

35. Klandermans and Oegema, "Potentials, Networks," 520.

36. "Report of Committee on Resolutions," God Hath Spoken, 15. For individual committee reports, see ibid., 15–24.

37. See "Pre-Philadelphia Conferences," S&C 2, 10 (1919): 170.

38. "Report of Committee on Correlation of Bible Conferences," God Hath Spoken, 22.

39. See Szasz, Divided Mind, 90–91. See also Trollinger, God's Empire, 39–40.

40. T. R. Horton, quoted in "Continent-Wide Conferences," S&C 2, 10 (1919): 282.

41. "Conferences on Christian Fundamentals," S&C 2, 13 (1920): 339.

42. "The Christian Fundamentals Movement," CF in S&C 4, 2 (1922): 22.

43. "Membership in the Christian Fundamentals Association," CF in S&C 4, 2 (1922): 23.

44. See Szasz, Divided Mind, 94.

45. "Christian Fundamentals Movement," 22.

46. See "The Christian Fundamentals Movement and State Organizations," CF in S&C 4, 1 (1921): 18.

47. "The Christian Fundamentals Movement," CF in S&C 4, 4 (1922): 6.

48. Riley, "Christian Fundamentals Movement: Its Battles, Its Achievements," 7.

49. On the Baptist Fundamentalist Fellowship, see Curtis Lee Laws, "Fundamentalism in the Northern Convention," Watchman-Examiner 10, 24 (1922): 745–48. See also Szasz, Divided Mind, 95–96. Among the reasons given for working within the existing Baptist denominations was concern over the direction of their foreign missions, which were frequently described as strongholds of modernism and evolutionary thinking. See, e.g., "Modernism in China," CF in S&C 3, 3 (1921): 21–22; John Roach Straton, "Our Foreign Mission Society and the Fundamentalist League," Watchman-Examiner 11, 46 (1923): 1466–68; and "Baptist Foreign Missions Shot Through with Evolution," Searchlight 6, 20 (1923): 1. See also Szasz, Divided Mind, 97–98.

50. On the BBU, see T. T. Shields, "The Baptist Bible Union," Watchman-Examiner 11, 32 (1923): 1018–19; William Bell Riley, "The Baptist Bible Union of America," Searchlight 6, 24 (1923): 6, and

"Why the Baptist Bible Union?" *Searchlight* 6, 25 (1923): 4; "Some Reasons Why I Am a Member of the Baptist Bible Union," *Baptist Beacon* 1, 4 (1924): 6. See also Stewart G. Cole, *The History of Fundamentalism* (Hamden, Conn.: Archon Books, 1963), 281–94. On its state associations, see "State Organization of the Baptist Bible Union," *Baptist Beacon* 1, 4 (1924): 6, and Cole, *History of Fundamentalism*, 288.

51. See Russell, *Voices of American Fundamentalism*, 52.

52. "The Fifth Annual Convention of the Christian Fundamentals Association," CF in S&C 5, 4 (1923): 5.

53. See William Bell Riley, "Whipping Fundamentalist Leaders into Line," CF in S&C 5, 2 (1923): 6–7. See also Trollinger, *God's Empire*, 56.

54. "The Anti-Evolution League," CF in S&C 5, 2 (1923): 16–17.

55. "Organization of Anti-Evolution League," CF in S&C 5, 2 (1923): 66–67.

56. "Minnesota Anti-Evolution League," CF in S&C 5, 6 (1923): 32; see also 31–32.

57. See Furniss, *Fundamentalist Controversy*, 69.

58. "Anti-Evolution League," 16.

59. See Klandermans and Oegema, "Potentials, Networks," 520. On social choice theory, and the assumption that participation in mass movements is rarely a rational choice, see Mancur Olson, *The Logic of Collective Action: Public Goods and the Theory of Groups* (Cambridge: Harvard University Press, 1965). Social movement theorists who argue that activists are more (rather than less) likely to participate when they assume others are participating include Klandermans ("Mobilization and Participation," 583–600), who writes: "On a collective level, the expectation that others will participate works as a self-fulfilling prophecy" (p. 597). In their work on the Dutch peace movement, Klandermans and Oegema ("Potentials, Networks," 527–29) found that the behavior of participants confirmed the theory.

60. "Fundamentals Conferences, Oct. to Jan.," CF in S&C 3, 2 (1921): 37.

61. "Minutes of the Meeting of the Executive Committee of Christian Fundamentals Association, June 16, 1921," CF in S&C 3, 4 (1921): 16.

62. "Support of Christian Fundamentals," CF in S&C 3, 5 (1921): 18.

63. "The Christian Fundamentals Movement," CF in S&C 4, 4 (1922): 5. See also "Back to Orthodoxy—The Denver Times Editorial," CF in S&C 3, 4 (1921): 19.

64. Other fundamentalist papers included T. T. Shield's *Gospel Witness*, published by his Jarvis Street Baptist Church in Toronto, and the *Western Recorder*, a Louisville publication edited by J. W. Porter (later by Victor I. Masters) and sponsored by the Baptist Board of Missions in Kentucky. Publications that were sympathetic to the movement included the *Presbyterian of the South* (Richmond, Va.), the *Christian Advocate* (Nashville, Tenn.), and the Methodist *Pentecostal Herald* (Louisville, Ky.).

65. For the first appearance of the seal and motto, see S&C 2, 9 (1919): 168.

66. On Laws, see John W. Bradbury, "Curtis Lee Laws and the Fundamentalist Movement," *Foundations* 5 (1962): 52–58.

67. "Dr. A. C. Dixon Speaks," *Searchlight* 3, 28 (1921): 2. Other admiring letters, printed on the same page, came from Riley, Torrey, evangelist T. T. Martin, and Southern Methodist bishop Warren A. Candler. Most fundamentalist editors followed the practice. Thus when the *Western*

Recorder published a sermon of T. T. Shields, Shields praised the publication and encouraged his readers to subscribe to it. See "The Western Recorder," *Gospel Witness* 2, 26 (1923): 10. At times the editors suggested that the papers were in a friendly competition. Commenting on the new *Baptist Beacon*, Norris put it this way: " 'The Beacon' makes the reading of 'The Searchlight' appear tame, and this will never do. So in a short time, we are going to put a little more fire, ginger, 'spizzerink-tum' or something or other to create a little more interest. For if that isn't done, 'The Beacon' will take away the crowd from 'The Searchlight.' " "Dr. Norris on the 'Baptist Beacon,' " *Baptist Beacon* 1, 3 (1924): 6.

68. An example of the WCFA advertising campaign is in *Searchlight* 7, 26 (1924): 7.

69. *Searchlight* 4, 1 (1921): 2. See also letters to the editor in ibid. 3, 51 (1921): 2.

70. See "Baptists and Fundamentalists," *Watchman-Examiner* 8, 30 (1920): 925–26; "What Does the Fundamentalist Movement Portend?," ibid. 9, 23 (1921): 709–10; "Fundamentalism Is Very Much Alive," ibid. 9, 30 (1921): 941; "Has Fundamentalism Helped or Hurt?," ibid. 10, 7 (1921): 197; and "Fundamentalism in the Northern Convention," ibid. 10, 24 (1921): 745–48.

71. Riley, "Whipping Fundamentalist Leaders into Line," 7. See also Riley, "Dr. Gambrell's Stalwart Faith in Christian Fundamentals," *CF in S&C* 5, 1 (1923): 23–26.

72. Quoted in William Bell Riley, "Frank Groner vs. Frank Norris, or Some Fundamental Facts," *CF in S&C* 5, 4 (1923): 19. See also "J. Frank Norris and the Texas Convention," *Baptist Beacon* 2, 5 (1926): 14.

73. William Bell Riley, "The Baptist Bible Union of America," *Searchlight* 6, 24 (1923): 6.

74. "Methodists Stirred Up," *Searchlight* 3, 28 (1921): 2. It should be noted that some Baptists saw fundamentalism as a vehicle for attracting more Baptists. According to T. T. Shields, "The Baptist Denomination in America, at this present hour, is facing one of the greatest opportunities of its existence. The denomination that will magnify the Word of the Lord and insist upon the authority of Scripture will command the attention of true believers of every name in this day of religious declension." Shields, "The Baptist Bible Union Urgently Needed," *Gospel Witness* 2, 17 (1923): 9.

75. "The Papal Spirit in Methodism," *CF in S&C* 4, 2 (1922): 8.

76. "His Brethren vs. His Bishop," reprinted in *CF in S&C* 4, 2 (1922): 12.

77. "The World's Fundamental Convention—April 29th to May 6th 1923," *Searchlight* 6, 20 (1923): 1.

78. See "Back to Fundamentals," *Watchman-Examiner* 11, 42 (1923): 1326. On efforts to remove Fosdick, see Szasz, *Divided Mind*, 99–100.

79. See "Southern Christians Repudiate 'The Christian Century,' " *CF in S&C* 4, 2 (1922): 16–17.

80. See Szasz, *Divided Mind*, 101–2.

81. "The Christian Fundamentals Movement," *CF in S&C* 4, 4 (1922): 6.

82. Riley, "Dr. Gambrell's Stalwart Faith," 29.

83. Charles Gallaudet Trumbull, "Fundamentalists Expose Modernism in the South," *Searchlight* 6, 28 (1923): 1.

84. Quoted in "Fifth Annual Convention of the Christian Fundamentals Association," 7.

85. "Resolutions of the Fundamentals Convention," *CF in S&C* 5, 3 (1923): 9. Also printed in *Searchlight* 6, 26 (1923): 6.

86. See Klandermans and Oegema, "Potentials, Networks," 520–21. In their study of the Dutch peace movement, Klandermans and Oegema found that 60 percent of already motivated individuals actually did not participate (p. 529).

87. Riley, "World Premillennial Conference," 92.

88. "The Interchurch World Movement," S&C 2, 13 (1920): 323. According to Riley, the absence of clear doctrinal or denominational boundaries theoretically opened the interchurch movements to non-Christians as well: "If there is to be no doctrinal basis for an interchurch movement why keep out the dear Mohammedans?," "The Interchurch World Movement," S&C 2, 12 (1920): 288.

89. Riley, "World Premillennial Conference," 94. Southern Baptist Robert Tandy tried to clarify the confusion: "Baptists are in favor of church union any day upon the basis of the teachings of Jesus and his apostles, but are opposed to all forms of compromise to attain that end." Robert H. Tandy, "Why Southern Baptists Did Not Enter the Interchurch World Movement," Western Recorder 95, 41 (1920): 5.

90. Quoted in "Is There To Be a Division in the Baptist Denomination?," CF in S&C 2, 12 (1920): 292.

91. Riley, "World Premillennial Conference," 96.

92. "The Fundamentals Movement," CF in S&C 3, 2 (1921): 19.

93. "The Northern Baptist Convention," CF in S&C 2, 13 (1920): 333.

94. "The Interchurch World Movement," S&C 2, 12 (1920): 289. According to J. W. Porter, the Interchurch World Movement was an attempt to create an "ecclesiastical trust." See "The Interchurch Movement," Western Recorder 95, 13 (1920): 8. Porter wrote, "Should the Interchurch Movement succeed, convictions will be crushed and all rivals put out of business. Quoted in "Quite True," Western Recorder 95, 31 (1920): 9. Some fundamentalists, however, were not in the least reticent to organize. T. T. Shields ("Baptist Bible Union Urgently Needed," 10) observed, "We are not organizing for a picnic but for war."

95. "The Interchurch World Movement," S&C 2, 12 (1920): 290.

96. Riley, "Christian Fundamentals Movement: Its Battles, Its Achievements," 4, 5, 6, 7, 5, 6.

97. "Support of Christian Fundamentals," 18.

98. Riley, "Christian Fundamentals Movement: Its Battles, Its Achievements," 7.

99. Ibid., 11. See also Riley's editorial "The Rule of the Rockefeller Foundation Fund," CF in S&C 4, 2 (1922): 4–6.

100. "Support of Christian Fundamentals," 18. According to Szasz (Divided Mind, 78, 94), Lyman and Milton Stewart contributed $300,000 for publication of The Fundamentals and "provided a steady influx of money" to the fundamentalist movement. On Lyman's support for the premillennial prophecy movement, which apparently ran into millions of dollars, see Szasz, Divided Mind, 80–81.

101. Riley, "Christian Fundamentals Movement: Its Battles, Its Achievements," 8.

102. Ibid. On Riley's appeal for "fifty millionaires" to support an orthodox premillennial seminary, see Szasz, Divided Mind, 94. On movement finances, see Ferenc Morton Szasz, "Three Fundamentalist Leaders" (Ph.D. diss., University of Rochester, 1969), 197–98.

103. On these divisions, see Trollinger, God's Empire, 41–42; Szasz, Divided Mind, 93; Cole, History of Fundamentalism, 80–81; and Russell, Voices of American Fundamentalism, 33–44. Russell found it

ironic "that Bryan, who had supported many a fundamentalist cause, and who had been used widely by the fundamentalists to champion their programs, was practically boycotted by the fundamentalist leaders at the Scopes Trial" (pp. 184–85).

104. On tensions between the Fundamentalist Fellowship and the BBU, see "The Fundamentalists and the Bible Union," *Watchman-Examiner* 11, 16 (1923): 487–88. See also Szasz, *Divided Mind*, 96.

105. "The Christian Fundamentals Movement," CF in S&C 4, 4 (1922): 5.

106. Charles T. Alexander, "Fundamentalism versus Modernism," reprinted from *Western Recorder* in CF in S&C 5, 2 (1923): 41. At least some fundamentalists seemed to oppose not just modernism but modern culture as a whole, including "asphalt streets, porcelain bath tubs, steam heat, social reform, clinics in social organization, super-statesmanship of so-called religious experts, germicides, vaccines, radiophones, and the like." "Southern Baptists and Northern Fundamentalists," reprinted from *Western Recorder* in ibid., 31.

107. "To My Brethren, Fundamentalist Editors," CF in S&C 6, 3 (1924): 11.

108. "World Conference Resolutions," CF in S&C 5, 1 (1922): 18.

109. See "100,000 New Members for Christian Fundamentals Association," CF in S&C 6, 2 (1924): 1. See also the advertisement for 100,000 new members in *Searchlight* 6, 34 (1923), 1.

110. "The Editor's Restoration and Return," CF in S&C 7, 3 (1925): 6–7. The same story appeared in *Baptist Beacon* 1, 8 (1925): 9–10.

111. "Moderator of the Presbyterian General Assembly," CF in S&C 7, 4 (1925): 21.

CHAPTER THREE

1. William Jennings Bryan and Mary Baird Bryan, *The Memoirs of William Jennings Bryan* (Philadelphia: John C. Winston Co., [1925], 459.

2. See Erving Goffman, *Frame Analysis: An Essay on the Organization of Experience* (Cambridge: Harvard University Press, 1974).

3. See William A. Gamson, *Talking Politics* (Cambridge: Cambridge University Press, 1992), 31–58. See also Bert Klandermans, "Mobilization and Participation: Social Psychological Expansions of Resource Mobilization Theory," *American Sociological Review* 49 (1984): 583–90; Doug McAdam, *Political Process and the Development of Black Insurgency* (Chicago: University of Chicago Press, 1982); and Frances Fox Piven and Richard Cloward, *Poor People's Movements: Why They Succeed, How They Fail* (New York: Pantheon, 1977).

4. David A. Snow and Robert D. Benford, "Ideology, Frame Resonance, and Participant Mobilization," *International Social Movement Research* 1 (1988): 199–204.

5. Robert D. Benford and David Snow, "Framing Processes and Social Movements: An Overview and Assessment," *Annual Review of Sociology* 26 (2000): 615. See also David A. Snow and Robert D. Benford, "Master Frames and Cycles of Protest," in Aldon D. Morris and Carol McClurg Mueller, eds., *Frontiers in Social Movement Theory* (New Haven: Yale University Press, 1992), 133–55; Benford, "'You Could Be the Hundredth Monkey': Collective Action Frames and Vocabularies of Motive within the Nuclear Disarmament Movement," *Sociological Quarterly* 34 (1993): 195–216; and Benford, "An Insider's Critique of Social Movement Framing Perspective," *Sociological Inquiry* 67 (1997): 409–30.

6. See Stewart G. Cole, *The History of Fundamentalism* (Hamden, Conn.: Archon Books, 1963); Ernest R. Sandeen, *The Roots of Fundamentalism: British and American Millenarianism, 1800–1930* (Chicago: University of Chicago Press, 1970); Norman F. Furniss, *The Fundamentalist Controversy, 1918–1931* (New Haven: Yale University Press, 1954); and George E. Webb, *The Evolution Controversy in America* (Lexington: University Press of Kentucky, 1994).

7. On diagnostic framing, see Snow and Benford, "Ideology, Frame Resonance," 200. On "injustice frames," see Gamson, *Talking Politics*, 31–58.

8. For background, see George M. Marsden, *The Soul of the American University: From Protestant Establishment to Established Nonbelief* (New York: Oxford University Press, 1994), 332–56.

9. Among the critics was American philosopher James Bisset Pratt, a professor at Williams College: "Most important of all, they are not interested in the religious things that interested the older generation. Their grandfathers believed in the Creed; their fathers a little doubted the Creed; they have never read it." Pratt, "Religion and the Younger Generation," *Yale Review* 12 (1923): 594.

10. The most comprehensive study was Robert Cooley Angell's *The Campus: A Study of Contemporary Undergraduate Life in the American University* (New York: Appleton, 1928).

11. Among the denominations announcing college initiatives were the Southern Baptists, as part of their "Seventy-Five Million Campaign." See Suzanne Cameron Linder, "William Louis Poteat and the Evolution Controversy," *North Carolina Historical Review* 40 (1963): 139.

12. William Bell Riley, *The Menace of Modernism* (New York: Christian Alliance Publishing Co., [1917]), 115.

13. See Michael Kazin, *A Godly Hero: The Life of William Jennings Bryan* (New York: Knopf, 2006), 131–41. See also Donald K. Springen, *William Jennings Bryan: Orator of Small-Town America* (New York: Greenwood Press, 1991), 73. On the Chautauqua circuit, see Victoria Case and Robert Ormond Case, *We Called It Culture: The Story of Chautauqua* (Garden City, N.Y.: Doubleday, 1948); Harry P. Harrison, *Culture under Canvas: The Story of Tent Chautauqua* (New York: Hastings House, 1958); and Andrew C. Rieser, *The Chautauqua Movement: Protestants, Progressives, and the Culture of Modern Liberalism* (New York: Columbia University Press, 2003). The lecture circuit contributed substantially to Bryan's livelihood. For every speech, he received the sum of single admissions up to $250; then circuit organizers received $250, and any additional amount was divided equally between the two. See Springen, *William Jennings Bryan*, 83.

14. See Springen, *William Jennings Bryan*, 73; Case and Case, *We Called It Culture*, 112; and Rieser, *Chautauqua Movement*, 263–64. For a view of Bryan's oratory through the eyes of a contemporary critic, see Glenn Frank, "William Jennings Bryan: A Mind Divided against Itself," *Century* 106 (1923): 796. Frank wrote: "Mr. Bryan has always been dominated by an audience. He is essentially an orator. He must have an audience. An audience is to Mr. Bryan what air is to the lungs. He cannot function without it."

15. See Case and Case, *We Called It Culture*, 90. See also Rieser, *Chautauqua Movement*, 51.

16. At one time, *The Commoner* published an average of 100,000 copies per month. See Lawrence W. Levine, *Defender of the Faith: William Jennings Bryan: The Last Decade, 1915–1925* (New York: Oxford University Press, 1965), 23. On the "Bryan Bible Talks," see ibid., 272.

17. Bryan, "The Menace of Darwinism," *Commoner* 21, 4 (1921): 7. The same passages reappear in Bryan's 1921 James Sprunt lectures, delivered at Union Theological Seminary in Virginia and

reprinted as Bryan's best-selling book *In His Image* (New York: Fleming H. Revell Co., 1922), 111–12. A slightly different version appears in *The Bible and Its Enemies*, 4th ed. (Chicago: Bible Institute Colportage Assn., 1921), 33–35, as well as in other speeches published as pamphlets.

18. Bryan, "Menace of Darwinism," 8.

19. Bryan, *Bible and Its Enemies*, 35.

20. Alfred Fairhurst, *Atheism in Our Universities* (Cincinnati: Standard Publishing Co., 1923), 32, 33, 32.

21. T. T. Martin, *Hell and the High Schools: Christ or Evolution Which?* (Kansas City, Mo.: Western Baptist Publishing Co., 1923), 155.

22. Bryan, *Bible and Its Enemies*, 35.

23. Bryan, *In His Image*, 120.

24. Quoted in "Straton to Fight Darwin in Schools," *NYT*, 9 February 1922. Straton wrote: "The shock that woke me up came when my own son, a high school boy, who has always believed the Bible, came home one day with figures about the antiquity of man and with theories in conflict with the Bible. I said, 'My son, where did you get that?' He told me it had been taught to him. I only had to go to the library and take down a few books to show him that the theories as to the age of the earth and the antiquity of man contain the wildest guesses. . . . My son quickly saw he had been misled, but many fathers have not the books handy or the time to controvert such teachings in the schools." Ibid. Riley had a similar experience when he sent his son to a Chicago school. See William Bell Riley, "Corporate Control, the Peril of Christian Education," *Commoner* 21, 8 (1921): 8.

25. Fairhurst, *Atheism in Our Universities*, 32. Similar complaints were expressed even before the 1920s. For years, Methodist evangelist L. H. Munhall had been describing parents with tear-dimmed eyes who told him of how they had sent their children to Methodist schools only to find them graduating confirmed infidels. Munhall is cited in Riley, *Menace of Modernism*, 115–16.

26. J. W. Porter, *Evolution—A Menace* (Nashville, Tenn.: Sunday School Board, Southern Baptist Convention, 1922), 84–85. Porter concentrated his criticism on the teaching of evolution. He went on: "In a recent meeting of our state board a prominent business man wept, as he told of the damage done his daughter's faith by this teaching. This is not an unusual, but an almost every day occurrence" (p. 85). Porter's associate Victor Masters reported that his secretary told him "that her own children were slimed with this miserable theory [evolution] in the High School system of Louisville." Quoted in "Baptist Schools Infected with Evolution Theory," *Western Recorder* 9, 22 (1921): 5.

27. Martin, *Hell and the High Schools*, 151.

28. Ibid., 154.

29. Quoted from *Monroe Daily Journal*, 3 September 1921, in Irvin G. Wyllie, "Bryan, Birge, and the Wisconsin Evolution Controversy, 1921–1922," *Wisconsin Magazine of History* 35 (1951): 297.

30. William Jennings Bryan, *Is the Bible True?* (Nashville, Tenn.: Published by the Friends of William Jennings Bryan, 1924), 4.

31. William Jennings Bryan, "The Modern Arena," *Commoner* 21, 6 (1921): 3. These and other examples are also in Bryan, "Evolution as Applied to Man," *Commoner* 22: 3 (1922): 3. Another rendition is in Bryan, *Bible and Its Enemies*, 36–37.

32. Bryan, "Evolution as Applied to Man," 4. See also Bryan, *Bible and Its Enemies*, 30.

33. Bryan, *Is the Bible True?*, 12.

34. Bryan, "Modern Arena," 3.

35. Fairhurst, *Atheism in Our Universities*, 211; Martin, *Hell and the High Schools*, 154; Bryan, "Menace of Darwinism," 7.

36. Quoted in "White-Washing Infidelity," *CF in S&C* 4, 2 (1922): 7.

37. See Fairhurst, *Atheism in Our Universities*, 72–195. A few years earlier Wheaton College president Charles A. Blanchard had circulated a questionnaire among a selected group of presidents of Midwestern colleges. He found that nearly three-fourths of them reported that their science faculty taught evolution, whereas less than 10 percent indicated that their colleges were strictly creationist. See Ronald L. Numbers, *The Creationists: The Evolution of Scientific Creationism* (Berkeley: University of California Press, 1992), 40.

38. See Bryan, "Modern Arena," 3; "Evolution as Applied to Man," 3; *Bible and Its Enemies*, 40–41; and *In His Image*, 116–18; and James H. Leuba, *The Belief in God and Immortality: A Psychological, Anthropological and Statistical Study* (Chicago: Open Court Publishing Co., 1921), 213–80. See also William Jennings Bryan, "The Real Issue Is Darwinism," *Commoner* 22, 2 (1922): 5.

39. Bryan, *In His Image*, 117.

40. On prognostic framing, see Snow and Benford, "Ideology, Frame Resonance," 201. See also Benford and Snow, "Framing Processes," 616–17. In "Ideology, Frame Resonance" (p. 201), Snow and Benford argue that the antinuclear movement was fragmented because of a failure in prognostic framing, with some groups advocating unilateral disarmament, others proposing arms control negotiations and treaties, and still others suggesting working through international institutions such as the World Court.

41. See Marsden, *Soul of the American University*, 150–59.

42. James M. Gray, "Bible Institutes and Theological Seminaries," *CF in S&C* 3, 3 (1921): 25. For background, see Jon H. Roberts, "Conservative Evangelicals and Science Education in American Colleges and Universities, 1890–1940," *Journal of the Historical Society* 5 (2005): 297–329.

43. Riley, *Menace of Modernism*, 118. On Dixon, see Ferenc Morton Szasz, *The Divided Mind of Protestant America, 1880–1930* (University, Ala.: University of Alabama Press, 1982), 109. See also Benjamin Kidd, *The Science of Power* (New York: Putnam, 1918).

44. "Resolutions of Fundamental Convention," *Searchlight* 6, 26 (1923): 6.

45. Fairhurst, *Atheism in Our Universities*, 199, 200, 201.

46. T. T. Shields, "The Baptist Bible Union at New York: An Address by the Pastor," *Gospel Witness* 2, 31 (1923): 7.

47. William Jennings Bryan, "Brother or Brute?," *Commoner* 20, 11 (1920): 11. See also Kidd, *Science of Power*. Bryan was also influenced by his reading of Vernon L. Kellogg's *Headquarters Nights* (Boston: Atlantic Monthly Press, 1917), which recounted the author's wartime conversations with German officers and described what he took to be the influence of Darwin on their thinking. Ironically, as a leading American biologist, Kellogg would become an active opponent of Bryan's antievolution campaign. See Szasz, *Divided Mind*, 109.

48. "Definition of Evolution," *Searchlight* 4, 2 (1921): 4.

49. Bryan, "Menace of Darwinism," 5–6.

50. William Jennings Bryan, "Back to God," *Commoner* 21, 8 (1921): 2.

51. Bryan, "Modern Arena," 3.

52. Bryan, *In His Image*, 200. He repeated the remark frequently in his speeches of the early 1920s, adding that it applied not only to Harvard but also "to Yale, or Columbia, or Princeton, or to any other great university, or even smaller colleges." Ibid.

53. Bryan, "Modern Arena," 3.

54. Bryan, "Back to God," 2.

55. Bryan, *In His Image*, 187. On another occasion, he contended that Darwinism was being taught by "not all of our teachers but many of them." Bryan, "Real Issue Is Darwinism," 5.

56. Fairhurst, *Atheism in Our Universities*, 211.

57. Martin, *Hell and the High Schools*, 13, 150. For more on the "high-brows," see Andrew Johnson, "Scholarship and Evolution," *Pentecostal Herald* 34, 12 (1922): 6.

58. "Evolution Is Now Taught at Baylor University," *Searchlight* 6, 48 (1923): 3.

59. Quoted in Martin, *Hell and the High Schools*, 149.

60. See Marsden, *Soul of the American University*, 319. As late as 1923, Brown University president William H. P. Faunce could announce with some confidence that "every boy or girl attending High School north of Mason and Dixon's line is now being taught some form of the doctrine of Evolution." Faunce, "Freedom in School and Church," *World's Work* 45 (1923): 510.

61. Martin, *Hell and the High Schools*, 9. For Bryan's views, see *Bible and Its Enemies*, 39.

62. Martin, *Hell and the High Schools*, 9, 9–10, 10, 11.

63. Bryan, "Back to God," 2, and *In His Image*, 121 (quotation).

64. Bryan, "Back to God," 2.

65. Bryan, "Real Issue Is Darwinism," 5. In one of his more thoughtful essays, Bryan argued: "When Christians want to teach Christianity they build their own schools and employ their own teachers." The same should apply to evolutionists, who had every right to "build their own colleges, and employ their own teachers for the training of their own children in their brute doctrine." Bryan, "Darwinism in Public Schools," *Commoner* 23, 1 (1923): 2.

66. Fairhurst, *Atheism in Our Universities*, 30.

67. Martin, *Hell and the High Schools*, 164. In fact, Martin was not convinced that parents would play this role, seeing them as either complacent or cowed by the educational establishment and unwilling to "go to the limit to protect their children" (p. 165).

68. Bryan, "Darwinism in Public Schools," 1. "The hand that writes the pay check rules the school," one of Bryan's favorite phrases, became something of a slogan in the antievolution campaign of the early 1920s. See Bryan, "Belief in God," *Commoner* 22, 5 (1922): 10. See also his speech to the West Virginia legislature, in "Science vs. Evolution," *Commoner* 23, 4 (1923): 3. The expression also appears in Bryan, *Orthodox Christianity vs. Modernism* (Chicago: Fleming H. Revell Co., 1923), 29.

69. On motivational frames, see Snow and Benford, "Ideology, Frame Resonance," 201–4. See also Benford and Snow, "Framing Processes," 617–18.

70. See Marsden, *Soul of the American University*, 296–301, 317–21. For an excellent study of the changes brought by compulsory education and rural southerners' resistance to them, see Jeanette Keith, *Country People in the New South: Tennessee's Upper Cumberland* (Chapel Hill: University of North Carolina Press, 1995), 118–42.

71. T. T. Shields, "The Baptist Bible Union Urgently Needed," *Gospel Witness* 2, 17 (1923): 9, 10. See also Shields, "Why Some Individuals and Institutions Need to Be Blown Up with Dynamite," *Gospel Witness* 2, 38 (1924): 1–8.

72. T. T. Martin, "The Three Fatal Teachings of President Poteat of Wake Forest College," *Western Recorder* 95, 16 (1920): 4. The series appeared in four parts on 22 January, 29 January, 5 February, and 12 February 1920. For background on the controversy, see Willard B. Gatewood Jr., *Preachers, Pedagogues and Politicians: The Evolution Controversy in North Carolina, 1920–1927* (Chapel Hill: University of North Carolina Press, 1966), 27–38.

73. T. T. Martin, "Evolution—Allegorial or Figurative Language," *Searchlight* 5, 52 (1922): 1.

74. Quoted from *Monroe Daily Journal*, 3 September 1921, in Wyllie, "Bryan, Birge, and the Wisconsin Evolution Controversy," 297; see also 294–301.

75. William Jennings Bryan, "Dr. Birge: Autocrat," *Commoner* 22, 5 (1922): 2

76. Quoted in "Another Explosion by Dr. Brooks," *Searchlight* 6, 35 (1923): 1.

77. See Samuel Proctor, "William Jennings Bryan and the University of Florida," *Florida Historical Quarterly* 39 (1960): 8–9.

78. William Jennings Bryan "Tampering with the Mainspring," *Commoner* 22, 7 (1922): 6.

79. Bryan, "Dr. Birge: Autocrat," 2. On popular reaction to the Bryan-Birge fight, see Wyllie, "Bryan, Birge, and the Wisconsin Evolution Controversy," 298–301. Equally embarrassing was a similar offer, made by Bryan at the same time, of one hundred dollars to any professor who would sign a statement declaring that he was the descendant of an ape. On the ensuing flap, see Paolo E. Coletta, *William Jennings Bryan: Political Puritan, 1915–1925* (Lincoln: University of Nebraska Press, 1969), 219–20. The exchange can also be followed in the *New York Times*: "Bryan Sends $100 Check," 28 April 1922; "Bryan Makes a New Offer," 13 June 1922; and "Bryan Critic Boasts of His Ape Ancestors," 13 June 1922.

80. See James J. Thompson Jr., *Tried as by Fire: Southern Baptists and the Religious Controversies of the 1920s* (Macon, Ga.: Mercer University Press, 1982), 102. See also Numbers, *Creationists*, 48.

81. See Numbers, *Creationists*, 48. For background, see Kenneth K. Bailey, *Southern White Protestantism in the Twentieth Century* (New York: Harper and Row, 1964), 64. At the same time, local Baptist associations passed resolutions condemning evolution and demanding that all Baptist teachers be required to produce statements of their faith. See Gatewood, *Preachers, Pedagogues*, 70–71.

82. For the Baylor story, see Patsy Ledbetter, "Defense of the Faith: J. Frank Norris and Texas Fundamentalism, 1920–1929," *Arizona and the West* 15 (1973): 52–54. The struggle between Norris and the Texas association was legendary. See Barry Hankins, *God's Rascal: J. Frank Norris and the Beginnings of Southern Fundamentalism* (Lexington: University Press of Kentucky, 1996), 26–30. The case against Norris can be found in F. S. Groner, "Records Reveal Pastor Norris in True Light as Denominational Agitator and Self-Promoter," *Baptist Standard* 35, 16 (1923): 1, 16.

83. William O. Saunders, "Dr. Poteat and the Monkeys," *Elizabeth City (N.C.) Independent*, 19 December 1922. See also Gatewood, *Preachers, Pedagogues*, 75–76. Bryan suffered a similar failure in his attempt to be elected moderator of the 1923 Presbyterian General Assembly. See Coletta, *Bryan*, 220–25. The story can be followed in "Bryan Fails to Get Conference Posts," NYT, 19 May 1923, and "Bryan Loses Fight to Ban Darwinism in Church Schools," NYT, 23 May 1923.

84. The headline is from *Searchlight* 3, 49 (1921): 1.

85. "Prof. Dow and Baylor University," *Searchlight* 3, 52 (1921): 1.

86. See Ledbetter, "Defense of the Faith," 52–54. Also resigning as a result of Norris's campaign was zoologist O. C. Bradbury. Professor Lula Pace, a botanist who was the subject of repeated attacks, refused to step down and remained on the Baylor faculty until her death in 1925. See ibid., 53–54.

87. See the letter from C. C. Hayley, editor of the *Carrollton Chronicle*, in *Searchlight* 4, 2 (1921): 4.

88. "The Western Recorder on Infidelity in Baylor University," *Searchlight* 4, 3 (1921): 4.

89. See " 'Tornado' Norris Converts Many," *Searchlight* 4, 10 (1922): 5.

90. "The Circulation of the 'Searchlight,' " *Searchlight* 4, 13 (1922): 1.

91. "Stenographic Report of the Famous Investigation of Methodist Schools," *Searchlight* 6, 26 (1923): 3, 2, 3.

92. Charles Gallaudet Trumbull, "Fundamentalists Expose Modernism in the South," *Searchlight* 6, 28 (1923): 4.

93. Bryan, "Aristocracy of Brains," *Commoner* 22, 11 (1922): 3.

94. See Alonzo W. Fortune, "The Kentucky Campaign against the Teaching of Evolution," *Journal of Religion* 2 (1922): 226–27.

95. See Ferenc M. Szasz, "William B. Riley and the Fight against Teaching Evolution in Minnesota," *Minnesota History* 41 (1969): 205–7.

96. See J. Frank Norris, "Address on Evolution before the Texas Legislature," *Searchlight* 6, 15 (1923): 1.

97. See "Controversy on Evolution Theory Carried to U. of T.," *NT*, 7 April 1923. The best source of the Tennessee firings is "Report on the University of Tennessee," *Bulletin of the American Association of University Professors* 10 (1924): 213–60. Dismissed at the same time, though apparently for unrelated reasons, was John R. Neal, who later became a member of the defense team at the Scopes trial. See Marsden, *Soul of the American University*, 325–26.

98. See George O. Smith, "Opposition to Evolution in Minnesota," *Science* 56 (1922): 520. The text of the resolutions is also available in Willard B. Gatewood Jr., *Controversy in the Twenties: Fundamentalism, Modernism, and Evolution* (Nashville, Tenn.: Vanderbilt University Press, 1969), 143–44.

99. "Order Darwin Inquiry in Baltimore School," *NYT*, 27 June 1923.

100. Norris, "Address on Evolution before the Texas Legislature," 1.

CHAPTER FOUR

1. For a full report on the Metcalf-Riley debate, see "Vociferous Demonstrations Accompany Evolution Debate," *Raleigh News and Observer*, 18 May 1922. See also Willard B. Gatewood Jr., *Preachers, Pedagogues and Politicians: The Evolution Controversy in North Carolina, 1920–1927* (Chapel Hill: University of North Carolina Press, 1966), 52–56.

2. See Bryan, "God and Evolution," *NYT*, 26 February 1922; Henry Fairfield Osborn, "Evolution and Religion," *NYT*, 5 March 1922; and Edwin Grant Conklin, "Bryan and Evolution," *NYT*, 5 March 1922. Also contributing to the debate was Harry Emerson Fosdick, "Attacks W. J. B.," *NYT*, 12 March 1922. See also "Reply from Mr. Bryan," *NYT*, 14 March 1922, and Henry Fairfield Osborn, *Evolution and Religion in Education* (New York: Scribner, 1926), 3–23.

3. On the "pamphlet wars" begun by Fosdick, see Ferenc Morton Szasz, *The Divided Mind of Protestant America, 1880–1930* (University, Ala.: University of Alabama Press, 1982), 100. On the popularity of books on evolution in the 1920s, see Constance Areson Clark, "Evolution for John Doe: Pictures, the Public, and the Scopes Trial Debate," *Journal of American History* 87 (2001): 1282.

4. For background on the stage debates, see Szasz, *Divided Mind*, 127; C. Allyn Russell, *Voices of American Fundamentalism: Seven Biographical Studies* (Philadelphia: Westminster Press, 1976), 94–95; and Introduction to Ronald L. Numbers, ed., *Creation-Evolution Debates* (New York: Garland Publishing Co., 1995), ix–xiv.

5. See David A. Snow, E. Burke Rochford Jr., Steven K. Worden, and Robert D. Benford, "Frame Alignment Process, Micromobilization, and Movement Participation," *American Sociological Review* 51 (1986): 464–81. The alignment process has been studied in several different settings. See Jurgen Gerhards and Dieter Rucht, "Mesomobilization: Organizing and Framing in Two Protest Campaigns in West Germany," *American Journal of Sociology* 98 (1992): 555–95; Stella M. Capek, "The 'Environmental Justice' Frame: A Conceptual Discussion and Application," *Social Problems* 40 (1993): 5–24; Rita K. Noonan, "Women against the State: Political Opportunities and Collective Action Frames in Chile's Transition to Democracy," *Sociological Forum* 19 (1995): 81–111; Mario Diani, "Linking Mobilization Frames and Political Opportunities: Insights from Regional Populism in Italy," *American Sociological Review* 61 (1996): 1053–69; Mitch Berbrier, " 'Half the Battle': Cultural Resonance, Framing Processes, and Ethnic Affectations in Contemporary White Separatist Rhetoric," *Social Problems* 45 (1998): 431–50; and Dawn McCaffrey and Jennifer Keys, "Competitive Framing Processes in the Abortion Debate: Polarization-Vilification, Frame Saving, and Frame Debunking," *Sociological Quarterly* 41 (2000): 41–61.

6. Szasz, *Divided Mind*, 126. Szasz adds: "People read just about anything they wished into the idea of evolution" (p. 128). On the "fifty-seven" varieties of evolution, see "Concerning Evolution," *Alabama Baptist* 58, 15 (1925): 3.

7. On frame bridging, see Snow et al., "Frame Alignment Processes," 467–69.

8. See Edward J. Larson, *Evolution: The Remarkable History of a Scientific Theory* (New York: Modern Library, 2004), esp. 105–29. See also Ronald L. Numbers, *Darwinism Comes to America* (Cambridge: Harvard University Press, 1998), 24–48; A. Hunter Dupree, "Christianity and the Scientific Community in the Age of Darwin," in David C. Lindberg and Ronald L. Numbers, eds., *God and Nature: Historical Essays on the Encounter between Christianity and Science* (Berkeley: University of California Press, 1986), 351–68; and Peter J. Bowler, *The Eclipse of Darwinism: Anti-Darwinian Evolution Theories in the Decades around 1900* (Baltimore: Johns Hopkins University Press, 1983), 3–19.

9. See Jon H. Roberts, *Darwinism and the Divine in America: Protestant Intellectuals and Organic Evolution, 1859–1900* (Madison: University of Wisconsin Press, 1988), 3–31, 146–73, 209–31. See also Paul K. Conkin, *When All the Gods Trembled: Darwinism, Scopes, and American Intellectuals* (Lanham, Md.: Rowman and Littlefield Publishers, Inc., 1998), 21–47.

10. See Lawrence W. Levine, *Defender of the Faith: William Jennings Bryan: The Last Decade, 1915–1925* (New York: Oxford University Press, 1965), 268–70.

11. See George M. Marsden, *Fundamentalism and American Culture: The Shaping of Twentieth-Century Evangelicalism, 1870–1925* (Oxford: Oxford University Press, 1980), 153–64.

12. See Willard B. Gatewood Jr., *Controversy in the Twenties: Fundamentalism, Modernism, and Evolution* (Nashville, Tenn.: Vanderbilt University Press, 1969), 23–26.

13. Bryan, "The Fundamentals," *Forum* 70 (1923): 1679.

14. George McCready Price, *Back to the Bible, or The New Protestantism* (Washington, D.C.: Review and Herald Publishing Assn., 1920), 124. Arthur I. Brown made the same case: "If there be no Fall, then no Redemption is required. If no Redemption, no Christ as Saviour. In fact, the essential Deity of the Son of God is denied." A. I. Brown, *Evolution and the Bible* (Vancouver: Arcade Printers, [1922]), 31. The pamphlet is reprinted in Ronald L. Numbers, ed., *The Antievolution Works of Arthur I. Brown* (New York: Garland Publishing Co., 1995), 1–28. See also Eldred C. Vanderlaan, ed. *Fundamentalism versus Modernism* (New York: H. H. Wilson Co., 1925), 9.

15. Bryan, "The Fundamentals," 1680. Bryan wrote succinctly, "Darwin's Christ was nobody."

16. See "Dr. Dixon Claims Evolution Started in Unscientific Age," *Raleigh News and Observer*, 13 December 1922. See also C. C. Carrol, "Evolution Grounded in Pantheism," *Western Recorder* 97, 22 (1922): 4.

17. J. W. Porter, *Evolution—A Menace* (Nashville, Tenn.: Sunday School Board, Southern Baptist Convention, 1922), 28. Porter wrote: "Tom Paine was a theist, and so are Jews and Unitarians. It is but just to assume that theistic evolutionists with their boasted wisdom, have rightly named themselves. It is possible to conceive of a theistic evolutionist, but impossible to conceive of a Christian evolutionist of the Darwinian type." See also Porter, "Can an Evolutionist Be a Christian?," *Western Recorder* 97, 30 (1921): 2.

18. John Roach Straton, *Evolution versus Creation: Second in the Series of Fundamentalist-Modernist Debates* (New York: George G. Doran Co., 1924), 34. Even Bryan, who tended to be among the most religiously tolerant in the movement, described theistic evolution as only one step removed from atheism. Writing in "The Fundamentals," he explained that the theistic evolutionist and the atheistic evolutionist "travel together until they reach the origin of life; at this point the theistic evolutionist embraces the atheist, tolerantly if not affectionately, and says, 'I beg your pardon, but here I must assume a Creator'" (p. 1678). He used a slightly different metaphor in *In His Image*: "The theistic evolutionist who tries to occupy a middle ground between those who accept the Bible account of creation and those who reject God entirely reminds one of a traveler in the mountains, who, having fallen half-way down a steep slope, catches hold of a frail bush. It takes so much of his strength to keep from going lower that he is useless as an aid to others." Bryan, *In His Image* (New York: Fleming H. Revell Co., 1922), 127.

19. Straton, *Evolution versus Creation*, 35. See also J. W. Porter, "Christianity and Evolution," *Western Recorder* 96, 38 (1921): 4.

20. Bryan, *In His Image*, 107, 125, 126. On Bryan's opposition to the eugenics movement, see Edward J. Larson, *Sex, Race, and Science: Eugenics in the Deep South* (Baltimore: Johns Hopkins University Press, 1995), 113. Lawrence Levine (*Defender of the Faith*, 270) writes: "Bryan continued to struggle for political, social, and economic reforms even after he entered the fundamentalist movement. It should be added that Bryan joined the anti-evolutionists not in order to retreat from politics but in order to combat a force which he held responsible for sapping American politics of its idealism and progressive spirit."

21. Quoted in "Straton to Fight Darwin in Schools," NYT, 9 February 1922. On Straton's moral reformism, see Hillyer H. Straton, "John Roach Straton, Prophet of Social Righteousness," *Foundations* 5 (1962): 17–38. For background on conservative moral reform, see Gaines M. Foster, *Moral Reconstruction: Christian Lobbyists and the Federal Legislation of Morality, 1865–1920* (Chapel Hill: University of North Carolina Press, 2002).

22. The quotation is from the *New York Tribune* report of the second debate as it appears verbatim in "Straton Wins Evolution Debate," *Searchlight* 7, 12 (1924): 4.

23. "Dr. Dixon Claims Evolution Started in Unscientific Age," 6. For the claim that evolution encouraged divorce and "the 'Free-love' doctrine," see R. M. Hunter, "Evolution and Denominational Debt," *Alabama Baptist* 58, 15 (1925): 8

24. Betty A. DeBerg, *Ungodly Women: Gender and the First Wave of American Fundamentalism* (Minneapolis, Minn.: Fortress Press, 1990), 135–39.

25. Quoted in "Ham Begins Seventh Week with Three Large Crowds," *Raleigh News and Observer*, 24 March 1924. See also Mrs. H. C. Morrison, "How About It, Girls?" *Pentecostal Herald* 35, 36 (1923): 9.

26. Quoted in "Governor Vetoes Evolution and Board Cuts Out Books," *Raleigh News and Observer*, 24 January 1924.

27. "The 'Blue Sunday' Agitation," *Western Recorder* 96, 27 (1921): 8.

28. William Bell Riley, "The Conflict of Christianity with Its Counterfeit," CF in S&C 3, 4 (1921), 6. See also William Vance Trollinger Jr., *God's Empire: William Bell Riley and Midwestern Fundamentalism* (Madison: University of Wisconsin Press, 1990), 68–69.

29. On Straton, see C. Allyn Russell, *Voices of American Fundamentalism: Seven Biographical Studies* (Philadelphia: Westminster Press, 1976), 64; on Bryan, see Levine, *Defender of the Faith*, 257–58; on Norris, see Barry Hankins, *God's Rascal: J. Frank Norris and the Beginnings of Southern Fundamentalism* (Lexington: University Press of Kentucky, 1996), 165–66.

30. J. Frank Norris, "Address on Evolution before the Texas Legislature," *Searchlight* 6, 15 (1923): 4.

31. Bryan, "Darwinism in the Public Schools," *Commoner* 23, 1 (1923): 2. For Bryan's views on race, see Levine, *Defender of the Faith*, 257.

32. See Jeffrey P. Moran, "Reading Race into the Scopes Trial: African American Elites, Science, and Fundamentalism," *Journal of American History* 90 (2003): 902. For background, see Larson, *Sex, Race, and Science*, 1–4; Clark, "Evolution for John Doe," 1294–96; and Eric D. Anderson, "Black Responses to Darwinism, 1859–1915," in Ronald L. Numbers and John Stenhouse, eds., *Disseminating Darwinism: The Role of Place, Race, Religion, and Gender* (Cambridge: Cambridge University Press, 1999), 247–66.

33. Norris, "Address on Evolution before the Texas Legislature," 3.

34. W. J. Cash, *The Mind of the South* (New York: Knopf, 1941), 347. On Cash, see Numbers, *Darwinism Comes to America*, 67.

35. See Moran, "Reading Race into the Scopes Trial," 902.

36. Quoted from *Waco News Tribune*, 19 January 1923, in Patsy Ledbetter, "Defense of the Faith: J. Frank Norris and Texas Fundamentalism, 1920–1929," *Arizona and the West* 15 (1973): 58.

37. Norris, "Address on Evolution before the Texas Legislature," 4.

38. Ibid.

39. James M. Gray, "Modernism a Foe to Good Government," *Moody Bible Institute Monthly* 24 (1924): 547.

40. William Bell Riley, "Civilization—Is It an Evolution," *Western Recorder* 99, 11 (1923): 29.

41. Quoted in "Evangelist Ham Finds His Audience Fundamentalists," *Raleigh News and Observer*, 29 February 1924. North Carolina Presbyterian Albert S. Johnson predicted that evolution would eventuate in "carnality, sensuality, bolshevism, and the red flag." Quoted in "Evolution Idea on False Basis," *Charlotte Observer*, 23 February 1925.

42. On frame amplification, see Snow et al., "Frame Alignment Processes," 469–72.

43. See Gatewood, *Controversy in the Twenties*, 147. Gatewood writes: "Science had been raised to the level of a national cult in the United States. Indeed, it appeared as if the new national criterion had become 'Is it scientific?' "

44. On the influence of Einstein and his theories on American culture in the 1920s, see Paul A. Carter, "Science and the Common Man," *American Scholar* 45 (1975–76): 778–94. See also Ronald C. Tobey, *The American Ideology of National Science, 1919–1930* (Pittsburgh, Pa.: University of Pittsburgh Press, 1971).

45. See George Daniels, "The Pure-Science Ideal and Democratic Culture," *Science* 156 (1967): 1699–1705. According to Daniels, "Science had long since passed so completely beyond the common understanding that there was little chance of meaningful contact with the public on an intellectual level" (p. 1701).

46. Ibid., 1701. On the moral status of science at that time, see David A. Hollinger, "Inquiry and Uplift: Late Nineteenth-Century American Academics and the Moral Efficacy of Scientific Practice," in Thomas L. Haskell, ed., *The Authority of Experts: Studies in History and Theory* (Bloomington: Indiana University Press, 1984), 142–56.

47. Bryan, *In His Image*, 93.

48. Quoted in "Dr. Dixon Claims Evolution Started in Unscientific Age," 5. On Scottish commonsense realism and its effect on American evangelicals, see Marsden, *Fundamentalism and American Culture*, 14–21. On the "Baconian Ideal," see ibid., 55–62. See also Ronald L. Numbers, *The Creationists: The Evolution of Scientific Creationism* (Berkeley: University of California Press, 1992), 50–51.

49. William Bell Riley, *The Scientific Accuracy of the Sacred Scriptures* (Minneapolis, Minn.: N.p., [1920]), 8, 8–9. Riley concluded that the chances of such agreement were no fewer than one in 1,307,674,367,900. This essay, as well as several others written by Riley in the 1920s, appear in William Vance Trollinger Jr., ed., *The Antievolution Pamphlets of William Bell Riley* (New York: Garland Publishing, Inc., 1995).

50. Riley, *Scientific Accuracy*, 13–14, 17.

51. Bryan, *In His Image*, 94.

52. For background, see Larson, *Evolution*, 105–29, 165–74.

53. Arthur Brown (*Evolution and the Bible*) was typical in referring to "the opinions of world-renowned men like Virchow of Berlin, Dawson of Montreal, Etheridge of the British Museum, Groette of Strassburg University, Paulson of Berlin, Clerk Maxwell, Dana, Naegeli, Holliker, Wagner, Snell, Tovel, Bunge the physiological chemist, Brown, Hoffman, and Askernazy, botanists,

Oswald Heer, the geologist, Carl Ernst von Baer, the eminent zoologist and anthropologist, Du Bois Reymond, Stuckenburg, and Zockler, and a host of others" (p. 14). Among those constructing the first lists were Luther L. Townsend, *Collapse of Evolution* (Boston: National Magazine Co. and American Bible League, 1905), 47–53, and Alexander Patterson, *The Other Side of Evolution: Its Effects and Fallacy* (Chicago: Bible Institute Colportage Assn., 1903), 7–11. For the use of such lists, see Numbers, *Creationists*, 51–53.

54. T. T. Martin, "The Three Fatal Teachings of President Poteat of Wake Forest College," *Western Recorder* 95, 16 (1920): 5.

55. T. T. Martin, *Hell and the High Schools: Christ or Evolution Which?* (Kansas City, Mo.: Western Baptist Publishing Co., 1923), 131. Poteat's reply was reprinted in the *Biblical Recorder*: "Two do not appear in the biographical dictionaries, five are misrepresented, seven won reputation in other than biological fields, and six have been in their graves more than forty years, two of these having died long before Darwin's great book was published." William Louis Poteat, "Evolution," *Biblical Recorder* 87 (1922): 3.

56. William Jennings Bryan, "Evolution as Applied to Man," *Commoner* 22, 3 (1922): 3.

57. Brown, *Evolution and the Bible*, 20. Surprised by the popular reaction to Bateson's speech, the AAAS passed resolutions at its next annual meeting emphasizing its support for evolution and denouncing the antievolution movement for "misleading public opinion." *Summarized Proceedings of the American Association for the Advancement of Science . . . June, 1921, to June, 1925* (Washington, D.C.: AAAS, 1925): 66. On Bateson, see also Numbers, *Creationists*, 52–53; George E. Webb, *The Evolution Controversy in America* (Lexington: University Press of Kentucky, 1994), 61–62; and Paul A. Carter, "The Fundamentalist Defense of the Faith," in John Braeman, Robert H. Bremner, and David Brody, eds., *Change and Continuity in Twentieth-Century America: The 1920s* (Columbus: Ohio State University Press, 1968), 208. On Brown, see Introduction to Numbers, *Antievolution Works of Arthur I. Brown*, ix–xiii.

58. Quoted in "Dr. Dixon Claims Evolution Started in Unscientific Age," 5.

59. Porter, *Evolution—A Menace*, 28; "Random Remarks on Evolution," *Western Recorder* 95, 37 (1920): 8.

60. Brown, *Evolution and the Bible*, 11; W. W. Everts, "Evolution," *Watchman-Examiner* 10, 13 (1922): 396.

61. Straton, *Evolution versus Creation*, 30.

62. Bryan, *In His Image*, 91. According to Lawrence Levine (*Defender of the Faith*), Bryan "understood, or more properly, wanted to understand, very little of Darwinian evolution. No matter how much the scientists might protest, no matter how clearly they might explain, evolution to Bryan and most of his followers simply meant that man had descended directly from the ape and that every living organism was related to every other living organism" (p. 291). By contrast, Ron Numbers (*Creationists*, 41–44) has shown that Bryan was fairly well informed when it came to evolutionary theory, having read Darwin and some of his defenders, and having followed the public statements of contemporary scientists.

63. Bryan, "Evolution as Applied to Man," 2. For a thoughtful treatment of the meaning of "hypothesis" and the methodology of hypothesis testing in Darwinian science, see Edward L. Rice, "Darwin and Bryan—A Study in Method," *Science* 61 (1925): esp. 244–45.

64. Bryan, "Evolution as Applied to Man," 2; Bryan, *In His Image*, 94; Bryan, "The Modern Arena," *Commoner* 21, 6 (1921): 3; Bryan, *In His Image*, 24.

65. Bryan, *In His Image*, 91–92.

66. Brown, *Evolution and the Bible*, 15. "Just to make the matter interesting," J. W. Porter offered cash rewards for anyone who could provide examples of such speciation:

1. For a single example of a change of species into a different species . . . $25

2. For a new species within the past 500 years . . . 25

3. For one instance of natural selection, improving specie . . . 25

4. For one example of acquired characteristics being inherited . . . 25

5. For a single achievement of evolution within the past 1,000 years . . . 25

Porter, "Colonel W. J. Bryan and His Critics," *Searchlight* 7, 11 (1924): 4.

67. Bryan, "Evolution as Applied to Man," 3.

68. William Jennings Bryan, *The Bible and Its Enemies*, 4th ed. (Chicago: Bible Institute Colportage Assn., 1921), 26.

69. Quoted from *North Carolina Lutheran* 1 (1923): 4, in Gatewood, *Preachers, Pedagogues*, 42.

70. Norris, "Address on Evolution before the Texas Legislature," 2.

71. Bryan, *Bible and Its Enemies*, 31.

72. Bryan, *In His Image*, 102–3.

73. Andrew Johnson, "Reply to Dr. E. L. Powell's Sermon on Evolution," *Pentecostal Herald* 34, 11 (1922): 6.

74. Bryan, *In His Image*, 103.

75. Quoted in "Evangelist Ham Raps Evolution," *Raleigh News and Observer*, 6 November 1923. By contrast, Ham described creation as a divine design, proven by the prevalence of "heptads," the perfect number seven, as seen in snowflakes, leaves, and the "elements of chemistry."

76. Quoted in "Evangelist Ham Preaches His Sermon on Evolution," *Raleigh News and Observer*, 14 March 1924.

77. On frame extension, see Snow et al., "Frame Alignment Process," 472–73. See also William A. Gamson, "The Political Culture of Arab-Israeli Conflict," *Conflict Management and Peace Science* 5 (1982): 81–82; Gamson, "Political Discourse and Collective Action," *International Social Movement Research* 1 (1988): 219–41; and Gamson, *Talking Politics* (Cambridge: Cambridge University Press, 1992), esp. 135–62.

78. Quoted in "Scientists Uphold Evolution Theory," NYT, 27 December 1922.

79. See "Gorilla Most Like Us, Say Scientists," NYT, 18 May 1922.

80. Lloyd C. Douglas, "Mr. Bryan's New Crusade," *Christian Century* 37, 48 (1920): 11.

81. William Jennings Bryan, "Belief in God," *Commoner* 22, 5 (1922): 10.

82. Bryan, *In His Image*, 107.

83. Bryan, *Bible and Its Enemies*, 34, 39.

84. Rev. Emil Lund of Minneapolis, quoted in "Shall Moses or Darwin Rule Minnesota Schools?," *Literary Digest* 76, 2 (1923): 56.

85. Quoted in ibid.

86. As the University of Chicago's T. V. Smith wrote in 1923, the average American expressed everything he knew about evolution in the retort that "*you* may claim the monkey for an ancestor if

you wish, but as for him, he prefers another line of descent." T. V. Smith, "Bases of Bryanism," *Scientific Monthly* 16 (1923): 512.

87. Quoted in "Bryan Flays Darwinists," NYT, 6 March 1922.

88. Norris, "Address on Evolution before the Texas Legislature," 3.

89. Straton, *Evolution versus Creation*, 95–96.

90. Johnson, "Reply to Dr. E. L. Powell's Sermon on Evolution," 6.

91. "Address of Rev. J. Frank Norris at Waco, Texas, May 29, 1923," *Searchlight* 6, 47 (1923): 3.

92. J. D. Croft, letter to *Western Recorder* 98, 14 (1923): 23.

93. Quoted in "Heckler Harasses Bryan at Lecture," NYT, 3 May 1922. For another view of the "monkey or mud" thesis, see the comments of Dr. George Elliot, a theistic evolutionist and editor of the *Methodist Review*: "Personally, I like to think that I am related to the worm in the sod, the birds in the air, and all the animals. I never want to go back on my poor relations. I would rather think we came from the monkey than from mud." Quoted in "Calls Bryan Superficial," NYT, 16 July 1923. See also "Is Man More Than Mud?," *Literary Digest* 77, 8 (1923): 34.

94. Straton, *Evolution versus Creation*, 59.

95. Quoted in "Straton Wins Evolution Debate," 4.

96. Bryan, *In His Image*, 192. See also Bryan, "Belief in God," 10.

97. Quoted in "Monkey in a Pulpit Acts as Text Exhibit," NYT, 26 August 1924.

98. Quoted in " 'Monkeying' with Evolution," *Literary Digest* 82, 12 (1924): 36. The *Portland Oregonian* added: "You can not drive home a moral with a monkey. He simply isn't adapted to such employment." Quoted in ibid. See also "An Absurdity Even If Not Cruelty," NYT, 28 August 1924.

99. For background, see Larson, *Evolution*, 133–50. For a contemporary view, see "The Missing Link Is Still Missing," *Literary Digest* 72, 4 (1922): 21. See also Carter, "Fundamentalist Defense of the Faith," 207–8.

100. See "Scientists Find New Clews in Search for Missing Link," NYT, 7 October 1923. On the Central Asiatic Expeditions, see Ronald Rainger, *An Agenda for Antiquity: Henry Fairfield Osborn and Vertebrate Paleontology at the American Museum of Natural History, 1890–1935* (Tuscaloosa: University of Alabama Press, 1991), 99–104.

101. See "African Skull a Link in Evolution," *Literary Digest* 84, 10 (1925): 24, and "Hornaday Elated by Ape-Man Skull," NYT, 7 February 1925.

102. Quoted in "Missing Link's Jaw Shown at Museum," NYT, 15 April 1924.

103. "To Seek 'Missing Link,' " NYT, 14 September 1922. The story can be followed in "Finds a 'Dry' Tribe of Island Pygmies," NYT, 15 June 1923.

104. Bryan, *Bible and Its Enemies*, 22–23, 23. Bryan demonstrated the argument's reach in a 1925 article in *The Forum*: "Darwin admitted,—even expressed surprise and disappointment,—that no species had ever been traced to another, but he thought his hypothesis should be accepted even though the 'missing links' had not been found. He did not say link, as some seem to think, but links. If there is such a thing as evolution, it is not just one link,—the link between man and the lower forms of life,—that is missing, but all the millions of links between millions of species. Our case is even stronger; it has been pointed out that evolution, if there is such a force, would act so slowly that there would be an infinite number of links between each two species; or a million times

a million links in all, every one of which is missing." Bryan, "Mr. Bryan Speaks to Darwin," *Forum* 74 (July 1925): 103.

105. Bryan, *Bible and Its Enemies*, 22.

106. Arthur Watterson McCann, *God—or Gorilla: How the Monkey Theory of Evolution Exposes Its Own Methods, Refutes Its Own Principles, Denies Its Own Inferences, Disproves Its Own Case* (New York: Devin-Adair Co., 1922), 163.

107. Arthur I. Brown, *Men, Monkeys, and Missing Links* (Glendale, Calif.: Glendale Printers [1923]), 10. Brown suggested that the Hall of Man might better be termed the "Hall of Confusion," since the cranial capacity of most of the reproductions was superior to almost all modern humans (p. 11). The pamphlet is reprinted in Numbers, *Antievolution Works of Arthur I. Brown*, 97–127.

108. Straton, *Evolution versus Creation*, 69, 71–72. "So fragmentary and unreliable is this 'evidence' that no judge or jury would convict even a horse-thief on such evidence, and certainly we ought not on it to convict man of a brute ancestry or convict the Bible of lying" (p. 71).

109. Straton, *Evolution versus Creation*, 68. See ibid., 68–69; McCann, *God—or Gorilla*, 1–18; and Brown, *Men, Monkeys, and Missing Links*, 25–28. See also Stephen J. Gould, *Hen's Teeth and Horse's Toes* (New York: Norton, 1983), 201–40. On Osborn's defense of Piltdown Man, see Rainger, *Agenda for Antiquity*, 145–46, 225.

110. Henry Fairfield Osborn, "Hesperopithecus: The First Anthropoid Primate Found in America," *Proceedings of the National Academy of Sciences* 8 (1922): 245–46.

111. Bryan, "Mr. Bryan Speaks to Darwin," 105.

112. Quoted in "Dr. Straton Offers a 'Pig-Tooth' Debate," NYT, 27 February 1928. A more thorough treatment of the incident is John Wolf and James S. Mellett, "The Role of 'Nebraska Man' in the Creation-Evolution Debate," *Creation/Evolution* 5 (1985): 31–43.

113. Quoted in "Governor Vetoes Evolution and Board Cuts Out Book," *Raleigh News and Observer*, 24 January 1924.

114. Quoted in "Author of Evolution Law Attacks 'Monkey Theory' in Stanzas about Creation," NT, 1 June 1925.

115. For examples of Pace's work, see his illustrations to William Jennings Bryan, *Seven Questions in Dispute* (New York: Fleming H. Revell Co., 1924). Full color slides of these and other Pace originals are available at the E. J. Pace Collection, Billy Graham Center, Wheaton, Ill.

116. Potter described Akeley's statue: "He took me to where he had it and pulled off a covering cloth, revealing a sculpture of a fine-looking young man, naked to the waist. Below the waist and twined around what would have been the man's legs was the suggestion of a gorilla figure and below that other dimly seen representations of primitive life until the broad base of the statue seemed to be the primal rocky shore on which life originated. The obvious and inspiring motif was the evolution of man struggling up from and yet supported by his animal predecessors." Charles Francis Potter, *The Preacher and I: An Autobiography* (New York: Crown Publishers, 1951), 221.

117. See "Akeley Bronze Ape to Stand in Church," NYT, 9 April 1924. According to Potter, who described the remarks in his autobiography, Akeley "wished to make it plain that by this statue he did not mean to suggest that man sprang from the gorilla. They undoubtedly had a common ancestor. Science is on the trail of this ancestor and will locate it." Ibid.,

223. A critical account of Akeley's career can be found in Donna Haraway, *Primate Visions: Gender, Race, and Nature in the World of Modern Science* (New York: Routledge, 1989), 26–58.

118. John Roach Straton, *Was Christ Both God and Man?: Fourth in a Series of Fundamentalist-Modernist Debates....* (New York: George H. Doran Co., 1924), 85, 86.

119. Clark, "Evolution for John Doe," 1283–94. Clark notes that these popularizations, which were primarily created to educate the public, failed to capture the disagreements that existed between paleontologists over the exact character of the human evolutionary process (see pp. 1296–97).

120. Hillyer Straton, "John Roach Straton: The Great Evolution Debate," *Foundations* 10 (1967): 140. The quotation is from a large sign erected outside Straton's Calvary Baptist Church. See ibid.

121. For a description, see Rainger, *Agenda for Antiquity*, 169–78.

122. Quoted in "Calls the Museum a Traitor to God," NYT, 10 March 1924. In his visit to the American Museum, Straton was personally guided through the Hall of Man by Professor William King Gregory, a Columbia paleontologist who was also director of the museum's department of comparative anatomy, and who explained the evidence showing that the different specimens followed separate lines of development. See Ranger, *Agenda for Antiquity*, 170–71, and Straton, "Great Evolution Debate," 141.

123. Straton, "Great Evolution Debate," 142.

124. Ibid., 141. See "Dr. Straton Assails Museum of History," NYT, 9 March 1924, and John Roach Straton, "The Fancies of the Evolutionists," *Forum* 75 (1926): 245–51.

125. See Straton, "Great Evolution Debate," 143.

126. Straton, "Fancies of the Evolutionists," 249; see also 248–51.

127. On frame transformation, see Snow et al., "Frame Alignment Process," 473–76. See also Erving Goffman, *Frame Analysis: An Essay on the Organization of Experience* (Cambridge: Harvard University Press, 1974), 301–38.

128. Bryan, *Is the Bible True?*, 5.

129. Professor R. C. Osburn, quoted in "Critics of Evolution Are Called Ignorant," NYT, 18 May 1922. Osburn was a geologist at Ohio State University and president of the Ohio Academy of Sciences. See also NYT: "Bryan's Ideas 'Buffoonery,'" 5 May 1922; "Argues Adam Bred All Disease Germs," 1 March 1923; "Calls Evolution a Fact," 4 June 1923; "Declares Evolution Greatest Discovery," 28 December 1923; and "Bryan Is Attacked before Scientists," 31 December 1924. For a discussion, see Webb, *Evolution Controversy*, 76–77.

130. See "Carbon from the Air Baffles Scientists," NYT, 28 February 1923. Robinson stated: "The sudden grotesque opposition to modern scientific discoveries which are included under the term evolution has been so impressed on us that scientific men and others suddenly realized that scientific discovery had gone on without really impressing effectively any great number of people in our country."

131. See "Want Evolution Taught," NYT, 16 November 1924, reporting on a mass meeting at San Francisco's Native Son's Hall, attended by Burbank, Dr. David Starr Jordan, chancellor of Stanford University, Maynard Shipley, president of the Science League, and others.

132. Bryan, *Seven Questions in Dispute*, 154. Bryan described this tiny elite as "the smallest, the most impudent, and the most tyrannical oligarchy that ever attempted to exercise arbitrary power."

133. Bryan, *Is the Bible True?*, 9. In 1924 Bryan himself paid five dollars to join the AAAS, which was open to all who had an interest in scientific topics. On his motivations for joining and on the reception he received from the organization, see James Gilbert, *Redeeming Culture: American Religion in an Age of Science* (Chicago: University of Chicago Press, 1997), 23–35.

134. Bryan, "A New Oligarchy," *Commoner* 23, 1 (1923): 3.

135. "Bryan Calls Scientists Dishonest Scoundrels," NYT, 14 May 1925. Bryan was not the only one to denounce the elitism of the evolutionists. Minnesota minister and antievolution activist August Samuelson said: "Let these so-called scientists who sit in a soft leather couch and smoke a cigar or ride a five-thousand-dollar car, who spend their nights at banquets and a few hours in the daytime trying to make their brains find some method by which they can make people believe that two times two is three, show some proof." "Shall Moses or Darwin Rule Minnesota Schools?," 54–55. See also Levine, *Defender of the Faith*, 288–89.

136. See Douglas, "Mr. Bryan's New Crusade," 11–12. See also "The Passing of Mr. Bryan," *Christian Century* 38, 41 (1921): 6–7.

137. Quoted in "Attacks W. J. B.," NYT, 12 March 1922. For more on the controversy, see Paolo E. Coletta, *William Jennings Bryan: Political Puritan, 1915–1925* (Lincoln: University of Nebraska Press, 1969), 214–16. For more on Fosdick, see Robert Moats Miller, *Harry Emerson Fosdick: Preacher, Pastor, Prophet* (Oxford: Oxford University Press, 1985).

138. Quoted in "Declares Bryan Befogs the Issue," NYT, 18 May 1925. Potter said: "Scientists should join the liberal churches, as indeed some of them are already doing. There should be a general moving together of the forces of liberalism. A common danger tends to bring about an integration of the menaced groups." Ibid.

139. Bryan, *Seven Questions in Dispute*, 150–51.

140. Bryan, *Is the Bible True?*, 3, 3–4, 15.

141. Bryan, *Seven Questions in Dispute*, 157.

142. See "Paint W. J. Bryan as a 'Medievalist,'" NYT, 22 March 1922. Professor Edwin R. A. Seligman, of Columbia University, one of America's leading educational reformers said: "Opposition to the theory of evolution expresses the ideas of the childhood of society. Now, if we are going back to childhood, let's go all the way. Let's teach that the earth is flat, and that the sun moves around it." Seligman suggested the creation of a traveling exhibit containing the remains of extinct dinosaurs, to be carried by a special train "to the benighted section of the country where it is most needed." Ibid.

143. See "Mr. Bryan at Dartmouth," NYT, 23 December 1923; "Dartmouth Charts Mr. Bryan's Arguments," NYT, 1 January 1924; and the published report of the survey by Malcolm M. Willey and Stuart A. Rice, "William Jennings Bryan as a Social Force," *Journal of Social Forces* 2 (1924): 338–44.

144. "Skull of Bryan Is Neanderthal Type, Luther Burbank Avers," *New York World*, 23 December 1924. The article includes side-by-side photographs of Bryan and Neanderthal Man.

145. Bryan, *Is the Bible True?*, 8. For a discussion, see Levine, *Defender of the Faith*, 290, and Numbers, *Creationists*, 43.

146. Bryan, *Is the Bible True?*, 8–9.

147. Ibid., 16. Bryan applied the example of the jury: "We have juries and we do not require that they shall have diplomas. There is not a statute in this Union that requires that a man shall be a

college graduate or even a high school graduate to serve on a jury, and yet those juries decide all the great questions. They decide the questions between the millionaire and the pauper; they decide the question of marriage and divorce, descent of property and the care of children. We use the experts; the expert gives his testimony, but the jury decides."

148. Quoted in "Evolution Is Now Taught at Baylor University," *Searchlight* 6, 48 (1923): 3.

149. Quoted from *Tyler (Texas) Courier Times*, 10 July 1925, in Ledbetter, "Defense of the Faith," 47.

150. See Hankins, *God's Rascal*, 51–54. See, e.g., "The Purple, Scarlet-Robed Woman of Prophecy and History," *Searchlight* 7, 36 (1924): 1–3; "Roman Catholics Issue Call for Military Force," *Searchlight* 7, 37 (1924): 1–3; and "The Menace of Roman Catholicism in Politics," *Searchlight* 7, 38 (1924): 1–4. In addition to Catholics, Norris criticized "the Mexican hordes" for their opposition to Prohibition. J. Frank Norris, "Robertson vs. Jim Ferguson: Rum, Romanism, Russianism the Issue," *Searchlight* 7, 38 (1924): 1.

151. See Gatewood, *Preachers, Pedagogues*, 43. In his sermons, Norris also criticized "Russian Jews," distinguishing them from "the highest class of Jews." Norris, "Robertson vs. Jim Ferguson," 1.

152. See Levine, *Defender of the Faith*, 307–16.

153. Quoted in "The Bryan Quality," *NYT*, 20 May 1925.

154. Bryan, "Mr. Bryan Speaks to Darwin," 104. See also Straton's views on degeneration in his *Evolution versus Creation*, 82. On Bryan's reading of Slosson, see Levine, *Defender of the Faith*, 276.

155. James M. Gray, *Why a Christian Cannot Be an Evolutionist* (Chicago: Moody Bible Institute, 1925), 11.

CHAPTER FIVE

1. Butler to McVey, 27 January 1922, McVey Papers.

2. See Richard David Wilhelm, "A Chronology and Analysis of Regulatory Actions Relating to the Teaching of Evolution in the Public Schools" (Ph.D. diss., University of Texas at Austin, 1978), 61–63. State legislatures debated evolution in Kentucky in 1922 and 1926; South Carolina in 1922, 1927, and 1928; Alabama in 1923 and 1927; Florida in 1923, 1925, and 1927; Georgia and Tennessee in 1923 and 1925; Oklahoma in 1923 and 1927; Texas in 1923, 1925, and 1929; North Carolina in 1925 and 1927; Louisiana and Mississippi in 1926; and Arkansas in 1927. See Kenneth K. Bailey, *Southern White Protestantism in the Twentieth Century* (New York: Harper and Row, 1964), 78.

3. For background on the study of political opportunity structures, see Doug McAdam, "Conceptual Origins, Current Problems, Future Directions," in Doug McAdam, John D. McCarthy, and Mayer Zald, eds., *Comparative Perspectives on Social Movements: Political Opportunities, Mobilizing Structures, and Cultural Framings* (Cambridge: Cambridge University Press, 1996), 23–24.

4. Sidney Tarrow, "National Politics and Collective Action: Recent Theory and Research in Western Europe and the United States," *Annual Review of Sociology* 14 (1988): 430. Tarrow defines political opportunity structures as "consistent—but not necessarily formal or permanent—dimensions of the political environment that provide incentives for collective action by affecting people's expectations for success or failure." Quoted in Tarrow, *Power in Movement: Social Movements, Collective Action and Politics*, 2nd ed. (Cambridge: Cambridge University Press, 1998), 77–78. For a

slightly different definition, see Tarrow, "States and Opportunities: The Political Structuring of Social Movements," in McAdam, McCarthy, and Zald, *Comparative Perspectives*, 54.

5. Sidney Tarrow, *Power in Movement: Social Movements, Collective Action and Politics* (Cambridge: Cambridge University Press, 1994), 85–89. Tarrow is not alone in conceptualizing opportunity in these ways. Analyzing the work of four social movement scholars (Charles Brockett, Hanspeter Kriesi, Dieter Rucht, and Tarrow), Doug McAdam finds striking similarity in how the authors define these four dimensions. See McAdam, "Conceptual Origins, Current Problems, Future Directions," in McAdam, McCarthy, and Zald, *Comparative Perspectives*, 26–29.

6. See Tarrow, "States and Opportunities," 53–56.

7. See Norman F. Furniss, *The Fundamentalist Controversy, 1918–1931* (New Haven: Yale University Press, 1954), 76–100; George E. Webb, *The Evolution Controversy in America* (Lexington: University Press of Kentucky, 1994), 70–108; and Edward J. Larson, *Trial and Error: The American Controversy over Creation and Evolution*, 3rd ed. (Oxford: Oxford University Press, 2003), 28–92. Although far from scholarly, Maynard Shipley's *The War on Modern Science: A Short History of the Fundamentalist Attacks on Evolution and Modernism* (New York: Knopf, 1927) can be considered the first of the state-by-state studies.

8. See Willard B. Gatewood Jr., *Preachers, Pedagogues and Politicians: The Evolution Controversy in North Carolina, 1920–1927* (Chapel Hill: University of North Carolina Press, 1966). Also among the state studies are Kenneth K. Bailey, "The Enactment of Tennessee's Antievolution Law," *Journal of Southern History* 16 (1950): 472–90; Virginia Gray, "Anti-Evolution Sentiment and Behavior: The Case of Arkansas," *Journal of American History* 57 (1970): 352–66; and several articles by R. Halliburton Jr.: "The Nation's First Anti-Darwin Law: Passage and Repeal," *Southwestern Social Science Quarterly* 41 (1960): 123–34; "Kentucky's Anti-Evolution Controversy," *Register of the Kentucky Historical Society* 66 (1968): 97–107; "Mississippi's Contribution to the Anti-Evolution Movement," *Journal of Mississippi History* 35 (1973): 175–82; and "The Adoption of Arkansas' Anti-Evolution Law," *Arkansas Historical Quarterly* 23 (1964): 271–83.

9. See Tarrow, *Power in Movement* (1994), 86.

10. For figures on school enrollment and state expenditures, see *Historical Statistics of the United States*, ser. H429–507 and H587–601 (Washington, D.C.: U.S. Bureau of the Census, 1975), 1:373, 379. See also *Digest of Educational Statistics*, National Center for Education Statistics, 2004, <http://nces.ed.gov/programs/digest/> (22 May 2006).

11. Quoted in Kenneth K. Bailey, "The Antievolution Crusade of the Nineteen-Twenties," (Ph.D. diss., Vanderbilt University, 1953), 51; see also 49–52. On the 1923 survey carried out by the Department of Interior's Bureau of Education, see 52n.

12. For background, see George Brown Tindall, *The Emergence of the New South, 1913–1945* (Baton Rouge: Louisiana State University Press, 1967), 1–32.

13. Jeanette Keith, *Country People in the New South: Tennessee's Upper Cumberland* (Chapel Hill: University of North Carolina Press, 1995), 208; see also 118–42.

14. See V. O. Key, *Southern Politics in State and Nation* (New York: Knopf, 1949), 298–311.

15. See Dewey W. Grantham, *The Life and Death of the Solid South: A Political History* (Lexington: University Press of Kentucky, 1988), 78.

16. See Key, *Southern Politics*, 302–10.

17. Grantham, *Life and Death of the Solid South*, 84. See also Grantham, *The South in Modern America: A Region at Odds* (New York: HarperCollins, 1994), 88–115.

18. See Halliburton, "First Anti-Darwin Law," 124–25.

19. Quoted in "House Puts Knife to Darwinism" (Oklahoma City) *Daily Oklahoman*, 22 February 1923. See also Halliburton, "First Anti-Darwin Law," 126–27, and Larson, *Trial and Error*, 50–51.

20. Senator John Golobie, Senator Jed Johnson, quoted in "Darwin Theory Excluded from Public Schools," *Tulsa Tribune*, 21 March 1923. See also Halliburton, "First Anti-Darwin Law," 128.

21. See Larson, *Trial and Error*, 51.

22. See "Free Textbook Bill Is Passed to Governor," *Tulsa Tribune*, 23 March 1923; Larson, *Trial and Error*, 51–52; and Elbert L. Watson, "Oklahoma and the Anti-Evolution Movement of the 1920's," *Chronicles of Oklahoma* 42 (1964): 396–407.

23. State Superintendent of Public Instruction M. A. Nash, quoted in "Regardless of the Verdict in Dayton's Unusual Trial Darwin's Theory Is Ruled Out of Oklahoma for at Least Four Years," *Tulsa Tribune*, 17 July 1925. See also Halliburton, "First Anti-Darwin Law," 130.

24. See Halliburton, "First Anti-Darwin Law," 130.

25. See ibid. See also Larson, *Trial and Error*, 52. On later efforts to revive the antievolution bill, see Watson, "Oklahoma and the Anti-Evolution Movement," 401–7. On Walton, see Tindall, *Emergence of the New South*, 234–36.

26. Bryan to Hylan, 12 June 1923, Bryan Papers. See also Larson, *Trial and Error*, 52.

27. See Frances Fox Piven and Richard Cloward, *Poor People's Movements: Why They Succeed, How They Fail* (New York: Pantheon, 1977), 1–40; Charles D. Brockett, "The Structure of Political Opportunities and Peasant Mobilization in Central America," *Comparative Politics* (1991): 253–74; and Tarrow, "States and Opportunities," 55.

28. Grantham, *Life and Death of the Solid South*, 97; see also 78–101.

29. For background, see Bailey, *Southern White Protestantism*, 1–24. As Bailey describes, the denominations often acted through complex committee structures, and antievolutionists often used Foreign Mission or Sunday School Boards to call for investigations or to issue resolutions.

30. Quoted in Halliburton, "First Anti-Darwin Law," 124.

31. See John C. Edwards, "Bryan's Role in the Evolution Controversy" (M.A. thesis, University of Georgia, 1966), 60.

32. See Bailey, "Antievolution Crusade," 61–62.

33. Quoted from a 1924 address by Edgar W. Knight, "Monkey or Mud in North Carolina?," *Independent*, 118 (1927): 515. See also Halliburton, "Kentucky's Anti-Evolution Controversy," 104–5.

34. Quoted in Royce Jordan, "Tennessee Goes Fundamentalist," *New Republic* 42 (1925): 258.

35. For background on Sunday and the "sawdust trail," see William G. McLoughlin, *Revivals, Awakenings, and Reform: An Essay on Religion and Social Change in America, 1607–1977* (Chicago: University of Chicago Press, 1978), 400–454.

36. See Gatewood, *Preachers, Pedagogues*, 40–42.

37. On Ham, see ibid., 42–48. See also Gerald W. Johnson, "Saving Souls," *American Mercury* 1 (1924): 364–68. For the view of a contemporary critic, see W. O. Saunders, *The Book of Ham*

(Elizabeth City, N.C.: The Independent, 1924). In 1934 Billy Graham would undergo a conversion experience when he answered an altar call at one of Ham's revivals. See Billy Graham, *Just as I Am* (San Francisco: HarperSanFrancisco/Zondervan, 1997), 21–32.

38. See Willard B. Gatewood Jr., "The Evolution Controversy in North Carolina, 1920–1927," *Mississippi Quarterly* 17 (1964): 200. See also Bailey, "Antievolution Crusade," 68–69.

39. Quoted in "Morrison Gets Big Ovation in Ham-Ramsay Tabernacle," *Raleigh News and Observer*, 25 February 1924. See also Gatewood, *Preachers, Pedagogues*, 107.

40. On Kentucky politics of the 1920s, see Grantham, *Life and Death of the Solid South*, 95–96; on Baptists in the state, see Bailey, *Southern White Protestantism*, 64; and on the antievolution campaign there, see LeRoy Johnson, "The Evolution Controversy during the 1920's" (Ph.D. diss., New York University, 1953), 101–9; Ferenc Morton Szasz, *The Divided Mind of Protestant America, 1880–1930* (University, Ala.: University of Alabama Press, 1982), 111; and Webb, *Evolution Controversy*, 72.

41. See LeRoy Johnson, "Evolution Controversy," 108. See also Alonzo W. Fortune, "The Kentucky Campaign against the Teaching of Evolution," *Journal of Religion* 2 (1922): 226–27; Halliburton, "First Anti-Darwin Law," 98; and Larson, *Trial and Error*, 48.

42. See Fortune, "Kentucky Campaign," 228.

43. Quoted in Gaines to Frank L. McVey, 16 March 1922, McVey Papers. See also "Noel Gaines of Kentucky Challenges the Evolutionists," 23 May 1922, McVey Papers.

44. "Anti-Darwin Bill Killed in House," *Louisville Courier-Journal*, 10 March 1922. See also Bailey, "Antievolution Crusade," 59. In a letter written shortly afterward, bill sponsor George W. Ellis told how Gaines had "literally lashed our opponents to pieces with proof, truth, powerful oratory, ridicule and earnest pleading." The performance, he concluded, "created a sensation and profound impression upon this huge audience." Ellis to William Jennings Bryan and J. W. Porter, 13 March 1922, McVey Papers.

45. "Women and Evolution," *Lexington Herald*, 11 February 1922. See also LeRoy Johnson, "Evolution Controversy," 117.

46. Quoted in Fortune, "Kentucky Campaign," 232.

47. On McVey, see Jerry Harvill, "The Monkey Trial That Wasn't: University President Frank LeRond McVey's Role in Kentucky's Anti-Evolution Controversy, 1921–1926" (Ph.D. diss., University of Kentucky, 1985).

48. Eliot to McVey, 1 March 1922, McVey Papers. At the time Eliot was Harvard's president emeritus. In an earlier note, Butler had written wryly about the antievolution efforts: "I take it for granted that the introducer of the bill is in close communion with the rulers of Soviet Russia, since he is faithfully reproducing one of their fundamental policies. Truly we are getting on." Butler to McVey, 27 January 1922, McVey Papers.

49. Abbott to McVey, Western Union telegram, 27 January 1922, McVey Papers.

50. Frank L. McVey, *The Gates Open Slowly: A History of Education in Kentucky* (Lexington: University of Kentucky Press, 1949), 292. The text of McVey's statement is included in an appendix to his autobiography; see 292–95.

51. See Mullins to McVey, 2 March 1922, McVey Papers. See also Halliburton, "Kentucky's Anti-Evolution Controversy," 102–3; William E. Ellis, "The Fundamentalist-Moderate Schism over Evo-

lution in the 1920's," *Register of the Kentucky Historical Society* 74 (1976): 113–16; and Ellis, "Frank LeRond McVey: His Defense of Academic Freedom," *Register of the Kentucky Historical Society* 67 (1969): 50.

52. McVey to Emery L. Frazier, 11 March 1922, McVey Papers.

53. Quoted in Arthur M. Miller, "Kentucky and the Theory of Evolution," *Science* 55 (1922): 178. See also Bailey, "Antievolution Crusade," 60.

54. See Tarrow, "States and Opportunities," 55. See also William Gamson, *The Strategy of Social Protest* (Homewood, Ill.: Dorsey Press, 1975).

55. Bryan to S. C. Singleton, 23 December 1921, Bryan Papers. See also Larson, *Trial and Error*, 31. On Bryan's continuing influence within the Democratic Party, see Lawrence W. Levine, *Defender of the Faith: William Jennings Bryan: The Last Decade, 1915–1925* (New York, Oxford University Press, 1965), 181–88.

56. See Levine, *Defender of the Faith*, 278.

57. See ibid., 272. In 1924 Bryan rejected a request to broadcast his Bible Talks, insisting that he could reach a larger audience by print. See Bryan to Fred Mizer, 8 March 1924, Bryan Papers.

58. Bryan to Norris, 1 May 1923, Bryan Papers. See also Bryan to Riley, 3 May 1923; Porter to Bryan, 14 April 1923; and Norris to Bryan, 24 April 1923—all in Bryan Papers. Antievolutionists were not the only ones seeking Bryan's support. When Bryan expressed approval of the work of the National Federated Evangelistic Committee, its general secretary appointed him president of the committee, typing his name over that of the previous president on its letterhead and scheduling and publicizing a cross-country tour for him, all without his knowledge. See Szasz, *Divided Mind*, 114.

59. On Bryan's views, see Ronald L. Numbers, *Darwinism Comes to America* (Cambridge: Harvard University Press, 1998), 79–84. Numbers makes the point that many fundamentalists subscribed to the "day-age" interpretation.

60. Glenn Frank, "William Jennings Bryan: A Mind Divided against Itself," *Century* 106 (1923): 794. It should be kept in mind that the meaning of fundamentalist was anything but stable at the time, and that while Bryan did not consider himself a fundamentalist, many fundamentalists considered him one of them. See Numbers, *Darwinism Comes to America*, 79–84; Szasz, *Divided Mind*, 113–16; and C. Allyn Russell, *Voices of American Fundamentalism: Seven Biographical Studies* (Philadelphia: Westminster Press, 1976), 188–89.

61. See Levine, *Defender of the Faith*, 286.

62. See Edwards, "Bryan's Role," 62.

63. See Paolo E. Coletta, *William Jennings Bryan: Political Puritan, 1915–1925* (Lincoln: University of Nebraska Press, 1969), 220–24. At the 1925 Presbyterian General Assembly, Bryan again alienated many of his followers when he supported William O. Thompson, former president of Ohio State University, for assembly moderator, thereby splitting the fundamentalist vote and allowing the election of the moderate candidate, Charles R. Erdman. See Edwards, "Bryan's Role," 78–81.

64. See Edwards, "Bryan's Role," 77. Bryan's poor showing at the Democratic convention was compounded by his attempt to float the name of his old friend A. A. Murphree, president of the University of Florida, as a compromise candidate for U.S. president. See Levine, *Defender of the Faith*, 301–3, and Michael Kazin, *A Godly Hero: The Life of William Jennings Bryan* (New York: Knopf, 2006), 283–85.

65. Bryan to Grace Bryan Hargreaves, 3 June 1923, Bryan Papers. See also Levine, *Defender of the Faith*, 285.

66. See, e.g., Frank, "William Jennings Bryan," 793–800. Coming to Bryan's defense was C. V. Dunn, "Mr. Bryan and His Critics," *Bible Champion* 29 (1923): 489–96.

67. See T. V. Smith, "Bases of Bryanism," *Scientific Monthly* 16 (1923): 505–13. Typical of the personal attacks was George Bernard Shaw's description of Bryan as "a man with an extraordinary uplift and no discernable brains of any kind." Quoted in "Bryan's 'Infantilism' Mark of Blockhead, Says Bernard Shaw," *New York Evening Post*, 10 June 1925.

68. See Szaz, *Divided Mind*, 114.

69. Viskniskki to Bryan, 9, 13, and 14 June 1923, Bryan Papers.

70. Bryan to Republic Syndicate, 15 June 1923, Bryan Papers. See also Levine, *Defender of the Faith*, 289.

71. On Bryan's ties to Miami real estate interests, as well as his own holdings, see Levine, *Defender of the Faith*, 238–39.

72. See Russell, *Voices of American Fundamentalism*, 179.

73. See Mary Duncan France, " 'A Year of Monkey War': The Anti-Evolution Campaign and the Florida Legislature," *Florida Historical Quarterly* 54 (1975): 156–77. See also Samuel Proctor, "William Jennings Bryan and the University of Florida," *Florida Historical Quarterly* 39 (1960): 1–15.

74. See France, "Monkey War," 159.

75. Quoted in "W.G.N. Put 'On Carpet': Gets a Bryan Lashing," *Chicago Daily Tribune*, 20 June 1923. See also Larson, *Trial and Error*, 53.

76. See Bailey, "Antievolution Crusade," 64.

77. See Edwards, "Bryan's Role," 62.

78. See "Anti-Darwin Campaign Stirs South and West," NYT, 10 June 1923.

79. See Gatewood, *Preachers, Pedagogues*, 100–101.

80. J. Speed Rogers, "The Teaching of Evolution at the University of Florida," *Science* 59 (1924): 126.

81. Tarrow, "States and Opportunities," 56.

82. Joseph Wood Krutch, "Tennessee: Where Cowards Rule," *Nation* 121 (1925): 88.

83. See Bailey, "Antievolution Crusade," 58. See also Webb, *Evolution Controversy*, 105. Along with the NEA, education groups including the AAUP, the Association of American Colleges, and the American Federation of Teachers went on record to oppose the movement. The AAAS and the Science Service news bureau, a scientific news syndicate modeled on the Associated Press, were especially effective in reporting on the status of antievolution legislation and organizing opposition to it. See LeRoy Johnson, "Evolution Controversy," 134. See also Paul A. Carter, *Another Part of the Twenties* (New York: Columbia University Press, 1977), 73–75. In 1924 Maynard Shipley established the Science League of America to counter the appearance of state Anti-Evolution Leagues. See LeRoy Johnson, "Evolution Controversy," 77. Roger Baldwin's ACLU, still a fledgling operation, advertised for opponents to test state laws in the courts, precipitating the famous Scopes case. See LeRoy Johnson, "Evolution Controversy," 85.

84. See Gatewood, "Evolution Controversy in North Carolina," 199. See also Edwards, "Bryan's Role," 63.

85. Although business, trade, and educational groups tended to be opposed, in some states they gave strong support for antievolution measures. In his study of North Carolina, for instance, Gatewood found antievolution broadsides from chambers of commerce, trade organizations (including the State Convention of the American Federation of Labor), and parent-teacher associations. Chapters of the Ku Klux Klan and related white supremacy groups tended to be supportive as well. See Gatewood, *Preachers, Pedagogues*, 22–25, 116, 121, 202, 211–12, and Gatewood, "Evolution Controversy in North Carolina," 200.

86. See Bailey, "Antievolution Crusade," 62n–63n.

87. See Bailey, *Southern White Protestantism*, 44–71, and Szasz, *Divided Mind*, 92–106. It remains a matter of speculation how seriously most church members were invested in these issues. Commenting on the fundamentalist-modernist debates, one Methodist bishop estimated in 1926 that in his denomination no more than 6 percent of clergy and 2 percent of laity were involved in the controversy in any way. See Bailey, "Antievolution Crusade," 44.

88. Southern Baptists were more divided than most. See Furniss, *Fundamentalist Controversy*, 119–26. See also James J. Thompson Jr., *Tried as by Fire: Southern Baptists and the Religious Controversies of the 1920s* (Macon, Ga.: Mercer University Press, 1982), 112–22. Among Baptist publications, the more moderate included Georgia's *Christian Index*, North Carolina's *Baptist Recorder*, South Carolina's *Baptist Courier*, and Virginia's *Religious Herald*. See Thompson, *Tried as by Fire*, 125–29.

89. "Concerning Evolution," *Alabama Baptist* 58, 15 (1925): 3.

90. See John L. Morrison, "American Catholics and the Crusade against Evolution," *American Catholic Historical Society of Philadelphia Records* 64 (1953): 64–68. Catholics played almost no part in the antievolution campaigns of the 1920s. Most considered themselves to be theistic evolutionists who, in keeping with church teachings, saw no inherent conflict between faith and science. In addition, there was little love lost between Catholics and the Protestant fundamentalists who made up the bulk of the antievolution movement, many of whom were thoroughly antagonistic toward Catholicism. (Ironically, those few Catholics who supported the antievolution movement sometimes became targets of anti-Catholic criticism from liberal Protestants.) According to Edward Larson, some Catholic newspapers depicted the movement as a fundamentalist scheme to gain control over public education. See Larson, *Summer for the Gods: The Scopes Trial and America's Continuing Debate over Science and Religion* (New York: BasicBooks, 1997), 126–27. See also Edwards, "Bryan's Role," 65–67.

91. See Wilhelm, "Chronology and Analysis," 61–65.

92. See Bailey, *Southern White Protestantism*, 79–80.

93. Ibid. When advocates of an antievolution bill in Florida sought to bypass the senate education committee by having the bill placed on the senate calendar by number only, committee members retaliated by voting to reconsider, effectively killing the bill since only eight days were left in the session. France, "Monkey War," 169.

94. See Bailey, *Southern White Protestantism*, 79.

95. As reported in the NT, much of the opposition to antievolution measures in the 1923 session of the Tennessee legislature came from political leaders who "profess to see great danger in the bills as regards the consumption of time. They are fearful the debate on the mooted question may continue for days, thus using up valuable time needed for the completion of the legislative pro-

gram." "Bryan Is Asked to Aid Fight on Darwin Theory," NT, 20 March 1923. See also Bailey, "Antievolution Crusade," 79.

96. Representative F. L. D. Carr, quoted in France, "Monkey War," 169. Carr put his thoughts in verse form:

To gain my next election,
   I know the bill must pass,
So I guess I'll ape the monkey
   By voting like an ass.

97. See Wilhelm, "Chronology and Analysis," vii.

98. See Bailey, "Antievolution Crusade," 59, 61, 66–67, 69.

99. See Wilhelm, "Chronology and Analysis," 67.

100. Quoted in Bailey, "Antievolution Crusade," 59. See also Wilhelm, "Chronology and Analysis," 68.

101. See Wilhelm, "Chronology and Analysis," 68.

102. John A. Shelton to Bryan, 5 February 1925, Bryan Papers.

103. Quoted in "Poole Bill Up in House Tonight," *Raleigh News and Observer*, 17 February 1925. The best single source on North Carolina's antievolution campaign is Gatewood, *Preachers, Pedagogues*: on Martin and Poteat, see 30–37; on Ham and other revivalists, 38–48; and on critics of Chase, Odum, and the university, 109–22. See also Willard B. Gatewood Jr., "Embattled Scholar: Howard B. Odum and the Fundamentalists, 1925–1927," *Journal of Southern History* 31 (1965): 375–92.

104. Quoted in Gatewood, *Preachers, Pedagogues*, 133. In a letter to University of North Carolina professor Collier Cobb, Chase advised faculty members not to attend the hearings, since it would be "better for me to be the Goat." Chase to Cobb, 7 February 1925, UNC Papers. See also Gatewood, *Preachers, Pedagogues*, 124–34.

105. According to Willard Gatewood (*Preachers, Pedagogues*, 146), region and religion factored in the vote, with legislators from mountain counties giving the resolution its strongest support, followed by those from piedmont and coastal counties, while Baptists and Presbyterians were the most supportive of the measure. He calculated that the bill drew support from 52 percent of the Baptists in the legislature, 45 percent of the Presbyterians, 40 percent of the Methodists, and 15 percent of the Episcopalians.

106. Chase to Walter Murphy, 13 March 1925, UNC Papers. See also Gatewood, *Preachers, Pedagogues*, 135–47.

107. Chase to Edwin Mims, 14 May 1926, UNC Papers. Anticipating the next legislative session, Chase prevailed upon geologist Collier Cobb to postpone publication of his forthcoming book on evolutionary geology. "The purposes for which we must contend are so large, and the importance of the victory is so great," Chase wrote Cobb, "that I think we can well afford for the moment to refrain from doing anything, when no matter of principle is involved, that tends to raise the issue in any concrete form or which might add to the perplexities of those who will have to be on the firing line for the University during these next few months." Chase to Cobb, 16 April 1926, UNC Papers. Cobb's book was never published.

108. See Bryan, *Is the Bible True?* (Nashville, Tenn.: Published by the Friends of William Jennings

Bryan, 1924). On the role of Nashville lawyer W. B. Marr and his associates in having the speech printed and distributed, see Bailey, "Enactment of Tennessee's Antievolution Law," 472–75.

109. See Larson, *Trial and Error*, 56. For a historical perspective, see Charles A. Israel, *Before Scopes: Evangelicalism, Education, and Evolution in Tennessee, 1870–1925* (Athens: University of Georgia Press, 2004).

110. "Bar Teaching of Evolution," NB, 28 January 1925. See also Bailey, "Tennessee's Antievolution Law," 476.

111. J. Mack Ellis to NB, "The People's Attitude," 7 February 1925. But compare the letter of Thomas Page Gore, printed in the same column, in which he blasts Tennessee's "silly, incompetent and bigoted legislators." Gore, "State Legislature vs. Truth," ibid.

112. Quoted in "Huge Throng Joins in Welcome to Sunday at Opening Meeting," MCA, 6 February 1925. When he left the state on the eve of the senate vote, Sunday was replaced by J. Frank Norris. On Sunday's Memphis crusade, see Larson, *Summer for the Gods*, 55. Among the bill's opponents was a group of prominent Nashville pastors who petitioned the senate to defeat the proposed legislation. See "Proceedings of Legislature," NT, 14 March 1925. Conservative clergy countered by criticizing the pastors and adding their own enthusiastic endorsement of the bill. See "Pastor Attacks Darwin Theory," NT, 22 March 1925. See also Bailey, "Antievolution Crusade," 95–96.

113. On Mims, see Paul K. Conkin, *When All the Gods Trembled: Darwinism, Scopes, and American Intellectuals* (Lanham, Md.: Rowman and Littlefield Publishers, Inc., 1998), 154–55. Some leaders, including Fisk University dean James L. Graham, expressed their opposition in private letters to Governor Peay. Graham to Peay, 18 March 1925, Peay Papers. Although teachers' groups were silent, a few public school officials did write requesting that the bill be rejected. See Jeanette Moore King to Austin Peay, 23 March 1925, Peay Papers. Also opposed were student groups, including the Tennessee Christian Student Conference. See Wilson L. Newman to Peay, 5 December 1925, Peay Papers.

114. See Larson, *Summer for the Gods*, 57–58.

115. Morgan to Peay, 9 February 1925, Peay Papers. See also James R. Montgomery and Gerald Gaither, "Evolution and Education in Tennessee: Decisions and Dilemmas," *Tennessee Historical Quarterly* 28 (1969): 141–55.

116. Quoted in "Senate Amends Law on Quail," NB, 5 February 1925. See also Bailey, "Tennessee's Antievolution Law," 478ff.

117. See Larson, *Summer for the Gods*, 55.

118. In analyzing the final vote, Bailey ("Tennessee's Antievolution Law," 488–89) finds that while delegates from urban districts were more inclined than those from rural ones to oppose the measure, a majority of those from Memphis, Nashville, Chattanooga, and Knoxville (except the Davidson County delegation in the senate) voted for the bill.

119. On the claim that Peay received "tens of thousands of letters," see T. H. Alexander, *Austin Peay: Governor of Tennessee* (Kingsport, Tenn.: Southern Publishers, 1929), 359. Although the claim is certainly exaggerated, he did receive hundreds of letters, many of them handwritten, from every part of the country.

120. On Peay's private opposition, see Ray Ginger, *Six Days or Forever?: Tennessee v. John Thomas*

Scopes (Boston: Beacon Press, 1958), 7. But compare his correspondence in which he expresses strong support for the bill. See, e.g., Peay to Noel Gaines, 21 August 1925; Peay to Dr. French E. Oliver, 17 October 1925; and Peay to J. Fred Johnson, 1 September 1925—all in Peay Papers.

121. S. F. Hinson to Peay, 17 August 1925, Peay Papers. See also Bailey, "Tennessee's Evolution Law," 483. Among the civic groups writing in support of the Butler bill was Klan Number 103 of the Knights of the Ku Klux Klan. See W. J. Bokin, Exalted Cyclops, St. Francis County Knights of the Kuklux Klan, Realm of Arkansas to Peay, 21 August 1925, Peay Papers.

122. On Peay's desire to protect his educational proposals, see Conkin, *When All the Gods Trembled*, 82–83.

123. Krutch, "Tennessee: Where Cowards Rule," 88. Peay's health was also a consideration, since he was out of the state undergoing treatment at a Battle Creek, Mich., sanatorium during much of the debate over the Butler bill. Reelected governor in 1926, he died in office a year later. See David W. Lee, *Tennessee in Turmoil: Politics in the Volunteer State, 1920–1932* (Memphis: Memphis State University Press, 1979), 57–58

124. Austin Peay, "Message from the Governor," *Journal of the House of Representatives of Tennessee* (1925 regular sess.): 745. Peay's sentiments were shared by many critics of the statute, who took consolation that its effect would be purely symbolic. Thus the *Literary Digest* concluded that Tennessee newspapers were "not frightfully worried over the new law. . . . Some of them do not even mention it editorially, while one is not averse to the advertising the State is getting, on the ground, perhaps, that any advertising is better than none." "No Monkeying with Evolution in Tennessee," *Literary Digest* 85, 3 (1925): 30–31. By contrast, as Edward Larson (*Summer for the Gods*, 276n) notes, antievolutionists took the statute seriously and expected it to be enforced.

CHAPTER SIX

1. John T. Scopes and James Presley, *Center of the Storm: Memoirs of John T. Scopes* (New York: Holt, Rinehart and Winston, 1967), 60.

2. Doug McAdam, "The Framing Function of Movement Tactics: Strategic Dramaturgy in the American Civil Rights Movement," in Doug McAdam, John D. McCarthy, and Mayer Zald, eds., *Comparative Perspectives on Social Movements: Political Opportunities, Mobilizing Structures, and Cultural Framings* (Cambridge: Cambridge University Press, 1996), 338–55.

3. See Doug McAdam, *Political Process and the Development of Black Insurgency*, 2nd ed. (Chicago: University of Chicago Press, 1999), and McAdam, *Freedom Summer* (New York: Oxford University Press, 1988). See also McAdam, "Strategic Dramaturgy," 345–54.

4. See McAdam, "Strategic Dramaturgy," 350–52.

5. See Ferenc Morton Szasz, *The Divided Mind of Protestant America, 1880–1930* (University, Ala.: University of Alabama Press, 1982), 119. The best trial studies are Edward J. Larson, *Summer for the Gods: The Scopes Trial and America's Continuing Debate over Science and Religion* (New York: BasicBooks, 1997); Ray Ginger, *Six Days or Forever?: Tennessee v. John Thomas Scopes* (Boston: Beacon Press, 1958), and L. Sprague de Camp, *The Great Monkey Trial* (Garden City, N.Y.: Doubleday, 1968). Insightful shorter treatments include Ronald L. Numbers, *Darwinism Comes to America* (Cambridge: Harvard University Press, 1998), 76–91; Paul K. Conkin, *When All the Gods Trembled: Darwinism, Scopes, and American Intellectuals* (Lanham, Md.: Rowman and Littlefield Publishers, Inc., 1998), 79–109; and

Garry Wills, *Under God: Religion and American Politics* (New York: Simon and Schuster, 1990), 79–124. See also Paolo E. Coletta, *William Jennings Bryan: Political Puritan, 1915–1925* (Lincoln: University of Nebraska Press, 1969), 240–81; Lawrence W. Levine, *Defender of the Faith: William Jennings Bryan: The Last Decade, 1915–1925* (New York: Oxford University Press, 1965), 324–57; and Michael Kazin, *A Godly Hero: The Life of William Jennings Bryan* (New York: Knopf, 2006), 285–95. On the trial as a modern media event, see Marjorie Garber, *Symptoms of Culture* (New York: Routledge, 1998), 107–39. The trial transcript can be found in *The World's Most Famous Court Trial: Tennessee Evolution Case* (Cincinnati: National Book Co., [ca. 1925]). Additional documents are in Jeffrey P. Moran, *The Scopes Trial: A Brief History with Documents* (Boston: Bedford/St. Martin's, 2002), and Sheldon Norman Grebstein, ed., *Monkey Trial: The State of Tennessee vs. John Thomas Scopes* (Boston: Houghton Mifflin, 1960). Photographs with text are in Edward Caudill, Edward J. Larson, and Jesse Fox Mayshark, *The Scopes Trial: A Photographic History* (Knoxville: University of Tennessee Press, 2000).

6. Martin Marty, *Righteous Empire: The Protestant Experience in America* (New York: Dial Press, 1970), 220.

7. One recent exception is Andrew Shane Nolan, "A Defining Moment for Dayton: The Scopes Trial as an Act in the Theater of the Modern" (Ph.D. diss., University of Illinois at Urbana-Champaign, 2001). Nolan describes the trial as a stage for the presentation of what he calls "multiple modernities," or competing conceptions of the meanings of an emerging modern nation (pp. 4–5).

8. See McAdam, "Strategic Dramaturgy," 346–49.

9. White's comment was reported by A. C. Stribling to Warren Allem. See Allem, "Backgrounds of the Scopes Trial at Dayton, Tennessee" (M.A. thesis, University of Tennessee, 1959), 61. On the events leading up to the trial, see Larson, *Summer for the Gods*, 87–96; Ginger, *Six Days or Forever?*, 68–74; and de Camp, *Great Monkey Trial*, 114–50.

10. Scopes describes the events of the day, along with his personal views, in Scopes and Presley, *Center of the Storm*, 58–60. See also George William Hunter, *A Civic Biology: Presented in Problems* (New York: American Book Co., 1914), esp. 194–96.

11. "Arrest under Evolution Law," NB, 6 May 1925. According to the account, Scopes was "placed under arrest." In fact, Rappleyea swore out a warrant for his arrest with a justice of the peace, who handed it over to the local constable, who handed it to Scopes, but all of these events took place at the drugstore. See Larson, *Summer for the Gods*, 91.

12. See "Set Stage for Evolution Case," NB, 24 May 1925. At one point, some of the planners advocated building a roof over the local baseball field or erecting a gigantic circus tent to house the trial. See "Dayton Seeks Pup Tents and Loud Speakers for Scopes Trial Crowd," NT, 23 May 1925.

13. See "Dayton Jolly as Evolution Trial Looms," CT, 21 May 1925, and Corinne Rich, "Jail Polished Up," MCA, 1 July 1925.

14. *Why Dayton—of All Places?* (Chattanooga, Tenn.: Andrews Printery, Inc., 1925), 17.

15. See "H. G. Wells May Fight Bryan in Scopes Case," MCA, 15 May 1925. Wells declined to accept the offer, suggesting that the invitation must have been meant for some other Wells, since he had never heard of Dayton. See "Can't Mean Me, Says H. G. Wells to Scopes Case," CN, 15 May 1925.

16. "Cheap Publicity," NT, 23 June 1925. For the 19 May scuffle between Rappleyea and the "man-biting barber" Reed, see Nolan, "Defining Moment for Dayton," 167–78.

17. Quoted in William Bell Riley, "The World's Christian Fundamentals Association and the Scopes Trial," *CF in S&C* 7, 5 (1925): 37–38. For the invitation itself, see L. M. Aldridge to Bryan, 12 May 1925, Bryan Papers. See also "Commoner Believes Evolution Tommyrot," *MCA*, 11 May 1925; "Radical Enemies of Evolution Forced to Acknowledge Defeat," *MCA*, 15 May 1925; and "Bryan May Be in Case," *NB*, 12 May 1925.

18. See Bryan to L. M. Aldridge, n.d. [May 1925], Bryan Papers. See also Larson, *Summer for the Gods*, 99–100, and Coletta, *Bryan*, 235. On the 1925 Presbyterian General Assembly, see Levine, *Defender of the Faith*, 333.

19. Norris to Bryan, n.d. [June 1925], Bryan Papers. Larson (*Summer for the Gods*, 96) makes the point that trial organizers saw the case in the same way. Even before Bryan entered the picture, he writes, "Daytonites envisioned the upcoming trial more as a public debate centered around Scopes than as a criminal prosecution. Indeed, it had all the trappings of a summer Chautauqua lecture series, then a popular form of education and entertainment in communities throughout America. In mid-May their vision began crystallizing into reality when Bryan—a top draw on the Chautauqua circuit—volunteered his services for the prosecution."

20. Earl L. Shaub, "Lines Drawn Tighter," *MCA*, 15 May 1925. Evolutionists saw Bryan's decision to appear at Dayton as offering them opportunities of their own. Rappleyea said: "I am glad Bryan has entered the case. The Lord has delivered him into my hands" (quoted in "H. G. Wells May Fight Bryan").

21. On the ACLU's early role, see Larson, *Summer for the Gods*, 60–83, 100–102; Ginger, *Six Days or Forever?*, 74–80; and Pearl Kluger, "New Light on the Scopes Trial" (M.A. thesis, Columbia University, 1957), 63–77.

22. See "Darrow Takes Sharp Rap at W. J. Bryan," *MCA*, 18 May 1925.

23. Larson (*Summer for the Gods*, 103) points out the irony that whereas Darrow described the threat to individual liberty as the product of religious bigotry, the ACLU had previously seen the threat as coming from wartime superpatriotism and postwar capitalism, both of which Bryan had opposed.

24. See "Darrow an Atheist, Is Bryan's Answer," *MCA*, 23 May 1925. For an excellent discussion of Darrow's religious views, see Larson, *Summer for the Gods*, 71–73.

25. Roger N. Baldwin, "Dayton's First Issue," in Jerry R. Tompkins, ed., *D-Days at Dayton: Reflections on the Scopes Trial* (Baton Rouge: Louisiana State University Press, 1965), 57.

26. "Darrow versus Bryan in Evolution Test Case," *MCA*, 17 May 1925.

27. For background on Dayton, see Allem, "Backgrounds of the Scopes Trial," 6–25; Ginger, *Six Days or Forever?*, 69–74; de Camp, *Great Monkey Trial*, 114–21; and Larson, *Summer for the Gods*, 87–88. "Dayton is an average small town," according to the *Nashville Tennessean*, "half southern, half northern and fairly evenly divided politically. . . . Its people are prosperous and well dressed, although some of the younger set do play slide trombones." See "Scopes Taught Bug Was Father of Man, State Will Charge," *NT*, 11 July 1925.

28. H. L. Mencken, "The Monkey Trial: A Reporter's Account," in Tompkins, *D-Days at Dayton*, 36 (reprinted from *Baltimore Evening Sun*, 9 July 1925).

29. "Outside the court room most of the town's interest was centered in the chimpanzees, but there continued, despite the strong counter-attraction, plenty of open-air evangelism, street hawk-

ing and mere loafing." "Two Apes and 'Link' Arrive at Dayton," NYT, 15 July 1925. Some of the best descriptions of the events surrounding the trial were provided by correspondents from the *New York Times*: see Charles McD. Puckette, "The Evolution Arena at Dayton" (5 July 1925), "Mountaineers Won't Hear Arguments on Evolution (7 July 1925), "Dayton Keyed Up for Scopes Trial" (10 July 1925), "Cranks and Freaks Flock to Dayton" (11 July 1925), and "Dayton's Police Suppress Skeptics" (12 July 1925). See also de Camp, *Great Monkey Trial*, 160–65.

30. Sterling Tracy, "Dayton Stage Set for Bryan-Darrow Tilt on Riddle of Ages," MCA, 10 July 1925. Voting to raise a $5,000 advertising fund, the Dayton Progressive Club also adopted a resolution condemning the frivolous attitude being taken toward the trial, asking Daytonians to remove all " 'monkey business' advertisements" and "save their humor for the Sunday comics." "Dayton to Raise Advertising Fund," CT, 23 May 1925.

31. "Bryan Here on Evolution Case," NT, 5 June 1925.

32. See "Darrow Declares He Is Always Seeking Truth," *Knoxville Journal*, 23 June 1925. On Darrow's reception, attorney Sue K. Hicks wrote to Bryan, "People of Dayton like his personality and think he is a great man, but they are all shaking their heads about his beliefs." Hicks to Bryan, 23 June 1925, Hicks Papers. Bryan replied: "It is a very able speech but contains nothing that need frighten us in this case." Bryan to Hicks and Hicks, 25 June 1925, Hicks Papers. Attorney Wallace C. Haggard also wrote of Darrow's warm reception but assured Bryan that "despite his intelligence and his magnetism, he cannot prevail among our people." Haggard to Bryan, 23 June 1925, Bryan Papers.

33. See "Scopes Dined, Says Fight Is for Liberty," NYT, 11 June 1925. On his return from New York, Scopes stopped off in Washington, D.C., where he visited the Supreme Court and was photographed viewing the original copy of the Constitution. See "Scopes Rests Hope in U.S. Constitution and Supreme Court," *Washington Post*, 13 June 1925.

34. John P. Fort, "Bryan vs. Darrow in Battle of Giants," CN, 10 July 1925. George M. Milton, editor of the *Chattanooga News* and a friend and admirer of Bryan, commented on the comparison to a prizefight: "It isn't exactly that, it is more like a sacrifice to Jehovah, with John Thomas Scopes in the role of the sacrificial lamb. . . . Dayton is filled with a serene confidence that Bryan will take Darrow . . . and all the others of the Scopes tribe of free speakers and eat them up alive." Milton, "Bryan Has Won Case before It Gets Underway," CN, 10 July 1925.

35. See Tracy, "Dayton Stage Set."

36. "Evolution Trial Opens This Morning; Raulston Relies on Divine Guidance," CT, 10 July 1925. "When the three-ring circus opens tomorrow in the first ring will be Mr. Bryan. In the second ring will be Mr. Bryan, and Mr. Bryan will be in the third ring. Mr. Bryan occupies the center of the stage and all the corners." Ibid.

37. Fort, "Bryan vs. Darrow."

38. "2,000,000 Words Wired to the Press," NYT, 22 July 1925. See also Donald F. Brod, "The Scopes Trial: A Look at Press Coverage after Forty Years," *Journalism Quarterly* 42 (1965): 219–26. The *New York Times* alone received an average of 10,000 words daily from its reporters on the scene.

39. See "Scopes Trial Reports Keep the Wires Hot," CN, 7 July 1925.

40. See James Walter Wesolowski, "Before Canon 35: WGN Broadcasts the Monkey Trial," *Tennessee Historical Quarterly* 34 (1975): 392–406. "For the first time in the history of American

jurisprudence," observed the *Chicago Tribune* (15 July 1925), "radio went into a court of law and broadcast . . . the entire proceedings of a criminal trial." "Science Brings Scopes Trial to Midwest's Ears."

41. See Coletta, *Bryan*, 240. See also "News Cameramen Emerge Victors from Scramble," *Knoxville Journal*, 14 July 1925.

42. "A Titanic Conflict," *CN*, 10 July 1925. Sociologist Howard W. Odum estimated that the trial was discussed in over 2,300 daily newspapers in the United States, as well as in 4,000 monthly and quarterly publications. In a search carried out shortly after the trial ended, he could find "no periodical of any sort, agricultural or trade as well, which has ignored the subject." Odum, "The Duel to the Death," *Social Forces* 4 (1925): 190.

43. On the importance of reaching these publics, see McAdam, "Strategic Dramaturgy," 349–50. See also McAdam, *Freedom Summer*, 150–54.

44. Ira E. Hicks to Sue K. Hicks, n.d., Hicks Papers. See also Larson, *Summer for the Gods*, 125–26.

45. "Bryan Speaks at Miami on Evolution," *NB*, 3 July 1925.

46. In a study of several metropolitan papers covering the trial, Edward Caudill found bias in favor of Darrow. See Caudill, "The Roots of Bias: An Empiricist Press and Coverage of the Scopes Trial," *Journalism Monographs* 114 (1989): 32–33.

47. Heywood Broun, "It Seems to Me," *New York World*, 29 June 1925.

48. Dudley Nichols, "The Bigot's Progress," *New York World*, 3 June 1925.

49. Mencken, "Monkey Trial," 46, 48 (reprinted from *Baltimore Evening Sun*, 16, 17 July 1925).

50. "Real Issue of Scopes Case Is Control of Schools, Says Bryan," *CN*, 25 May 1925.

51. "Commoner's Plea Sways Plain Folk," *NYT*, 13 July 1925.

52. According to the *Knoxville Journal* ("Darrow Mixer, Bryan Is Aloof," 12 July 1925), Darrow's skills at street corner banter were actually superior to Bryan's, whose "aloof dignity renders him impressive and awe-inspiring as he sometimes stops at the curb in his chauffered Reo sedan to talk to friends on the sidewalk."

53. Frank R. Kent, "Dayton Bears Fame in Seemly Manner," *Baltimore Sun*, 10 July 1925. Bryan missed few opportunities to endear himself to the town. In his Progressive Club speech he went out of his way to remind its members that the big-city papers had spoken disparagingly of Dayton, having suggested that it was too small to be the setting for such an important case. "Why should the size of the town be a matter of importance in the trial of a religious case?" he asked indignantly. "Christianity began in a small town," he went on, "whether we date the beginning with the birth of Christ in Bethlehem or with the youth of Christ spent in Nazareth. Why should not this peaceful community furnish a fitting environment for the trial of a case that involves the two greatest subjects that interest mankind—education and religion?" Quoted in "Religion Dies If Evolution Wins, Bryan Declares," *NT*, 8 July 1925.

54. Quoted in "Bryan Here On Evolution Case," 10.

55. "Peay Has Contempt for Slurs at State," *MCA*, 27 June 1925. Among those leveling the criticism was native son Joseph Wood Krutch, who chastised the failure of Tennessee leaders to stand up to unenlightened public opinion: "There is no State of the Union, no country of the world, which does not have communities as simple-minded as this one, and if Tennessee has become the

laughing-stock of the world it is because among her sons who know better there is scarcely one who has the courage to stand up for what he thinks and knows instead of flying quickly to cover lest he might have to sacrifice to his conviction some political advantage or some material gain." Krutch, "Tennessee: Where Cowards Rule," *Nation* 121 (1925): 88–89.

56. "Christianity Goes If Evolution Wins, Bryan Tells Dayton," *CT*, 8 July 1925.

57. Quoted in "Hostility Grows in Dayton Crowds; Champions Clash," *NYT*, 12 July 1925.

58. "Trial at Dayton Battle of Wolves," *CT*, 15 July 1925. Darrow was a frequent target: "The notorious Clarence Darrow . . . has been spreading his doctrine of Pessimism over the state and shrewdly, by suggestion and by bold statement, he has sought to turn the youth of Tennessee to open rebellion against the laws of their commonwealth." Quoted in "Evolution Issue Warm," *Baptist and Reflector* 91 (1925): 3.

59. Mencken, "Monkey Trial," 42, 46 (reprinted from *Baltimore Evening Sun*, 14, 16 July 1925). On the reports, never substantiated, that Mencken was forced to leave town because of threats from local citizens, see Coletta, *Bryan*, 257. See also "Dr. Pickard Raps Darrow, Mencken," *CT*, 20 July 1925.

60. "Pikeville Speech by Bryan Assails Critics of State," *NT*, 20 July 1925.

61. Agnostic Plot against Bible Seen by Bryan," *CN*, 20 July 1925. Bryan's strategy won support among many Tennesseans. The *Baptist and Reflector*, a Nashville publication, wrote: "It is about time that a free people should rise up and say to the rest of the Union, 'When it comes to the conduct of our own internal affairs, we do not need your help.' . . . Tennessee has never been ashamed of her scholarship nor of her statesmanship and she is not going to be abashed by the mental effervescence of a lot of front-page seekers nor by a deluge of ecclesiastical and theological and scientific rant." "Young Professor Scopes," *Baptist and Reflector* 91 (1925): 3.

62. "Christianity Goes If Evolution Wins, Bryan Tells Dayton."

63. Bryan Answers Scopes' Attorney, *CT*, 13 July 1925.

64. "Bryan Scores Agnostics and Denies Campaign to Make Bible Law of Land," *MCA*, 15 July 1925.

65. "Is Conspiracy against Bible Bryan Asserts," *CT*, 19 July 1925.

66. "Bryan, at Pikeville, Scores Newspaper Men," *CT*, 20 July 1925.

67. "Calls Scopes Trial 'Pitiful Drama,' " *NB*, 20 July 1925.

68. Quoted in " 'Christ and Devil' at Dayton Trial," *CT*, 20 July 1925.

69. "Darrow's Paradise!," *MCA*, 15 July 1925.

70. Quoted in " 'Christ and Devil' at Dayton Trial," 12. See also "Straton Attacks Darrow," *NYT*, 17 July 1925.

71. "Bryan Threatens National Campaign to Bar Evolution," *NYT*, 8 July 1925. Bryan was adamant that any suggestion that he favored a constitutional amendment to outlaw the teaching of evolution was a misrepresentation of his views. "I have never in my life used any phrase in speech or writing in favor of putting God into the Constitution," he told the *New York Times*. "I have never advocated teaching the Bible in public schools. I have advocated reading the Bible, but not teaching it." Quoted in "Dayton's One Pro-Evolution Pastor Quits," *NYT*, 13 July 1925.

72. Quoted in "Jury System Defended," *CT*, 9 July 1925.

73. Quoted in "Dayton's One Pro-Evolution Pastor Quits." Others on the prosecution team

elaborated on the theme of the "militant minority," sometimes taking the low road. "The Scopes defense has linked itself up with the agnostics, the socialists, and the communists who are trying to tear down the United States government," attorney Sue Hicks informed an interviewer from the *New York Herald-Tribune*. "Scopes Defense Allied to 'Reds,' State Aide Holds," *New York Herald-Tribune*, 11 June 1925. Hicks was quoted as being "especially pleased to note" that the ACLU "represents the pro-communists." Ibid. The prosecution was not alone in making this point. An editorial in the *New York Commercial* ("Not Apish—Fishy," 9 June 1925) pointed out that the ACLU had "engaged in aiding Communists and I.W.W. lawbreakers" and that Roger Baldwin had "served a term for obstructing the draft." The *New York Evening Post* ("The Super-Sideshow in Tennessee," 11 June 1925) warned as well of the "professional martyrs" who would soon be arriving at Dayton, including not only "agnostics, atheists, Communists, Syndicalists and New Dawners," but also "long-haired men, short-haired women, feminists, neurotics, free-thinkers and free-lovers."

74. "Rusby's Suggestion Scouted By Bryan," NYT, 13 July 1925. Addressing the Methodist Sunday school in Dayton, Bryan elaborated on his views. "The God I worship," he concluded his talk, "is the God of the ignorant as well as the learned." "Thousands Hear Bryan," CT, 13 July 1925.

75. "No Compromise for Mr. Bryan," NB, 20 July 1925. See also "Pikeville Speech by Bryan Assails Critics of State," NT, 20 July 1925.

76. Bryan to Howe, 20 June 1925, Bryan Papers.

77. Western Union telegrams to Bryan from Brockman, 9 July 1925; Schnebly and Cannon, 8 July 1925; Wharton, n.d. [July 1925]; C. L. Montgomery, 12 July 1925; Arkansas Baptist State Assembly and Convention, 10 July 1925; Aimee Semple McPherson, 12 July 1925; Gulf Coast Missionary Baptist Association, 10 July 1925; and Mead, 15 July 1925—all in Bryan Papers.

78. McAdam, "Strategic Dramaturgy," 350–52.

79. Ira E. Hicks to Sue K. Hicks, n.d., Hicks Papers.

80. Quoted in "Nation Divided on Darwinism as Trial Looms," CT, 26 May 1925. On the prosecution, see de Camp, *Great Monkey Trial*, 124–26. On Untermyer and Walsh, see Larson, *Summer for the Gods*, 131–32.

81. "Jesus' Precepts At Issue in Scopes Case, Says Bryan," NT, 20 June 1925.

82. Sue K. Hicks to Ira E. Hicks, 8 June 1925, Hicks Papers.

83. Quoted in W. C. Ross Jr., "Bryan, Noted Orator, in Favor at Dayton," *Knoxville Journal*, 10 July 1925. Here there were certain parallels between defense and prosecution strategies, with most of the members of both teams concentrating on the courtroom, while Bryan and Darrow addressed a larger public audience. See Larson, *Summer for the Gods*, 136–37.

84. Although the testimony of defense experts was eventually disallowed in the courtroom, eight scientists provided written statements for the trial record: anthropologist Faye-Cooper Cole (University of Chicago), zoologist Winterton C. Curtis (University of Missouri), zoologist Horatio Hackett Newman and psychologist Charles Hubbard Judd (University of Chicago), agronomist Jacob G. Lipman (Rutgers), geologist Kirtley F. Mather (Harvard), zoologist Maynard M. Metcalf (Johns Hopkins), and geologist Hubert A. Nelson (state geologist of Tennessee). Four experts on religion submitted statements: Shailer Matthews, dean of the University of Chicago's Divinity School and one of America's leading liberal theologians; Rabbi Herman Rosenwasser, of San Francisco, a biblical scholar and linguist; and two Tennessee modernists, Methodist minister

Herbert E. Murkett of Chattanooga and Episcopal priest Walter C. Whitaker of Knoxville. See Larson, *Summer for the Gods*, 186.

85. Burbank posed a special problem, since his success in breeding hybrid plant varieties was admired widely, particularly by farmers like those who might comprise much of the jury. For months, Bryan had been trying to undermine his reputation, at one point suggesting to W. B. Riley that antievolutionists posing as atheists write laudatory letters to Burbank in an attempt to "draw out from him a declaration of his atheistic views." Bryan to Riley, 27 March 1925, Bryan Papers. Burbank did not testify and apparently never had any plans to travel to Dayton. See Larson, *Summer for the Gods*, 134–35.

86. Quoted in " 'God or Gorilla' Author Refused to Have Any Part in Dayton Trial," MCA, 19 July 1925. To Bryan's consternation, McCann proceeded to leak his letter to the press; his denunciation appeared prominently in Tennessee newspapers during the closing days of the trial.

87. See Larson, *Summer for the Gods*, 131, 156. Riley and Norris were committed to attending the annual meeting of the Northern Baptist Convention in Seattle in July; Straton was preoccupied at home with a dispute with his congregation concerning church property. Norris did send a court stenographer to Dayton so trial reports could "be put in book form and used as propaganda by the Christians Fundamental [sic] Association." Norris to Bryan, 3 June 1925, Bryan Papers. Billy Sunday, who was also invited by Bryan, sent his regrets but added a few "ideas that may suggest a line of thought": "If man evolved from a monkey why are there any monkeys left. Why didn't they all evolve into humans?" Sunday to Bryan, 4 July 1925, Bryan Papers. See also "Billy Sunday Not to Go to Dayton," NB, 7 July 1925. The wealthy George F. Washburn, who would later take up Bryan's mantle as leader of the Bible Crusaders of America, chose not to go to Dayton because he could not be assured of "good accommodations." Washburn to W. B. Riley, 13 July 1925, Riley Papers.

88. Price to Bryan, 1 July 1925, Bryan Papers.

89. Bryan to Marr, 15 July 1925, Clarence Darrow Papers, Manuscript Division, Library of Congress, Washington, D.C. Bryan's letter came into Darrow's possession in 1934, years after the case had been closed. See Ewing C. Baskette to Darrow, 6 January 1934, ibid.

90. Bryan to Kelly, 22 June 1925, Bryan Papers.

91. *Public Acts of the State of Tennessee, Passed by the Sixty-Fourth General Assembly, 1925* (Nashville: N.p., 1925), 50.

92. "Bryan Answers Scopes' Attorney." In an earlier statement, Attorney General Stewart argued that the trial could become a battle between experts that continued for weeks or months and "in the end be but a babel of tongues." Quoted in "Narrows Scope of Scopes Trial," CT, 11 July 1925.

93. In grand jury proceedings and at the trial, students testified that Scopes had taught them evolution. But Larson (*Summer for the Gods*, 107–8) points out that Scopes had coached them in their answers, and that few seemed to have any understanding of the concept. In preparing for the case, the prosecution collected student examinations from the biology classes in which Scopes substituted. Although some of the exams refer to cell division, none discuss evolution directly or even use the word. At the same time, as Andrew Nolan argues, the answers showed some awareness of the scientific principles of eugenics. See the exams of Margaret Allen, Orvillle Gannaway, Jack Hudson, and Charles Stomley, n.d. [April 1925], Hicks Papers, and Nolan, "Defining Moment for

Dayton," 47–50. The defense showed no desire to put Scopes on the stand either: rather than deny that he had taught evolution, it wanted to make the case that the teaching of evolution did not violate the law. See Larson, *Summer for the Gods*, 173–74.

94. Scopes was originally represented by Dayton attorney John L. Godsey, who filed pretrial motions, but Godsey bowed out of the case once Darrow took charge. Concerned about Darrow, the ACLU had added former secretary of state Bainbridge Colby to the team, but he resigned before the trial began. In addition to Malone, Hays, and Neal, the defense team also relied on several Nashville lawyers for assistance. See de Camp, *Great Monkey Trial*, 126; on Neal, see Larson, *Summer for the Gods*, 79–80; and on Colby, see Larson, 102–3, 139.

95. Robert T. Small, "Scopes Nominal Prisoner at Bar," CT, 18 July 1925. "Scarcely a word has been spoken of Scopes," Small added. "Occasionally his name creeps in, but when it does everyone in the courtroom appears puzzled and concerned."

96. Quoted in *World's Most Famous Court Trial*, 90. The *Chicago Tribune*'s Philip Kinsley said, "If Mr. Darrow ever had a chance to save his client, he lost it at that moment." Kinsley, "Prayer Jars Darrow; 'I Object,' He Says," MCA, 15 July 1925.

97. Quoted in Sterling Tracy, "Another Barrage Fired in Bryan-Darrow Battle over Issues in Trial of Scopes," MCA, 19 July 1925.

98. Quoted in *World's Most Famous Court Trial*, 170. For Stewart's objection, see ibid., 117.

99. "Bryan Says Exclusion of Scientists Only Thing Judge Raulston Could Do; Darrow Says Bryan Has Dodged Issue," CT, 18 July 1925. For the exchange on the Leopold-Loeb case, see *World's Most Famous Court Trial*, 179–82.

100. Scopes had coincidentally grown up in Bryan's birthplace of Salem, Ill., and at his high school graduation Bryan had delivered the commencement address. At their first meeting in Dayton, Bryan recalled the occasion, and the two expressed their mutual respect, agreeing to remain friends. See Scopes and Presley, *Center of the Storm*, 85–86.

101. Quotations in *World's Most Famous Court Trial*, 170, 181–82, 182, 197. For Malone's reply, see 183–88.

102. "Darrow Asks W. J. Bryan to Answer These," *Chicago Daily Tribune*, 4 July 1923.

103. R. H. Perry, "Scopes Defense Facing Defeat," NB, 19 July 1925.

104. Quoted in *World's Most Famous Court Trial*, 284, 288.

105. Ibid., 287, 298–99, 299, 304. Newspaper accounts quoted Darrow as saying "examining" rather than "exempting." See, e.g., "Bryan Called as a Witness for Scopes," CT, 21 July 1925.

106. Quoted in "Bryan Called as a Witness."

107. Philip Kinsley, "Darrow Puts Agnosticism on Defense," MCA, 21 July 1925. For the conventional view, see Ginger, *Six Days or Forever?*, 173–74, and de Camp, *Great Monkey Trial*, 410. See also Numbers, *Darwinism Comes to America*, 79–84.

108. W. S. Keese, "Declares Bryan Shorn of Strength," CT, 22 July 1925.

109. See McAdam, "Strategic Dramaturgy," 352–54.

110. Quoted in "Says States Will Put Ban on Evolution," CT, 23 July 1925.

111. Quoted in *World's Most Famous Court Trial*, 316, 316–17, 317. Darrow responded: "I think this case will be remembered because it is the first case of this sort since we stopped trying people in

America for witchcraft because here we have done our best to turn back the tide that has sought to force itself upon this—upon this modern world, of testing every fact in science by a religious dictum." Ibid., 317.

112. Quoted in "New Battle Opens on Bryan-Darrow Front," MCA, 22 July 1925.

113. See "Commoner Propounds 9 Specific Questions to Chicago Attorney," Knoxville Journal, 22 July 1925. Within the hour, Darrow had issued replies to Bryan's questions. See "Darrow Replies to Bryan Quiz," CT, 22 July 1925.

114. Bryan, quoted in "Dayton Hears Parting Shots," NB, 22 July 1925.

115. "Evolutionist First to Call Him Ignorant, Bryan Says; Admits He Is No Scientist," NT, 23 July 1925.

116. "Bryan Plans to Talk Here in Few Days," CT, 25 July 1925.

117. "Bryan's Final Speech Eloquent in Defense of Faith of His Fathers," MCA, 29 July 1925.

118. "Says Atheists Seek to Usurp State Schools," CT, 26 July 1925. See also "Bryan Draws Record Crowd for Winchester," CT, 26 July 1925.

119. Small, "Believe Bryan Again Seeking Public Office," CT, 26 July 1925.

120. Doris Stevens, "Fears Bryan Soon to Wield Great Power," CT, 26 July 1925.

121. "The Week," New Republic 43 (1925): 219.

122. See Numbers, Darwinism Comes to America, 87. See also Mary Baird Bryan's description of her last conversation with her husband, in which they discussed his ability to control his fundamentalist followers. William Jennings Bryan and Mary Baird Bryan, The Memoirs of William Jennings Bryan (Philadelphia: John C. Winston Co., [1925]), 485–86.

123. Quoted in "Bryan Plans to Talk Here in Few Days," CT, 25 July 1925.

124. Washburn to Bryan, 24 July 1925, Bryan Papers.

125. M. F. Dunlap to Bryan, Western Union telegram, 22 July 1925, Bryan Papers.

126. "W. J. Bryan Dies in His Sleep at Dayton," NYT, 27 July 1925.

127. On Bryan's death, see Coletta, Bryan, 273–75; Levine, Defender of the Faith, 356–57; and Kazin, A Godly Hero, 294–95.

128. "Darrow Conflict Brought on End," NT, 28 July 1925.

129. George F. Milton, "A Dayton Postscript," Outlook 140 (1925): 551.

130. "The Cost of Bad Manners," Independent 115 (1925): 113–14. See also "Peay Sees Bryan Martyr to Faith," NT, 28 July 1925.

131. "Malone Talks at Follies," NYT, 24 July 1925.

132. "Darrow Makes Brief Reply," NB, 29 July 1925. See also "Clarence Darrow Back in Chicago," NB, 1 August 1925. Defending the defense strategy, Arthur Hays wrote of his hopes that, as a result of the case, "laws of this kind will hereafter meet the opposition of an aroused public opinion." Hays, "The Strategy of the Scopes Defense," Nation 121 (1925): 157–58.

133. Herbert E. Hicks to Ira E. Hicks, 22 July 1925, Hicks Papers.

134. "Deep Gloom in Tennessee," San Francisco Bulletin, 21 July 1925.

135. "Hot Dog Men Gloomy as Dayton Trial Ends," CT, 22 July 1925. A few local merchants did profit from the trial, including the owners of the Aqua Hotel, which served some 6,000 meals while the court was in session and netted an estimated $3,500. See Allem, "Backgrounds of the Scopes Trial," 97.

136. "'Let's Finish This Evolution Fight,' Peay Determines," NT, 6 August 1925. On international criticism, see "Foreign Amazement at Tennessee," *Literary Digest* 86, 4 (1925): 18–19; "The Evolution Trial," *Forum* 74 (1925): 320; and Michael Williams, "At Dayton, Tennessee," *Commonweal* 2 (1925): 264.

137. Quoted in "The Scopes Trial," *Independent* 115 (1925): 86. The editors of the *Independent* elaborated: "In the deep, dark fog created by the special writers, correspondents, sob-sisters, Fundamentalist pulpit orators, scientific snobs, human-interest reporters, and the miscellaneous crew of crackbrains and publicity seekers, the original idea of the Dayton drama becomes daily more obscure and incoherent" (p. 85).

138. *Scopes v. State*, 154 Tenn. 105 (1927), 367. See also Larson, *Summer for the Gods*, 207–21.

139. "The End of the Scopes Case," *Literary Digest* 92, 6 (1927): 14. See also "Scopes Goes Free, but Law Is Upheld," NYT, 16 January 1927.

140. Quoted in "End of the Scopes Case," 15. See also Darrow's comment that the decision left the case in an "unsettled condition," in "Scopes Goes Free, but Law Is Upheld."

CHAPTER SEVEN

1. Advertisement in *Searchlight* 8, 38 (1925): 1. See "Body of Commoner Viewed by Thousands," *Chattanooga Daily Times*, 30 July 1925. The report captured the moment: "Eyes upturned in quiet grief, hymns intoned by reverent lips, love expressed in simple form, sped the pilgrim home." See also Paolo E. Coletta, *William Jennings Bryan: Political Puritan, 1915–1925* (Lincoln: University of Nebraska Press, 1969), 273–77, and Michael Kazin, *A Godly Hero: The Life of William Jennings Bryan* (New York: Knopf, 2006), 296–97.

2. Sidney Tarrow, *Power in Movement: Social Movements and Contentious Politics*, 2nd ed. (Cambridge: Cambridge University Press, 1998), 144–47. Tarrow has also argued that once past the peak of protest, the cycle will proceed through a series of stages that include exhaustion, institutionalization, and selective facilitation and repression by the state (pp. 147–50).

3. Norman F. Furniss, *The Fundamentalist Controversy, 1918–1931* (New Haven: Yale University Press, 1954), 178–81. See also Louis Gasper, *The Fundamentalist Movement* (The Hague: Mouton and Co., 1963), 18. George Marsden agrees that fundamentalism sank rapidly from sight after 1925, a "fad" that had "played itself out." Marsden, *Fundamentalism and American Culture: The Shaping of Twentieth-Century Evangelicalism, 1870–1925* (Oxford: Oxford University Press, 1980), 191.

4. Ferenc Morton Szasz, "The Scopes Trial in Perspective," *Tennessee Historical Quarterly* 30 (1971): 288–98 (quotation, 290). See also Paul M. Waggoner, "The Historiography of the Scopes Trial: A Critical Re-Evaluation," *Trinity Journal* 5 (1984): 154–74, and Ronald L. Numbers, *Darwinism Comes to America* (Cambridge: Harvard University Press, 1998), 76–79.

5. Tarrow, *Power in Movement* (1998), 144–45. On these peak moments, see Aristide R. Zolberg, "Moments of Madness," *Politics and Society* 2 (1972): 183–207.

6. See Richard David Wilhelm, "A Chronology and Analysis of Regulatory Actions Relating to the Teaching of Evolution in the Public Schools" (Ph.D. diss., University of Texas at Austin, 1978), 62. See also Edward J. Larson, *Trial and Error: The American Controversy over Creation and Evolution*, 3rd ed. (Oxford: Oxford University Press, 2003), 75.

7. See, e.g., "Virginia To Have Evolution Fight," NB, 12 August 1925.

8. See "Evolution Battle To Go to Congress," NYT, 24 July 1925, 1.

9. Quoted in "Dayton Fight Will Move Up," NB, 19 July 1925. See also Ferenc Morton Szasz, *The Divided Mind of Protestant America, 1880–1930* (University, Ala.: University of Alabama Press, 1982), 124.

10. "Dayton—and After," *Nation* 121 (1925): 155. As Ron Numbers (*Darwinism Comes to America*) has shown, in the immediate aftermath of the Scopes trial, few if any critics assumed the imminent demise of the antievolution crusade. On the contrary, in an examination of trial coverage in five geographically scattered newspapers and over a dozen national magazines, Numbers found "not a single declaration of victory by the opponents of antievolutionism, in the sense of their claiming that the crusade was nearing an end" (p. 85).

11. See "William Jennings Bryan University," CF in S&C 7, 5 (1925): 52.

12. "Undelivered Address of Bryan Is Released," NB, 28 July 1925. The speech was also published as *The Last Message of William Jennings Bryan* (New York: Fleming H. Revell Co., 1925).

13. "Bryan Speaks in Death in Address Never Delivered," NT, 29 July 1925.

14. "William Jennings Bryan," *Watchman-Examiner* 13, 32 (1925): 1005.

15. Quoted in "Religion and Science in Tennessee," *Round Table* 15 (1925): 740. See also Numbers, *Darwinism Comes to America*, 88.

16. "Dr. J. Roach Straton Challenges Darrow," *Chicago Daily News*, 18 August 1925. See also Szasz, *Divided Mind*, 125.

17. See William Bell Riley, "Bryan the Great Commoner and Christian," *Baptist Beacon* 1, 12 (1925): 11–15. See also Stewart G. Cole, *The History of Fundamentalism* (Hamden, Conn.: Archon Books, 1963), 309.

18. See Furniss, *Fundamentalist Controversy*, 70.

19. On the Bible Crusaders, see Cole, *History of Fundamentalism*, 270–75; Furniss, *Fundamentalist Controversy*, 57–61; and "Announcing the Bible Crusaders of America," *Crusaders' Champion* 1, 1 (1925): 6, 12. The first edition of Washburn's *Crusaders' Champion* includes numerous testimonials endorsing him as Bryan's successor, including one from Straton declaring him to be "God's man to take the place of our lamented leader." Quoted in "Greetings to the Bible Crusaders," *Crusaders' Champion* 1, 1 (1925): 7.

20. "William Jennings Bryan's Successor," CF in S&C 7, 5 (1925): 56–57. At least one observer suggested that the entire enterprise of replacing Bryan may have been misguided from the start. Noting that national newspapers had commonly depicted Bryan as the leading figure in American fundamentalism, fundamentalist editor Curtis Lee Laws observed that he had been a leader only to the extent that the press had labeled him one. "Fundamentalism," he commented, "has never had a leader. Any man can assume the leadership of a small or a large portion of the fundamentalists when they are willing to be led. It has been our experience and observation that the leadership of the fundamentalists is a pretty hard job." Quoted in *Watchman-Examiner* 13, 36 (1925): 1131.

21. "Announcing the Bible Crusaders of America," *Crusaders' Champion* 1, 1 (1925): 6; 12. The organization included an International Advisory Council made up of business and political leaders. Among Washburn's other innovations was the introduction of Junior Bible Crusaders for children. See Furniss, *Fundamentalist Controversy*, 58.

22. The idea of "flying squadrons" had been popularized by the Prohibition movement. See "The 'Flying Defenders,'" *Defender* 1, 2 (1926): 1. In the year 1927 alone, Winrod estimated that he delivered 358 addresses in 240 communities to some 130,000 persons. "Items of Interest to Defenders," *Defender* 2, 9 (1928): 2.

23. See "The Key-Note Address," *Defender* 2, 2 (1927): 1. See also Leo B. Ribuffo, *The Old Christian Right: The Protestant Far Right from the Great Depression to the Cold War* (Philadelphia: Temple University Press, 1983), 80–93.

24. The Supreme Kingdom also boasted a musical division called the "Lydian Singers of America" and its own magazine, *Dynamite*. Donors were listed according to the size of their gifts as pioneer, crusader, alpha, mystic knight, life, charter, and foundation members. See Furniss, *Fundamentalist Controversy*, 62–66.

25. Quoted in "Constitution, By-Laws, Articles of Incorporation of American Anti-Evolution Association Soon Ready for Distribution," *Baptist and Commoner* 10, 43 (1927): 3. See also "American Anti-Evolution Association," ibid., 2.

26. See Cole, *History of Fundamentalism*, 262–67; Furniss, *Fundamentalist Controversy*, 71, 98–99; and Maynard Shipley, *The War on Modern Science: A Short History of the Fundamentalist Attacks on Evolution and Modernism* (New York: Knopf, 1927), 239–81.

27. See Furniss, *Fundamentalist Controversy*, 71.

28. "Editorial," *American Mercury* 6 (1925): 160.

29. See Wilhelm, "Chronology and Analysis," 68–69.

30. See Furniss, *Fundamentalist Controversy*, 93–94; Shipley, *War on Modern Science*, 63–74; Harbor Allen, "The Anti-Evolution Campaign in America," *Current History* 24 (1926): 893–94; and Edwin Bernard Massey Jr., "Development of the Anti-Evolution Bill in the Mississippi Legislature in 1926" (M.A. thesis, University of Mississippi, 1966).

31. "Townsend and Connor, Foes of Klan and Poole Bill, Win," *Greensboro Daily News*, 9 June 1926. See also Willard B. Gatewood Jr., *Preachers, Pedagogues and Politicians: The Evolution Controversy in North Carolina, 1920–1927* (Chapel Hill: University of North Carolina Press, 1966), 201–5.

32. See Wilhelm, "Chronology and Analysis," 64–65.

33. "Antievolutionists Still Fighting," *Literary Digest* 95, 11 (1927): 29. See also Furniss, *Fundamentalist Controversy*, 78.

34. See Mary Duncan France, "'A Year of Monkey War': The Anti-Evolution Campaign and the Florida Legislature," *Florida Historical Quarterly* 54 (1975): 169.

35. Riley and Clarke quoted in Allen, "Anti-Evolution Campaign," 893, 897.

36. See Gatewood, *Preachers, Pedagogues*, 106.

37. See Larson, *Trial and Error*, 75. See also Shipley, *War on Modern Science*, 239–45.

38. See Larson, *Trial and Error*, 85.

39. See Judith V. Grabiner and Peter D. Miller, "Effects of the Scopes Trial," *Science* 185 (1974): 832–37. As one example, the 1921 edition of Truman Moon's best-selling *Biology for Beginners* had been explicitly premised on evolutionary principles, going so far as to include Darwin's portrait on the frontispiece. In the 1926 edition, references to evolution were dropped from the preface, Darwin's photograph was replaced with a diagram of the digestive system, and religious quotations were added to the text. See Grabiner and Miller, 833–34.

40. Quoted in Shipley, *War on Modern Science*, 174. See also Furniss, *Fundamentalist Controversy*, 93–94.

41. On the Riley-Metcalf debates, see Gatewood, *Preachers, Pedagogues*, 48–58; on the Potter-Straton debates, see C. Allyn Russell, *Voices of American Fundamentalism: Seven Biographical Studies* (Philadelphia: Westminster Press, 1976), 65–75; and on these and other debates see also Szasz, *Divided Mind*, 127. Several of these contests are collected in Ronald L. Numbers, ed., *Creation-Evolution Debates* (New York: Garland Publishing Co., 1995).

42. See, e.g., William Bell Riley to Maynard Shipley, 25 May, 5 June 1925, and Shipley to Riley, 30 May, 2 June 1925, Riley Papers. After the Scopes trial, attempts were made by several antievolution speakers to schedule debates with Clarence Darrow, who adamantly refused their offers. See "Dr. J. Roach Straton Challenges Darrow." Unable to debate Darrow, Straton confronted him in absentia in his popular sermon "Monkey Men and Monkey Morals—What I Would Have Testified Had I Been a Witness at the Scopes Trial." Ibid.

43. Admission was charged, typically twenty-five cents for general admission and fifty cents for reserved seats. On occasion, crowds were asked to make contributions to a collection plate, with the proceeds divided equally between the two debaters. See "Hisses, Howls End Evolution Debate at Bible Institute," *Los Angeles Examiner*, 20 June 1925. See also the collection of debate materials in Science League of America Clippings, Rare Book Room, Wilson Library, University of North Carolina, Chapel Hill.

44. See "The Riley-McCabe Toronto Debate," *Christian Fundamentalist* 2, 5 (1928): 20. See also William Vance Trollinger Jr., *God's Empire: William Bell Riley and Midwestern Fundamentalism* (Madison: University of Wisconsin Press, 1990), 47, and Russell, *Voices of American Fundamentalism*, 94–95.

45. See Willard B. Gatewood Jr., "The Evolution Controversy in North Carolina, 1920–1927," *Mississippi Quarterly* 17 (1964): 205.

46. See "Charles Smith, Atheist, in Jail," *Christian Fundamentalist* 2, 5 (1928): 21. See also Szasz, *Divided Mind*, 127–28.

47. Quoted in "Defense of Defeated Debaters," *Christian Fundamentalist* 2, 9 (1929): 88. On the California debates, see Edward J. Larson, *Summer for the Gods: The Scopes Trial and America's Continuing Debate over Science and Religion* (New York: BasicBooks, 1997), 123–25.

48. See Shipley, *War on Modern Science*, 135–36; Kenneth K. Bailey, *Southern White Protestantism in the Twentieth Century* (New York: Harper and Row, 1964), 89; and George E. Webb, *The Evolution Controversy in America* (Lexington: University Press of Kentucky, 1994), 80. See also Howard K. Beale, *Are American Teachers Free? An Analysis of Restraints upon the Freedom of Teaching in American Schools* (New York: Scribner, [1936]), 229–30.

49. See L. Sprague de Camp, *The Great Monkey Trial* (Garden City, N.Y.: Doubleday, 1968), 135–36. See also Howard K. Beale, *Are American Teachers Free?*, 231.

50. See France, "Monkey War," 171.

51. Allen, "Anti-Evolution Campaign," 896.

52. "Students Hear Sermons, Burn Evolution at the Stake," CF in S&C 8, 1 (1926): 56–57. On a similar event in Morristown, N.J., see Allen, "Anti-Evolution Campaign," 896. See also Shipley, *War on Modern Science*, 126.

53. Quoted in Shipley, *War on Modern Science*, 48. See also "Clarke Heard by 200 Persons,"

Birmingham Post, 1 March 1926. For similar predictions from the other side, see Maynard Shipley, "A Year of the Monkey War," *Independent* 119 (1927): 326.

54. Tarrow, *Power in Movement* (1998), 145–46.

55. "Editorial Notes and Comments," *Watchman-Examiner* 13, 34 (1925): 1071. Two months earlier, South Carolina Baptist B. P. Robertson had made a similar, though less sweeping argument in "The Giant Fighting the Man of Straw," *Baptist Courier* 56, 24 (1925): 11. See also Szasz, *Divided Mind*, 131–32.

56. Billy Sunday, "Back to the Old-Time Religion," *Collier's* 76 (1926): 24.

57. Andrew Johnson, "The Evolution Articles," *Pentecostal Herald* 38, 39 (1926): 6. For Johnson's thinking, see also Numbers, *Darwinism Comes to America*, 124–25.

58. See Willard B. Gatewood Jr., *Controversy in the Twenties: Fundamentalism, Modernism, and Evolution* (Nashville, Tenn.: Vanderbilt University Press, 1969), 224. Gatewood made the point that for many state legislators, such statutes provided alternatives to more narrowly defined antievolution bills. He wrote: "For legislators concerned about the image of their states and cognizant of the popular anxiety regarding the moral content of education, laws requiring some form of religious instruction in the public schools seemed to avoid the risk of ridicule and to satisfy the desires of their anxious constituents" (p. 287). On laws requiring daily reading of the Bible, see Allen, "Anti-Evolution Campaign," 896–97.

59. "Minority Report on H.B. no. 77," *Journal of the House of Representatives of the State of Mississippi*, 1926 (Jackson, Mich.: Herderman Brothers, 1926): 330–31. Reprinted in Gatewood, *Controversy in the Twenties*, 304.

60. For examples of southern stereotypes in trial reporting, see H. L. Mencken, "Darrow's Eloquent Appeal Wasted on Ears That Heed Only Bryan, Says Mencken," *Baltimore Evening Sun*, 14 July 1925. See also his famous description of a Church of God revival—"the Holy Roller communion," in Mencken, "Yearning Mountaineers' Souls Need Reconversion Nightly, Mencken Finds," *Baltimore Evening Sun*, 13 July 1925. It should be stressed that many reporters at Dayton went out of their way to avoid regional stereotypes. See "Dayton's Amazing Trial," *Literary Digest* 86, 4 (1925): 5. On Mencken's continuing commentary on the South, see Larson, *Summer for the Gods*, 222.

61. "Why the Dayton Trial Will Resound to the South's Good," *Manufacturers' Record* 88 (1925): 70.

62. Warren A. Candler, "Liberalism Proposing to Liberate the South," *Christian Advocate* 86, 38 (1925): 5. See also Bailey, *Southern White Protestantism*, 91.

63. See Donald Davidson, "First Fruits of Dayton: The Intellectual Evolution in Dixie," *Forum* 79 (1928): 898. See also Paul K. Conkin, *When All the Gods Trembled: Darwinism, Scopes, and American Intellectuals* (Lanham, Md.: Rowman and Littlefield Publishers, Inc., 1998), 155–56.

64. Quoted in Shipley, *War on Modern Science*, 63–64. See also R. Halliburton Jr., "Mississippi's Contribution to the Anti-Evolution Movement," *Journal of Mississippi History* 35 (1973): 177–78.

65. John Roach Straton, "The Most Sinister Movement in the United States," *American Fundamentalist* 2, 22 (1925): 9.

66. H. L. Mencken, *Prejudices: Fifth Series* (New York: Knopf, 1926), 74. Fundamentalists, he continued, "are thick in the mean streets behind the gas-works. They are everywhere where learning is too heavy a burden for mortal minds to carry, even the vague, pathetic learning on tap in the

little red schoolhouses. They march with the Klan, with the Christian Endeavor Society, with the Junior Order of United American Mechanics, with the Epworth League, with all the rococo bands that poor and unhappy folk organize to bring some new light of purpose into their lives. They have had a thrill, and they are ready for more."

67. George F. Milton, "A Dayton Postscript," *Outlook* 140 (1925): 552.

68. T. T. Martin, quoted in "Ben M'Kenzie Will Speak Here Sunday," *Jackson Daily Clarion Ledger*, 2 February 1926.

69. See Gatewood, *Preachers, Pedagogues*, 215.

70. Quoted in "The Gazette Begins Its Contemptible Opposition to Our Anti-Evolution Law," *Baptist and Commoner* 11, 2 (1927): 1. See also "The Arkansas Law against Evolution," *Christian Fundamentalist* 2, 8 (1929): 58.

71. Quoted in Shipley, *War on Modern Science*, 129. Lindsay added: "When a man gets so smart that he can't believe in the Bible he is just too smart to know that he's a fool." See also "Clause in Appropriations Bill Hitting at Evolution Is Snowed Under in House," *Atlanta Constitution*, 30 July 1925.

72. See Cole, *History of Fundamentalism*, 269.

73. See R. S. Beal, "The Eternal Searchlight Turned On Modern Socialism," CF in S&C 8, 1 (1926): 42.

74. Quoted in "The Bible Crusaders' Challenge," *Crusaders' Champion* 1, 7 (1926): 12–13.

75. See "The Week," *New Republic* 49 (1926): 123. On Straton's ambivalent relationship to the Klan, see Hillyer H. Straton, "John Roach Straton and the Ku Klux Klan," *Andover-Newton Quarterly* 9 (1968): 124–34.

76. Quoted in "Virginia To Have Evolution Fight," NB, 12 August 1925. Critics suggested that the strategy may have been encouraged by financial conservatives, who saw fundamentalism as hostile to labor and committed to industrial stability. See Kirsopp Lake, *The Religion of Yesterday and To-Morrow* (Boston: Houghton Mifflin, 1925), 162–63. See also Gatewood, *Evolution in the Twenties*, 25.

77. "Dr. J. Roach Straton Challenges Darrow."

78. William Bell Riley, "How and Why I Was Denied a Building on the University of Minnesota Campus for an Address on Evolution," *Baptist Beacon* 2, 8 (1926): 7. See also Ferenc M. Szasz, "William B. Riley and the Fight against Teaching of Evolution in Minnesota," *Minnesota History* 41 (1969): 209. On Riley's views of the state, see Trollinger, *God's Empire*, 66–68. See also Marsden, *Fundamentalism and American Culture*, 127–32.

79. Tarrow, *Power in Movement: Social Movements and Contentious Politics* (Cambridge: Cambridge University Press, 1994), 157. On "early risers" and latecomers, see p. 145.

80. Quoted in "Rev. Paul W. Rood, Christian Fundamentalist," CF in S&C 7, 5 (1925): 52.

81. See "Multiplying Fundamentalist Organizations," CF in S&C 8, 1 (1926): 28.

82. See Cole, *History of Fundamentalism*, 312. At this time the WCFA also began to collaborate more actively with other groups; by 1927 it was joining with Winrod's Defenders to sponsor teams of "flying fundamentalists." See ibid., 313.

83. See Furniss, *Fundamentalist Controversy*, 54–55.

84. Quoted in "Multiplying Fundamentalist Organizations," 28.

85. See Trollinger, *God's Empire*, 42–43. Despite the personal resentments, as late as 1928 Riley

commended Norris in public, saying that he could "not recall any case in which he has been on the wrong side of an important public or church question." See "Frank Norris and Hoover Election," *Christian Fundamentalist* 2,6 (1928): 14.

86. On this conflict, see Cole, *History of Fundamentalism*, 310–11. President Charles A. Blanchard complicated the situation by offering to have Wheaton College change its name and become the nucleus for the institution. Ibid. Others countered with plans for a Bryan Foundation for the Promotion of Biblical Science, a fund of "not less than $10,000,000" to aid "departments of science in every standard college where materialistic evolutionary theories are not taught." Quoted in "A New Fundamentalist College," *Baptist and Reflector* 91, 32 (1925): 3. In 1926 the WCFA resolved to create a Bryan foundation with an endowment of $25 million, modeled on the Carnegie Foundation for the Advancement of Teaching, to advance Christian fundamentalist education. See Furniss, *Fundamentalist Controversy*, 54. With Washburn as chair of the finance committee, Dayton's Bryan Memorial University Association was able to raise nearly a million dollars in its first five years, and the town became the chosen site. See "Offer of $10,000 to Start Bryan 'University' Opens Dayton Campaign for $1,000,000 Fund," NYT, 17 July 1925.

87. See Russell, *Voices of American Fundamentalism*, 100.

88. See Bailey, *Southern White Protestantism*, 66–67.

89. For this story, see Cole, *History of Fundamentalism*, 293; Marsden, *Fundamentalism and American Culture*, 90–91; and David O. Beale, *In Pursuit of Purity: American Fundamentalism since 1850* (Greenville, S.C.: Unusual Publications, 1986), 237–42.

90. Quoted in "Fundamentalism and the Fundamentalists," *Christian Fundamentalist* 2, 12 (1929): 207.

91. J. R. Clark, "Monkeyism Compounded," *Baptist and Commoner* 10, 48 (1927): 3.

92. Quoted from *Harlow's Weekly*, 14 January 1928, 14, in Elbert L. Watson, "Oklahoma and the Anti-Evolution Movement of the 1920's," *Chronicles of Oklahoma* 52 (1964–65): 403.

93. See "In the Name of God We Will Set Up Our Banners," *Defender* 3, 10 (1929): 5.

94. See Marsden, *Fundamentalism and American Culture*, 210. On Ford's role in popularizing the *Protocols*, see Ribuffo, *Old Christian Right*, 10–13.

95. On this episode, see Barry Hankins, *God's Rascal: J. Frank Norris and the Beginnings of Southern Fundamentalism* (Lexington: University Press of Kentucky, 1996), 118–20. See also Russell, *Voices of American Fundamentalism*, 35–36; Bailey, *Southern White Protestantism*, 60–62; David O. Beale, *In Pursuit of Purity*, 232–35; and Patsy Ledbetter, "Defense of the Faith: J. Frank Norris and Texas Fundamentalism, 1920–1929," *Arizona and the West* 15 (1973): 60. See also "The Shooting Parson of Texas," *New Republic* 48 (1926): 35–37.

96. T. T. Shields, "The Convention as Seen by the Toronto Newspaper Reporters," CF in S&C 8, 2 (1926): 8.

97. Quoted in "The Bible Crusaders' Challenge," CF in S&C 8, 2 (1926): 64.

98. Gatewood, *Preachers, Pedagogues*, 201–5 (quotation, 203).

99. Quoted in Jonathan Daniels, "Evolution Battle May Break Out at Raleigh Meeting," *Raleigh News and Observer*, 25 April 1926. See also Gatewood, *Preachers, Pedagogues*, 184–85.

100. See "Stormy Scenes Mark Meeting of 'Committee of One Hundred' Here," *Charlotte Observer*, 5 May 1926. See also Gatewood, *Preachers, Pedagogues*, 186–201.

101. See Gatewood, *Preachers, Pedagogues*, 203. See also Gatewood, "The Evolution Controversy in North Carolina," 203–4.

102. "Undignified Exhibition," *Charlotte Observer*, 2 June 1926.

103. Tarrow, *Power in Movement* (1998), 146–47.

104. See Constance Areson Clark, "Evolution for John Doe: Pictures, the Public, and the Scopes Trial Debate," *Journal of* American History 87 (2001): 1282. In an analysis of some four thousand articles from fourteen daily papers of the time, Paul A. Carter found that American newspapers were "more up-to-date in things biological than are college and high-school texts on the subject." Carter, "Science and the Common Man," *American Scholar* 45 (1975–76): 787. See also Henshaw Ward, *Evolution for John Doe* (Indianapolis: Bobbs-Merrill, 1925).

105. Maynard Shipley, "The Menace to Science from the Fundamentalist Movement," *Current History* 25 (1926): 339.

106. See de Camp, *Great Monkey Trial*, 478–79.

107. See "The Fundamentalists Retreat," *New Republic* 52 (1927): 8–9.

108. See Duncan Aikman, "Ape Laws as Political Medicine," *Independent* 116 (1926): 544, 558.

109. Tennessee attorney Franklin Reynolds, quoted in Larson, *Summer for the Gods*, 212.

110. For a description of the campaign, see Szasz, "Riley and the Fight against Teaching of Evolution in Minnesota," 212–16. The senate vote was 55 to 7.

111. Quoted in "The Anti-Evolution Fight in Minnesota," *CF in S&C* 9, 2 (1927): 14. See also Szasz, "Riley and the Fight against Teaching of Evolution in Minnesota," 215.

112. Quoted in "The Evolution Fight Is Now On to Arkansas," *Baptist and Commoner* 11, 4 (1927): 3.

113. "The Bible or Atheism, Which?" *Arkansas Gazette*, 4 November 1928. The same advertisement appeared in the *Arkansas Democrat* on the same day.

114. On the Arkansas vote, see Larson, *Trial and Error*, 79–81; R. Halliburton Jr., "The Adoption of Arkansas' Anti-Evolution Law," *Arkansas Historical Quarterly* 23 (1964): 271–83; and Virginia Sue Hickman, "The Enactment of the Arkansas Anti-Evolution Law" (B.A. thesis, Hendrix College, 1967).

115. Quoted in "The Arkansas Law against Evolution," *Christian Fundamentalist* 2,8 (1929): 58. Also responding to the Arkansas vote, Maynard Shipley predicted that the antievolution movement would take advantage of the initiative system to mount a "big drive" in 1929. Shipley, "Evolution Still a Live Issue in the Schools," *Current History* 27 (1928): 801.

116. Virginia Gray, "Anti-Evolution Sentiment and Behavior: The Case of Arkansas," *Journal of American History* 57 (1970): 355–57.

117. Quoted in "Al Smith and the Presidency," *Baptist and Commoner* 11, 43 (1928): 5. On the politics of the 1928 Arkansas primary, see Hickman, "Enactment of the Arkansas Anti-Evolution Law," 82–84.

118. See Bailey, *Southern White Protestantism*, 101. According to Bailey, Prohibition was a unifying factor within the churches as well, serving "to calm and moderate internal dissensions and to draw warring factions into a common cause and purpose" (p. 95).

119. "Editorial Note," *Western Recorder* 102, 30 (1928): 6. See also Louie D. Newton, "Vital Moral Facts of Politics Plainly Stated for Christian Citizens," ibid., 6, 9, 28; J. B. Lawrence, "Let Us Save

the Democratic Party," ibid., 10; and Bailey, *Southern White Protestantism*, 99. On the connections between the preachers and the Republican Party, see Allan J. Lichtman, *Prejudice and the Old Politics: The Presidential Election of 1928* (Chapel Hill: University of North Carolina Press, 1979), 57–70.

120. Norris to Ham, 17 September 1928, Norris Papers.

121. Quoted in "Reasons Why Al Smith Should Not Be Elected President of the United States," *Christian Fundamentalist* 2, 4 (1928): 8.

122. See James J. Thompson Jr., *Tried as by Fire: Southern Baptists and the Religious Controversies of the 1920s* (Macon, Ga.: Mercer University Press, 1982), 192. For a description of other anti-Catholic scandal sheets, see ibid., 59. On Norris's role, see also Hankins, *God's Rascal*, 54–63.

123. Ham to J. Frank Norris, 12 March 1928, Norris Papers.

124. "Who Would Be the President If Al Smith Should Be Elected?," *Baptist and Commoner* 10, 7 (1926): 3.

125. "An Organized Fight to Be Made on Al Smith," *Baptist and Commoner* 12, 2 (1928): 11.

126. Even so, Norris enjoyed strong Klan support. Mrs. W. A. Ashe, Excellent Commander of the Women of the Ku Klux Klan, complimented him on a recent sermon. "While you did not say that it was a Klan Sermon but those of us who were fortunate enough to have heard it, both over the Radio and in the Church feel like it was." Ashe to Norris, 27 March 1928, Norris Papers.

127. "The Question of Motives," *Baptist Record* 30, 34 (1928): 5.

128. "Who Loves the Negro?" *Baptist Record* 30, 35 (1928): 2.

129. "Smith, Hoover, and the Negro," *Baptist Record* 30, 41 (1928): 1, 5. See also Bailey, *Southern White Protestantism*, 105.

130. "Startling, Disgusting Facts: Al Smith and Tammany Hall Negro Equality," *Baptist and Commoner* 12, 26 (1928): 2. In other articles Bogard insisted that Hoover opposed all efforts to achieve radical equality, assuring readers that "SMITH IS THE MAN WHO FAVORS THE NEGROES AND THAT HOOVER IS NOT FOR THEM." See "Negro Equality and Al Smith," *Baptist and Commoner* 12, 23 (1928): 3.

131. See Bailey, *Southern White Protestantism*, 106. On the role of religion in the 1928 election, see Lichtman, *Prejudice and the Old Politics*, 40–57. The five southern states carried by Hoover were Florida, North Carolina, Virginia, Tennessee, and Texas.

132. Quoted in "Says Bishop Was Known as 'One-Quart Cannon,' " *NYT*, 24 October 1928. See also Bailey, *Southern White Protestantism*, 107.

133. W. M. Miles, "Let Hooverites Pay Preachers," letter to the editor, *MCA*, 4 November 1928. See also Bailey, *Southern White Protestantism*, 107.

134. "Laymen Protest Church Entrance in Party Politics," *New Orleans Times-Picayune*, 7 October 1928.

135. See Bailey, *Southern White Protestantism*, 107–9.

136. See Russell, *Voices of American Fundamentalism*, 99.

137. For the Riley-Rimmer debate, see "A Debate: Resolved That the Creative Days in Genesis Were Aeons, Not Solar Days," in Ronald L. Numbers, ed., *Creation-Evolution Debates* (New York: Garland Publishing Co., 1995), 393–425. See also Numbers, *The Creationists: The Evolution of Scientific Creationism* (Berkeley: University of California Press, 1992), 66–67. Over the course of the 1920s, says C. Allyn Russell (*Voices of American Fundamentalism*, 94), audiences had begun to come less to

hear the debate than to see the show, and "many persons who attended seem to have done so for entertainment rather than for enlightenment."

138. Quoted in "The Fraternity of Fundamentalists," *Christian Fundamentalist* 3, 11 (1930): 658.

139. Paul W. Rood, "The Future of Fundamentalism," *Christian Fundamentalist* 3, 3 (1929): 327.

140. Tarrow, *Power in Movement* (1998), 147–50.

141. An example of cooperation was the joint publication after 1926 of the *Bryan Broadcaster* and the *Defender*. See Cole, *History of Fundamentalism*, 263–64.

142. See Cole, *History of Fundamentalism*, 275, 270, 278. See also "Let Everyone Do His Bit; None Will Be Burdened," *Defender* 2, 7 (1927): 2.

143. "Evolution Propaganda," *Christian Fundamentalist* 2, 8 (1929): 59.

CHAPTER EIGHT

1. Riley fund-raising letter, 17 July 1933, Norris Papers.

2. Riley, "Is Quitting the Sign of Courage?," sermon [1935], Riley Papers.

3. On the limits of the Weber-Michels model and for a more fluid view of growth and change, see Mayer N. Zald and Roberta Ash, "Social Movement Organizations: Growth, Decay, and Change," *Social Forces* 44 (1966): 327–41.

4. Joseph R. Gusfield, "Social Movements and Social Change: Perspectives of Linearity and Fluidity," *Research in Social Movements, Conflict and Change* 4 (1981): 324–25. See also Gusfield, *Symbolic Crusade: Status Politics and the American Temperance Movement* (Urbana: University of Illinois Press, 1963).

5. See Anne N. Costain, *Inviting Women's Rebellion: A Political Process Interpretation of the Women's Movement* (Baltimore: Johns Hopkins University Press, 1992); Debra C. Minkoff, "Bending with the Wind: Strategic Change and Adaptation by Women's and Racial Minority Organizations," *American Journal of Sociology* 104 (1999): 1666–1703; Leila J. Rupp, "The Survival of American Feminism," in Robert H. Bremner and Gary W. Reichard, eds., *Reshaping America: Society and Institutions, 1945–1960* (Columbus: Ohio State University Press, 1982), 33–65; Leila J. Rupp and Verta Taylor, *Survival in the Doldrums: The American Women's Rights Movement, 1945 to the 1960s* (New York: Oxford University Press, 1987); Suzanne Staggenborg, "The Survival of the Women's Movement: Turnover and Continuity in Bloomington, Indiana," *Mobilization* 1 (1996): 143–58; Staggenborg and Verta Taylor, "Whatever Happened to the Women's Movement?," *Mobilization* 10 (2005): 37–52; Verta Taylor, "Social Movement Continuity: The Women's Movement in Abeyance," *American Sociological Review* 54 (1989): 761–75; Nancy Whittier, "Political Generations, Micro-Cohorts, and the Transformation of Social Movements," *American Sociological Review* 62 (1997): 760–78; and Whittier, *Feminist Generations: The Persistence of the Radical Women's Movement* (Philadelphia: Temple University Press, 1995).

6. See Staggenborg and Taylor, "Whatever Happened to the Women's Movement?," 41–47. On "spillover," see David S. Meyer and Nancy Whittier, "Social Movement Spillover," *Social Problems* 41 (1994): 277–98. See also Doug McAdam, " 'Initiator' and 'Spin-off' Movements: Diffusion Processes in Protest Cycles," in Mark Traugott, ed., *Repertoires and Cycles of Collective Action* (Durham, N.C.: Duke University Press, 1995), 217–39.

7. George E. Webb, *The Evolution Controversy in America* (Lexington: University Press of Kentucky, 1994), xi.

8. Ronald L. Numbers, *The Creationists: The Evolution of Scientific Creationism* (Berkeley: University of California Press, 1992), xi; see also 242–43.

9. See Taylor, "Social Movement Continuity," 764–70; Rupp, "Survival of American Feminism," 33–55; and Rupp and Taylor, *Survival in the Doldrums*, 187–206. See also Bob Edwards and Sam Marullo, "Organizational Mortality in a Declining Social Movement: The Demise of Peace Movement Organizations in the End of the Cold War Era," *American Sociological Review* 60 (1995): 908–27.

10. See Richard David Wilhelm, "A Chronology and Analysis of Regulatory Actions Relating to the Teaching of Evolution in the Public Schools" (Ph.D. diss., University of Texas at Austin, 1978), 64.

11. See Kenneth K. Bailey, *Southern White Protestantism in the Twentieth Century* (New York: Harper and Row, 1964), 87. See also Edward J. Larson, *Trial and Error: The American Controversy over Creation and Evolution*, 3rd ed. (Oxford: Oxford University Press, 2003), 82.

12. See Larson, *Trial and Error*, 82.

13. On Riley, see William Bell Riley, *Protocols and Communism* (Minneapolis, Minn.: L. W. Camp, 1934); Riley, "Why Recognize Russia and Rag Germany?," *Pilot* 14, 4 (1934): 109–10; Riley, "The Blood of the Jew vs. the Blood of Jesus," *Pilot* 15, 2 (1934): 24–25; and Riley, "The Jewish Web for the Gentile Fly," *Pilot* 15, 5 (1935): 124–25. *The Pilot* was a monthly magazine published by Riley's Northwestern Bible School; in 1932 it merged with *The Christian Fundamentalist*. On Riley's anti-Semitism and attraction to fascism, see also William Vance Trollinger Jr., *God's Empire: William Bell Riley and Midwestern Fundamentalism* (Madison: University of Wisconsin Press, 1990), 68–82. On Winrod, see Gerald B. Winrod, "Unmasking 'The Hidden Hand'—A World Conspiracy," *Defender* 7, 10 (1933): 3, 5; Winrod, "More Evidence of the World Conspiracy," *Defender* 7, 11 (1933): 9, 11, 13; Winrod, "Is America Seeing Red?," *Defender* 8, 6 (1933): 3, 13, 15; and Winrod, "Jewish Conspirators Expect to Destroy All Governments and Set Up International Dictatorship," *Defender* 8, 11 (1933): 2, 21–22. See also Leo B. Ribuffo, *The Old Christian Right: The Protestant Far Right from the Great Depression to the Cold War* (Philadelphia: Temple University Press, 1983), 80–127.

14. See George M. Marsden, *Fundamentalism and American Culture: The Shaping of Twentieth-Century Evangelicalism, 1870–1925* (Oxford: Oxford University Press, 1980), 191–93.

15. Riley fund-raising letter, 17 July 1933, Norris Papers.

16. On fundamentalism at this time, see Marsden, *Fundamentalism and American Culture*, 193–96. For background on the development of fundamentalist institutions, see Joel Carpenter, *Revive Us Again: The Reawakening of American Fundamentalism* (New York: Oxford University Press, 1997), 13–32. A more concise statement of the argument is Carpenter's "Fundamentalist Institutions and the Rise of Evangelical Protestantism, 1929–1942," *Church History* 49 (1980): 62–75.

17. See Carpenter, *Revive Us Again*, 23. See also David O. Beale, *In Pursuit of Purity: American Fundamentalism since 1850* (Greenville, S.C.: Unusual Publications, 1986), 252–53. On fundamentalism's emphasis on attracting youth, see Paul A. Carter, "The Fundamentalist Defense of the Faith," in John Braeman, Robert H. Bremner, and David Brody, eds., *Change and Continuity in Twentieth-Century America: The 1920s* (Columbus: Ohio State University Press, 1968), 184.

18. See Carpenter, *Revive Us Again*, 25–27. See also David O. Beale, *In Pursuit of Purity*, 255–56.

19. Carpenter, *Revive Us Again*, 23–24. See also Tona J. Hangen, *Redeeming the Dial: Radio, Religion, and Popular Culture in America* (Chapel Hill: University of North Carolina Press, 2002).

20. See Carpenter, *Revive Us Again*, 16–22. By the mid-1930s Riley's Northwestern Bible and Missionary Training School could report that seventy-five of its alumni were serving as pastors in Minnesota alone, and that all of them were recruiting others. On the influence of Northwestern alumni among Minnesota Baptists and on their success at capturing the state convention, see Trollinger, *God's Empire*, 133–50. By the time of Riley's death in 1947, there were approximately two thousand alumni of the Northwestern Bible and Missionary Training School, Northwestern Evangelical Seminary, and Northwestern College. See Jerry Falwell, *The Fundamentalist Phenomenon* (Garden City, N.Y.: Doubleday, 1981), 99. Among the seminaries, the most important was Westminster Theological Seminary, in Philadelphia, founded when conservative faculty led by J. Gresham Machen broke from Princeton Theological Seminary. At the same time, Machen was active in organizing the Independent Board for Presbyterian Foreign Missions, and he eventually played a leading role in the creation of a new denomination, the Presbyterian Church of America. See Carpenter, *Revive Us Again*, 20; David O. Beale, *In Pursuit of Purity*, 315–22; Marsden, *Fundamentalism and American Culture*, 192; and C. Allyn Russell, *Voices of American Fundamentalism: Seven Biographical Studies* (Philadelphia: Westminster Press, 1976), 153–58.

21. Carpenter, *Revive Us Again*, 72–73.

22. On Rimmer, see Numbers, *Creationists*, 60–71. See also Edward B. Davis, ed., *The Antievolution Pamphlets of Harry Rimmer* (New York: Garland Publishing, Inc., 1995). On Irwin Moon, see Carpenter, *Revive Us Again*, 73.

23. Morris describes his discovery in Henry M. Morris, *A History of Modern Creationism* (San Diego, Calif.: Master Book Publishers, 1984), 79–109.

24. See Ronald L. Numbers, "Creationism in 20th-Century America," *Science* 218 (1982): 541. On the Religion and Science Association, Deluge Geology Society, and American Scientific Affiliation, see Numbers, *Creationists*, 102–39, 158–81. See also Edward J. Larson, *Summer for the Gods: The Scopes Trial and America's Continuing Debate over Science and Religion* (New York: BasicBooks, 1997), 233–34.

25. Numbers, "Creationism in 20th-Century America," 541.

26. On post-1920s debates, see also Numbers, *Creationists*, 66–67, 142, 151–52, 287; Morris, *Modern Creationism*, 261–66; and Ronald L. Numbers, ed., *Creation-Evolution Debates* (New York: Garland Publishing Co., 1995), 426–503.

27. On the growth of religious radio, see Carpenter, *Revive Us Again*, 124–40; Hangen, *Redeeming the Dial*, 37–56; and Jeffrey K. Hadden and Charles E. Swann, *Prime-Time Preachers: The Rising Power of Televangelism* (Reading, Mass.: Addison-Wesley, 1981), 69–83. On Armstrong, see Numbers, *Creationists*, 317.

28. See Carpenter, *Revive Us Again*, 73. See also Willard B. Gatewood Jr., "From Scopes to Creation Science: The Decline and Revival of the Evolution Controversy," *South Atlantic Quarterly* 83 (1984): 368–69. For more on Moon, see James Gilbert, *Redeeming Culture: American Religion in an Age of Science* (Chicago: University of Chicago Press, 1997), 121–45.

29. On Morris's ties to Falwell and LaHaye, see Numbers, *Creationists*, 212, 283–84.

30. Morris, *Modern Creationism*, 79. See also Larson, *Summer for the Gods*, 233–34.

31. Louis Gasper, *The Fundamentalist Movement* (The Hague: Mouton and Co., 1963), 15; on the divisions, see pp. 21–37; Carpenter, *Revive Us Again*, 144–47; and Gary J. Clabaugh, *Thunder on the Right: The Protestant Fundamentalists* (Chicago: Nelson-Hall Co., 1974), 69–97.

32. Ron Numbers (*Creationists*, 102–17) has argued that such divisions have characterized virtually every subsequent creationist society. See also Gatewood, "From Scopes to Creation Science," 370–73. For a comparison of the main creationist theories, see Eugenie C. Scott, "The Creation/Evolution Continuum," *Reports of the National Center for Science Education* 19 (1999): 16–23.

33. Numbers, "Creationism in 20th-Century America," 541. See also Morris, *Modern Creationism*, 133. On the ASA, see Numbers, *Creationists*, 158–83, and Gatewood, "From Scopes to Creation Science," 373.

34. See Frederick Lewis Allen, *Only Yesterday: An Informal History of the Nineteen-Twenties* (1931; repr. New York: Harper, 1964), 163–71. See also Larson, *Summer for the Gods*, 225–30.

35. Price elaborated: "Although this trial might not have contributed so much to the hilarity of the unbelievers in all the nations of the civilized world, the subsequent history of all human thinking would inevitably have been radically different." Price, "What Christians Believe about Creation," *Bulletin of Deluge Geology* 2 (1942): 76. The article is included in Ronald L. Numbers, ed., *Early Creationist Journals* (New York: Garland Publishing, Inc., 1995), 269–88. See also Edward J. Larson, *Summer for the Gods*, 236–37.

36. On the failure of the scientific community to take seriously science education in the public schools in this period, see Judith V. Grabiner and Peter D. Miller, "Effects of the Scopes Trial," *Science* 185 (1974): 833. See also Garry Wills, *Under God: Religion and American Politics* (New York: Simon and Schuster, 1990), 108–14. It should be said that after 1929 pro-evolution organizations faced many of the same financial and organizational issues as their antievolution opponents. Maynard Shipley, for example, writing for the Science League of America, sent out plaintive letters to supporters during the 1930s asking them to "send what you can, however small, to help us." Science League fund-raising letter, 6 August 1932, Science League of America Clippings, Rare Book Room, Wilson Library, University of North Carolina, Chapel Hill.

37. Numbers, "Creationism in 20th-Century America," 540. See also Maynard Shipley, "Growth of the Anti-Evolution Movement," *Current History* 32 (1930): 330.

38. See Raymond A. Eve and Francis B. Harrold, *The Creationist Movement in Modern America* (Boston: Twayne Publishers, 1991), 27.

39. Arthur O. Baker and Lewis H. Mills, *Dynamic Biology* (New York: Rand McNally, 1933), 681.

40. Larson, *Trial and Error*, 85–86.

41. Howard K. Beale, *Are American Teachers Free? An Analysis of Restraints upon the Freedom of Teaching in American Schools* (New York: Scribner, [1936]), 238.

42. Dorothy Nelkin, *The Creation Controversy: Science or Scripture in the Schools* (New York: Norton, 1982), 34. See also Webb, *Evolution Controversy*, 109–14.

43. Staggenborg, "Survival of the Women's Movement," 145. See also Suzanne Staggenborg, "Critical Events and the Mobilization of the Pro-Choice Movement," *Research in Political Sociology* 9 (1993): 319–45. On the idea of "citizen surges," see John Lofland, *Polite Protesters: The American Peace Movement of the 1980s* (Syracuse, N.Y.: Syracuse University Press, 1993), 187–212.

44. See Larson, *Trial and Error*, 91; Eve and Harrold, *Creationist Movement*, 28–29; and Nelkin, *Creation Controversy*, 39ff.

45. On the NSF initiatives, including BSCS, see Nelkin, *Creation Controversy*, 40–44. See also Gerald Skoog, "The Topic of Evolution in Secondary School Biology Textbooks, 1900–1977," *Science*

Education 63 (1979): 622–23. In addition to BSCS, the NSF funded "Man: A Course of Study" (MACOS), a social studies program emphasizing the biological basis of human society, which would be adopted by schools in forty-seven states. See Nelkin, *Creation Controversy*, 47–51.

46. On the *Epperson* case, the best analysis is Larson, *Trial and Error*, 98–119. See also "The Ban on the Teaching of Evolution Reaches the Supreme Court," *American Biology Teacher* 60 (1998): 650–60. Another treatment is Peter Irons, *The Courage of Their Convictions* (New York: Free Press, 1988), 207–30. In 1967 Tennessee's Butler bill was repealed, and three years later the Mississippi Supreme Court, citing *Epperson*, declared that state's antievolution statute unconstitutional. See Larson, *Trial and Error*, 104–7, 119–22.

47. Larson, *Trial and Error*, 92. In describing the context for these changes, Larson notes not only the growing numbers of scientists but also the increasing federal support for scientific research (pp. 89–91). Also important was the expanding network of professional scientific societies. See Thomas F. Gieryn, George M. Bevins, and Stephen C. Zehr, "Professionalization of American Scientists: Public Science in the Creation/Evolution Trials," *American Sociological Review* 50 (1985): 392–409.

48. Nelkin, *Creation Controversy*, 46–47.

49. Skoog, "The Topic of Evolution," 634.

50. Quoted in Nelkin, *Creation Controversy*, 47. As Nelkin notes, the fact that the assassination took place from the Texas Schoolbook Depository "was not ignored by textbook opponents."

51. On Price, see Ronald L. Numbers, ed., *Selected Works of George McCready Price* (New York: Garland Publishing, Inc., 1995).

52. See John C. Whitcomb Jr. and Henry M. Morris, *The Genesis Flood: The Biblical Record and Its Scientific Implications* (Philadelphia, Pa.: Presbyterian and Reformed Publishing Co., 1961). For background on the book, see Numbers, *Creationists*, 184–213.

53. Ron Numbers has shown that although the term "creationism" is older than Darwin, it was first popularized by Harold Clark in his 1929 book *Back to Creationism*. In the 1930s Dudley Joseph Whitney of Wheaton College began circulating a newsletter called *The Creationist*. Willard Gatewood notes that the term was popularized in the 1940s by Frank Lewis Marsh in his *Evolution, Creation and Science*. All were students of George McCready Price. See Ronald L. Numbers, "Creating Creationism: Meanings and Uses since the Age of Agassiz," in David Livingstone, D. G. Hart, and Mark A. Noll, eds., *Evangelicals and Science in Historical Perspective* (New York: Oxford University Press, 1999), 234–43. See also Gatewood, "From Scopes to Creation Science," 371–72.

54. R. H. Leitch, in *Bible-Science Newsletter* 18 (1980): 2, quoted in Numbers, "Creationism in 20th-Century America," 543. See also Christopher P. Toumey, *God's Own Scientists: Creationists in a Secular World* (New Brunswick, N.J.: Rutgers University Press, 1994), 31. On the *Bible-Science Newsletter* and its sponsor, the Bible-Science Association based in Caldwell, Idaho, see Morris, *Modern Creationism*, 212–19. On creation science discourse, see Susan Harding, *The Book of Jerry Falwell: Fundamentalist Language and Politics* (Princeton, N.J.: Princeton University Press, 2000), 217–18.

55. Morris, *Modern Creationism*, 222.

56. The story of the C-SRC is told in Numbers, "Creationism in 20th-Century America," 543. See also Nelkin, *Creation Controversy*, 79–80.

57. On the split between the C-SRC and the ICR, see Larson, *Trial and Error*, 128–29. At one point

in the early 1980s, the two organizations became so estranged that the ICR threatened to bring suit for defamation against any media source that misidentified it as the C-SRC. See Toumey, *God's Own Scientists*, 116–17.

58. On the early days of the ICR, see Morris, *Modern Creationism*, 235–61.

59. See Morris, *Modern Creationism*, 261–66. For these figures, see Marvin L. Lubenow, "From Fish to Gish" (San Diego, Calif.: CLP Publishers, 1983), 254–60. On Gish, see Numbers, *Creationists*, 287.

60. On the ICR, see Numbers, *Creationists*, 283–90; Nelkin, *Creation Controversy*, 80–83; Eve and Harrold, *Creationist Movement*, 121–24; and James Moore, "The Creationist Cosmos of Protestant Fundamentalism," in Martin E. Marty and R. Scott Appleby, eds., *Fundamentalisms and Society: Reclaiming the Sciences, the Family, and Education* (Chicago: University of Chicago Press, 1993), 49. See also Toumey, *God's Own Scientists*, 116.

61. Henry Morris, "The ICR Scientists," *Impact* 86 (1980), <http://www.icr.org/index.php?module=articles&action=view&page=163> (23 May 2006).

62. See Larson, *Trial and Error*, 96–97.

63. On the FCC fairness doctrine, see Larson, *Trial and Error*, 97–98. See also Nelkin, *Creation Controversy*, 174–75.

64. On Artist, see Larson, *Trial and Error*, 134–39.

65. Richard Wilhelm ("Chronology and Analysis," 64–65) identifies twenty-four creationism bills introduced in twelve states from 1971 to 1977. Edward Larson (*Trial and Error*, 221) describes the approval of creationist texts or teaching by state agencies in Georgia, Idaho, Indiana, Oklahoma, Oregon, and Tennessee. On the adoption of the "two model" approach by local school districts, see Dean R. Fowler, "The Creationist Movement," *American Biology Teacher* 44 (1982): 540.

66. Henry M. Morris and Donald H. Rohrer, eds., *The Decade of Creation* (San Diego, Calif.: Creation-Life Publishers, 1981), 9. See also Eve and Harrold, *Creationist Movement*, 148–49.

67. See Larson, *Trial and Error*, 131–33, and Eve and Harrold, *Creationist Movement*, 145.

68. See Larson, *Trial and Error*, 133, and Eve and Harrold, *Creationist Movement*, 145.

69. Henry Morris, "Introducing Creationism into Public Schools," *Impact* 20 (1974), <http://www.icr.org/index.php?module=articles&action=view&page=66> (23 May 2006).

70. On the Tennessee decision, see Larson, *Trial and Error*, 137–39. On the "Lemon test," see *Lemon v. Kurzman* 403 US 602 (1971), 612–13.

71. Wendell R. Bird, "Freedom of Religion and Science Instruction in Public Schools," *Yale Law Journal* 83 (1978): 515–70. On the article's importance, see Larson, *Trial and Error*, 147–55; Eve and Harrold, *Creationist Movement*, 147–48; and Nelkin, *Creation Controversy*, 99–100.

72. See Larson, *Trial and Error*, 150–51; Eve and Harrold, *Creationist Movement*, 148–49; and Nelkin, *Creation Controversy*, 100. On the significance of Bird and Ellwanger, see Eugenie C. Scott, "Antievolutionism and Creationism in the United States," *Annual Review of Anthropology* 26 (1997): 273.

73. Quoted from correspondence with Paul Ellwanger, 2 July 1981, in Larson, *Trial and Error*, 151.

74. On the effect of the Scopes trial on *Epperson v. Arkansas*, and especially for Fortas's role, see Larson, *Summer for the Gods*, 253–58.

75. Wendell R. Bird, "Creation-Science and Evolution-Science in Public Schools," *Northern Kentucky Law Review* 9 (1982): 162. Although a similar statement was made at the trial by Darrow

associate Dudley Field Malone, Edward Larson (*Summer for the Gods*, 258) has pointed out that the argument was not in keeping with Darrow's legal strategy, since he was arguing that Tennessee schools should teach only one view, which was evolution. See also Tom McIver, "Creationist Misquotation of Darrow," *Creation/Evolution* 23 (1988): 9.

76. Norman L. Geisler, "Creationism: A Case for Equal Time," *Christianity Today* 26 (1982): 29.

77. In fact, the "Scopes II" label was applied by the press to several cases involving creationist claims from the 1960s on, leading historian Leo P. Ribuffo to ruminate that Scopes II ought to be followed "by 'Scopes III,' 'Scopes IV,' and so on." Ribuffo, "Monkey Trials, Past and Present," *Dissent* 28 (1981): 361.

78. See Charles A. Taylor and Celeste Michelle Condit, "Objectivity and Elites: A Creation Science Trial," *Critical Studies in Mass Communication* 5 (1988): 292–312. See also Marcel C. La Follette, "Creationism in the News: Mass Media Coverage of the Arkansas Trial," in La Follette, ed., *Creationism, Science, and the Law* (Cambridge: MIT Press, 1983), 189–207. For the media's role in shaping these perceptions, see Larry A. Witham, *Where Darwin Meets the Bible: Creationists and Evolutionists in America* (New York: Oxford University Press, 2002), 227–41.

79. Geisler believed that mainstream news sources failed to critically analyze the beliefs of the defense witnesses, which were "either liberal, agnostic, atheistic, or Marxist." Norman L. Geisler, A. F. Brooke II, and Mark J. Keough, *The Creator in the Courtroom: Scopes II* (Milford, Mich.: Mott Media, 1982), 17; see also 14–17. An analysis of the competing rhetorical strategies used in the McLean case is Kary Doyle Smout, *The Creation/Evolution Controversy: A Battle for Cultural Power* (Westport, Conn: Praeger, 1998), 103–78.

80. Quoted in Toumey, *God's Own Scientists*, 45. See also Larson, *Trial and Error*, 162.

81. La Follette, "Creationism in the News," 194.

82. On *McLean*, see Larson, *Trial and Error*, 159–66; Eve and Harrold, *Creationist Movement*, 149–51; and Randy Moore, "The McLean Decision Destroys the Credibility of 'Creation Science,'" *American Biology Teacher* 61 (1999): 92–101.

83. Geisler et al., *Creator in the Courtroom*, 19.

84. Quoted in "Sponsor Sees Victory in End on Act," *Arkansas Gazette*, 6 January 1982. Even before the court's decision was announced, Holsted spoke about future plans: "But if we lose it won't matter that much," he told a reporter for the *Washington Post*. "If the law is unconstitutional it'll be because of something in the language that's wrong. So we'll just change the wording and try again with another bill. . . . We got a lot of time. Eventually we'll get one that's constitutional." Quoted in Philip J. Hilts, "Law Requiring Teaching Creation Faces Trial Today," *Washington Post*, 7 December 1981.

85. See Meyer and Whittier, "Social Movement Spillover," 277–93. See also Staggenborg and Taylor, "Whatever Happened to the Women's Movement?," 43–44; Whittier, *Feminist Generations*, 248–50; and David S. Meyer, "Protest Cycles and Political Process: American Peace Movements in the Nuclear Age," *Political Research Quarterly* 46 (1993): 454–57. See also Meyer, *A Winter of Discontent: The Nuclear Freeze and American Politics* (New York: Praeger, 1990).

86. Quoted in "Republican Candidate Picks Fight with Darwin," *Science* 209 (1980): 1214.

87. John W. Whitehead and John Conlan, "The Establishment of the Religion of Secular Humanism and Its First Amendment Implications," *Texas Tech Law Review* 10 (1978): 1–66.

88. See Tim LaHaye, *The Battle for the Mind* (Old Tappan, N.J.: Fleming H. Revell Co., 1980). On LaHaye and the idea of secular humanism in the NCR, see Michael Lienesch, *Redeeming America: Piety and Politics in the New Christian Right* (Chapel Hill: University of North Carolina Press, 1993), 160–69.

89. Jerry Bergman, "Does Academic Freedom Apply to Both Secular Humanists and Christians?," *Impact* 80 (1980), <http://www.icr.org/index.php?module=articles&action=view&page=162> (23 May 2006).

90. Henry M. Morris, *The Twilight of Evolution* (Grand Rapids, Mich.: Baker Book House, 1963), 24.

91. Quoted in a C-SRC report by Toumey, *God's Own Scientists*, 94. See also Christopher P. Toumey, *Conjuring Science: Scientific Symbols and Cultural Meanings in American Life* (New Brunswick, N.J.: Rutgers University Press, 1996), 117–19.

92. Bergman, "Does Academic Freedom Apply to Both Secular Humanists and Christians?"

93. Quoted in Toumey, *God's Own Scientists*, 203. See also ibid., 48–49; Toumey, *Conjuring Science*, 121–25; and Christopher P. Toumey, "Evolution and Secular Humanism," *Journal of the American Academy of Religion* 61 (1993): 275–301.

94. See Fowler, "Creationist Movement," 539. On the televangelists, see Eve and Harrold, *Creationist Movement*, 134. Another organization that produced antievolutionist films was "Films for Christ" of Mesa, Ariz., which brought out a six-part series called "Origins," featuring creation scientists from the ICR. Ibid.

95. See Eve and Harrold, *Creationist Movement*, 134.

96. On the Gablers, see Nelkin, *Creation Controversy*, 63–65; Eve and Harold, *Creationist Movement in Modern America*, 158–60; Steven Shafersman, "Censorship of Evolution in Texas," *Creation/Evolution* 10 (1982): 30–38; and Eugene F. Provenzo Jr., *Religious Fundamentalism and American Education: The Battle for the Public Schools* (Albany: State University of New York Press, 1990), 31–50. In Texas, as a result of lobbying led by the Gablers, BSCS books were removed from state-approved textbook lists, while biology texts were required to identify evolution as theory rather than fact and as only one of several explanations of origins. In addition to their stand against reading material for being biased against the Bible, reflecting nontraditional gender roles, and encouraging disrespect of America and its capitalist system, the Gablers have opposed the "new math," classroom role-playing, and dictionaries that include colloquial or vulgar language. They once objected to the story of Robin Hood on the grounds that it encouraged socialism. See Eve and Harrold, *Creationist Movement*, 133. On Simonds and Wildmon, see Edward H. Berman, "Fundamentalism, the Schools, and Cultural Politics," *Educational Foundations* 2 (1997): 79. Also emerging as an important voice at this time was James Dobson's Focus on the Family. See Frances R. A. Paterson and Lawrence F. Rossow, " 'Chained to the Devil's Throne': Evolution and Creation Science as a Religio-Political Issue," *American Biology Teacher* 61 (1999): 360.

97. See Larson, *Summer for the Gods*, 258. The survey most often cited was an AP-NBC poll reporting that 76 percent of respondents favored classroom treatment of both creationist and evolutionary theories, while 10 percent supported the exclusive presentation of creationism and 8 percent endorsed the teaching of evolution alone. See Nelkin, *Creation Controversy*, 145–46. The 1988 Williamsburg Charter Survey reported similar findings. See Larson, *Trial and Error*, 157.

98. Morris, *Modern Creationism*, 13.

99. On *Smith v. Mobile*, see Toumey, *God's Own Scientists*, 83–84.

100. For a treatment of this complex series of cases, see Larson, *Trial and Error*, 166–84. See also Eve and Harrold, *Creationist Movement*, 151–545; Randy Moore, "Demanding 'Balanced Treatment,'" *American Biology Teacher* 61 (1999): 175–80; and Bill Keith, *Scopes II: The Great Debate* (Shreveport, La.: Huntington House, Inc., 1982). A Louisiana legislator and creationist writer, Keith applied the "Scopes II" terminology to political and legal proceedings in both Arkansas and Louisiana.

101. Quoted in Stuart Taylor Jr., "Evolution Debate Started by Darwin," NYT, 20 June 1987. Stephen Jay Gould was even more expansive in commenting that *Edwards v. Aguillard* had "ended an important chapter in American social history, one that stretched back to the Scopes trial of 1925." Gould, "Genesis and Geology," *Natural History* 97 (1988): 12. See also Larson, *Trial and Error*, 181–82.

102. *Edwards v. Aguillard*, 482 US 578 (1987), 594.

103. Ibid., 578, 634.

104. Quoted from "Robertson: Court Ruling Disgraceful," *Shreveport (La.) Times*, 20 June 1987, in Larson, *Trial and Error*, 183.

105. For this story, see Toumey, *God's Own Scientists*, 57–59.

106. Ibid., 193, 204, 263.

107. On the Accelerated Christian Education (ACE) curriculum, see Eve and Harrold, *Creationist Movement*, 134.

108. Toumey, *God's Own Scientists*, 263.

109. Joseph Wood Krutch, "The Monkey Trial," *Commentary* 43 (1967): 83. For background, see Larson, *Summer for the Gods*, 239–46; Nicholas M. Aksionczyk, *A Second Look at Fundamentalism, the Scopes Trial, and Inherit the Wind* (El Cajon, Calif.: Institute for Creation Research, 1999), 48; and Elizabeth J. Hayba, "A Comparative Study of *Inherit the Wind* and the Scopes 'Monkey Trial'" (M.A. thesis, University of Tennessee, Knoxville, 1984).

110. Morris, *Modern Creationism*, 69.

111. R. M. Cornelius, "Their Stage Drew All the World," in R. M. Cornelius and John D. Morris, eds., *Scopes: Creation on Trial* (El Cajon, Calif.: Institute for Creation Research, 1995), 20.

112. D. James Kennedy, *The Case for Creation* (Fort Lauderdale, Fla.: Coral Ridge Ministries, and Mesa, Ariz.: Films for Christ, 1988). See also Lawrence Bernabo, "The Scopes Myth: The Scopes Trial in Rhetorical Perspective" (Ph.D. diss., University of Iowa, 1990), 430.

113. On Reed's stealth strategy, see Melissa M. Deckman, *School Board Battles: The Christian Right in Local Politics* (Washington, D.C.: Georgetown University Press, 2004), 83–85. Creationists had been active in local school politics for years, collaborating with other conservative critics in campaigns to censor texts and change offensive curricula. As early as 1974, following violent protests that took place in Kanawha County, West Va., ministers and parents had combined forces in hundreds of school districts across the country to campaign in support of school prayer and opposition to evolution, sex education, and teaching techniques stressing "values clarification." See Eve and Harrold, *Creationist Movement*, 94–99. On the Kanawha protests, see Ann L. Page and Donald A. Clelland, "The Kanawha County Textbook Controversy: A Study of the Politics of Lifestyle Concern," *Social Forces* 57 (1978): 265–81.

114. CEE president Robert Simonds claimed that his organization had helped over five thousand

candidates win school board seats from 1989 to 1992. Following the 1992 elections, he estimated that CEE sympathizers held a majority on over 2,250 local school boards. See "Three R's in California School District Include Religious Right," *Washington Post*, 12 May 1994.

115. See "Judgment Day Approaches for Vista Schools," *Los Angeles Times*, 16 November 1992.

116. Ken Blalack, quoted in Jill Smolowe, "Outfoxing the Right," *Time* 146 (1995): 38. See also Michael Granberry, "New Vision for Vista Schools," *Los Angeles Times*, 14 March 1995. On how Christian conservatives act as school board members, see Deckman, *School Board Battles*, 135–65.

117. Minkoff, "Bending with the Wind," 1689, 1694–1700. Contrary to conventional expectations, the study showed that the oldest and most established organizations were able to act with the greatest flexibility, often adopting the most activist-oriented strategies and the least conservative goals (p. 1689). For a discussion of the concept of "strategy," see ibid., 1668–69. On how activists innovate within repertoires, see Doug McAdam, Sidney Tarrow, and Charles Tilly, *Dynamics of Contention* (Cambridge: Cambridge University Press, 2001), 48–50. See also Colin Barker and Michael Lavalette, "Strategizing and the Sense of Context: Reflections on the First Two Weeks of the Liverpool Docks Lockout, September–October 1995," in David S. Meyer, Nancy Whittier, and Belinda Robnett, eds., *Social Movements: Identity, Culture, and the State* (New York: Oxford University Press, 2002), 142–43.

118. In *Webster v. New Lennox School District* (1990), the U.S. Court of Appeals for the Seventh Circuit declared that school boards could prevent high school science teachers from providing instruction in creation science. In *Peloza v. Capistrano School District* (1994), the Ninth Circuit Court determined that the right to the free exercise of religion for teachers who believed in creationism was not violated when they were required to cover evolution as an accepted scientific theory. In *Freiler v. Tangipahoa Parish Board of Education* (1999), the Fifth Circuit found it unconstitutional for school boards to require teachers to read a disclaimer in class whenever evolution was taught. See Carl Schnee, "Evolution v. Creationism: Fundamentalism, the Scopes Trial, and the Impact of the Recent Creationist Movement" (M.A. thesis, University of Delaware, 2000), 59.

119. On the "wedge strategy," see Barbara Forrest, "The Wedge at Work: How Intelligent Design Creationism Is Wedging Its Way into the Cultural and Academic Mainstream," in Robert T. Pennock, ed., *Intelligent Design Creationism and Its Critics: Philosophical, Theological, and Scientific Perspectives* (Cambridge: MIT Press, 2001), 5–53. Johnson has also applied military metaphors to the strategy, describing the shift from defending creation science to attacking evolution as "leaving the fortress, and heading behind the lines to blow up the other side's headquarters, its ammunition store." Quoted in Nancy Pearcey, "We're Not in Kansas Anymore," *Christianity Today* 44 (2000): 45. See also Pearcey, "The Evolution Backlash," *World* 11 (1997): 12–15. Johnson's books include *Darwin on Trial* (Washington, D.C.: Regnery Gateway, 1991) and the following works published by Inter-Varsity Press (Downers Grove, Ill.): *Reason in the Balance: The Case against Naturalism in Science, Law and Education* (1995); *Defeating Darwinism by Opening Minds* (1997); *Objections Sustained: Subversive Essays on Evolution, Law and Culture* (1998); *The Wedge of Truth: Splitting the Foundations of Naturalism* (1998); and *The Right Questions: Truth, Meaning and Public Debate* (2002). For more on Johnson, see Witham, *Where Darwin Meets the Bible*, 65–70.

120. See Charles B. Thaxton, Walter L. Bradley, and Roger L. Olson, *The Mystery of Life's Origin: Reassessing Current Theories* (New York: Philosophical Library, 1984); Michael Behe, *Darwin's Black Box:*

The *Biochemical Challenge to Evolution* (New York: Free Press, 1996); and William A. Dembski, *The Design Inference: Eliminating Chance through Small Probabilities* (Cambridge: Cambridge University Press, 1998). The best critical view is Robert T. Pennock, *Tower of Babel: The Evidence against the New Creationism* (Cambridge: MIT Press, 1998).

121. For background on ID, see Francis Harrold, Raymond Eve, and John Taylor, "Creationism, American Style: Ideology, Tactics and Rhetoric in a Social Movement," in Simon Coleman and Leslie Carlin, eds., *The Cultures of Creationism: Anti-Evolutionism in English-Speaking Countries* (Aldershot, Hance, England: Ashgate, 2004), 76–81. See also Witham, *Where Darwin Meets the Bible*, 219–23; Frederick Crews, "Saving Us from Darwin," *New York Review of Books*, 48, 16 (2001): 24–27; and Pearcey, "We're Not in Kansas Anymore," 43–49.

122. Phillip E. Johnson, "Review of W. R. Bird, *The Origin of Species Revisited: The Theories of Evolution and of Abrupt Appearance*," *Constitutional Commentary* 7 (1990): 430. On the role of the Foundation for Thought and Ethics, see Witham, *Where Darwin Meets the Bible*, 220–21. For the origin of the term "intelligent design," see Witham, 221.

123. William A. Dembski, "Is Intelligent Design Testable?," *Access Research Network*, 5 October 2001, <http://www.arn.org/docs/dembski/wd_isidtestable.htm> (23 May 2006).

124. "Presenting evidence against evolution *per se* is only bad science, which the First Amendment does not forbid," explained Eugenie Scott, executive director of the National Center for Science Education, a group that tracks creationist efforts. Scott, "Antievolutionism and Creationism," 278. With the adoption of the strategy, wrote Eve and Harrold (*Creationist Movement*, 187), "creationism is being sanitized, until it is no longer overtly recognizable as religious in origin."

125. Quoted in Forrest, "The Wedge at Work," 30.

126. Johnson elaborated on the possibilities: "Whenever I see anybody who's interested in pursuing this question, then I want them to be in our movement," he told Larry Witham (*Where Darwin Meets the Bible*, 68). "We are not the kind of movement that has a doctrine."

127. See, e.g., "A Scientific Dissent from Darwinism," *New York Review of Books*, 48, 17 (2001): 23. Printed as a full-page advertisement in national magazines including the *New Republic* and the *New York Review of Books*, the statement was a short, relatively unspecific expression of skepticism about Darwinian theory that called for careful examination of the evidence. The signers represented a variety of creationist views and came from numerous fields in the natural and social sciences. Most were affiliated in some way with mainstream and secular institutes and universities. For a critical view, see Skip Evans, "Doubting Darwinism through Creative License," *National Center for Science Education*, 8 April 2002, <http://www.ncseweb.org/resources/articles/3416_doubting_darwinism _through_cre_4_8_2002.asp> (23 May 2006). "The most striking thing about the intelligent design folks," said Eugenie Scott, "is their potential to really make anti-evolutionism intellectually respectable." Quoted in James Glanz, "Darwin vs. Design: Evolutionists' New Battle," NYT, 8 April 2001. See also Randy Moore, "Here Come the Secular Creationists," *American Biology Teacher* 62 (2000): 2.

128. On the CRSC, see Forrest, "The Wedge at Work," 6–16; Witham, *Where Darwin Meets the Bible*, 222; and Larry Witham, "Contesting Science's Anti-Religious Bias," *Washington Times*, 29 December 1999. The CRSC has held briefings for members of Congress and their staffs, lobbied at the state level on education and science issues, and sometimes encouraged local groups in efforts

to include ID curricula in science classrooms. See Larry Arnhart, "Chimpanzee Politics and Intelligent Design Theory," paper presented to the 2001 Annual Meeting of the American Political Science Association, August 2001, 3–4, 10. For more on the Discovery Institute, see Karen L. Willoughby, "Discovery Institute Emerging as Force in Creation, Public Policy," *BP (Baptist Press) News*, 15 May 2001, <http://www.bpnews.net/bpnews.asp?ID=10888> (23 May 2006).

129. Johnson, "Review of W. R. Bird," 430.

130. Quoted from "Original Warning Label" (1996–2001), *Alabama Citizens for Science Education*, <http://www.alscience.org/disclaimer.html#pictures> (23 May 2006). See Larson, *Trial and Error*, 202. In November 1999 Oklahoma's State Textbook Committee voted to require a similar disclaimer for any science book that discussed evolution. Three months later, the state's attorney general issued an opinion that the committee had no authority to require such a disclaimer. "Creationism in 2001: A State-by-State Report," People for the American Way (2001), 9. For the report, see <http://www.law.umkc.edu/faculty/projects/ftrials/conlaw/creationismreport.pdf> (23 May 2006).

131. Scott, "Antievolution and Creationism," 284. In response, the National Center for Science Education, the National Association of Biology Teachers, and People for the American Way sent a mailing to the same Alabama teachers that included a critical review of the book. See Karen Schmidt, "Creationists Evolve New Strategy," *Science* 273 (1996): 422.

132. Randy Moore, "Creationism in the United States: The Lingering Threat," *American Biology Teacher* 61 (1999): 335. See also Glanz, "Darwin vs. Design," 1, 32. See also Scott, "Antievolutionism and Creationism," 277–78. At the same time activists appearing before the Illinois Board of Education successfully fought for evolution to be placed in the "controversial issues" category, allowing local school districts to decide how to approach it. See Larson, *Trial and Error*, 201. For more recent examples of "evidence against evolution" efforts, see Larson, 207.

133. See Larson, *Trial and Error*, 196–200.

134. Quoted in Suzanne Perez Tobias, "Standards' Effects Could Evolve Slowly," *Wichita Eagle*, 12 August 1999. On the Kansas controversy, see Larson, *Trial and Error*, 202–5; Edward Larson and Larry Witham, "Inherit an Ill Wind," *Nation* 269 (1999): 26–29; and Pearcey, "We're Not in Kansas Anymore," 42–50. Meanwhile, local school boards began to allow students to initiate discussions of theories of alternative origins. In fact, no sooner had the Georgia legislature defeated a bill that would have given teachers the right to present alternative theories than similar measures appeared before local school boards in Hall, Cobb, Clayton, Oconee, and Valdosta Counties, leading a concerned Eugenie Scott to comment on the "direct relationship between the state level assault and these local level brush-fires" (quoted in Schmidt, "Creationists Evolve New Strategy," 420).

135. See Scott, "Antievolutionism and Creationism," 283–84. See also Percival Davis and Dean H. Kenyon, *Of Pandas and People: The Central Question of Biological Origins*, 2nd ed. (Dallas, Tex.: Haughton Publishing Co., 1993).

136. See Larson, *Trial and Error*, 207.

137. See Larson and Witham, "Inherit an Ill Wind," 27.

138. Glanz, "Darwin vs. Design," 32.

139. See Paterson and Rossow, " 'Chained to the Devil's Throne,' " 361. The Santorum resolution, originally offered as an amendment to the 2001 education funding bill, passed the Senate but

was later shifted by a conference committee from the legislative text to an explanatory conference report. See Larson, *Trial and Error*, 209.

140. See Moore, "The Lingering Threat," 334–35.

141. The report was commissioned by the Discovery Institute. For its findings, see <http://www.discovery.org/articleFiles/PDFs/ZogbyFinalReport.pdf> (23 May 2006).

142. Minkoff, "Bending with the Wind," 1647.

143. Wise quoted from a personal interview with Witham, *Where Darwin Meets the Bible*, 68. See also the criticism of Henry M. Morris, "Neocreationism," *Impact* 296 (1980), <http://www.icr.org/pubs/imp/imp-296.htm> (23 May 2006).

144. See Glanz, "Darwin vs. Design," 32.

145. Pearcey, "We're Not in Kansas Anymore," 47–48.

146. See Larson and Witham, "Inherit an Ill Wind," 32. Among other worries, Graves expressed concern that the debates on evolution would prove harmful to Kansas's ability to compete for economic development. Mike Matson, speaking for the governor, declared: "They'll hear three words: Kansas, evolution and creationism, and will wonder, 'Didn't we deal with this issue in the 1920s?'" Suzanne Perez Tobias and Lillian Zier Martell, "Evolution Debate Puts Kansas in the Spotlight," *Wichita Eagle*, 13 August 1999.

147. Quoted in Larry Witham, "Creationists on Kansas School Panel Defeated," *Washington Times*, 3 August 2000.

148. See Eugenie Scott, "The Struggle for the Schools," *Natural History* 103 (1994): 12. See also Barbara Forrest and Paul R. Gross, *Creationism's Trojan Horse: The Wedge of Intelligent Design* (New York: Oxford University Press, 2004).

149. Quoted in Schmidt, "Creationists Evolve New Strategy," 420.

150. See Witham, *Where Darwin Meets the Bible*, 236–37. See also Cynthia A. McCune, "Framing Reality: Shaping News Coverage of the 1996 Tennessee Debate on Evolution" (M.A. thesis, San Diego State University, 1998).

151. The play was timed to appear during "Scopes Week," a series of events that commemorated the seventy-fifth anniversary of the trial, sponsored in part by the pro-evolution group Kansas Citizens for Science. In response, the Intelligent Design Network convened its own conference on "Darwin, Design, and Democracy" at a local high school. Kate Beem, "Play, Debate to Study Evolution Dispute," *Kansas City Star*, 28 June 2000.

152. Nancy Pearcey, "Scopes in Reverse," *Washington Times*, 24 July 2000.

153. Phillip Johnson, "The Wedge: A Progress Report," *Access Research Network*, 16 April 2001, <http://www.arn.org/docs/pjweekly/pj_wedgeprogress041601.htm> (23 May 2006).

154. Phillip Johnson, "Weekly Wedge Update," *Access Research Network*, 2 July 2001, <http://www.arn.org/docs/pjweekly/pj_weekly_010702.htm> (23 May 2006).

CONCLUSION

1. For a summary of recent surveys, see Glenn Branch, "The Latest Polls on Creationism and Evolution," *National Center for Science Education*, <http://www.ncseweb.org/resources/rncse_content/vol24/7937_the_latest_polls_on_creationis_12_30_1899.asp> (23 May 2006).

2. See Christoph Schoenborn, "Finding Design in Nature," NYT, 7 July 2005. See Cornelia Dean and Laurie Goodstein, "Leading Cardinal Redefines Church's View on Evolution," NYT, 9 July 2005.

3. "Public Divided on Origins of Life," *Pew Forum on Religion and Public Life*, <http://www.ncseweb.org/resources/rncse_content/vol24/7937_the_latest_polls_on_creationis_12_30_1899.asp> (23 May 2006).

4. Randy Moore, "Here Come the Secular Creationists," *American Biology Teacher* 62 (2004): 2–3. On the shift of creationist epistemology from Baconian empiricism to the more critical and subjective conceptions of science advocated by Karl Popper and Thomas Kuhn, see James Moore, "The Creationist Cosmos of Protestant Fundamentalism," in Martin E. Marty and R. Scott Appleby, eds., *Fundamentalisms and Society: Reclaiming the Sciences, the Family, and Education* (Chicago: University of Chicago Press, 1993), 53.

5. For the best overall review, see Ron Number's chapter "Creationism Goes Global" in his *The Creationists: From Scientific Creationism to Intelligent Design*, expanded ed. (Cambridge: Harvard University Press, 2006), 399–431. On creationism in England, Canada, Australia, and New Zealand, see Simon Coleman and Leslie Carlin, eds., *The Cultures of Creationism: Anti-Evolutionism in English-Speaking Countries* (Aldershot, U.K.: Ashgate, 2004), 29–44, 85–164; in Europe, see Fedor Steeman, "Creationism in Europe," *Therefore: Evolution*, <http://www.geocities.com/fedor_steeman/Europe.html> (23 May 2006); in Mexico, see Antonio Lazcano, "Evolution in Mexico," *Reports of the National Center for Science Education* 24 (2004): 22–23; in Kenya, see Peter Fulljames and Leslie Francis, "Creationism among Young People in Kenya and Britain," in Coleman and Carlin, *Cultures of Creationism*, 165–73; and in Turkey, see Ümit Sayin and Aykut Kence, "Islamic Scientific Creationism: A New Challenge in Turkey," *Reports of the National Center for Science Education* 19 (1999): 18–20, 25–29. See also Moore, "Creationist Cosmos," 51–52. It has been reported that one of the Discovery Institute's five-year objectives is the creation of an active intelligent design movement "in Israel, the UK and other influential countries outside the US." See "The Wedge Strategy," <http://www.antievolution.org/features/wedge.html> (23 May 2006).

6. According to the Web site "Charity Navigator," total revenue for Answers in Genesis (FY 2004) was $10,423,222; for the Institute for Creation Research (FY 2005), $4,341,000; and for the Discovery Institute (FY 2004), $3,504,062. For these figures, see <http://www.charitynavigator.org/index.cfm/bay/search.summary/orgid/5214.htm>; <http://www.charitynavigator.org/index.cfm/bay/search.summary/orgid/7485.htm>; and <http://www.charitynavigator.org/index.cfm/bay/search.summary/orgid/9757.htm> (23 May 2006). A 2006 news report lists the annual budget of the U.S. branch of Answers in Genesis as $15 million. See Stephanie Simon, "Their Own Version of a Big Bang," *Los Angeles Times*, 11 February 2006. Of the Discovery Institute's annual budget, approximately $1.2 million goes to the Center for the Renewal of Science and Culture. See Karen L. Willoughby, "Discovery Institute Emerging as Force in Creation, Public Policy," BP (*Baptist Press*) *News*, 15 May 2001, <http://www.bpnews.net/bpnews.asp?ID=10888> (23 May 2006). The Discovery Institute and its center is heavily funded by evangelical Christian foundations such as the MacLellan Foundation of Chattanooga, Tenn., the Henry P. and Susan C. Crowell Trust of Colorado Springs, and the Stewardship Foundation of Tacoma, Wash. According to a 2005 report, the Discovery Institute has received some financial support from 22 foundations, at least two-thirds of

which have explicitly religious missions. Among the most active contributors were conservative philanthropists Howard and Roberta Ahmanson, of Irvine, Calif., whose gifts were estimated to account for one-fourth of Discovery's annual operations. See Jodi Wilgoren, "Politicized Scholars Put Evolution on the Defensive," NYT, 21 August 2005.

7. See Kevin Eigelbach, "Answers in Genesis' Message Being Heard," Kentucky Post, 26 October 2002, <http://www.kypost.com/2002/10/26/genes102602.html> (23 May 2006). See also Randy Moore, "The Business of Creationism," American Biology Teacher 59, 4 (1997): 196. A more recent update is in Moore, "The Dark Side of Creationism," American Biology Teacher 66 (2004): 66. A native of Australia, Ken Ham is no relation to Mordecai Ham, the Baptist evangelist and antievolution campaigner of the 1920s.

8. James Langton, "In the Beginning . . . Adam Walked with Dinosaurs," News.Telegraph, 1 February 2005, <http://www.telegraph.co.uk/news/main.jhtml?xml=/news/2005/01/02/wedeno2. xml&sSheet=/news/2005/01/02/ixworld.html> (23 May 2006).

9. For the Center for Science and Culture, see <http://www.csc.org/>. The International Society for Complexity, Information, and Design is at <http://www.iscid.org/>. The Web address for Access Research Network is <http://www.iscid.org/>. Most of the forty fellows of the Center for Science and Culture are not in residence.

10. See Robert E. Kofahl, Handy Dandy Evolution Refuter (San Diego, Calif.: Beta Books, 1977). In his bibliography of antievolutionist literature, Tom McIver lists over 1,850 books and pamphlets, most of them published since 1920. McIver, Anti-Evolution: An Annotated Bibliography (Jefferson, N.C.: McFarland and Co., Inc., Publishers, 1988).

11. See "Fossil Hominids," Talk.Origins Archive, 7 September 2005, <http://www.talkorigins.org/ faqs/homs/> (23 May 2006).

12. See Raymond A. Eve and Francis B. Harrold, The Creationist Movement in Modern America (Boston: Twayne Publishers, 1991), 68–93. An extensive list of other arguments, together with rebuttals, is "An Index to Creationist Claims," Talk.Origins Archive, 12 May 2006, <http://www. talkorigins.org/indexcc/list.html> (23 May 2006).

13. See, e.g., Tom Wagner, "Darwin vs. the Eye," Creation 16 (1994): 10–13.

14. David N. Menton, "Making Monkeys Out of Man," Answers in Genesis, 28 August 2000, <http://www.answersingenesis.org/docs2/4371gc8-28-2000.asp> (23 May 2006).

15. Quoted in Evan Ratliff, "The Crusade against Evolution," Wired Magazine, 18 October 2004, <http://www.wired.com/wired/archive/12.10/evolution.html> (23 May 2006).

16. Bruce Chapman and Jay W. Richards, "Scopes Trial Symbolism Holds Today," Daily Oklahoman, 26 August 2000, archived at Access Research Network, <http://www.arn.org/docs/richards/jr_ scopessymbolism.htm> (23 May 2006). See also G. Jeffrey MacDonald, "Now Evolving in Biology Classes: A Testier Climate," Christian Science Monitor, 3 May 2005.

17. See "U.S. Congressional Leader Castigated for Creationism Comments," Answers in Genesis, 25 April 2002, <http://www.answersingenesis.org/docs2002/0425delay.asp> (23 May 2006).

18. See David Stout, "Frist Urges 2 Teachings on Life Origin," NYT, 20 August 2005. Democrats like Senator Robert Byrd of West Virginia have expressed support for the teaching of ID as well. See "Primer: History of Intelligent Design and the Creation-Evolution Controversy," IDEA: Intelligent

Design and Evolution Awareness Center, <http://www.ideacenter.org/contentmgr/showdetails.php/id/1119> (23 May 2006).

19. See Elisabeth Bumiller, "Bush Remarks Roil Debate on Teaching of Evolution," *NYT*, 3 August 2005. The statement was not his first endorsement. When asked in the 2000 election campaign about the decision of the Kansas Board of Education, a spokeswoman stated that candidate Bush "believes both [evolution and creationism] ought to be taught." A representative of Democratic candidate Al Gore replied to a similar question in similar terms, saying that Gore "favors the teaching of evolution in the public schools" but that "localities should be free to teach creationism as well." Quoted in Edward Larson and Larry Witham, "Inherit an Ill Wind," *Nation* 269 (1999): 29.

20. See Nick Matzke, "Intelligent Design Bill Proposed in Pennsylvania," *National Center for Science Education*, <http://www.ncseweb.org/resources/news/2005/PA/929_intelligent _design_ bill_propos_4_1_2005.asp> (23 May 2006).

21. See Peter Slevin, "In Kansas, a Sharp Debate on Evolution: Educators Consider Intelligent Design," *Washington Post*, 6 May 2005.

22. Quoted in Claudia Wallis, "The Evolution Wars," *Time*, 15 August 2005, 30. By working at the state level, suggests Wallis, advocates of ID can sometimes avoid being compromised by the religious statements of local activists.

23. See Carey Gillam, "Kansas Moves to Stem Role of Evolution in Teaching," *CNN.com*, 11 August 2005, <http://www.cnn.com/2005/EDUCATION/08/10/life.evolution.reut/> (23 May 2006). See also Jodi Wilgoren, "In Kansas, Darwinism Goes on Trial Once More," *NYT*, 6 May 2005.

24. Quoted in Karen Schmidt, "Creationists Evolve New Strategy," *Science* 273 (1996): 422.

25. According to People for the American Way, the Thomas More Center in 2000 offered to provide free legal services to the Kanawha County, West Va., School Board if it agreed to purchase the antievolution textbook *Pandas and People* for use by teachers. See "Creationism in 2001: A State-By State Report," People for the American Way, 2001, 14, found at <http://www.law.umkc.edu/faculty/projects/ftrials/conlaw/creationismreport.pdf> (23 May 2006).

26. Quoted in Schmidt, "Creationists Evolve New Strategy," 421.

27. Quoted in Cornelia Dean, "Evolution Takes a Back Seat in U.S. Classes," *NYT*, 1 February 2005.

28. For a summary, see Lawrence S. Lerner, "Teaching Evolution, State by State," *Freethought Today* 18 (2001), <http://www.ffrf.org/fttoday/2001/jan_feb01/lerner.html> (23 May 2006). The complete report is Lawrence S. Lerner, "Good Science, Bad Science: Teaching Evolution in the States," *Thomas B. Fordham Foundation*, 1 September 2000, <http://www.edexcellence.net/FOUN DATION/publication/publication.cfm?id=42&pubsubid=662> (23 May 2006).

29. See Michael L. Rutledge and Melissa A. Warden, "Evolutionary Theory, the Nature of Science, and High School Biology Teachers: Critical Relationships," *American Biology Teacher* 62 (2000): 23–31, and Rutledge and Melissa A. Mitchell, "High School Biology Teachers' Knowledge Structure, Acceptance, and Teaching of Evolution," *American Biology Teacher* 64 (2002): 21–28. Similar findings for teachers in Pennsylvania, Oklahoma, South Dakota, and Tennessee can be found in Jeffrey Weld and Jill C. McNew, "Attitudes toward Evolution," *Science Teacher* 66 (1999): 27–31. See

also Randy Moore, "Educational Malpractice: Why Do So Many Biology Teachers Endorse Creationism?," *Skeptical Inquirer* 25 (2001): 40–41.

30. Quoted in Dean, "Evolution Takes a Back Seat."

31. Moore, "Educational Malpractice," 39.

32. See, e.g., Donald Aguillard, "Evolution Education in Louisiana Public Schools: A Decade Following *Edwards v. Aguillard*," *American Biology Teacher* 61 (1999): 182–88; P. G. Eglin, "Creationism versus Evolution: A Study of the Opinions of Georgia Science Teachers" (Ph.D. diss., Georgia State University, 1983); B. A. Osif, "Evolution and Religious Beliefs: A Survey of Pennsylvania High School Teachers," *American Biology Teacher* 59 (1997): 552–56; Ganga Shankar and Gerald D. Skoog, "Emphasis Given Evolution and Creationism by Texas High School Biology Teachers," *Science Education* 77 (1993): 221–33; Robert Tatina, "South Dakota High School Biology Teachers and the Teaching of Evolution," *American Biology Teacher* 51 (1989): 275–80; Weld and McNew, "Attitudes toward Evolution," 27–31; and Michael Zimmerman, "The Evolution-Creation Controversy: Opinions of Ohio High School Biology Teachers," *Ohio Journal of Science* 87 (1987): 115–25.

33. See Randy Moore and Karen Kramer, "The Teaching of Evolution and Creationism in Minnesota," *American Biology Teacher* 67 (2005): 457–66.

34. Quoted in Steven Kemper, "Evolution On Trial," *Smithsonian* 35 (2005): 56, 54.

35. See Aguillard, "Evolution Education in Louisiana," 186, 184. See also Moore, "Educational Malpractice," 42.

36. Moore and Kramer, "Teaching of Evolution and Creationism in Minnesota," 462.

37. Quoted in Dean, "Evolution Takes a Back Seat."

38. Quoted in MacDonald, "Now Evolving in Biology Classes."

39. See Jonathan Wells, "Ten Questions to Ask Your Biology Teacher about Evolution," *Icons of Evolution*, <http://www.iconsofevolution.com/tools/questions.php3> (23 May 2006). See also Wells, *Icons of Evolution* (Washington, D.C.: Regnery Publishing, Inc., 2000).

40. Williamson and Wachholz quoted in MacDonald, "Now Evolving in Biology Classes."

41. Quoted in Laurie Goodstein, "Issuing Rebuke, Judge Rejects Teaching of Intelligent Design," NYT, 21 December 2005. For the full decision, see <http://www.pamd.uscourts.gov/kitzmiller/kitzmiller_342.pdf> (23 May 2006). See also Margaret Talbot, "Darwin in the Dock," *New Yorker* 81, 39 (2005): 66–77.

42. Quoted in "Dover Intelligent Design Decision Criticized as a Futile Attempt to Censor Science Education," *Discovery Institute News*, 20 December 2005, <http://www.discovery.org/scripts/viewDB/index.php?command=view&id=3107&program=News&callingPage=discoMainPage> (23 May 2006).

43. Quoted in ibid. See also William Dembski's comment on the ruling: "I think the big lesson is, let's go to work and really develop this theory and not try to win this in the court of public opinion." Quoted in Goodstein, "Issuing Rebuke."

44. See "Public View of Creationism and Evolution Unchanged, Says Gallup," *National Center for Science Education*, 19 November 2004, <http://www.ncseweb.org/resources/news/2004/US/724_public_view_of_creationism_and_11_19_2004.asp> (23 May 2006).

45. Quoted in Pam Belluck, "Evolution Dealt a Defeat in Kansas Vote," NYT, 3 August 2000.

46. See Talbot, "Darwin in the Dock," 77.

47. Quoted in Laurie Goodstein, "Evolution Slate Outpolls Rivals," NYT, 9 November 2005. See also Gary Gately, "A Town in the Spotlight Wants Out of It," NYT, 21 December 2005.

48. Quoted in John Hurdle, "Leading Republican Differs with Bush on Evolution," *Free Republic,* 4 August 2005, <http://www.freerepublic.com/focus/f-news/1457027/posts> (23 May 2006).

49. Ross Douthat, "How Intelligent Design Hurts Conservatives (by Making Us Look Like Crackpots)," *New Republic Online,* 16 August 2005, <https://ssl.tnr.com/p/docsub.mhtml?i=w050 815&s=douthat081605> (23 May 2006). Douthat called ID a "poisoned chalice for conservatives." He continued: "There's already a public perception, nurtured by the media and by scientists themselves, that conservatives oppose the 'scientific' position on most bioethical issues. Once intelligent design runs out of steam, leaving its conservative defenders marooned in a dinner-theater version of *Inherit the Wind,* this liberal advantage is likely to swell considerably."

50. Quoted in Amy Worden, "Robertson Says Dover Deserves Snub from God," *Philadelphia Inquirer,* 11 November 2005.

51. Jonathan Wells, "Why I Went for My Second Ph.D.," *The Words of the Wells Family,* <http://www.tparents.org/library/unification/talks/wells/DARWIN.htm> (23 May 2006).

52. Quoted in Laurie Goodstein, "Intelligent Design Might Be Meeting Its Maker," NYT, 4 December 2005. See also Carl Wieland, "AiG's views on the Intelligent Design Movement," *Answers in Genesis,* 30 August 2002, <http://www.answersingenesis.org/docs2002/0830_IDM.asp> (23 May 2006); and Henry Morris, "The Design Revelation," *Back to Genesis,* 1 February 2005, <http://www.icr.org/index.php?module=articles&action=print&ID=476> (23 May 2006).

53. Morris, "The Design Revelation."

54. See George F. Bishop, "The Religious Worldview and American Beliefs about Human Origins," *The Public Perspective* 9 (1998): 39–44.

55. See "CWRU Faculty Report Findings on Evolution, Intelligent Design Poll of Ohio's Scientists," *Case Western Reserve University,* 4 October 2002, <http://www.cwru.edu/pubaff/univcomm/2002/10-02/inteldesign.htm> (23 May 2006). See also "Survey of Scientists Supports Evolution, Rejects 'Intelligent Design,'" *National Center for Science Education,* 11 October 2002, <http://www.ncseweb.org/resources/news/2002/OH/878_survey_of_scientists_supports__10_11_2002.asp> (23 May 2006). On the religious views of contemporary scientists, see Edward J. Larson and Larry Witham, "Scientists Are Still Keeping the Faith," *Nature* 386 (1997): 435–36. See also Larson and Witham, "Leading Scientists Still Reject God," *Nature* 394 (1998): 313.

56. See Moore and Kramer, "Teaching of Evolution and Creationism in Minnesota," 462. In this study of Minnesota science teachers, the authors found that the percentage of biology teachers including evolution in their courses increased from 69 percent in 1994 to 88 percent in 2003. They also found that the percentage of teachers who gave at least six class hours to evolution increased from 43 percent in 1994 to 57 percent in 2000.

57. Of those supporting the teaching of evolutionary theory, 20 percent stated that evolution only should be taught; 17 percent indicated that evolution only should be taught in science classes, but that other religious views on the origins of humans should be allowed in other nonscience courses; and 29 percent were of the opinion that both evolution and creationism should be taught in science classes, but that it should be made clear that evolution is a scientific theory whereas creationism is "a belief, not science." See "Public Wants Evolution, Not Creation, in Science

Class, National Poll Shows," *People for the American Way*, 10 March 2000, <http://www.pfaw.org/pfaw/general/default.aspx?oid=1903> (23 May 2006). It should be noted that the poll was commissioned by People for the American Way, an organization that is strongly opposed to admitting creationism into public school science classes.

58. Quoted in "Reading the Polls on Evolution and Creationism," Pew Research Center Pollwatch, *Pew Research Center for People and the Press*, 28 September 2005, <http://people-press.org/commentary/display.php3?AnalysisID=118> (23 May 2006). On the 2005 Gallup survey, see ibid.

59. Quoted in Jim Brown and Jody Brown, "Intelligent Design Introduced in PA Town While ACLU Watches," *Agape Press*, 24 January 2005, <http://headlines.agapepress.org/archive/1/242005b.asp> (23 May 2006).

60. See "NCSE Project Steve," *National Center for Science Education*, 16 February 2003, <http://www.ncseweb.org/resources/articles/3541_project_steve_2_16_2003.asp> (23 May 2006). For a current count, see the "Steve-O-Meter" at <http://www.ncseweb.org/resources/articles/meter.html> (23 May 2006). Lists of creation scientists can be found at the Discovery Institute, <http://www.dissentfromdarwin.org>; at the Institute for Creation Research (which has separate listings for physical and biological scientists), <http://www.icr.org/research/index/research_physci/> and <http://www.icr.org/research/index/research_biosci/>; and at Answers in Genesis, <http://www.answersingenesis.org/home/area/bios/#presentsci> (23 May 2006).

61. "The Evolution Controversy in Our Schools," *National Academy of Sciences*, 4 March 2005, <http://www.nasonline.org/site/PageServer?JServSessionIdr010=otfb119ac2.app1a&pagename=NEWS_letter_president_03042005_BA_evolution> (23 May 2006).

62. Quoted in Richard Monastersky, "On the Front Lines in the War over Evolution," *Chronicle of Higher Education* 52 (2006): A14.

63. Stephen C. Meyer, "Teach the Controversy on Origins," *Center for Science and Culture*, <http://www.discovery.org/scripts/viewDB/index.php?program=CSC&command=view&id=1134> (23 May 2006). See also David K. DeWolf, Stephen C. Meyer, and Mark Edward DeForrest, "Teaching the Origins Controversy: Science, Religion, or Speech," *Utah Law Review* 39 (2000): 39–110. Critics of the concept are Eugenie C. Scott and Glenn Branch, "Evolution: What's Wrong with Teaching the Controversy,' " *Trends in Ecology and Evolution* 18 (2003): 499–502, and Charles Haynes, " 'Teaching the Controversy' over Evolution Could Be Disastrous," *First Amendment Freedom Forum*, 27 October 2002, <http://www.freedomforum.org/templates/document.asp?documentID=17157> (23 May 2006).

64. See "Cobb County Policy on Objective Origins Science," *Center for Science and Culture*, <http://www.discovery.org/scripts/viewDB/index.php?command=view&id=1396> (23 May 2006).

65. Quoted in Jerry Adler, "Doubting Darwin," *Discovery Institute News*, 30 January 2005, <http://www.discovery.org/scripts/viewDB/index.php?command=view&program=CSC%20-%20Views%20and%20News&id=2404> (23 May 2006). For Meyer's view that the stickers were a "dumb idea," see Linda Shaw, "Theory of Intelligent Design: A Debate Evolves," *Seattle Times*, 31 March 2005.

66. Quoted in Kim Minugh, "Father of Intelligent Design," *Sacramento Bee*, 11 May 2006.

67. Next time, said Eugenie Scott, "they'll be smarter about concealing their religious intent" (quoted in Goodstein, "Issuing Rebuke").

68. Quoted in Peter Slevin, "Battle on Teaching Evolution Sharpens," *Washington Post*, 14 March 2005.

69. See Jodi Wilgoren, "Kansas Approves Challenges to Evolution," NYT, 9 November 2005.

70. "Nothing Wrong with Kansas: State Voters Move Science Education Out of the Victorian Era," *Washington Post*, 6 August 2006. See also Monica Davey and Ralph Blumenthal, "Fight over Evolution Shifts in Kansas School Board," NYT, 3 August 2006.

71. Quoted in *The World's Most Famous Court Trial: Tennessee Evolution Case* (Cincinnati, Ohio: National Book Co., [ca. 1925]), 316.

Index

ture of, 198, 199, 200–205, 226; development of issues, 199, 205–12, 226; connections with other movements, 205, 212–19, 226; strategies and goals of, 205, 219–22, 224–26; collective identity of, 226, 227; cyclical course of, 234. *See also* Cycle of contention; Evolution--issue; Political opportunities and antievolution movement

Anti-immigrant agitation, 89, 118

Antinuclear movement, 258 (n. 40)

Anti-Semitism, 89, 113–14, 183, 186, 200

Archaeological science, 22, 246 (n. 34)

Arizona, 208

Arkansas: antievolution bills in, 115, 191, 205, 272 (n. 2); and teaching of evolution, 171; antievolution movement in, 183, 185–86, 190–91, 193; and balanced treatment bill, 210, 211–12, 215, 216; intelligent design bills in, 231

Armstrong, Herbert W., 202

Artist, Russell, 208

Ash, Roberta, 199

Association of American Colleges, 126, 277 (n. 83)

Atheism: and secular society, 61; higher education associated with, 64, 69; and college faculty, 65, 66, 67, 68, 72, 75; evolution associated with, 70, 72, 91, 125, 183, 263 (n. 18); and college presidents, 77; scientific community associated with, 110, 111; Darrow accused of, 144; and Scopes trial, 145, 151; and evolution debates, 178; and secular humanism, 213, 215

Bacon, Francis, 21, 30, 92, 95, 110

Bailey, Kenneth K., 195–96, 274 (n. 29), 298 (n. 118)

Baker, Arthur O., 204

Baldwin, Roger, 118, 144, 277 (n. 83), 287 (n. 73)

Baptist Bible Union (BBU), 45, 51, 56

Baptists: and fundamentalism, 44–45, 49, 51–52, 54, 56, 251 (n. 49), 253 (n. 74); and teaching of evolution in colleges, 79; and teaching of evolution in public schools, 119; and divisions among elites, 132; and antievolution movement, 185

Bateson, William, 94–95, 229, 266 (n. 57)

Bauer, Gary, 213

Baylor University, 77, 79–80, 236

Beach, Henry, 31

Beale, Charles H., 151

Behe, Michael, 220, 228

Bendroth, Margaret, 38

Benford, Robert, 60, 258 (n. 40)

Bennetta, William, 232

Bergman, Jerry, 213–14

Bible colleges, 36–37, 42, 201

Bible conferences, 11, 36–38, 40–44, 47, 201, 202

Bible Crusaders of America, 174, 175, 176, 188, 196, 292 (n. 21)

Bible Institute of Los Angeles (Biola), 36, 42, 43

Biblical criticism, 18–19, 25, 69

Biological Science Curriculum Study (BSCS), 205, 206, 209

Bird, Wendell, 210, 215

Birge, Edward A., 77, 78

Bishop, George, 25

Blanchard, Charles A., 43, 258 (n. 37), 297 (n. 86)

Blount, A. A., 210

Blue laws, 27, 88

Bogard, Ben, 191, 193, 194, 195

Bolshevism, 91, 123

Boundaries of social movements and collective identity, 9, 16–24, 27–28, 33

Bradbury, O. C., 261 (n. 86)

Brennan, William, 216

Bridging of issues, 84, 85–91, 114

Brockman, W. F., 154

Brooks, Eugene C., 135

Brooks, Samuel P., 77–78, 80

and evolution issue, 132, 228; and divisions among elites, 132, 278 (n. 90); and intelligent design, 224; and creationism, 236

Center for Science and Culture, 228, 229

Center for the Renewal of Science and Culture (CRSC), 221, 228, 310–11 (n. 128), 313 (n. 6)

Cerulo, Karen, 9

Chapman, Bruce, 230

Chase, Harry W., 134, 135, 136, 279 (nn. 104, 107)

Chautauqua circuit, 43, 62, 148, 256 (n. 13), 283 (n. 19)

Christian Coalition, 218–19

Christian Heritage College, 207

Christian schools, 217

Christian Science, 25

Christy, John R., 232–33

Citizens for Excellence in Education, 219, 308–9 (n. 114)

Citizens for Fairness in Education, 210

Civil Rights Act of 1964, 165

Civil rights groups, 121

Civil rights movement, 140, 141, 147, 165, 214

Clark, Constance Areson, 106, 108, 270 (n. 119)

Clark, Harold, 304 (n. 53)

Clark, J. R., 186

Clarke, E. Y., 177, 180, 189, 196

Class issues, 38, 39, 73, 87, 182–83

Cloward, Richard, 121

Cobb, Collier, 279 (nn. 104, 107)

Cochran, Michael, 230

Cohen, Jean, 9

Colby, Bainbridge, 289 (n. 94)

Cole, Stewart G., 9, 60

Collective identity: and social movements, 5; role of discourse in, 7; of fundamentalists, 9, 10, 33, 34, 36; and consciousness, 9, 10–14, 16, 33; and boundaries of movements, 9, 16–24, 27–28, 33; and politicization, 9, 24–33, 34; adaptation of, 219; of antievolution movement, 226, 227

College students: lack of interest in religion, 59, 61, 65, 66, 67, 68, 69, 72, 80, 256 (n. 9); Protestant churches' programs for, 59, 61–62; temptations of, 62, 64, 73; firsthand accounts of, 64, 65, 80–81; social surveys of, 67–68. See also Higher education

Committee for Excellence in Education/ National Association of Christian Educators, 215

Commonsense philosophy, 92

Communities of discourse, 7

Concerned Women for America, 215

Congregationalists, 52

Conklin, Edwin Grant, 84, 101–2

Connally, John, 206

Connor, Eugene "Bull," 154

Connor, Henry Grove, 134–35

Consciousness, and collective identity, 9, 10–14, 16, 33

Conservative evangelicals: concerns of, 8; fragmentation of, 9; collective consciousness of, 10; and Christ's Second Coming, 14; and boundaries, 17; and social reform, 32, 248 (nn. 65, 66); collective identity of, 34; institutions of, 36; and intelligent design, 220, 221, 222, 236; and antievolution movement, 227. See also Fundamentalism

Conservative social reformers, 4–5, 88, 89, 117, 122

Conversion narratives, 13–14, 245 (n. 15)

Coolidge, Calvin, 151

Costain, Anne, 199

Court cases, 205, 208–13, 215–16, 219–20, 234, 235, 238, 308 (n. 101), 309 (n. 118), 316 (n. 43)

Creationism: and public opinion, 1, 212, 215, 225, 235, 307 (n. 97), 317 (n. 57); as subject in public schools, 1–2, 231, 232, 233, 234; and fundamentalism, 9, 221; and themes of speeches and pamphlets, 30; and science and inerrancy of Bible, 94; divisions in, 200, 203, 221, 224, 236, 303

(n. 32); and antievolution movement, 200, 203, 227; political potential of, 208, 234–35; and balanced treatment bills, 210–12; and New Christian Right, 212–17; and political conservatives, 213, 215–19, 231, 234–36; and secular humanism, 213–16; decline in, 216–17; and *Inherit the Wind*, 217–18; and local school board politics, 218–19, 308 (n. 113), 308–9 (n. 114); strategies and goals of, 219–22, 224–26, 238, 309 (n. 119), 310 (nn. 124, 127); as international movement, 228; organizations of, 228–29; intelligent design as relabeled version of, 234; allies of, 235; public support for, 237; continued commitment of, 238–39; history of, 304 (n. 53). *See also* Antievolution movement; Creation science; Intelligent design

Creation science, 198, 200, 202, 206, 207–12, 215–17, 219–22, 228

Creation-Science Research Center (C-SRC), 207, 208, 214, 304–5 (n. 75)

Creation story, 1, 86, 93, 263 (n. 14)

Croft, J. D., 101

Crosby, Howard, 25, 27–28, 246 (n. 44)

Curriculum: creationism's effect on, 2–3, 208, 215, 219, 232–33; Sunday school, 44; and state education boards, 73–74; Bryan on, 110; commissions on, 118; and Scopes trial, 155; censorship of, 178; evolution excluded from, 204–5; evolution included in, 205–6, 210; of Christian schools, 217; and intelligent design, 224; and antievolution movement, 232

Cycle of contention: between new and old organizations, 171, 184–86, 188, 226, 228–29, 313–14 (n. 6); and acceleration and diffusion of conflict, 172, 173–78, 180, 227; and social movements, 172, 180, 184, 188, 291 (n. 2); and new frames and repertoires, 180–84, 226; and interaction between activists and authorities, 188–91, 193–97

Cyclical theory of protest. *See* Cycle of contention

Daniels, Josephus, 135

Darby, John Nelson, 14

Darrow, Clarence: and confrontation with Bryan, 139, 144, 158–59, 160, 162–64, 165, 168, 169; interviews on Scopes trial, 145–46; public support of, 149, 285 (n. 52); characterization of, 151, 286 (n. 58); strategy of, 156, 157–60, 162, 306 (n. 75); characterization of Scopes trial, 168–69, 211, 212, 289–90 (n. 111), 305–6 (n. 75); dramatic portrayals of, 217, 218; reception in Dayton, 284 (n. 32); media as supportive of, 285 (n. 46); and evolution debates, 294 (n. 42)

Dart, Raymond, 103

Darwin, Charles, 8, 28–30, 70, 85, 248 (n. 59)

Darwinism: and theistic evolution, 22–23, 28; scientific critics of, 29, 30; fundamentalist critics of, 29–31; application of, 31; Social Darwinism confused with, 31, 70, 85–86, 87, 214; and higher education, 60, 69–70, 71, 72; political radicalism associated with, 90–91; and teaching of evolution, 230–31. *See also* Evolution

David Lipscomb College, 208

Davidson, Donald, 181

Davis, Derek, 236

Davis, Watson, 147

Dawson, John William, 94

"Day-age" theory, 23, 128, 196, 203, 204, 276 (n. 49)

Dayton, Tenn., 141–42, 145, 169, 185, 283 (n. 27), 285 (n. 53)

Dayton Progressive Club, 142, 145, 146, 149, 150, 153, 284 (n. 30), 285 (n. 53)

DeBerg, Betty, 38, 88

Delaware, 176

DeLay, Tom, 231

Dembski, William, 220, 221, 228, 316 (n. 43)

Democratic National Convention (1924), 129, 276 (n. 64)

Democratic Party, 122, 123, 147, 194

Dennert, Eberhard, 29

Destiny in Dayton (play), 218

Discourse: communities of, 7; of fundamentalism, 9, 16, 32–33; and martial metaphors, 32–33, 45, 54, 55, 77, 150, 225, 309 (n. 119)

Discovery Institute, 221, 222, 228, 230, 231, 234, 238, 313–14 (nn. 5, 6)

Dispensationalism, 14, 16, 36, 39, 41, 128

Divisions among elites: and political opportunity structures, 116, 117; and antievolution movement, 131–38

Dixon, A. C: and Stewart, 8, 10; as editor of *The Fundamentals*, 11, 25; as fundamentalist minister, 37; and founding of fundamentalism, 40; and networks, 43; and Fundamentalist Fellowship, 44; and Norris, 49; and teaching of evolution, 69; on evolution as grounded in Greek philosophy, 86; on family issues, 88; and Ku Klux Klan, 90; on science, 92–93, 95; and inerrancy of Bible, 206

Dixon, Thomas, Jr., 90

Dobson, James, 307 (n. 96)

Douglas, Lloyd, 99–100, 111

Douthat, Ross, 235, 317 (n. 49)

Dow, G. S., 80

Dubois, Eugene, 104

Eagle Forum, 215

Edinger, Steve, 231

Educational elite, 112–13, 271 (n. 142)

Educational Research Analysts, 215

Edwards v. Aguillard (1987), 215–16, 219, 220, 308 (n. 101)

Einstein, Albert, 92

Eisinger, Peter K., 116

Eldredge, Niles, 229

Eliot, Charles W., 126, 275 (n. 48)

Elliott, George, 268 (n. 93)

Ellis, George W., 275 (n. 44)

Ellwanger, Paul, 210

England, Howell, 178

Epperson v. Arkansas (1968), 205, 210

Erdman, Charles R., 26, 247 (n. 53)

Ervin, Sam, Jr., 135

Eugenics movement, 39, 87

Eve, Raymond, 229

Everson v. Board of Education (1947), 209

Everts, W. W., 95

Evolution

—debates over: and alignment of evolution issue, 83–85; Potter-Straton, 86–87, 95, 102, 104, 105, 106, 178; and monkey metaphor, 100; and public education campaign for evolution, 109; and state legislatures, 116, 133; and Scopes trial, 144, 153, 155, 283 (n. 19); Riley-Metcalf, 177–78; audiences of, 196, 299–300 (n. 137); and public awareness, 230; admission for, 294 (n. 43)

—issue: emergence as fundamentalist concern, 60, 61, 70, 76–77, 83; and political conservatives, 86, 88–91; public education campaign for, 109–10; and Catholic Church, 132, 228; declining interest in, 203; and creationists' "wedge" strategy, 220–22, 224–25, 310 (nn. 124, 127), 311 (n. 134). *See also* Alignment of evolution issue; Framing of evolution issue; Staging of evolution issue

—theory of: and public opinion, 1, 228, 235; critics of, 2, 8, 22, 85, 94–95, 229, 235, 238, 265–66 (n. 53); and *The Fundamentals*, 22–23, 28–32, 33; and fundamentalists' mobilization, 35–36; African Americans' concerns about, 39, 250–51 (n. 24); and higher education, 65, 69, 71–72; atheism associated with, 70, 72, 91, 125, 183, 263 (n. 18); secular society associated with, 70, 82, 227; in public schools, 73–74; fundamentalists' interpretation of, 84–85, 229;

and length of life on earth, 97–98; and
artistic depictions of evolution, 105–6,
108–9, 269 (n. 116), 269–70 (n. 117), 270
(n. 119); scientific status of, 209; support
for, 236–38. *See also* Darwinism; Teaching
of evolution
Extension of issues, 84, 99–106, 108–9, 114

Fairhurst, Alfred, 64–65, 67, 73
Faith-science differences, 21–23, 27–28, 35
Falwell, Jerry, 203, 213, 215, 216
Family issues, 88, 89. *See also* Parents
Faunce, William H. P., 259 (n. 60)
Federal Communications Commission (FCC),
208
Federal Council of Churches, 53, 55, 126, 128
Feminism, 38, 200, 212. *See also* Women's
movement
Ferguson, James E., 119
Ferguson, Miriam "Ma," 119, 177
Ferguson, W. F., 142
Feuerbach, Ludwig, 18
First Amendment, 209, 210, 213, 234
Florida, 115, 130, 131, 133, 176, 219, 278 (n. 93)
Florida Purity League, 180
Ford, Henry, 186
Fort, John P., 146
Fortas, Abe, 210
Fosdick, Harry Emerson, 51–52, 84, 111
Fossils, 103–5, 108, 204, 229–30, 269 (n. 107)
Fotergill, Charles, 80
Foundation for Thought and Ethics, 220, 222
Fowler, George, 100
Fox, Terry, 239
Frames: function of, 60; tasks of framing pro-
cess, 60, 84
Framing of evolution issue: and motivation,
60, 76–82; and diagnosis of problem, 61–
62, 64–68; and prognosis/solutions, 68–
76; and alignment, 84; and new frames and
repertoires, 180–84, 226. *See also* Align-
ment of evolution issue

Frandsen, John, 233
Frank, Glenn, 128
Freiler v. Tangipahoa Parish Board of Education
(1999), 309 (n. 118)
Frist, Bill, 231
Fuller, Charles E., 201
Fundamentalism: and antievolution movement, 8, 60, 201, 227; and collective identity, 9, 10, 33, 34, 36; discourse of, 9, 16,
32–33; and creationism, 9, 221; five points
of, 9–10, 128; network structures of, 36,
37, 42–46, 49, 57, 201; and secular society,
38, 57, 59, 61, 62, 70, 255 (n. 106); founding of, 40–42; doctrinal statement of, 41;
conflicts within, 56–57; evolution as issue
of, 60, 70, 76–77, 83; Mencken on, 182,
295–96 (n. 66); meaning of, 276 (n. 60).
See also Fundamentals, The; Mobilization;
Politicization
Fundamentalist Fellowship, 44–45, 49, 56
Fundamentalist League of Greater New York, 45
Fundamentalist publications: and activating
potential, 36, 37, 250 (n. 16); and networks, 42, 44, 49; and motivation to participate, 47, 49, 51, 252–53 (nn. 64, 67);
and Norris, 49, 253 (n. 67); and Bryan's
speeches, 62; and explanations of evolution, 70; and antievolution movement, 80;
and Scopes trial, 147; expansion of, 201
Fundamentals, The: and Stewart, 8, 9, 10–11, 55,
56, 254 (n. 100); and collective identity, 9,
10, 33, 34, 36; and consciousness, 10–14,
16, 33; biblical exegesis in, 11, 12, 18; and
inerrancy of Bible, 11, 12, 18–20, 25; personal testimonies in, 12–14, 245 (n. 15);
and secular society, 13–14, 26–27, 245
(n. 15); prophetic language of, 14, 16;
audience of, 17, 23–24; as movement, 17,
24, 245 (n. 21); and boundaries of fundamentals movement, 17–24, 27–28, 33; and
science, 21–22, 27–30; and evolutionary
theory, 22–23, 28–32, 33; essays in later

volumes of, 24–25, 28, 32; and politicization, 24–33, 34; and enemies of Christianity, 25–27, 28, 31–32, 33, 247 (n. 45);
combative conservatism in, 32

Furniss, Norman, 2, 3, 9, 35–36, 37, 60, 172

Gabler, Mel, 215, 307 (n. 96)
Gabler, Norma, 215, 307 (n. 96)
Gaebelein, Arno C., 32, 37, 41, 248 (n. 63)
Gaines, Noel, 125, 275 (n. 44)
Galileo, 21, 22
Gamson, William, 7, 60, 116
Gasper, Louis, 203
Gatewood, Willard, 117, 278 (n. 85), 279
    (n. 105), 295 (n. 58), 304 (n. 53)
Geisler, Norman, 211, 212, 306 (n. 79)
Georgia, 131, 173, 183, 222, 231, 232, 238, 272
    (n. 2), 311 (n. 134)
Ginger, Ray, 140
Gish, Duane, 208
Gladden, Washington, 128
Glass, Carter, 195
Glasser, Ira, 216
Goals 2000 legislation, 222
Godsey, John L., 289 (n. 94)
Goffman, Erving, 60
Gore, Al, 315 (n. 19)
Gould, Stephen Jay, 211, 229, 237, 308 (n. 101)
Graham, Billy, 275 (n. 37)
Graham, James L., 280 (n. 113)
Grantham, Dewey, 119, 122
Graves, Bill, 224, 225, 312 (n. 146)
Gray, Asa, 22
Gray, James M., 12, 37, 42, 69, 91, 114
Gray, Virginia, 191
Great Depression, 196, 198, 201, 203
Gregory, William King, 270 (n. 122)
Gusfield, Joseph R., 199
Guyot, Arnold, 94

Haggard, Wallace C., 155, 284 (n. 32)
Hague, Dyson, 12, 16, 18–19, 29–30

Ham, Ken, 228, 229
Ham, Mordecai, 88, 91, 98–99, 113–15, 123,
    134, 186, 193–94, 267 (n. 75), 275 (n. 37)
Hand, W. Brevard, 215
Harrold, Francis, 229
Hawkins, William E., Jr., 80–81
Hays, Arthur Garfield, 158, 160, 162, 166, 168,
    290 (n. 132)
Helms, Jesse, 213
Hicks, Herbert, 155, 168
Hicks, Ira, 148, 155, 168
Hicks, Sue K., 148, 155, 156, 284 (n. 32), 287
    (n. 73)
Higher education: and teaching of evolution,
    39, 66, 67, 69, 72, 75, 81–82, 258 (n. 37);
    and secular society, 59, 61, 64, 66, 68, 69,
    72, 76; Bryan on, 59, 62, 64, 66, 67, 68–69,
    72–73, 80; and Darwinism, 60, 69–70, 71,
    72; role of, 61, 72; critics of, 61–62, 64, 68–
    69, 76; role of faculty in, 64, 65–66, 68,
    72–73, 74, 76, 78, 259 (n. 52); and evolu-
    tionary theory, 66, 67, 71–72. See also Col-
    lege students
Hill, Lew D., 137
"Hired man" theory, 74, 78
Hodge, Charles, 11
Hofstadter, Richard, 36
Holsted, James L., 212, 306 (n. 84)
Home schooling, 217
Hoover, Herbert, 193, 195–96, 299 (n. 130)
Hunter, George William, 142, 177
Huxley, Thomas Henry, 29, 30
Hylan, John F., 121

Identity. See Collective identity
Identity theory and social movements, 5–6, 9
Indiana, 232
Inerrancy of Bible: and The Fundamentals, 11, 12,
    18–20, 25; and fundamentalist discourse,
    16; and Riley, 93, 206, 265 (n. 49); and role
    of science, 93, 206–7, 265 (n. 49); modern-
    ist campaigns against, 111; and creation-

Luskin, Casey, 234

Lusk laws, 118

Macartney, Clarence E., 37

Machen, J. Gresham, 302 (n. 20)

Malone, Dudley Field, 158, 159–60, 162, 166, 167, 168, 306 (n. 75)

Malthus, Thomas, 87

Marr, W. B., 157

Marsden, George, 2, 38, 92

Martial metaphors in fundamentalist discourse, 32–33, 45, 54, 55, 77, 150, 225, 309 (n. 119)

Martin, Daniel Hoffman, 27

Martin, T. T.: and Anti-Evolution League, 46; and Bryan, 56; and college students, 65, 66; and college faculty, 73; and high school teachers, 74; and parents' role, 75, 259 (n. 67); college presidents as target of, 77; and lists of scientific critics of evolution, 94; and lobbying of state legislatures, 115, 182; and antievolution bills, 134; and Scopes trial, 145, 157; and media, 147; and Bible Crusaders of America, 175, 176, 188; and evolution debates, 178; and networks, 252 (n. 67)

Marty, Martin, 140–41

Massee, Jasper C., 37, 43, 44, 56

Masters, Victor, 257 (n. 26)

Materialism, 28, 64, 69, 70, 72, 85, 220

Mather, Kirtley, 160

Mauro, Philip, 13–14, 20, 21, 245 (n. 15)

McAdam, Doug, 116, 140, 141, 147, 154, 273 (n. 5)

McCann, Alfred Watterson, 103–4, 156, 288 (n. 86)

McCarthy-era politics, 217

McClean, Angus W., 135

McDonald, Harry, 222

McGregor, J. Howard, 108

McKenzie, Ben G., 150, 155

McKenzie, Gordon, 155

McLean v. Arkansas Board of Education (1982), 211–12, 215, 216

McLendon, Baxter F. "Cyclone Mack," 97, 115, 123

McPherson, Aimee Semple, 175, 189

McVey, Frank, 115, 125–26

Media: antievolution movement's use of, 6, 227, 230; and fundamentalism, 43, 47; and secular society, 59; and Bryan's speeches, 62, 71, 130, 174; and evolution debates, 83–84; and monkey metaphor, 102, 148, 268 (n. 98); and public education campaign for evolution, 109; and state legislatures, 115–16, 125, 126; and divisions among elites, 132, 135, 136, 137; and staging of evolution issue, 139, 140, 141–47, 164, 168–69, 230, 285 (n. 42), 291 (n. 137); as unsympathetic toward Bryan, 147, 148, 285 (n. 46); and evolution advocates, 189; and creationism, 229, 230; as sympathetic toward Darrow, 285 (n. 46)

Melucci, Alberto, 9

Men: as leaders of fundamentalist movement, 38, 39; and divorce, 89. See also Women

Mencken, H. L., 145, 146, 147, 148, 150, 176, 181, 182, 189

Metcalf, Zeno B., 83, 177

Methodists, 51–52, 56, 185

Meyer, David S., 6, 116, 212

Meyer, Louis, 25

Meyer, Stephen, 238

Michels, Robert, 199

Midwest, 47, 52, 233

Millennialism, 60

Mills, Lewis H., 204

Milton, George F., 168, 284 (n. 34)

Mims, Edwin, 137

Ministers: and activating potential, 37, 39, 40, 41; and networks, 43, 228; lack of support for Bryan, 56, 254–55 (n. 103); and evolution as issue, 61; and secular society, 62; and college students, 64–66; and teaching of evolution, 75; and pulpit revelations, 79; antievolution rhetoric of, 112; and lobbying state legislatures, 115; and divisions among elites, 137, 280 (n. 112); and Scopes trial, 145, 151, 156–57; and book burnings, 180; and local school boards, 232

Minkoff, Debra, 199, 219, 224

Minnesota, 122, 190, 231, 233, 317 (n. 56)

Minority organizations, 219

Missing link, 29, 102–4, 105, 145, 229, 268–69 (n. 104)

Missionary organizations, 32, 42, 251 (n. 49)

Mississippi, 115, 171, 176, 181–83, 231, 272 (n. 2), 304 (n. 46)

Missouri, 231

Mobilization: factors influencing, 34–36; and networks, 35, 36, 42–46, 49; and activating potential, 35, 36–42; and motivation to participate, 35, 46–47, 49, 51–53, 60; and removing barriers, 35, 53–58, 254 (n. 86); and modernism, 35–36, 44, 51, 61, 255 (n. 106); and framing process, 60

Modernism: and fundamentalist boundary setting, 17; and fundamentalist mobilization, 35–36, 44, 51, 61, 255 (n. 106); and evolution advocates, 61, 111–12; and higher education, 69; evolutionary theory compared to, 70, 71, 72; and Scopes trial, 139, 150; and evolution debates, 178; and missionary organizations, 251 (n. 49)

Monkeys: and misrepresentation of Darwin, 29, 71, 75, 82, 99–102, 108, 120, 123, 148, 230, 267–68 (n. 86), 268 (nn. 93, 98). See also Scopes "monkey" trial

Moody, Dwight L., 12, 14, 37

Moody Bible Institute, 36, 41, 42, 65

Moon, Irwin, 202

Moon, Sun Myung, 236

Moore, Randy, 225, 233

Moral Majority, 215

Moral reform movements, 4, 86, 122, 214

Moran, Jeffrey, 39, 90

Morgan, G. Campbell, 14, 16

Morgan, Harcourt, 137

Mormonism, 25

Morris, Connie, 231

Morris, Henry, 202, 203, 206, 207–10, 214, 218, 228, 236

Morrison, Cameron, 88, 105, 118, 122–23, 135, 177

Morton, Ferdinan Q., 194

Motion pictures, 202, 218, 307 (n. 94)

Motivation to participate: and social movements, 35; and fundamentalist mobilization, 35, 46–47, 49, 51–53, 60; and fundamentalist publications, 47, 49, 51, 252–53 (n. 64); and framing of evolution issue, 60, 76–82

Mullins, E. Y., 20–21, 126

Munhall, Leander W., 37, 51, 257 (n. 25)

Murphree, A. A., 130, 276 (n. 64)

Murphy, Walter, 135–36

National Academy of Sciences, 238

National Association of Biology Teachers, 209, 311 (n. 131)

National Center for Science Education, 232, 237, 238, 311 (n. 131)

National Defense Education Act, 205

National Education Association, 112, 132, 277 (n. 83)

National Federated Evangelistic Committee, 276 (n. 58)

Nationalism, 183

National Reform Association, 176

National Science Foundation (NSF), 205, 209

Nativism, 89, 183

Naturalism, 69, 70

Natural selection: and Darwinists, 28; fundamentalist critics of, 31; and Bryan, 71, 96, 98, 214; scientific critics of, 85, 94; and textbooks, 177; and intelligent design, 220

Neal, John Randolph, 158, 261 (n. 97)

Negotiation. See Politicization

Race issues: and evolutionary theory, 39, 90; and antievolution movement, 194–95

Racial segregation, 118

Rader, Paul, 202

Radio, 146–47, 177, 178, 201, 202, 230, 284–85 (n. 40)

Ransom, John Crowe, 181

Rappleyea, George, 141–42, 143, 282 (n. 11), 283 (n. 20)

Raulston, John T., 150, 159, 160, 164, 165, 166

Reagan, Ronald, 213

Reed, Ralph, 213, 218

Reed, Thurlow, 143

Reeve, J. J., 19–20, 22

Reinking, Bernadette, 235

Republican Party, 122, 123, 195, 213, 224–25

Resource mobilization theory, 35

Revival ministries, 11–13, 16, 32, 40, 62, 115, 123, 134, 180–81, 248 (nn. 65, 66)

Ribuffo, Leo P., 306 (n. 77)

Rice, John R., 201

Rice, Stuart, 112

Richards, Jay, 230

Riley, William Bell: role in antievolution movement, 3, 41; as fundamentalist minister, 34, 37, 40; and mobilization, 40–45, 47, 52, 53–58; and fundamentalist publications, 47, 49, 51, 250 (n. 16), 252 (n. 67); and Norris, 51, 56, 185, 296–97 (n. 85); on interchurch movements, 53, 254 (n. 88); and doctrinal disagreements, 57; on college students, 62, 257 (n. 24); and modernism, 69; on evolution textbooks, 82; and debate with Metcalf, 83; and anti-Semitism, 89, 196, 200; on political radicalism, 91; and inerrancy of Bible, 93, 206, 265 (n. 49); and political alignment, 123, 125; and Bryan, 128, 288 (n. 85); and media, 147; and Scopes trial, 157, 288 (n. 87); as Bryan's successor, 174, 175; and state legislatures, 176, 190; and evolution debates, 177–78; and communists, 183,

200; and patriotism, 183–84; as WCFA president, 184–85, 198; and radicalism, 186; and Arkansas, 191; and Prohibition, 193; post-1930s activism of, 201; Northwestern Bible and Missionary Training School, 302 (n. 20)

Rimmer, Harry, 176, 184, 190, 201

Robertson, Pat, 213, 216, 218, 236

Robinson, James Harvey, 82, 110, 270 (n. 130)

Robinson, Joe T., 193

Rockefeller, John D., 55–56

Rood, Paul, 174, 175, 176, 184, 196

Roosevelt, Theodore, 72

Rosenwald, Julius, 114

Rossiter, Joseph P., 120

Rotenberry, A. L., 191

Rucht, Dieter, 116, 273 (n. 5)

Rudnick, Milton, 17

Rupp, Leila J., 199, 200

Rusby, Henry H., 153

Russell, C. Allyn, 254–55 (n. 103)

Rutherford Institute, 215

Ryan, Quin, 147

Ryle, J. C., 26, 247 (n. 47)

Salisbury, Edward, 103

Samuelson, August, 271 (n. 135)

Sandeen, Ernest, 14, 60

Sandefur, George Washington, 39, 250–51 (n. 24)

Santorum, Rick, 224, 231, 235, 311–12 (n. 139)

Scalia, Antonin, 216

Schlafly, Phyllis, 215

Schleiermacher, Friedrich, 18

Schnebly, C. J., 154

Scholars, 20, 21, 24, 26. See also Higher education; Scientific community

Science: and fundamentalists' boundary setting, 21–22, 27–30; differences with faith, 21–23, 27–28, 35; and college campuses, 61, 68; and influence of evolution, 71; and academic freedom of faculty, 78; role of,

Smith, Charles C., 178

Smith, T. V., 267–68 (n. 86)

Smithsonian Institution, 209

Smith v. Mobile (1987), 215

Snow, David, 60, 84, 258 (n. 40)

Social choice theory, 46

Social Darwinism, 31, 70, 85–86, 87, 214

Socialism, 26, 247 (n. 53)

Social movements: scholarly study of, 4–6, 9, 35, 46, 60, 199, 252 (n. 59); internal dynamics of, 5; boundaries of, 9, 16–24, 27–28, 33; mobilization of, 35, 36; and framing issues, 60, 68, 76, 84; and political opportunities, 116; and staging issues, 140, 154; and cycle of contention, 172, 180, 184, 188, 291 (n. 2); adaptability of, 219, 224, 309 (n. 117)

Social surveys of college students, 67–68

South: and antievolution movement, 3, 116–19, 181–82; and fundamentalist movement, 37, 38, 39, 47, 52; and evolution's association with racial equality, 90; and antievolutionist bills, 115, 171; and conservative social reformers, 118; and political access, 119–20, 138; and political alignment, 121–22, 138; and divisions among elites, 131–33, 138; and effects of Scopes trial, 171; and teaching of evolution, 233

South Carolina, 133, 231, 272 (n. 2)

Southern Agrarian School, 181

Southern Baptist Convention, 49, 51, 122, 126, 143

Southern Christian Leadership Conference (SCLC), 140, 141, 147, 154, 165

Southern Methodist General Conference, 122

Southern Methodist University (SMU), 51, 79

Southern Presbyterian General Assembly, 122

Speer, Robert E., 26, 32, 248 (n. 67)

Spencer, Herbert, 30, 85

Sprowls, J. W., 82

Staggenborg, Suzanne, 199, 205

Staging of evolution issue: and media atten-
tion, 139, 140, 141–47, 164, 168–69, 230, 285 (n. 42), 291 (n. 137); and public support, 139, 141, 147–51, 153–54; and public policy, 139, 141, 164–70; and constraint of opponents, 154–60, 162–64

State Association of Missionary Baptist Churches, 122

State legislatures: Norris's lobbying of, 82, 89, 90, 91, 97; Bryan's lobbying of, 82, 115, 121, 125, 126–27, 130–31, 134; and antievolution bills, 115, 119–21, 132–36, 171, 173, 176, 184, 190, 200, 231, 272 (n. 2), 277 (n. 83), 295 (n. 58); and media, 115–16, 125, 126; and evolution debates, 116, 133; and reform of public schools, 118; and Great Depression, 204; and creationist bills, 209, 305 (n. 65); and balanced treatment bills, 210–12; and intelligent design, 222

Stevens, Doris, 167

Stewart, A. T. "Tom," 155–56, 158, 160, 167, 288 (n. 92)

Stewart, Lyman, 8, 9, 10, 55, 56, 254 (n. 100)

Stewart, Milton, 8, 10, 56, 254 (n. 100)

Strategic staging, 6, 140, 141. See also Staging of evolution issue

Straton, John Roach: role in antievolution movement, 3; as fundamentalist minister, 37; and networks, 45; and Riley, 56; and teaching of evolution, 65, 257 (n. 24); and modernism, 69; debates with Potter, 86–87, 95, 102, 104, 105, 106, 178; and conservative reformers, 88; and Ku Klux Klan, 89, 183; and monkey metaphor, 101; on fossils, 104, 105, 269 (n. 108); on artistic representations of evolution, 106, 108–9, 270 (n. 122); and Scopes trial, 151, 153, 157, 288 (n. 87); and public policy, 165; as Bryan's successor, 174, 175, 292 (n. 19); and Bible Crusaders of America, 175; on South, 182; and radio, 202

Strauss, David Friedrich, 18

Stroder, J. T., 90
Sumrall, Jean, 208
Sunday, Billy, 115, 123, 137, 180, 288 (n. 87)
Sunday closing laws, 27, 88
Swidler, Ann, 7
Szasz, Ferenc Morton, 40, 84, 85, 172

Tarrow, Sidney, 116, 127, 131, 172–73, 180, 184, 188, 196, 272 (n. 4), 291 (n. 2)
Taxpayers, 46, 76, 108
Taylor, Verta, 9, 10, 24, 199, 200
Teaching of evolution: with creationism, 1, 228, 231, 232, 233; in public schools, 1–2, 31, 46, 65, 73–74, 217, 257 (n. 26), 259 (n. 60); and college faculty as targets, 20, 72–73, 79–80, 259 (nn. 52, 55), 260 (n. 81), 261 (n. 97); and higher education, 39, 66, 67, 69, 72, 75, 81–82, 258 (n. 37); and high school teachers as targets, 66, 73–75, 178, 180, 225, 232; Bryan on, 69–70, 74, 76, 77, 81–82, 130–31, 258 (n. 47); and college presidents as targets, 77–78, 80, 82; and public policy, 114, 117, 205; and Scopes, 139, 142, 158, 216, 288–89 (n. 93); removal of, from public schools, 171; antievolution movement's focus on, 180, 227, 230, 238; advocates for, 189, 236–38; decline in, 204–5, 232–34; and intelligent design, 221–22, 224, 311 (nn. 131, 132); and critical treatment of evolutionary theory, 222, 231, 311 (nn. 132, 134); and public opinion, 224, 228, 237, 317–18 (n. 57); increase in, 237, 317 (n. 56); public support for, 237, 317–18 (n. 57); and "teaching the controversy," 238. See also Scopes "monkey" trial
Television, 202–3, 215, 230
Tennessee: and antievolution movement, 3; and antievolution bills, 115, 131, 138, 272 (n. 2), 278–79 (n. 95), 281 (n. 124); and political alignment, 121; and divisions among elites, 136–38, 280 (n. 118); antievolution law, 139, 143, 149, 150, 157, 158–

59, 163, 165, 171, 173, 304 (n. 46); equal time law, 210; and teaching of evolution, 225. See also Dayton, Tenn.; Scopes "monkey" trial
Texas, 119, 122, 177, 200, 206, 219, 272 (n. 2), 307 (n. 96)
Textbooks: antievolution movement's call for removal of, 46, 82, 119, 123, 125; state education boards' control of, 73–74, 76, 177; and higher education, 82; selection of, 118, 125, 176, 222, 307 (n. 96); and antievolution bills, 119–21, 133–34; changes in, 177, 204, 293 (n. 39), 311 (n. 130); and custom publishing, 232; disclaimers in, 238, 311 (n. 130)
Thaxton, Charles B., 220
Theistic evolutionism: Orr on, 22–23; and The Fundamentals, 28, 29, 30; and Poteat, 77; and materialism, 85; Porter on, 86, 263 (n. 17); and day-age theory, 128; Bryan on, 150–51, 263 (n. 18); and scientific community, 236; and Catholics, 278 (n. 90)
Thomas, W. H. Griffith, 25
Thomas B. Fordham Foundation, 232
Thomas More Foundation, 237
Thomas More Law Center, 232, 315 (n. 25)
Thompson, Dick, 237
Thompson, William O., 276 (n. 63)
Tilly, Charles, 116
Tocqueville, Alexis de, 117
Torcaso v. Watkins (1961), 213
Torrey, Reuben A., 12, 13, 25, 37, 40, 252 (n. 67)
Toumey, Christopher, 214, 216
Touraine, Alain, 9
Townsend, Luther T., 29, 30
Transformation of issues, 84, 109–14
Transmutation of species, 29, 96–97, 98
Trumbull, Charles G., 32, 248 (n. 66)

Unification Church, 236
United Farm Workers, 127

H. Eugene and Lillian Youngs Lehman Series

Lamar Cecil, Wilhelm II: Prince and Emperor, 1859–1900 (1989).

Carolyn Merchant, Ecological Revolutions: Nature, Gender, and Science in New England (1989).

Gladys Engel Lang and Kurt Lang, Etched in Memory: The Building and Survival of Artistic Reputation (1990).

Howard Jones, Union in Peril: The Crisis over British Intervention in the Civil War (1992).

Robert L. Dorman, Revolt of the Provinces: The Regionalist Movement in America (1993).

Peter N. Stearns, Meaning Over Memory: Recasting the Teaching of Culture and History (1993).

Thomas Wolfe, The Good Child's River, edited with an introduction by Suzanne Stutman (1994).

Warren A. Nord, Religion and American Education: Rethinking a National Dilemma (1995).

David E. Whisnant, Rascally Signs in Sacred Places: The Politics of Culture in Nicaragua (1995).

Lamar Cecil, Wilhelm II: Emperor and Exile, 1900–1941 (1996).

Jonathan Hartlyn, The Struggle for Democratic Politics in the Dominican Republic (1998).

Louis A. Pérez Jr., On Becoming Cuban: Identity, Nationality, and Culture (1999).

Yaakov Ariel, Evangelizing the Chosen People: Missions to the Jews in America, 1880–2000 (2000).

Philip F. Gura, C. F. Martin and His Guitars, 1796–1873 (2003).

Louis A. Pérez Jr., To Die in Cuba: Suicide and Society (2005).

Peter Filene, The Joy of Teaching: A Practical Guide for New College Instructors (2005).

John Charles Boger and Gary Orfield, eds., School Resegregation: Must the South Turn Back? (2005).

Jock Lauterer, Community Journalism: Relentlessly Local (2006).

Michael Hunt, The American Ascendancy: How the United States Gained and Exercised Global Dominance (2007).

Michael Lienesch, In the Beginning: Fundamentalism, the Scopes Trial, and the Making of the Antievolution Movement (2007).